INTERMEDIATE LATIN

Andrew Pearson

INTERMEDIATE LATIN

A. T. Reyes

Drawings by Sheila Gibson

Oxbow Books

Published by

Oxbow Books, Oxford, UK

ISBN 978 1 84217 331 2

A CIP record for this book is available from the British Library

This book is available direct from

Oxbow Books, Oxford, UK

Phone: 44-(0)1865-241249; Fax: 44-(0)1865-794449

and

The David Brown Book Company

PO Box 511, Oakville, CT 06779, USA

Phone: 1-860-945 9329; Fax: 1-860-945 9468

or from our website

www.oxbowbooks.com

Front cover: The Forum of Augustus, showing its side porticoes, used as courts of justice, and the temple of Mars Ultor, 'the Avenger', inaugurated in 2 BC (Sheila Gibson).

Back cover: Classroom of LHS at Groton School in 2007 (Nathaniel Lovell-Smith).

Printed in Great Britain by
Maney Publishing, Leeds

Designed and typeset by
Gill Haddock, Woodlands, Ford, Midlothian, UK

DEDICATION

For over half a century, Hugh Sackett's dedication to Groton School has been vital to its well-being. It is hoped that he will take some pleasure from this omnium gatherum of Latin miscellanea from Classics handouts of bygone days. To him — and to the shades of previous Classics Masters at Groton School whose work finds some reflection here — this book is dedicated.

Et quasi cursōrēs vītāī lampada trādunt.

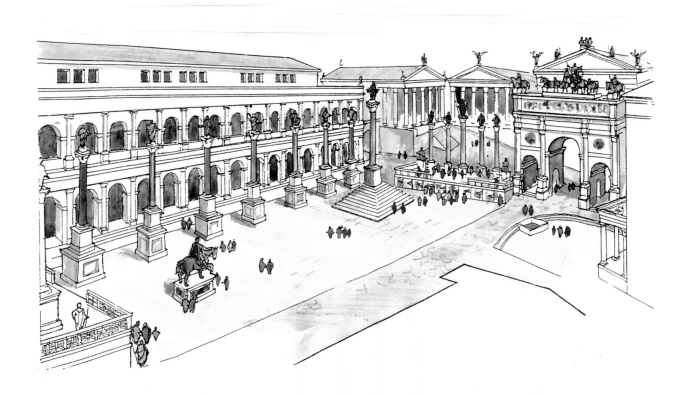

Sheila Gibson

Frontispiece: The Roman Forum in late antiquity (the fourth to seventh centuries AD). At the far right is the arch of Septimius Severus standing next to the Augustan Rostra on which are five honorific columns. There are seven further honorific columns along the side, in front of the Basilica Julia. The equestrian statue is of the emperor Marcus Aurelius.

CONTENTS

I followed Custom as my guide,
And found his field was wondrous wide.

A. B. Ramsay (1872–1955), 'Classical Education'

PART ONE: Grammar

CHAPTER 1. The alphabet : Sound and pronunciation

CHAPTER 2. Introducing nouns, verbs, and adjectives : The five declensions : The nominative as subject and predicate : The present tense in the active voice : The verb 'To be'

CHAPTER 3. **I-stem nouns of the third declension : More on the genitive and dative : The imperfect and future in the indicative active : The imperfect and future of esse : Adverbs and more on adjectives**

CHAPTER 8. **Deponents and semi-deponents : Further miscellaneous notes on verbs :**

Interrogative and indefinite pronouns : The subjunctive and its morphology

CHAPTER 9. **The subjunctive used independently : The subjunctive in subordinate clauses :**

Sequence of tenses

LIST OF ILLUSTRATIONS

MAPS

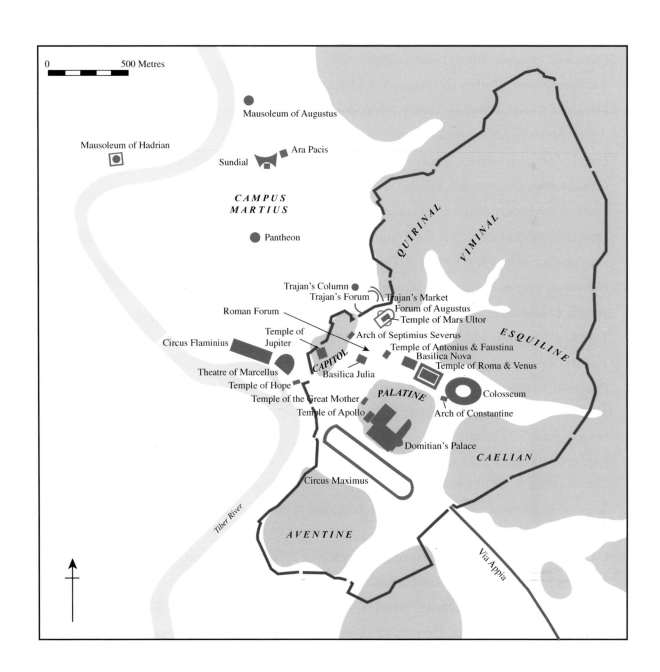

MAP 1. ROME

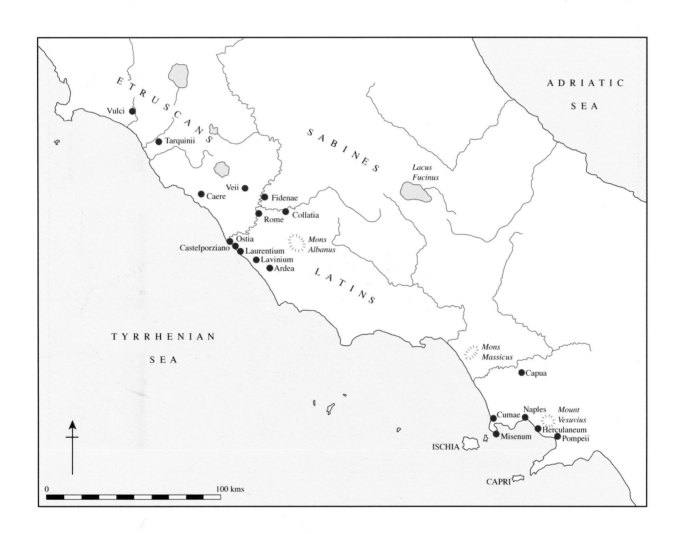

MAP 2. AREA AROUND ROME

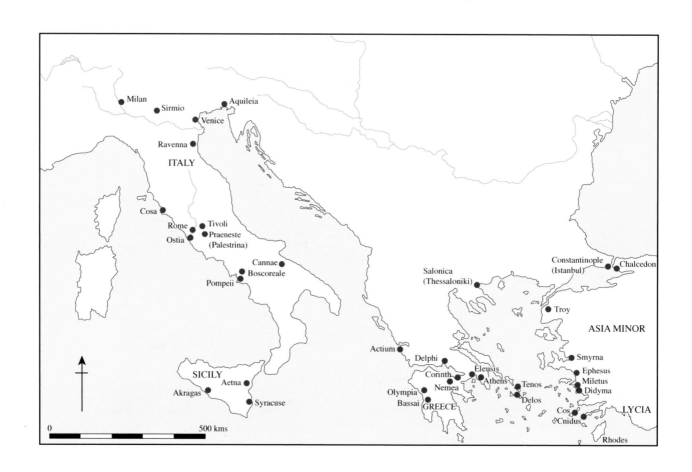

MAP 3. GREECE AND ITALY

MAP 4. EUROPE AND THE MEDITERRANEAN

Fig. 1. Amphitheatre at Arles in France, second half of first century AD, now used for bull-fighting.

Preface

Dare any call Permissiveness
An educational success?
Saner those class-rooms which I sat in,
Compelled to study Greek and Latin.

W. H. Auden (1907–1973), 'Doggerel by a Senior Citizen'

A generation or so after Auden's Senior Citizen posed his question, the answer seems to be 'yes,' and few now call 'sane' classes compelled to learn Latin, let alone Greek. Astonishing too is that, these days, amongst those who discourage the compulsory study of Latin at school are classicists themselves, some even eminent. The following, for example, is from a book apparently meant to encourage the study of the ancient world:

> Only a lunatic fringe now believes that the learning of grammatical rules
> has any positive effect on a pupil's logical thinking.

There is a glibness here that avoids the problem of how to understand the ancients without understanding their languages accurately, and it seems inconsiderate too to deny to a younger generation precisely those tools that made it possible for an older one to examine the world and its constituent words and syllables — as much fundamental particles and building-blocks of nature as molecules or quarks.

So this is a book that, from one perspective, may be described as radical or 'lunatic,' but from another, conservative and possibly 'sane.' It is an intermediate Latin grammar for those still coming to grips with the nuances and nuisances of the language. It is intended for boys and girls who have studied Latin for a year and reviews material learnt or allegedly learnt previously, providing additional information. Older, more mature students, however, may use the whole as a primer from which to learn the basics, since its approach is largely prescriptive: if 'x', then 'y', a formula peculiarly suited to an audience brought up in a world where information is acquired by the consumption of news-nuggets and 'sound-bites.'

Within so short a compass, of course, not all idiosyncrasies of the language can be covered. But as a further guide, cross-references have been made to *Gildersleeve's Latin Grammar* (abbreviated *GLG*), first published in 1895 and still in print, the most readily available grammar in English that aspires to completeness. At the very least, cross-referencing makes the point that learning Latin is complicated, and no matter how many the cartoon-drawings, conversational snippets, or contemporary references tossed into a text-book, there are still fundamental paradigms that a pupil must — as the old *Book of Common Prayer* put it in its second Advent collect — 'read, mark, learn, and inwardly digest.'

The medium, in other words, can only do so much for the message, and as every schoolmaster knows, within a classroom, there is a distinction to be made between education and entertainment or between the solemn and the serious. To put the matter in another way: it is generally accepted that teaching is a form of theatre — but it is rarely asked what type of theatre it is that teaching most closely resembles. For my money, that would be bull-fighting. In both, the audience is certainly critical, even hostile, for whom no turn is left unstoned. But with a certain grace and imagination, it is possible to win through to some general approval and even enjoyment. And the bull need not be slaughtered at the end.

• • • • •

The first part of this textbook presents a concise outline of Latin grammar and uses as exercises and sample-sentences texts from actual Roman authors. Each chapter concludes with two groups of readings, the first in Latin to be translated into English, the second in English to be translated back into Latin. For some sentences, I have excised certain subordinate clauses to allow pupils to concentrate more closely on the grammatical point to hand or to simplify somewhat a particularly harrowing group of words. But I have not created any sentences of my own, since most pupils will have read enough about girls loving sailors or farmers ploughing fields when they were first introduced to Latin.

But to maintain this policy of using essentially authentic Latin, readings at the end of each chapter have had to be drawn from authors who fall chronologically late within the spectrum of ancient literature, but whose writings have the twin advantages of a simple (enough) grammar and a straightforward (enough) narrative. The works of Aulus Gellius (second century AD), Eutropius (fourth century AD), and Macrobius (fifth century AD) — none a household name — have therefore been excerpted here. In a bygone era, Aulus Gellius was regarded highly for the elegance of his style and the capaciousness of his intellect, and it is hoped that, by a sort of mental osmosis, excerpted passages will encourage an appreciation of what constitutes clear writing. The intellectual quality of Eutropius has been frankly and succinctly given as 'low,' but his liking for constructions in the active indicative makes him an ideal foil for beginners. As for Macrobius, the *Oxford Classical Dictionary* puts it best, describing his style as 'elegant', but 'without the extravagance'.

Following the chapters on grammar are ten readings from the Augustan historian Livy, a difficult, often intractable, author. But by this point in the proceedings, the pupil should be able to puzzle out — perhaps even read — the Latin with a certain facility. The passages from Livy tell of the founding of Rome and the early history of the city. The text follows the Oxford edition without change or emendation. Glosses and grammatical help are given as footnotes.

The time it takes to work through this textbook will vary from class to class. Some may take a term or semester, others somewhat more than that. Afterwards, it will be possible to proceed to passages in any of the advanced readers available (for example, the textbooks edited by Jenney, Scudder *et al.*), or else they may continue with Livy or an author whose syntax is reasonably straightforward (*e.g.*, Caesar). By the end of the year, the more apt may be able to read a speech by Cicero.

• • • • •

The substance of this textbook has been determined in large measure by the Classical syllabus at Groton School which requires those in the Second and Third Forms to have achieved a certain competence in the reading of Latin and in the history of Rome. Since its early years, the School has maintained a tradition of producing Classics textbooks, beginning with *Exercises in Greek Composition Based on Xenophon's* Anabasis *and* Hellenica (1898) by Edwin Hall Higley (Professor of Classics at Middlebury College in Vermont before becoming a Groton schoolmaster) and *First Latin Writer* (1904) by Mather Abbot. I have inevitably learnt much from my predecessors, in particular, the revision of *Pearson's Essentials of Latin* (1966) by M. W. Mansur and N. M. Getty; *Selections from Ovid's Metamorphoses* (1968), edited by F. J. DeVeau and N. M. Getty; *Intermediate Latin* (1968) by R. J. Gula; and the revision of *Jenney's Latin Course* (1975 and over the years in several editions) by R. V. Scudder in four volumes. On matters of history and mythology, I still find useful *Mythology* (1977) by Gula and T. H. Carpenter.

School editions produced by the Groton School Press over the years have also been helpful. For students before the Second World War, the Classics Department produced *Latin Syntax*, a small booklet (47 pages of quarto size) giving the basic outlines of the language; the third revised edition appeared in 1938. Of roughly the same vintage is an equally short booklet prepared by DeVeau called *Questions on Virgil and Cicero*, useful for its inclusion of recondite information on Classical literature and its tradition. DeVeau had also published an edition of Virgil's *Eclogues* in 1935. After the war, there appeared, under the supervision of the then Press Master A. E. Olson, three volumes of Latin poetry edited by W. J. Myers — *Juvenal and Johnson* (1976); *Varieties of Latin Verse* (1977); and *Carmina Amatoria* (1978) — and a compendium of essential Latin words, *Basic Latin Vocabulary* (1966), edited by Getty and Mansur. The word-lists in *Basic Latin Vocabulary* are still the most concise and useful summary of meanings that I know, and I have taken the liberty of adopting definitions in that volume for the vocabulary and glossaries here.

With the demise of the Press and the advent of word-processing in the 1990s, members of the Department (then under the chairmanship of John Tulp) produced two binders, one a Latin primer, the other a reader with passages adapted from the texts of Livy and others. Both have been continually revised over the years and remain in use at the School, and I have gained much from them.

Most importantly, I have benefited from a large selection of classroom handouts written over the decades by my many distinguished predecessors in the Department. In many ways, in fact, this textbook is simply a compendium of these handouts with bits of connecting prose written by myself. I fortunately inherited when I arrived at Groton the classroom over which Hugh Sackett presided for forty years, and he generously left for my use his files of vocabulary lists, historical notes, sight passages, and grammatical aids.

Other handouts in my possession were probably written by Melvin Mansur and Norris Getty. Some (identifiable by their distinctive typesetting) were prepared by Warren Myers. In addition, I have been able to consult — through the kindness of Charles Alexander and Warren Myers — Getty and Mansur's handwritten notes for their own classes.

Finally, Mrs Maureen Beck, formerly of the Department, kindly gave me when she retired papers of Robert Gula, and I have made much use of his memoranda. Many, I think, were intended as a preliminary to a concise grammar that he hoped to write with Rogers Scudder, a project abandoned with Gula's untimely death in 1989. From these, I gather that the two had in conversation already gone some way toward deciding how the new grammar was to be organized, and in one sense, this textbook is what I imagine that volume would have been like, had it been completed.

Adding to the list of textbooks produced by School authors has been a daunting task, therefore, made even more daunting by the recent addition of *A Vergil Workbook* by K. Bradley (2006, with B. W. Boyd) and *Virgil's Aeneid: A Reader's Guide* by D. Ross (2007). I hope that I have maintained standards, not only with regard to grammatical exposition, but also in terms of Classical scholarship. It has always been one of the peculiarities of the Groton Classics Department that the task of teaching has gone hand in hand with the preparation of primary research. The papers on medieval history written in the 1950s by the younger Theodore Mommsen (grandson and namesake of the ancient historian who won the Nobel Prize in Literature in 1905 competing against Leo Tolstoy) remain a highlight of scholarship at the School. The texts of Catullus and Horace, prepared by Warren Myers and George Goold and printed at the Groton School Press in 1973 and 1977 respectively, were the best critical editions then available of either poet. These days, most famous of all are Hugh Sackett's several volumes and articles on his excavations at Lefkandi in Euboia (with Mervyn Popham) and Palaikastro in Crete, a body of work that will never fall out of date.

· · · · ·

This textbook was initially written when I was on leave from Groton School in the academic year 1998-1999, intermittently corrected afterwards, and then substantially revised when I was on sabbatical in 2004-2005. Since then, further changes have been made in the intervals between terms. For allowing absences from Groton, I need to thank W. M. Polk and R. Commons, successively Headmasters over this period. I am glad to acknowledge also the assistance of the trustees of the Dillon Fund at the School for subventions over the past decade that have gone toward the completion of this book. For criticism and logistical aid, I am grateful to all colleagues and teachers in the Classics Department, past and present. As ever, Warren and Micheline Myers provided freely of their knowledge and their refrigerator, and I have borrowed and stolen much from them, whether they were at Groton or, in retirement, Charlotte, North Carolina.

Others who have been crucial are Amanda Claridge and Judith McKenzie, both far more sure-footed in the high-ways and by-ways of Roman history and archaeology than I. The illustrations and drawings have been selected from their collections to show the wide geographical area in which Roman architecture may be found. Charles and Ann Alexander, Auguste Bannard (then Johns), Barbara Bispham, Douglas Brown, Vernon Cassin, John Conner, Henry Davis, Townsend Davis, Swift Edgar, Richard Fox, Byron Fuller, Galit Goldschmid, Tom Hardwick, Maja Kominko, Nathaniel Lovell-Smith, John MacEachern and his staff, Nick Milner, Kathleen Pond, Maggie Sasanow, Alison Siegenthaler, and the late Pat Smith assisted in various ways. Conversation on Latin with John DeStefano over the years has been instructive. Alison Wilkins kindly prepared the maps. Thanks are due also to Professor T. P. Wiseman who gave permission for the axonometric of the villa at Sirmio to be reprinted here in colour. The publishing exper-tise of Liz Rosindale, Gill Haddock and Janice Brett of Maney's has been greatly appreciated. I am very grateful to David Brown and Oxbow Books for having taken on this project. The different second year Latin classes have queried and complained over the years, and that has been to the good. Errors and nonsense that remain are, of course, my own fault.

• • • • •

Over the years during which I have worked on this volume, time and illness have claimed four extraordi-nary individuals from whom I had asked advice and help, always generously given:

Kevin Lee, formerly Professor of Classics at the University of Sydney, gave me the benefit of his expe-rience in teaching undergraduates, especially those entering university to study Latin and Greek without prior knowledge of either language. He showed me exercises that he used in his teaching and suggested that I would find the writings of Eutropius, Aulus Gellius, and Macrobius helpful.

To Roger Moorey is owed an incalculable debt. It was due to his advocacy, shortly before his death in 2004, that I was able to revise this textbook as a Visiting Scholar at Wolfson College, Oxford in 2004–2005.

Fig. 2. LHS in his dormitory, ca. 1968.

Conversation with him was always an education, and many of the locutions and references to be found here no doubt go back in some fashion to hints and ideas passed on to me over twenty years.

Rogers Scudder began teaching at Groton in 1968, although his relation with the School had begun in 1936, when he became Classics Master at Brooks School, founded in 1927 as a sort of adjunct to Groton. Over the past few years, from 1999 until shortly before his death in 2006, he looked over odd sections of this textbook and made gently encouraging (or distressed) noises as necessary. He approved the principles of the project, and I hope he would have approved its end. At his death, his classroom notes and files were passed on to me, and these have been instructive and helpful.

Sheila Gibson, a master of the art of archaeological draughtsmanship, happily agreed to the use of her illustrations here and added watercolouring especially for this textbook. In her 80s, her eye was still discerning, her talent undiminished. She died in early 2002, her work on the illustrations largely complete, and I am sorry that she did not live to see final publication. She did view, however, a prototype volume in the summer of 2001, and was glad to know then that the large number of her drawings collected together here would be of use to boys and girls beginning their study of the Roman world. I hope she would have been pleased by the final result.

Et lūx perpetua lūceat eīs.

• • • • •

The publication of this textbook marks the 80th birthday of Mr Sackett (often known at School simply by the initials LHS), Senior Classics Master at Groton. It coincides as well with the fortieth anniversary of his collaboration, now sadly concluded, with Rogers Scudder that began in 1968, when they were instructors in charge of the School's unique year-long class on Greek and Roman Archaeology. Mr Sackett arrived at Groton in 1955, and since then, he — together with Eleanor, more recently — has acted as guide and advisor (officially and unofficially) to innumerable boys and girls, many of whom have given me advice on this volume. Amongst these, Mr S. Considine, Mr H. Davis, Mr G. M. Hornblower and Mr H. Lewis, in particular, are to be thanked for their extreme generosity for providing the subvention that has made this publication possible.

Groton, Massachusetts   **A. T. R.**
St Jerome's Day
30 September 2007

Fig. 3. The Roman Forum.

PART ONE: Grammar

'Third boy, what's a horse?'

'A beast, sir,' replied the boy.

'So it is,' said Squeers. 'Ain't it, Nickleby?'

'I believe there is no doubt of that, sir,' answered Nicholas.

'Of course, there isn't,' said Squeers. 'A horse is a quadruped, and quadruped's Latin for beast,

as everyone that's gone through the grammar knows, or else where's the use of having grammars at all?'

Charles Dickens (1812–1870), *Nicholas Nickleby*

I wish you to gasp not only at what you read, but at the miracle of its being readable....

Vladimir Nabokov (1899–1977), *Pale Fire*

Fig. 4. Arch of Septimius Severus in Rome.

Chapter 1

The alphabet
Sound and pronunciation

Tis true, on Words is still our whole debate,
Disputes of Mē or Tē, of aut or at,
To sound or sink in canō, O or A,
Or give up Cicero to C or K.

Alexander Pope (1688-1744), *The Dunciad* 4. 219-222

ex sonīs linguae sunt compositae.
Languages are constituted of sounds.

Said to be inscribed above a Groton School classroom-door, but never sighted

Latin is a language, and like all languages, ancient or modern, it has to be spoken. If, to borrow Auden's phrase, to study Latin is 'to break bread with the dead', then as at any dinner party, we have to talk and converse, as well as watch and listen. Learning Latin is an auricular and oral exercise, not just an ocular one.

I. The Latin alphabet [GLG 1]

1. The Classical Latin alphabet is essentially the same as the English one, except that the letter I is used instead of the J, and V may also represent the letter U. W is not found, nor are X, Y, and Z seen, except in loan-words (words adopted by the Romans from other languages). In this book, J is not used, but V and U are distinguished.

II. Sounds [GLG 6]

2. Consonants are sounded as they are in English. But:

(a)   C is always pronounced as if it were K.

(b)   G is always a hard sound (as in 'gold,' not as in 'legion').

(c)   S is a soft sound (as in 'lass,' not as in 'measure').

(d)   T is always hard (as in 'ten,' not as in 'action').

(e)   V is pronounced as if it were the English W.

III. Quantity [GLG 2-3, 12]

3. The pronunciation of vowels depends upon quantity. Some syllables are long, others short. Long syllables are marked with the symbol ¯ over the vowel. This symbol is called a macron (macra in the plural). Short syllables are indicated by the symbol ˘ above the vowel or have no mark. Any Latin vowel in this book without a symbol above may be taken as short.

Dictionaries do not always agree on the quantities of vowels for particular words. I have generally followed notations in Lewis's *Elementary Latin Dictionary,* which helpfully marks quantities for all vowels. (*Cassell's Dictionary,* Lewis and Short's *Latin Dictionary*, and the *Oxford Latin Dictionary* only indicate quantities for metrically ambiguous syllables, and so enquiring minds should be wary.)

4. The pronunciation of the different long and short vowels is as follows:

ā	is sounded as in 'car';
ă	is sounded as in 'atone';
ē	is sounded as in 'neighbour';
ĕ	as in 'let';
ī	as in 'marine';
ĭ	as in 'quit';
ō	as in 'zone';
ŏ	as in 'dot';
ū	as in 'unit';
ŭ	as in 'consul'.

The meanings of words that appear similar are affected by a syllable's quantity:

cecidī: I fell	cecīdī: I killed
fugit: he flees	fūgit: he fled
hic: this	hīc: here
iacere: to throw	iacēre: to lie, lie slain
legit: he reads	lēgit: he has read
os: bone	ōs: face, mouth
venit: he comes	vēnit: he came

IV. Diphthongs [GLG 4]

5. Diphthongs are combinations of two vowels pronounced with one sound. Most common are:

> ae, sounded as in 'Taiwan;'
>
> au, sounded as in 'pound;'
>
> eu, sounded as in 'feud;'
>
> oe, sounded as in 'loiter.'

V. Stress [GLG 11, 15]

6. Stress refers to the emphasis on a particular syllable. Stress is indicated below by the symbol ' after the stressed syllable.

7. The final syllable of a word is called the ultimate; the second-to-last syllable is the penult; and the third-to-last syllable is the antepenult. In general, Latin words that have two syllables receive stress on the penult:

> ta' men (nevertheless)
>
> de' us (god).

Words with more than two syllables stress the penult if the penult is a long syllable; if the penult is short, the stress is on the antepenult:

> servā're (to save, guard)
>
> regē'bat (he was ruling)
>
> do' minus (master)
>
> fī' lius (son)

Added to the end of an individual word, -ne (the sign of a question) or -que (and) are counted as the ultima of that word. Because they become part of the word to which they are attached, -ne and -que are called enclitics.

Vocabulary

The words below should be pronounced following the rules of quantity and stress.

deinde	then
et	and, even, also
et ... et ... (et ...)	both ... and ... (and ...)
hodiē	today

iam	already, now, soon
igitur	therefore
ita	thus, so
mox	soon, subsequently
nam	for
nisi	unless, if not
posteā	afterward
quidem	indeed (*often not translated*)
quippe	in fact, for
sed	but
sī	if
sīc	thus, so
tamen	nevertheless
tamquam	just as, just as if, on the grounds that
tot	so many (*undeclinable*)
tum	then
ubi	when, where

Sheila Gibson

Fig. 5. The Altar of the Augustan Peace (Ara Pacis Augustae) in Rome. It was built to celebrate the return of Augustus from Spain and Gaul after three years. The monument was dedicated on 30 January 9 BC. It consists of an altar of marble atop a platform surrounded by a high enclosure elaborately carved with relief sculpture.

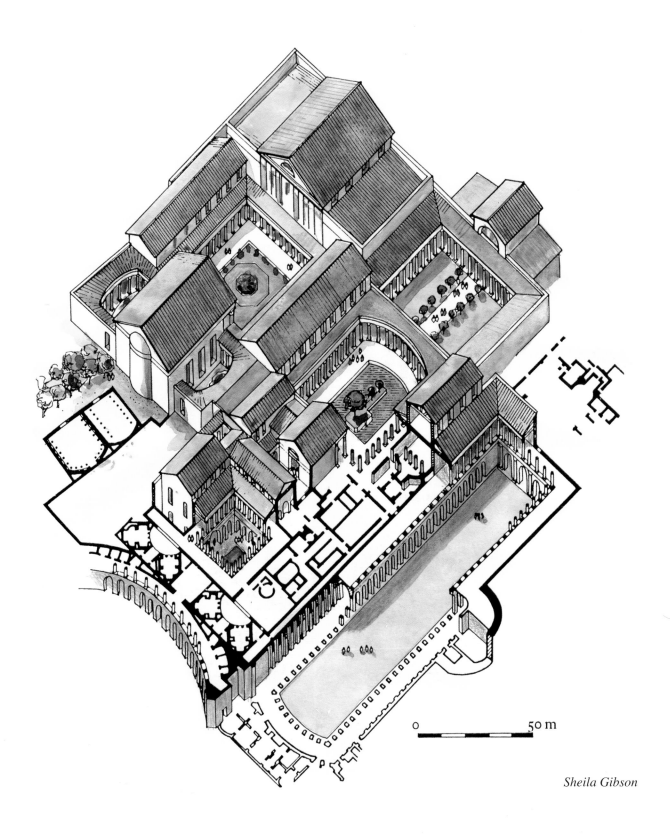

Fig. 6. The imperial residence on the Palatine in Rome, officially known as the Domus Augustana and less officially as Domitian's Palace. The palace was inaugurated in AD 92 and included state rooms, a colonnaded courtyard, and a banqueting hall.

Sheila Gibson

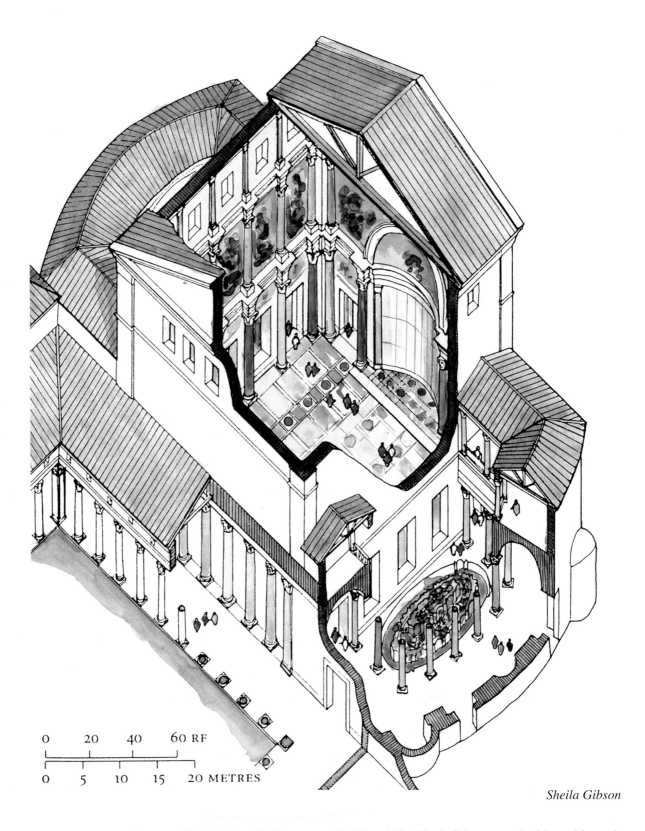

Sheila Gibson

Fig. 7. The Banquet Hall in Domitian's Palace, built between AD 81 and 92. The hall is veneered with marble, and there are mosaics above. In the court in front is an island-fountain, and to the side is the palace-complex's first court, apparently given the name 'Sicily' and also veneered entirely in marble. The poet Statius described the hall in AD 93/4: 'I think I am dining with Jupiter in mid-heaven.' (*Silvae* 4. 2. 18).

Chapter 2

Introducing nouns, verbs, and adjectives
The five declensions
The nominative as subject and predicate
The present tense in the active voice
The verb 'to be'

Declension, declension, declension,
I've forgotten my Latin declension.
Second or first?
Third is the worst,
Declension, declension, declension.

Traditional school-incantation at the start of the academic year

Grammar combines phonology, morphology, and syntax. Phonology is the science of vocal sounds. Morphology refers to the way different parts of speech are formed, and syntax is the ordering of these words. The essential building blocks for any grammar are nouns (words representing people, places, things, ideas, or other such), and verbs (words which explain what these nouns are up to). Nouns decline (politely); verbs (more robust on the whole) conjugate. As for adjectives, they describe nouns and follow their lead.

VI. Declensions and cases [GLG 23]

8. Nouns are divided into five declensions. Within a declension, the case of a noun identifies the function of that noun within a sentence. These cases are formed by attaching different endings to the stem of a noun.

(a) The nominative case identifies the subject or subjects of a sentence (*i.e.*, what the sentence is about).

(b) The genitive case indicates possession.

(c) The dative case identifies the indirect object or objects of a sentence, usually after verbs of giving, showing, or telling. In English, the indirect object often comes after either 'to' or 'for' which acts as a 'buffer' between the verb and the noun (hence the notion of indirectness).

(d) The accusative case identifies the direct object or objects of a sentence, that is, those items on which the verb acts and which are usually positioned immediately after the English verb. A verb that takes a direct object is called a transitive verb.

(e)   The ablative case indicates special relationships within a sentence; in English translations of Latin, it is always introduced by prepositions, words like 'by' (as in the usage known as the ablative of means) or 'with' (as in the ablative of manner or the ablative of accompaniment).

Thus, if the sentence

The serpent gave the apple of Paradise to Eve by guile.

were translated into Latin, 'serpent' would be in the nominative, 'apple' in the accusative, 'Paradise' in the genitive, 'Eve' in the dative, and 'guile' in the ablative.

VII. Gender and number [GLG 19-22]

9. Nouns have gender and are described as masculine, feminine, or neuter.

10. Nouns are either singular or plural.

11. Latin does not have a word for the English definite article 'the' or the indefinite article 'a' or 'an'. It is necessary to decide from context whether an author means a particular designation or a general one (*e.g.*, *a* hippopotamus or *the* hippopotamus)

VIII. Noun-stems [GLG 17, 25]

12. The stem of the noun is that part of the word to which different case-endings are attached. These endings change the function of a word within a sentence. The word is thereby said to be inflected. Latin, therefore, is an inflected language.

The noun-stem is usually found by dropping the genitive singular ending of the noun. For this reason, whenever vocabulary is studied, the genitive singular form of a noun must be memorized together with the nominative singular form and the gender of the noun.

IX. The first declension [GLG 29-30]

13. Nouns in the first declension are usually feminine. There are exceptions:

advena	stranger
agricola	farmer
nauta	sailor

perfuga		deserter
pīrāta		pirate
poēta		poet

These masculine first-declension nouns still use the same endings as any other first declension noun.

14. Any noun with the genitive-ending -ae is a first declension noun. The nominative singular ending is -a.

15. The endings for first declension nouns are as follows:

FIRST DECLENSION NOUNS

puella (girl)

	singular	plural	singular	plural
nom.	-a	-ae	puella	puellae
gen.	-ae	-ārum	puellae	puellārum
dat.	-ae	-īs	puellae	puellīs
acc.	-am	-ās	puellam	puellās
abl.	-ā	-īs	puellā	puellīs

16. The dative and ablative plurals of dea, deae (goddess) and fīlia, fīliae (daughter) are irregular, in that the forms deābus and fīliābus are used instead of the regular constructions.

X. The second declension [GLG 31-34]

17. Second declension nouns have the genitive singular ending in -ī; the nominative singular ends in -us or -r or -um.

18. Nouns with -us or -r in the nominative are masculine; those with -um are neuter.

19. The stem of a second declension noun ending in -r either loses or retains the vowel before the -r: puer, puerī (boy), but ager, agrī (field). The English cognate of the Latin noun will usually remind one whether or not the vowel is retained (*e.g.*, 'puerile' keeping the -e, 'agriculture' dropping it).

20. Endings for second declension nouns are as follows:

SECOND DECLENSION NOUNS

| | masculine | | neuter | |
	singular	plural	singular	plural
nom.	-us, -r	-ī	-um	-a
gen.	-ī	-ōrum	-ī	-ōrum
dat.	-ō	-īs	-ō	-īs
acc.	-um	-ōs	-um	-a
abl.	-ō	-īs	-ō	-īs

| **dominus (master)** | | | **bellum (war)** | |
| | masculine | | neuter | |
	singular	plural	singular	plural
nom.	dominus	dominī	bellum	bella
gen.	dominī	dominōrum	bellī	bellōrum
dat.	dominō	dominīs	bellō	bellīs
acc.	dominum	dominōs	bellum	bella
abl.	dominō	dominīs	bellō	bellīs

| **puer (boy)** | | |
	singular	plural
nom.	puer	puerī
gen.	puerī	puerōrum
dat.	puerō	puerīs
acc.	puerum	puerōs
abl.	puerō	puerīs

21. Second declension nouns ending in -ius and -ium generally have genitive singular forms ending in -ī, rather than -iī (*e.g.*, cōnsilī (plan), rather than cōnsiliī). The stress of the genitive will remain on the same syllable as in the nominative.

XI. The third declension [GLG 35-59]

22. Third declension nouns are identified by the genitive singular ending -is. There is no standard form for the nominative singular. Nouns are masculine, feminine, or neuter.

23. Noun-endings are attached to the third declension noun-stem found by dropping the -is ending of the genitive. Endings for the third declension are as follows:

THIRD DECLENSION NOUNS

| | masculine, feminine | | neuter | |
	singular	plural	singular	plural
nom.	?	-ēs	?	-a
gen.	-is	-um	-is	-um
dat.	-ī	-ibus	-ī	-ibus
acc.	-em	-ēs	= nom.	-a
abl.	-e	-ibus	-e	-ibus

| | **mīles, mīlitis (soldier)** | | **soror, sorōris (sister)** | | **iūs, iūris (justice, right, duty)** | |
| | masculine | | feminine | | neuter | |
	singular	plural	singular	plural	singular	plural
nom.	mīles	mīlitēs	soror	sorōrēs	iūs	iūra
gen.	mīlitis	mīlitum	sorōris	sorōrum	iūris	iūrum
dat.	mīlitī	mīlitibus	sorōrī	sorōribus	iūrī	iūribus
acc.	mīlitem	mīlitēs	sorōrem	sorōrēs	iūs	iūra
abl.	mīlite	mīlitibus	sorōre	sorōribus	iūre	iūribus

24. Third declension nouns in -iō, -tūdō, and -tās are generally feminine: dominātiō, dominātiōnis (lordship); multitūdō, multitūdinis (multitude) vānitās, vānitātis (vanity).

25. Third declension nouns in -or are generally masculine: vīctor, vīctōris (victor); but soror, sorōris (sister) and arbor, arboris (tree) are feminine.

26. Third declension nouns whose nominatives end in -n are neuter: nōmen, nōminis (name); carmen, carminis (song).

XII. The fourth declension [GLG 61-62]

27. Fourth declension nouns have -ūs in the genitive singular. Masculine and feminine nouns have -us in the nominative singular, and neuter ones have -ū.

28. Fourth declension endings are as follows:

FOURTH DECLENSION NOUNS

	masculine, feminine		neuter	
	singular	**plural**	**singular**	**plural**
nom.	-us	-ūs	-ū	-ua
gen.	-ūs	-uum	-ūs	-uum
dat.	-uī	-ibus	-ū	-ibus
acc.	-um	-ūs	-ū	-ua
abl.	-ū	-ibus	-ū	-ibus

	frūctus, -ūs (fruit, profit, enjoyment)		**manus, -ūs (hand, band of men)**		**cornū, -ūs (horn, wing of an army)**	
	masculine		feminine		neuter	
	singular	**plural**	**singular**	**plural**	**singular**	**plural**
nom.	frūctus	frūctūs	manus	manūs	cornū	cornua
gen.	frūctūs	frūctuum	manūs	manuum	cornūs	cornuum
dat.	frūctuī	frūctibus	manuī	manibus	cornū	cornibus
acc.	frūctum	frūctūs	manum	manūs	cornū	cornua
abl.	frūctū	frūctibus	manū	manibus	cornū	cornibus

Domus (f., house) is declined partly like a second declension noun and partly like a fourth declension noun.

nom.	domus	domūs
gen.	domūs	domōrum
dat.	domuī	domibus
acc.	domum	domōs, domūs
abl.	domō	domibus

29. Fourth declension nouns are often formed from the fourth principal part of a verb: adventus, -ūs, m. (arrival, from adveniō, to arrive).

XIII. The fifth declension [GLG 63-64]

30. Almost all nouns of the fifth declension are feminine. Diēs (day) is the principal exception. It is masculine normally, but feminine when referring to an appointed day or date. In the plural, diēs is always masculine. Fifth decleticals nouns are identified by the genitive singular ending -ēī. The nominative singular ends in -ēs.

31. Fifth-declension endings are as follows:

FIFTH DECLENSION NOUNS

diēs, -ēī (day)

	singular	plural	singular	plural
nom.	-ēs	-ēs	diēs	diēs
gen.	-ēī	-ērum	diēī	diērum
dat.	-ēī	-ēbus	diēī	diēbus
acc.	-em	-ēs	diem	diēs
abl.	-ē	-ēbus	diē	diēbus

Note that in the genitive and dative singulars, -ē shortens after a consonant.

XIV. Verbs and their moods [GLG 253]

32. Verbs denote the action taking place within a sentence. Mood in grammar refers to a verb's nature. Latin has three moods: the indicative in which verbs tend to be concerned with fact; the subjunctive in which verbs tend to be concerned with hypotheticals; and the imperative in which verbs appear as commands.

XV. Person and voice [GLG 212-214]

33. A verb is said to be in the active voice when it describes action done by the subject of the sentence. In the passive voice, the subject is the recipient of the action.

34. A verb may be in the first, second, or third person, depending on its subject. In the singular, if the verb is in the first person, its subject is 'I'; in the second person, its subject is 'you'; in the third, its subject is 'he,' 'she,' or 'it,' if unstated. In the plural, if the verb is in the first person, its subject is 'we'; in the second person, its subject is 'you'; and in the third person, the subject is 'they,' if not explicitly given.

XVI. Tenses [GLG 222-245]

35. Be sensitive to distinctions among tenses, which denote the times at which particular actions take place. In the indicative mood, there are six tenses.

(a) The present tense denotes action taking place at that moment.

(b) The imperfect tense denotes continuous action in the past. The imperfect may also have a conative sense ('tried to _____').

(c) The future tense denotes action that will take place.

(d) The perfect tense denotes completed action in the past.

(e) The pluperfect denotes action completed prior to another completed action.

(f) The future perfect denotes action to be completed at a particular moment in the future.

XVII. Conjugations and principal parts [GLG 17, 120]

36. Latin verbs are divided into four conjugations. Within a conjugation, each regular verb has four principal parts, from which one can derive all verbal forms. The second principal part identifies the conjugation under which a verb is classified.

(a) Verbs with a second principal part ending in -āre comprise the first conjugation: *e.g.,* amō, amāre, amāvī, amātum.

(b) Those with the ending -ēre and a first principal part ending in -eō comprise the second conjugation: *e.g.,* moneō, monēre, monuī, monitum.

(c) Those ending with -ere form the third conjugation: *e.g.,* regō, regere, rēxī, rēctum; capiō, capere, cēpī, captum.

(d) Those with the ending -īre form the fourth conjugation: *e.g.,* audiō, audīre, audīvī, audītum.

37. The first principal part is the first person singular form of the verb in the present tense, active voice (*e.g.,* I love, I do love, I am loving). The second principal part is the infinitive of the verb (*e.g.,* to love). The third is the first person singular form of the verb in the perfect tense, active voice (*e.g.,* I loved, I have loved). The fourth principal part is called the supine and forms part of a number of verb forms.

XVIII. The verbal-stem [GLG 120]

38. The stem of a verb is that part of the verb to which different endings are attached in order to change its meaning. The verbal-stem is normally found by dropping the -re of the second principal part.

XIX. Morphology of the present tense, active [GLG 122-127]

39. In the active, the first principal part of the verb gives the first-person singular form. To generate the remaining forms, take the verbal-stem, and add the endings shown below. But:

(a) for the third conjugation, the -e- of the verbal-stem shifts to -i- before endings are added;

(b) in the third person plural form of the third conjugation, however, the -e- shifts to -u- before endings are added;

(c) for the third person plural form of the fourth conjugation, -u- and the personal ending are added directly onto the stem;

(d) third conjugation verbs with first principal part ending in -iō (*e.g.*, faciō or capiō) are essentially conjugated in the present tense as if they were fourth-conjugation verbs.

FIRST CONJUGATION PRESENT ACTIVE

amō, amāre (love; stem: amā-)

	singular			**plural**	
1st	amō	I love, am loving, do love		amā**mus**	we love, are loving, do love
2d	amās	you love, are loving, do love		amā**tis**	you love, are loving, do love
3d	ama**t**	he, she, it loves, is loving, does love		ama**nt**	they love, are loving, do love

---

SECOND CONJUGATION PRESENT ACTIVE

moneō, monēre (warn, advise; stem: monē-)

1st	moneō	I warn, *etc.*		monē**mus**	we warn, *etc.*
2d	monē**s**	you warn, *etc.*		monē**tis**	you warn, *etc.*
3d	mone**t**	he, she, it warns, *etc.*		mone**nt**	they warn, *etc.*

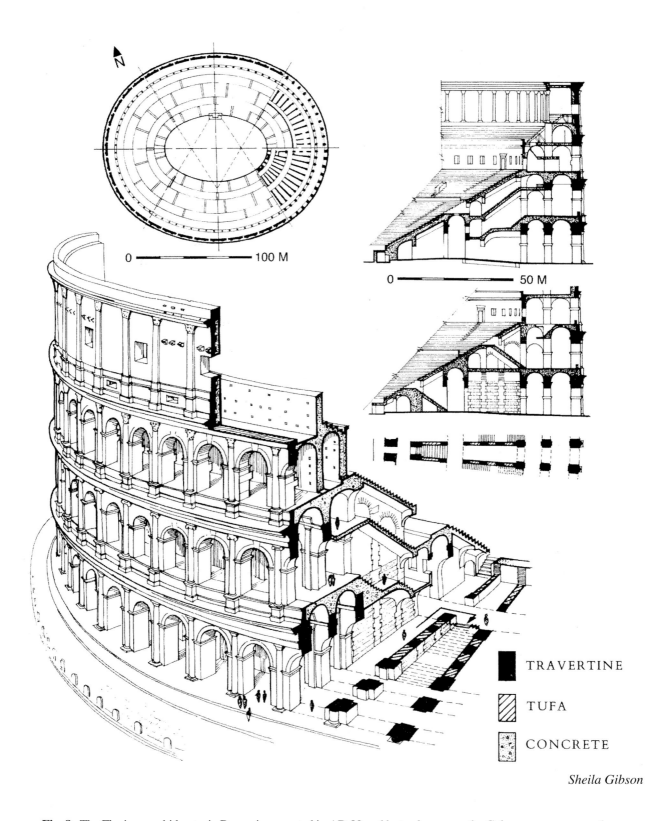

N

0   100 M

0   50 M

■ TRAVERTINE

▨ TUFA

▧ CONCRETE

Sheila Gibson

Fig. 8. The Flavian amphitheatre in Rome, inaugurated in AD 80 and better known as the Colosseum, a name perhaps derived from the Colossus of Nero, a statue which stood nearby. The amphitheatre seated between 45,000 and 55,000 people.

THIRD CONJUGATION PRESENT ACTIVE

regō, regere (rule; stem: rege-, shifting to regi-, regunt in the third plural)

1st	reg**ō**	I rule, *etc.*	regi**mus**	we rule, *etc.*
2d	regi**s**	you rule, *etc.*	regi**tis**	you rule, *etc.*
3d	regi**t**	he, she, it rules, *etc.*	reg**unt**	they rule, *etc.*

THIRD CONJUGATION (-IŌ) PRESENT ACTIVE

capiō, capere (take, form a plan or conspiracy
stem: cape-, shifting to capi-; capiunt in the third plural)

1st	capi**ō**	I take, *etc.*	capi**mus**	we take, *etc.*
2d	capi**s**	you take, *etc.*	capi**tis**	you take, *etc.*
3d	capi**t**	he, she, it takes, *etc.*	capi**unt**	they take, *etc.*

FOURTH CONJUGATION PRESENT ACTIVE

audiō (hear; stem: audī-; audiunt in the third plural)

1st	audi**ō**	I hear, *etc.*	audī**mus**	we hear, *etc.*
2d	audī**s**	you hear, *etc.*	audī**tis**	you hear, *etc.*
3d	audi**t**	he, she, it hears, *etc.*	audi**unt**	they hear, *etc.*

XX. The present tense of the verb esse (to be) [GLG 116]

40. The principal parts of the verb 'to be' are: sum, esse, fuī, futūrum. As in all languages, the present tense is irregular:

ESSE IN THE PRESENT

sum	I am	sumus	we are
es	you are	estis	you are
est	he, she, it is; there is	sunt	they are; there are

XXI. The nominative case and verbs [GLG 203-206]

41. The subject of a sentence is expressed in the nominative. It can appear in any position, even after the verb. If the subject is not explicitly stated, it is expressed in the verb.

> ārdēbant oculī.
>
> Their eyes were burning.   Cicero, *Verrine Orations* 2. 5. 62. 161
>
> Fīlium ūnicum adulēscentulum habeō.
>
> I have an only son, a rather young man.   Terence, *The Self-Tormentor* 94

42. Esse does not take a direct object. Instead, a nominative appears after it. This nominative is called a complement or predicate nominative. Similarly, an adjective after esse will be in the nominative and agree with the subject in case, number, and gender.

In addition to esse, these passive verb forms may take a predicate nominative:

appellor	be called
creor	be created
fiō	become
habeor	be considered
legor	be chosen
putor	be thought
videor	seem
vocor	be called

> ipsa Fōrtūna caeca est.
>
> Fortune herself is blind.   Cicero, *On Friendship* 15. 54
>
> rēx est dēclārātus.
>
> He was declared king.   Livy 1. 46. 1

XXII. Agreement of adjectives [GLG 72, 289-291]

43. Adjectives modify nouns and agree with the nouns they modify in case, number, and gender:

> bona dea
>
> bonus agricola

XXIII. Adjectives as substantives [GLG 204]

44. Adjectives are often used as nouns, particularly in the nominative and accusative plural. In such a case, the adjective is said to be used substantively. If the adjective has a masculine ending, supply a noun like 'man'; if feminine, supply a feminine noun like 'woman'; if neuter, supply a neuter noun like 'thing'.

Omnia ergō servāte et facite.

Therefore, preserve and keep all those things (*i.e.*, commandments).

Matthew 23: 3

XXIV. First and second declension adjectives [GLG 73]

45. First and second declension adjectives use endings of the first and second declension nouns.

FIRST AND SECOND DECLENSION ADJECTIVES

bonus, bona, bonum (good)

	singular			plural		
	masc.	*fem.*	*neut.*	*masc.*	*fem.*	*neut.*
nom.	bonus	bona	bonum	bonī	bonae	bona
gen.	bonī	bonae	bonī	bonōrum	bonārum	bonōrum
dat.	bonō	bonae	bonō	bonīs	bonīs	bonīs
acc.	bonum	bonam	bonum	bonōs	bonās	bona
abl.	bonō	bonā	bonō	bonīs	bonīs	bonīs

pulcher, pulchra, pulchrum (beautiful)

	singular			plural		
	masc.	*fem.*	*neut.*	*masc.*	*fem.*	*neut.*
nom.	pulcher	pulchra	pulchrum	pulchrī	pulchrae	pulchra
gen.	pulchrī	pulchrae	pulchrī	pulchrōrum	pulchrārum	pulchrōrum
dat.	pulchrō	pulchrae	pulchrō	pulchrīs	pulchrīs	pulchrīs
acc.	pulchrum	pulchram	pulchrum	pulchrōs	pulchrās	pulchra
abl.	pulchrō	pulchrā	pulchrō	pulchrīs	pulchrīs	pulchrīs

XXV. Third declension adjectives [GLG 77-83]

46. Third declension adjectives may have

(a)   three terminations (a separate form for each gender of the nominative singular);

ācer, ācris, ācre   sharp, eager, fierce

(b)   two terminations (the same form for the masculine and feminine nominative singular with a

different form for the neuter);

similis, simile   like

THIRD DECLENSION ADJECTIVES

ācer, ācris, ācre (eager, fierce)

	singular			plural		
	masc.	*fem.*	*neut.*	*masc.*	*fem.*	*neut.*
nom.	ācer	ācris	ācre	ācrēs	ācrēs	ācria
gen.	ācris	ācris	ācris	ācrium	ācrium	ācrium
dat.	ācrī	ācrī	ācrī	ācribus	ācribus	ācribus
acc.	ācrem	ācrem	ācre	ācrēs (-īs)	ācrēs (-īs)	ācria
abl.	ācrī	ācrī	ācrī	ācribus	ācribus	ācribus

similis, simile (like)

	singular		plural	
	masc., fem.	*neut.*	*masc., fem.*	*neut.*
nom.	similis	simile	similēs	similia
gen.	similis	similis	similium	similium
dat.	similī	similī	similibus	similibus
acc.	similem	simile	similēs (-īs)	similia
abl.	similī	similī	similibus	similibus

pār (equal, like)

	masc., fem.	*neut.*	*masc., fem.*	*neut.*
nom.	pār	pār	parēs	paria
gen.	paris	paris	parium	parium
dat.	parī	parī	paribus	paribus
acc.	parem	pār	parēs (-īs)	paria
abl.	parī	parī	paribus	paribus

(c)   one termination (the same form for the masculine, feminine, and neuter nominative singular)

pār (gen. pāris)   equal, like

The stem to which the endings are added is found by dropping the -e of the neuter nominative singular form. In the case of those adjectives with only one form for all genders, the stem has to be memorised.

Note:

(a)   in the genitive plural, the ending is -ium, not simply -um.

(b)   n the ablative singular, the third declension adjective-ending is -ī, not -e.

(c)   in the masculine and feminine accusative plural forms, -īs and -ēs are both found as endings.

(d)   in the accusative neuter plural, the ending is -ia, not simply -a.

EXERCISES

For the full range of semantic meanings available, consult a proper dictionary, such as the *Oxford Latin Dictionary* or the equally large volume edited by Lewis and Short. When parsing or considering the form of a word, always ask first: what part of speech is this? In translating from English into Latin, it is perhaps better not to leave it until the end to sprinkle the macra, like salt and pepper, over the noun and verb endings, but to mark lengths immediately, so as to force oneself to think about the appropriate cases or tenses.

A. Vocabulary

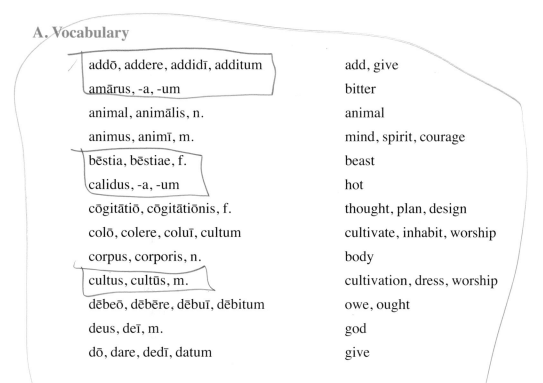

addō, addere, addidī, additum	add, give
amārus, -a, -um	bitter
animal, animālis, n.	animal
animus, animī, m.	mind, spirit, courage
bēstia, bēstiae, f.	beast
calidus, -a, -um	hot
cōgitātiō, cōgitātiōnis, f.	thought, plan, design
colō, colere, coluī, cultum	cultivate, inhabit, worship
corpus, corporis, n.	body
cultus, cultūs, m.	cultivation, dress, worship
dēbeō, dēbēre, dēbuī, dēbitum	owe, ought
deus, deī, m.	god
dō, dare, dedī, datum	give

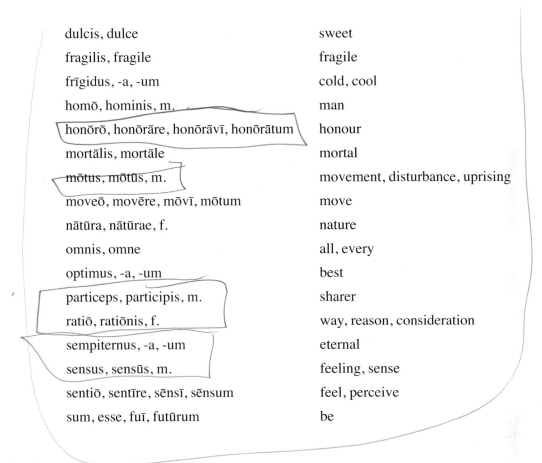

dulcis, dulce	sweet
fragilis, fragile	fragile
frīgidus, -a, -um	cold, cool
homō, hominis, m.	man
honōrō, honōrāre, honōrāvī, honōrātum	honour
mortālis, mortāle	mortal
mōtus, mōtūs, m.	movement, disturbance, uprising
moveō, movēre, mōvī, mōtum	move
nātūra, nātūrae, f.	nature
omnis, omne	all, every
optimus, -a, -um	best
particeps, participis, m.	sharer
ratiō, ratiōnis, f.	way, reason, consideration
sempiternus, -a, -um	eternal
sensus, sensūs, m.	feeling, sense
sentiō, sentīre, sēnsī, sēnsum	feel, perceive
sum, esse, fuī, futūrum	be

B. Sentences

The following sentences for translation are taken from philosophical and scientific works by Cicero, the greatest of the Classical Roman orators. Cicero's philosophy was once thought to be largely derivative of his Greek predecessors, but it has become increasingly clear how original he was, and his works were crucial to the development of a Latin philosophical vocabulary.

1. Omne animal sensūs habet; sentit igitur et calida, et frīgida, et dulcia, et amāra. (*On the Nature of Gods* 3. 13. 32)

2. Bēstiīs nātūra sensum et mōtum dat; hominī addit ratiōnem. (*On the Nature of Gods* 2. 12. 34)

3. Homō est animal mortāle, particeps ratiōnis et cōgitātiōnis. (*Laws* 1. 7. 22)

4. Sīc fragile corpus animus sempiternus movet. (*Dream of Scipio* 8 = *Republic* 6. 24. 26)

5. We ought to honour all gods; the worship of the gods is best. (*On the Nature of Gods* 2. 28. 71)

Fig. 9. Trajan's Column in Rome.

Sheila Gibson

Fig. 10. The hemicycle of Trajan's Market in Rome, built ca. AD 100-112. The market contained more than 150 shops and offices, and there were entrances at three different levels. The construction was of concrete, faced with brick.

Chapter 3

I-stem nouns of the third declension
More on the genitive and dative
The imperfect and future in the indicative, active
The imperfect and future of esse
Adverbs and more on adjectives

> *Some Grammarians treat the subject in so extensive and minute a manner as to confuse rather than edify, ... and by attempting to accomplish too much they frustrate their own plan.*

T. Smith, *The Eton Latin Grammar,* new ed. (1852), iii

> *Vēr'bŭm* pērsōnā'lĕ cōncōr'dăt* cŭm* nōminātī'vō nū'mĕrō et* pērsō'nā ....*

An explanation of verb use in the above grammar, 109

The point of taking a sentence apart analytically is to put the whole back together again. Like an auto-mechanic who spreads out carburetor and muffler and clutch onto the garage-floor to see what makes a car go or not go, a grammarian examines the parts of sentences to identify the thinking behind the whole. But driving is not simply a matter of turning a key and aiming the car. There are subtleties of steering and public laws to follow. In Latin too, there are nuances to different parts of speech. The trick of translation is to combine all the grammatical bits in such a way as to end with a coherent expression of thought.

XXVI. I-stem nouns of the third declension [GLG 56-58]

47. A third declension word is an i-stem noun if:

(a)   it is masculine or feminine, and the nominative singular ends in -is or -ēs, with the genitive having the same number of syllables:

      caedēs, caedis, f.   slaughter

      hostis, hostis, m. or f.   enemy

(b)   its nominative singular ends in two consonants (including x, the equivalent of ks) and its genitive singular also has two consonants before the case-ending:

      nox, noctis, f.   night

      pōns, pōntis, m.   bridge

(c)   it is a neuter word ending in -e, -al, or -ar:

animal, animālis, n.	animal
calcar, calcāris, n.	spur; incitement
mare, maris, n.	sea
sedīle, sedīlis, n.	seat

48. Masculine or feminine i-stem words can have -ēs or -īs in the accusative plural. The genitive plural ending is -ium, rather than -um, and -ia appears as the nominative and accusative neuter plural ending, not -a. Neuter i-stem nouns use -ī in the ablative singular, not -e.

THIRD DECLENSION I-STEM NOUNS

	fīnis, fīnis (end)		**mors, mortis (death)**		**mare, maris (sea)**	
	masculine		feminine		neuter	
	singular	**plural**	**singular**	**plural**	**singular**	**plural**
nom.	fīnis	fīnēs	mors	mortēs	mare	maria
gen.	fīnis	fīnium	mortis	mortium	maris	marium
dat.	fīnī	fīnibus	mortī	mortibus	marī	maribus
acc.	fīnem	fīnēs (-īs)	mortem	mortēs (-īs)	mare	maria
abl.	fīne	fīnibus	morte	mortibus	marī	maribus

49. Note the irregular declension of the noun vīs, —, f. (force, power; courage, strength, in the plural):

nom.	vīs	vīrēs
gen.	—	vīrium
dat.	—	vīribus
acc.	vim	vīrēs
abl.	vī	vīribus

Do not confuse this word with vir, virī, m. (man).

XXVII. The genitive case [GLG 360-383]

50. Most of the time, a genitive denotes possession, and the noun is translated with 'of' in front of it. But there are additional uses:

(a)   A noun modified by an adjective can express description in the genitive. This is called a descriptive genitive.

> T. Balventiō, virō māgnae auctōritātis, femur trāgulā trāicitur.

> The thigh of Titus Balventius, a man of great influence, was pierced by a dart.

> Caesar, *Gallic War* 5. 35. 6

(b)   The partitive genitive (or genitive of the whole) is used typically after pars, partis, f. (part, direction, side), and after certain adverbs. A noun denoting a part is followed by a noun in the genitive denoting the whole. In English, it is sometimes best to ignore the 'of' in translation.

> māxima pars hominum morbō iactātur eōdem.

> The greatest part of mankind is racked by the same illness.

> Horace, *Satires* 2. 3. 121

Note the following words that tend to take a partitive genitive:

aliquid novī	something new
minus pecūniae	less (of) money
nihil pecūniae	nothing (of) money, no money
plūrimum pecūniae	very much (of) money
plūs pecūniae	more (of) money
satis pecūniae	enough (of) money
tantum pecūniae	so much (of) money

The following words, which seem to take the genitive in English, are used in Latin as adjectives in agreement with the noun:

cēterī, cēterae, cētera (plural)	the rest of
extrēmus, -a, um	the end of
īmus, -a, -um	the bottom of
medius, -a, -um	the middle of
reliquus, -a, -um	the remainder of
summus, -a, -um	the top of

(c)   Occasionally, the genitive is best translated with 'for.' This is called an objective genitive.

      adsectābar mīrā studiōrum cupiditāte.

      I was attending closely because of a wonderful passion for studies.

Tacitus, Dialogue on Oratory 2. 1

In this sentence, 'studies' (studiōrum) identifies the object of the desire (cupiditās).

(d)   The genitive case may express measurement. This is known as the genitive of measurement.

      mūrum in altitūdīnem pedum sēdecim perdūcit.

      He constructs a wall to a height of sixteen feet.

Caesar, Gallic War 1. 8. 1

Note too that verbs of remembering (meminī) and forgetting (oblīvīscor) may take a genitive. Verbs of reminding (admoneō) have the person reminded in the accusative and the thing of which he is reminded in the genitive. Similarly, common verbs indicating a charge or penalty, such as accūsō (I accuse), damnō (I condemn), and absolvō (I acquit) may be followed by the accusative of the person, but the genitive of the charge or penalty.

XXVIII. The dative case [GLG 344-359]

51. The dative case identifies the indirect object of a sentence and is translated by 'to' or 'for'. It is used after words of giving, showing, and telling, such as dēmōnstrō (show), dīcō (say), dō (give), nūntiō (announce), or trādō (surrender).

      praedam mīlitibus dōnat.

      He grants booty to the soldiers.

Caesar, Gallic War 7. 11. 9

52. Other common uses are as follows:

(a)   A dative of purpose identifies the reasoning behind an action.

      castrīs idōneum locum dēligit.

      He selects a place suitable for camping.

Caesar, Gallic War 6. 10. 2

The most common words used as datives of purpose are:

auxiliō	as an aid
cūrae	as a concern

impedīmentō	as a hindrance
praesidiō	as a protection
subsidiō	as an aid
ūsuī	as a use

(b) A dative of possession may appear after a form of esse in the third person.

> contrōversiam dīiūdicābis quae mihi fuit cum avunculō tuō.

> You will adjudicate my debate with your uncle.

Cicero, *On Ends* 3. 2. 6

(c) After the gerundive with sum (*i.e.*, the passive periphrastic construction), the dative of agent is used.

> dēspēranda [est] tibi salvā concordia socrū.

> You must despair of concord if your mother-in-law is alive.

Juvenal 6. 231

53. The dative is often used after a compound verb (a verb whose meaning is completed by a prefix).

impōnō, impōnere, imposuī, impositum	to place (acc.) on (dat.)
īnferō, īnferre, intulī, inlātum	to bring (acc.) on (dat.)
occurrō, occurrere, occurrī, occursum	to run to meet (dat.)
praeficiō, praeficere, praefēcī, praefectum	to put (acc.) in charge of (dat.)
praestō, praestāre, praestitī, praestitum	to excel (dat.)
praesum, praeesse, praefuī, praefutūrum	to be in charge of (dat.)
subveniō, subvenīre, subvēnī, subventum	to come to aid (dat.)

54. When two words independent of each other are in the dative, the literal translation is 'as a _____ to _____'.

> cuī bonō?

> As an advantage to whom?

Traditional question asked during murder investigations

This construction is called the double dative. One part of the construction is a dative of purpose, the other a dative of reference.

55. The dative case also follows certain Latin verbs which are transitive in English but intransitive in Latin.

The 17 'sacred' verbs that take the dative are:

crēdō, crēdere, crēdidī, crēditum	believe, entrust
faveō, favēre, fāvī, fautum	favour
fīdō, fīdere, fīsus sum	trust
ignōscō, ignōscere, ignōvī, ignōtum	pardon
imperō, imperāre, imperāvī, imperātum	order
invideō, invidēre, invīdī, invīsum	envy
īrāscor, īrāscī, īrātus sum	be angry
minor, minārī, minātus sum	threaten
noceō, nocēre, nocuī, nocitum	injure
parcō, parcere, pepercī, parsum	spare
pāreō, pārēre, pāruī, —	obey
permittō, permittere, permīsī, permissum	permit, entrust
persuādeō, persuādēre, persuāsī, persuāsum	persuade
placeō, placēre, plācuī, placitum	please
resistō, resistere, restitī, —	resist
serviō, servīre, servīvī, servītum	serve
studeō, studēre, studuī, —	be eager

56. The dative completes the meaning of several adjectives:

amīcus, -a, -um	friendly to
cārus, -a, -um	dear to
dissimilis, dissimile	not similar to
fidēlis, fidēle	faithful, loyal to
fīnitimus, -a, -um	near to, neighbouring to
grātus, -a, -um	pleasing to
idōneus, -a, -um	suitable for
inimīcus, -a, -um	unfriendly, hostile to
inūtilis, -e	not useful for
pār, paris	equal to

propīnquus, -a, -um	near to
proximus, -a, -um	nearest to
similis, -e	similar to
ūtilis, -e	useful for

XXIX. Morphology of the imperfect tense, active [GLG 122-127]

57. The imperfect tense in the active voice is formed by adding the endings shown below to the verbal stems. Fourth conjugation verbs have -ē- after the verbal stem and then add the imperfect endings. Third conjugation verbs that have -iō in the first principal part use -iē- instead of -e- in the verbal stem.

FIRST CONJUGATION IMPERFECT ACTIVE

amō, amāre (stem: amā-)

	singular			**plural**	
1st	amā**bam**	I was loving, used to love, kept loving		amabā**mus**	we were loving, etc.
2d	amā**bās**	you were loving, etc.		amabā**tis**	you were loving, etc.
3d	amā**bat**	he, she, it was loving, etc.		amā**bant**	they were loving, etc.

SECOND CONJUGATION IMPERFECT ACTIVE

moneō, monēre (stem: monē-)

1st	monē**bam**	I was warning, etc.		monēbā**mus**	we were warning, etc.
2d	monē**bās**	you were warning, etc.		monēbā**tis**	you were warning, etc.
3d	monē**bat**	he, she, it was warning, etc.		monē**bant**	they were warning, etc.

THIRD CONJUGATION IMPERFECT ACTIVE

regō, regere (stem: rege- becomes regē-)

1st	regē**bam**	I was ruling, etc.		regēbā**mus**	we were ruling, etc.
2d	regē**bās**	you were ruling, etc.		regēbā**tis**	you were ruling, etc.
3d	regē**bat**	he, she, it was ruling, etc.		regē**bant**	they were ruling, etc.

THIRD CONJUGATION (-IŌ) IMPERFECT ACTIVE

capiō, capere (stem: cape-, shifts to capiē-)

1st	capiēbam	I was taking, etc.	capiēbāmus	we were taking, etc.
2d	capiēbās	you were taking, etc.	capiēbātis	you were taking, etc.
3d	capiēbat	he, she, it was taking, etc.	capiēbant	they were taking, etc.

FOURTH CONJUGATION IMPERFECT ACTIVE

audiō, audīre (stem: audī- shifts to audiē-)

1st	audiēbam	I was hearing, etc.	audiēbāmus	we were hearing, etc.
2d	audiēbās	you were hearing, etc.	audiēbātis	you were hearing, etc.
3d	audiēbat	he, she, it was hearing, etc.	audiēbant	they were hearing, etc.

XXX. Morphology of the future tense, active voice for the first and second conjugations [GLG 122-127]

58. The future tense of verbs in the first and second conjugations is formed by taking the verbal stem and adding the endings shown below:

FIRST CONJUGATION FUTURE ACTIVE

amō, amāre (stem: amā-)

	singular			plural	
1st	amābō	I shall love	amābimus	we shall love
2d	amābis	you will love	amābitis	you will love
3d	amābit	he, she, it will love	amābunt	they will love

SECOND CONJUGATION FUTURE ACTIVE

moneō, monēre (stem: monē-)

1st	monēbō	I shall warn	monēbimus	we shall warn
2d	monēbis	you will warn	monēbitis	you will warn
3d	monēbit	he, she, it will warn	monēbunt	they will warn

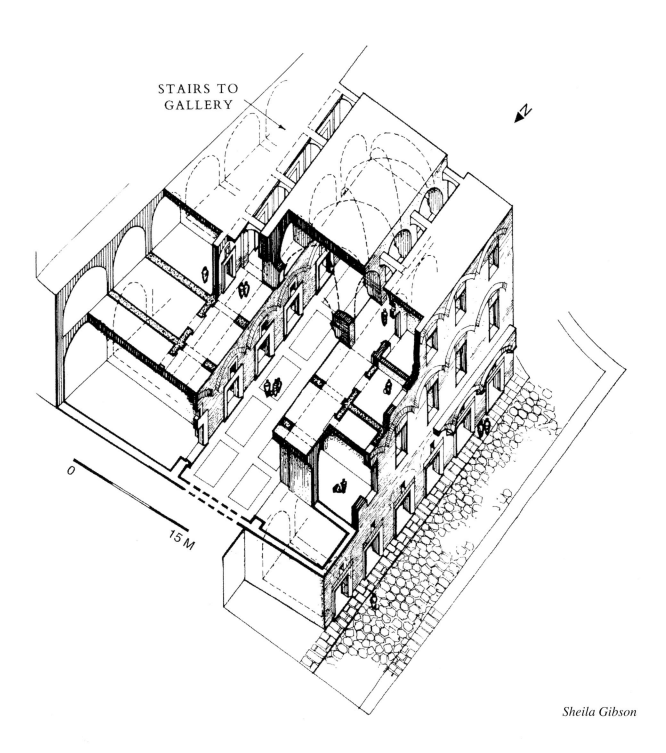

STAIRS TO
GALLERY

N

0

15 M

Sheila Gibson

Fig. 11. The main hall of Trajan's Market in Rome, built ca. AD 100-112, off the Via Biberatica. The market was covered, with shopping on three levels. The main hall is on the upper two storeys, with two rows of six shops opening off each side, beneath a vaulted roof.

XXXI. Formation of the future tense, active voice for the third and fourth conjugations [GLG 122-127]

59. To form the future tense of verbs in the third conjugation, take the second principal part of the verb, drop the -re, and add the endings shown below. Note, however, that in the first person singular of the future tense, active, the -e- of the verbal stem shifts to -a-.

THIRD CONJUGATION FUTURE ACTIVE

regō, regere (stem: rege-; regam in the first person singular)

	singular		**plural**	
1st	reg**am**	I shall rule	reg**ēmus**	we shall rule
2d	reg**ēs**	you will rule	reg**ētis**	you will rule
3d	reg**et**	he, she, it will rule	reg**ent**	they will rule

For the fourth conjugation, take the stem of the verb, and add the endings below.

FOURTH CONJUGATION FUTURE ACTIVE

audiō, audīre (stem: audī-, shortening to audi-)

1st	audi**am**	I shall hear	audi**ēmus**	we shall hear
2d	audi**ēs**	you will hear	audi**ētis**	you will hear
3d	audi**et**	he, she, it will hear	audi**ent**	they will hear

---

Third conjugation verbs with -iō in the first principal part have future tenses that resemble fourth conjugation verbs.

THIRD CONJUGATION (-IŌ) FUTURE ACTIVE

capiō, capere (stem: cape-, shifts to capi-)

1st	capi**am**	I shall take	capi**ēmus**	we shall take
2d	capi**ēs**	you will take	capi**ētis**	you will take
3d	capi**et**	he, she, it will take	capi**ent**	they will take

---

XXXII. The imperfect and future tenses of esse [GLG 116]

60. The imperfect and future tenses of esse are as follows:

<table>
<tr><td colspan="6" align="center">**IMPERFECT OF ESSE**</td></tr>
<tr><td></td><td colspan="2">**singular**</td><td></td><td colspan="2">**plural**</td></tr>
<tr><td>1st</td><td>eram</td><td>I was</td><td></td><td>erāmus</td><td>we were</td></tr>
<tr><td>2d</td><td>erās</td><td>you were</td><td></td><td>erātis</td><td>you were</td></tr>
<tr><td>3d</td><td>erat</td><td>he, she, it was</td><td></td><td>erant</td><td>they were</td></tr>
</table>

<table>
<tr><td colspan="6" align="center">**FUTURE OF ESSE**</td></tr>
<tr><td>1st</td><td>erō</td><td>I shall be</td><td></td><td>erimus</td><td>we shall be</td></tr>
<tr><td>2d</td><td>eris</td><td>you will be</td><td></td><td>eritis</td><td>you will be</td></tr>
<tr><td>3d</td><td>erit</td><td>he, she, it will be</td><td></td><td>erunt</td><td>they will be</td></tr>
</table>

XXXIII. The ablative case after certain adjectives [GLG 397, 401, 406]

61. Some adjectives require what is called an ablative of respect to complete their meanings; the following are especially important:

dīgnus, -a, -um	worthy (in respect to)
frētus, -a, -um	relying (on)
indīgnus, -a, -um	not worthy (in respect to)

> ita hāc opīniōne frētus tōtum sē facere posse exīstimābat.
>
> So, relying on this estimation, he was thinking he could do the whole.
>
> Caesar, *Spanish War* 28.3

Note also the following expression which uses a similar construction:

opus est (or erat, etc.)	there is need (in respect to)

XXXIV. Adjectives used as adverbs [GLG 91]

62. The accusative neuter singular of several adjectives is used adverbially.

minimum	least
minus	less
multum	much, quite
nihil	nothing
parum	too little
paulum	a little
plūrimum	very, very much
plūs	more, rather
tantum	so much

XXXV. Formation of comparative and superlative adjectives [GLG 86-89]

63. In English, the comparative form of the adjective is translated by adding '-er' to the basic English adjective (*e. g.*, 'wider'), or else by using the words 'more' or 'rather' or 'too' in front of the base or positive form of the adjective ('more difficult', 'rather difficult', 'too difficult').

The superlative form is translated by adding '-est' to the base form of the adjective ('widest'), or else by using the words 'most' or 'very' ('most difficult', 'very difficult').

64. In Latin, to form the comparative degree of a regular adjective:

(a)   find the stem of the adjective by dropping the ending from the genitive singular.

(b)   to this stem, add -ior (gen. -iōris) to form the masculine and feminine nominative singular of the comparative, and -ius (gen. -iōris) to form the neuter nominative singular of the comparative.

The comparative declines following the paradigm for third declension adjectives, but with -um, not -ium in the genitive plural. In Classical prose, however, the ablative singular of the comparative adjective ends in -e.

65. To form the superlative, add -issimus, -a, -um to the stem, and decline the superlative as if it were a first or second declension noun.

Thus:

lātus, lāta, lātum	wide or broad
lātior, lātius	wider or broader

lātissimus, -a, -um	widest or broadest
fortis, forte	brave
fortior, fortius	braver
fortissimus, -a, -um	bravest

66. For third declension adjectives that end in -er, add -ior (gen. -iōris) to the stem for the masculine and feminine forms of the comparative, and -ius (gen. -iōris) for the neuter form. Decline the adjectives using the third declension adjective endings, with -e in the ablative singular, and with -um, not -ium in the genitive plural.

To form the superlative, add -rimus, -rima, -rimum to the nominative, masculine, singular of the positive, and decline the adjective using first and second declension endings.

Thus:

ācer, ācris, ācre	sharp, bitter
ācrior, ācrius	sharper, more bitter
ācerrimus, ācerrima, ācerrimum	sharpest, most bitter.

67. The following adjectives add -limus, -lima, -limum to the stem to form the superlative adjective, and then decline using first and second declension adjective endings:

difficilis, -e (difficult)	difficilior, -ius	difficillimus, -a, -um
dissimilis, -e (not similar)	dissimilior, -ius	dissimillimus, -a, -um
facilis, -e (easy)	facilior, -ius	facillimus, -a, -um
gracilis, -e (slender)	gracilior, -ius	gracillimus, -a, um
humilis, -e (low)	humilior, -ius	humillimus, -a, -um
similis, -e (similar)	similior, -ius	simillimus, -a, -um

68. An adjective which has a vowel before the -us ending usually does not add another ending to form the comparative and superlative, but instead uses the positive form with magis (more) and maximē (very).

ēgregius (outstanding)	magis ēgregius	māximē ēgregius

XXXVI. Irregular comparative and superlative adjective forms [GLG 90]

69. The following irregular comparative and superlative forms should be noted:

IRREGULAR COMPARATIVE AND SUPERLATIVE ADJECTIVES

bonus, -a, -um (good)	melior, -ius (better)	optimus, -a, -um (best)
īnferus, -a, -um (low)	īnferior, -ius (lower)	īnfimus / īmus, -a, -um (lowest)
iuvenis, -e (young)	iūnior, -ius / minor nātū	minimus nātū (youngest)
māgnus, -a, -um (great)	māior, -ius (greater)	māximus, -a, -um (greatest)
malus, -a, -um (bad)	pēior, -ius (worse)	pessimus, -a, -um (worst)
multus, -a, -um (many)	—, plūs (more, stem: plūr-)	plūrimus, -a, -um (most)
parvus, -a, -um (little)	minor, minus (fewer)	minimus, -a, -um (fewest)
posterus, -a, -um (late)	posterior, -ius (later)	postrēmus, -a, -um (latest)
senex, senis (old)	senior, -ius /māior nātū (older)	māximus nātū (oldest)
superus, -a, -um (upper)	superior, -ius (higher, previous)	suprēmus, -a, -um / summus, -a, -um (highest, top of, last)
vetus, veteris (old)	vetustior, -ius (older)	veterrimus, -a, -um (oldest)

Plūs is declined as follows:

	singular		plural	
	masc. and fem.	*neut.*	*masc. and fem.*	*neut.*
nom.	—	plūs	plūrēs	plūra
gen.	—	plūris	plūrium	plūrium
dat.	—	—	plūribus	plūribus
acc.	—	plūs	plūrēs, plūrīs	plūra
abl.	—	—	plūribus	plūribus

XXXVII. Adverbs [GLG 91-92]

70. Adverbs qualify verbs. To form the Latin adverb:

(a)   take the stem of the adjective by dropping the ending of the genitive singular.

(b)   add -ē, if the adjective is in the first or second declension.

cārus, -a, -um (dear)	carē (dearly)
pulcher, pulchra, pulchrum (pretty)	pulchrē (prettily)

(c)   add -iter if the adjective is in the third declension:

celer, celeris, celere (swift, stem: celer-)	celeriter (swiftly)
fortis, forte (brave; stem: fort-)	fortiter (bravely)

If the stem ends in -nt, simply add -er:

potēns, potentis (powerful; stem: potent-)	potenter (powerfully)

71. Occasionally, the accusative singular neuter form of the adjective is used as an adverb:

facile	easily
trīste	sadly.

Sometimes, the adverb is taken from the ablative singular of the adjective:

prīmus (first)	prīmō (at first).

XXXVIII. The comparative and superlative adverb [GLG 93]

72. Adverbs form their comparative by using the neuter nominative singular of the comparative adjective from which they are derived. Regular comparative adverbs, therefore, will end in -ius.

Adverbs form their superlative by first dropping -us from the superlative of the adjective from which they were formed; then add -ē.

Thus:

pulchrē	beautifully
pulchrius	more beautifully
pulcherrimē	most beautifully

XXXIX. Irregular adverbs [GLG 93]

73. Note the following irregular adverbs:

bene, from bonus	well
māgnoperē, from māgnus	greatly

XL. Constructions using comparatives [GLG 296-301, 644]

74. Comparison can be expressed simply by using the ablative. This usage is known as the ablative of comparison. After a comparative adverb or adjective, translate the word in the ablative using 'than'.

nihil est enim virtūte amābilius.

For nothing is more lovable than virtue.

Cicero, *On Friendship* 8. 28

Similar to the ablative of comparison is the ablative of degree of difference which expresses a measured distinction between items:

turrēs dēnīs pedibus quam mūrus altiōrēs sunt.

The towers are higher than the wall by ten feet.

Curtius Rufus 5. 1. 26

75. Comparison may also be expressed by quam (than) used after a comparative. The items compared must be in the same case.

īgnōrātiō futūrōrum malōrum ūtilior est quam scientia.

Ignorance of future ills is more useful than knowledge of these.

Cicero, *On Divination* 2. 9. 23

XLI. Constructions using the superlative [GLG 303]

76. Quam with the superlative of an adjective or adverb is translated 'as _____ as possible'.

cīvitātibus māxima laus est quam lātissimē circum sē sōlitūdinēs habēre.

It is a very great distinction for states to have areas of wilderness as broadly

as possible around themselves.

Caesar, *Gallic War* 6. 23. 1

77. Sometimes the irregular verb posse (to be able) will appear in the quam-superlative construction, but it need not affect the translation.

> quam aequissimō locō potest castra commūnit.

> He fortified his camp in as favourable a place as possible.

Caesar, *Gallic War* 5. 49. 7

<h2 align="center">Exercises</h2>

A. Vocabulary

ad (*prep. with accus.*)	to, for, near, in respect to
administrō, administrāre, administrāvī, administrātum	manage
attentus, -a, -um	attentive
audiō, audīre, audīvī, audītum	hear
docilis, -e	easily taught
ferus, -a, -um	wild, fierce
immortālitās, immortālitātis, f.	immortality
māgnus, -a, -um	large, great
mors, mortis, f.	death
multus, -a, -um	much (*sing.*); many (*plur.*)
nec or neque	and ... not; nor
nēmō (gen. nūllīus; dat. nēminī; acc. nēminem; abl. nūllō) m, or f.	no one
nihil, —, n. (*undeclinable*)	nothing; not (*as adv.*)
patria, patriae, f.	fatherland
prō (*prep. with abl.*)	for, in front of
prōpāgō, prōpāgāre, prōpāgāvī, prōpāgātum	prolong, propagate
pūgnō, pūgnāre, pūgnāvī, pūgnātum	fight
quod	which, what, this, it, the fact that, because
sine (*prep. with abl.*)	without
spēs, speī, f.	hope
umquam	ever
vēlōx, vēlōcis	swift
vīctus, vīctūs, m.	food, way of life
vīs, —. f. (see § 49 for forms)	force, violence; strength (*in plural*)
vīta, vītae, f.	life

B. Sentences

The following sentences are again taken from the philosophical works of Cicero.

1.   Docilis erat, quod attentissimē audiēbat. (*On Invention* 1. 16. 23)

2.   Hominēs vīctū ferō vītam prōpāgābant, nec ratiōne animī, sed multa vīribus corporis
     administrābant. (*On Invention* 1. 2. 2)

3.   Nēmō umquam sine māgnā spē immortālitātis prō patriā pūgnābit ad mortem.
     (*Tusculan Disputes* 1. 15. 32)

4.   Nothing is swifter than the soul. (based on *Tusculan Disputes* 1. 19. 43)

Fig. 12. Island villa (called the 'Teatro Marittimo') of Hadrian's Villa, built AD 118-125, at Tivoli near Rome.

Fig. 13. Pantheon in Rome, ca. 118-128.

Chapter 4

More on the accusative and ablative
The perfect, pluperfect, and future perfect in the active
The vocative and locative cases
First, second, and third person pronouns

I do not feel that Greek and Latin
Are languages I'm safe to chat in;
At present all that I can say
Is 'φιλέω σέ' and 'amō tē'.

G. Boas, 'The Direct Method' in *Lays of Learning* (1926)

On the whole, it is better to be dative and giving, than accusative and objectionable. But both are necessary to life and Latin expression. Pronouns and the ablative, locative, and vocative cases also allow a wider latitude of expression, and new verb tenses express new ideas (perfection, pluperfection, and future perfection).

XLII. Further uses for the accusative case [GLG 329-343]

78. Since the accusative denotes the direct object of a sentence, it is best not to begin translating a sentence with a word in this case.

(a) If the direct object of an accusative is directly derived from the verb, this accusative is called a cognate accusative:

> somniāvī somnium.

> I dreamed a dream.

Plautus, *Rudēns* 597

(b) Verbs of asking, showing, and concealing often take two accusatives, one designating an object, the other a person. Translate by placing 'to' or 'from' before the word designating the person; place 'for' before the accusative designating the object.

> Rogā mē vīgintī minās.

> Ask me for twenty minas.

Plautus, *Pseudolus* 1070

In addition to rogō (ask), a double accusative may be found after appellō (name), creō (create), dēligō (choose), and faciō (do, make).

79. The accusative also expresses duration of time or extent of space.

> nam centum et novem vīxit annōs.

> For he lived for a hundred and nine years.

Quintilian 3. 1. 9

Contrast this with the ablative used to express a specific or definite time or place (§87).

80. 'Motion-toward' is expressed when the objects governed by the prepositions ad (to) or in (into) take the accusative. With the names of cities, and with domus (house) or rūs (country), there will usually be no preposition to express 'motion-toward'. With urbs (city) and oppidum (town), the preposition is normally used.

> Ego rūs ībō atque ibi manēbō.

> I shall go to the country, and I shall stay there.

Terence, *The Eunuch* 216

> pervēnit in oppidum māgnum atque opulentum.

> He came to a great and opulent town.

Sallust, *Jugurthine Wars* 75. 1

81. Certain prepositions require an accusative for the word or words that they govern. The most common are:

ad	to, towards
ante	before
circum	around
in	into
inter	among, between
ob	on account of
per	through
post	after
propter	on account of
sub	under (*when motion is understood*)
super	above (*when motion is understood*)
trāns	across

In moments of great emotion, an exclamation may be made in the accusative without a preposition:

> mē miserum!

> Me, poor me!

A standard Roman exclamation of sadness

XLIII. The ablative case with prepositions [GLG 384-410]

82. When a word appears in the ablative case, always use a preposition in English to translate that ablative, even when a preposition does not appear in the Latin.

83. An ablative after the preposition ā or ab (by) denotes agency and is often found after a passive verb. This is known as the ablative of personal agent.

84. An ablative after the preposition cum (with) denotes accompaniment. This is known as the ablative of accompaniment.

85. The ablative of separation expresses 'motion-away-from' when words after the preposition ab (from), dē (from, down from), ē or ex (from, out of) are in the ablative. With city-names, and with domus (house) or rūs (country), no prepositions appear.

> dēcēdit ex Galliā Rōmam simul Naevius.
>
> Naevius immediately withdrew from Gaul to Rome.
>
> > Cicero, *In Defence of Quinctius* 4. 16
>
> omnia domō ēius abstulit.
>
> He took everything away from his house.
>
> > Cicero, *Verrine Orations* 2. 2. 34. 83

After a word expressing a number, an ablative of separation is used to denote the whole from which something is a part. The preposition ex usually appears.

> paucōs ex suīs dēperdidērunt.
>
> They lost a few from their own side.
>
> > Caesar, *Gallic War* 3. 28. 4

Expressions signifying one's origins may take an ablative of source or origin with or without dē or ex.

> ōdērunt natōs dē paelice.
>
> They hate those born from concubines.
>
> > Juvenal 6. 627

86. 'Place-where' is indicated by the Latin in (in, on) with the ablative.

> pōns in Hibērō prope effectus nūntiābātur.
>
> The bridge on the Ebro was being reported as nearly finished.
>
> > Caesar, *Civil War* 1. 62. 3

XLIV.　The ablative without prepositions

87.　The following are the most common ablative constructions that do not involve a preposition in the Latin:

(a)　The ablative of time or distance denotes a specific time (either when or within what time) or a specific distance.

> tōtā nocte continenter īvērunt.
>
> That whole night they marched without stop.
>
> Caesar, Gallic War 1. 26. 5

(b)　The ablative of means identifies an instrument by which an action is done. In contrast, the agent or doer of the action is put in the ablative with the preposition ā or ab.

> ille sē lapidibus adpetītum dīxit.
>
> That one said he had been attacked with stones.
>
> Cicero, Concerning His House 5. 13

(c)　The ablative of cause expresses the reason behind an emotion.

> ōdērunt peccāre bonī virtūtis amōre.
>
> Good people hate to sin because of their love of virtue.
>
> Horace, Epistles 1. 16. 52

(d)　The ablative of respect answers the question 'in respect of what?' (§ 61).

(e)　The ablative of description uses an adjective and noun to express description.

> tōta mīlia mē decem poposcit,
>
> ista turpiculō puella nāsō.
>
> She demands a whole ten thousand from me, that girl with the disgusting little nose.
>
> Catullus 41. 2-3

(f)　The ablative of separation is found when the prepositions ā or ab, dē, ē or ex expresses separation from a tangible or concrete noun. When one separates oneself from an abstract or intangible noun, the preposition is usually omitted.

> rōbustus animus et excelsus omnī est līber cūrā et angōre.
>
> A robust and lofty mind is free from all care and anguish.
>
> Cicero, On Ends 1. 15. 49

(g)　The ablative of manner explains how something is done. This construction may use cum (with). But when an adjective modifies a noun in the ablative of manner, the preposition may be dropped.

When cum is not dropped, it must appear between the adjective in the ablative and the noun in the ablative.

circulōs suōs orbēsque cōnficiunt celeritāte mīrābilī.

They complete their circles and orbits with wonderful swiftness.

Cicero, *The Republic* 6. 15. 15

honestē, id est cum virtūte, vīvere.

To live honourably, that is to live with virtue.

Cicero, *On Ends* 3. 8. 29

cum laude, māgnā cum laude, summā cum laude

with distinction, with great distinction, with the greatest distinction

Traditional designations for undergraduate degrees in America and elsewhere

(h)   For the ablative of comparison and the ablative of degree of difference, see § 74.

XLV. The vocative case [GLG 33]

88. The vocative is used when people or personified objects and forces are addressed directly. The vocative is the same as the nominative in all declensions, except for masculine nouns ending in -us or -ius in the second declension. The vocative in Latin does not usually come first in a sentence.

(a)   If a noun ends in -us, change the -us to -e.

Marce! (from Marcus)

(b)   If a noun ends in -ius, simply drop the -us and lengthen the -i. The stress remains on the same syllable as in the nominative.

Antōnī! (from Antōnius).

The vocative singular and plural of deus are deus and dī, respectively.

XLVI. The locative case [GLG 386, 411]

89. With names of cities, the locative case is used to express 'place-in-which.' The locative is generally the same as the ablative except in the singular of the first and second declensions; here, it is the same as the genitive. Names of towns in the plural of the first or second declension resemble the ablative as normal. There is no locative in the fourth or fifth declensions. Note the locatives of domus, humus, and rūs.

Athenīs	in/at Athens
Carthāgine	in Carthage
Corinthī	in/at Corinth
domī	at home
humī	on the ground
Rōmae	in/at Rome
rūre	in the country

XLVII. Two further notes on nouns [GLG 320-325, 337]

90. When a preposition is used with the name of a city, that preposition may designate a general vicinity or general direction.

pōntem ad Genāvam iubet rescindī.

He orders the bridge near Geneva to be cut down.

Caesar, *Gallic War* 1. 7. 2

91. When a noun modifies another noun, the second noun is said to be in apposition with the first.

Ancum Marcium rēgem populus creāvit.

The people made Ancus Marcius king.

Livy 1. 32. 1

XLVIII. The formation of the perfect tense, active voice [GLG 122-127]

92. The third principal part of the verb is the first person singular active form of the perfect tense. For the other forms, drop the -ī of the third principal part, and add the endings shown below.

FIRST CONJUGATION PERFECT ACTIVE

amō, amāre, amāvī (perfect stem: amāv-)

		singular			**plural**	
1st	amāvī	I loved, have loved, did love		amāv**imus**	we loved, etc.
2d	amāv**istī**	you loved, etc.		amāv**istis**	you loved, etc.
3d	amāv**it**	he, she, it loved, etc.		amāv**ērunt**	they loved, etc.

SECOND CONJUGATION PERFECT ACTIVE

moneō, monēre, monuī (perfect stem: monu-)

1st	monu**ī**	I warned, etc.	monu**imus**	we warned, etc.
2d	monu**istī**	you warned, etc.	monu**istis**	you warned, etc.
3d	monu**it**	he, she, it warned, etc.	monu**ērunt**	they warned, etc.

THIRD CONJUGATION PERFECT ACTIVE

regō, regere, rēxī (perfect stem: rēx-)

1st	rēx**ī**	I ruled, etc.	rēx**imus**	we ruled, etc.
2d	rēx**istī**	you ruled, etc.	rēx**istis**	you ruled, etc.
3d	rēx**it**	he, she, it ruled, etc.	rēx**ērunt**	they ruled, etc.

THIRD CONJUGATION (-IŌ) PERFECT ACTIVE

capiō, capere, cēpī (perfect stem: cēp-)

1st	cēp**ī**	I took, etc.	cēp**imus**	we took, etc.
2d	cēp**istī**	you took, etc.	cēp**istis**	you took, etc.
3d	cēp**it**	he, she, it took, etc.	cēp**ērunt**	they took, etc.

FOURTH CONJUGATION PERFECT ACTIVE

audiō, audīre, audīvī (perfect stem: audīv-)

1st	audīv**ī**	I heard, etc.	audīv**imus**	we heard, etc.
2d	audīv**istī**	you heard, etc.	audīv**istis**	you heard, etc.
3d	audīv**it**	he, she, it heard, etc.	audīv**ērunt**	they heard, etc.

The same endings are added to the third principal part of esse (fuī) to form the perfect tense of the verb 'to be'.

XLIX. The formation of the pluperfect tense, active voice [GLG 122-127]

93. The active forms of the pluperfect are derived from the third principal part of the verb. Drop the final -ī, and add the endings shown below.

FIRST CONJUGATION PLUPERFECT ACTIVE

amō, amāre, amāvī (perfect stem: amāv-)

	singular		plural	
1st	amāv**eram**	I had loved	amāv**erāmus**	we had loved
2d	amāv**erās**	you had loved	amāv**erātis**	you had loved
3d	amāv**erat**	he, she, it had loved	amāv**erant**	they had loved

---

SECOND CONJUGATION PLUPERFECT ACTIVE

moneō, monēre, monuī (perfect stem: monu-)

1st	monu**eram**	I had warned	monu**erāmus**	we had warned
2d	monu**erās**	you had warned	monu**erātis**	you had warned
3d	monu**erat**	he, she, it has warned	monu**erant**	they had warned

---

THIRD CONJUGATION PLUPERFECT ACTIVE

regō, regere, rēxī (perfect stem: rēx-)

1st	rēx**eram**	I had ruled	rēx**erāmus**	we had ruled
2d	rēx**erās**	you had ruled	rēx**erātis**	you had ruled
3d	rēx**erat**	he, she, it had ruled	rēx**erant**	they had ruled

---

THIRD CONJUGATION (-IŌ) PLUPERFECT ACTIVE

capiō, capere, cēpī (perfect stem: cēp-)

1st	cēp**eram**	I had taken	cēp**erāmus**	we had taken
2d	cēp**erās**	you had taken	cēp**erātis**	you had taken
3d	cēp**erat**	he, she, it had taken	cēp**erant**	they had taken

FOURTH CONJUGATION PLUPERFECT ACTIVE

audiō, audīre, audīvī (perfect stem: audīv-)

1st	audīv**eram**	I had heard	audīv**erāmus**	we had heard
2d	audīv**erās**	you had heard	audīv**erātis**	you had heard
3d	audīv**erat**	he, she, it had heard	audīv**erant**	they had heard

The same endings are added to the third principal part of esse (fuī) to form the pluperfect tense of the verb 'to be'.

L. The formation of the future perfect tense, active voice [GLG 122-127]

94. In the active, the future perfect tense is formed by dropping the -ī of the third principal part and adding the endings shown below.

FIRST CONJUGATION FUTURE PERFECT ACTIVE

amō, amāre, amāvī (perfect stem: amāv-)

	singular		**plural**	
1st	amāv**erō**	I shall have loved	amāv**erimus**	we shall have loved
2d	amāv**eris**	you will have loved	amāv**eritis**	you will have loved
3d	amāv**erit**	he, she, it will have loved	amāv**erint**	they will have loved

SECOND CONJUGATION FUTURE PERFECT ACTIVE

moneō, monēre, monuī (perfect stem: monu-)

1st	monu**erō**	I shall have warned	monu**erimus**	we shall have warned
2d	monu**eris**	you will have warned	monu**eritis**	you will have warned
3d	monu**erit**	he, she, it will have warned	monu**erint**	they will have warned

THIRD CONJUGATION FUTURE PERFECT ACTIVE

regō, regere, rēxī (perfect stem: rēx-)

1st	rēx**erō**	I shall have ruled	rēx**erimus**	we shall have ruled
2d	rēx**eris**	you will have ruled	rēx**eritis**	you will have ruled
3d	rēx**erit**	he, she, it will have ruled	rēx**erint**	they will have ruled

THIRD CONJUGATION (-IŌ) FUTURE PERFECT ACTIVE

capiō, capere, cēpī (perfect stem: cēp-)

1st	cēp**erō**	I shall have taken	cēp**erimus**	we shall have taken
2d	cēp**eris**	you will have taken	cēp**eritis**	you will have taken
3d	cēp**erit**	he, she, it will have taken	cēp**erint**	they will have taken

FOURTH CONJUGATION FUTURE PERFECT ACTIVE

audiō, audīre, audīvī (perfect stem: audīv-)

1st	audīv**erō**	I shall have heard	audīv**erimus**	we shall have heard
2d	audīv**eris**	you will have heard	audīv**eritis**	you will have heard
3d	audīv**erit**	he, she, it will have heard	audīv**erint**	they will have heard

The same endings are added to the stem of the third principal part of esse (fuī) to form the future perfect tense of the verb 'to be'.

LI. Personal pronouns [GLG 100–103, 304]

95. Pronouns are substitutes for nouns. In a sense, they are irregular nouns, with forms in different cases that may not be guessed from the nominative. Compare the English use of 'I' as a subject, with 'me' as a direct object in the singular, and 'us' as a direct object in the plural. The personal pronouns are shown below. The third person personal pronoun has separate forms for the masculine, feminine, and neuter.

FIRST PERSON PERSONAL PRONOUN

	singular	**plural**
nom.	ego (I)	nōs (we)
gen.	meī (of me)	nostrī (nostrum) (of us)
dat.	mihi (to, for me)	nōbīs (to, for us)
acc.	mē (me)	nōs (us)
abl.	mē (by, with, etc. me)	nōbīs (by, with, etc. us)

SECOND PERSON PERSONAL PRONOUN

nom.	tū (you)	vōs (you)
gen.	tuī (of you)	vestrī (vestrum) (of you)
dat.	tibi (to, for you)	vōbīs (to, for you)
acc.	tē (you)	vōs (you)
abl.	tē (by, with, etc. you)	vōbīs (by, with, etc. you)

THIRD PERSON PERSONAL PRONOUN

Singular

	masculine	*feminine*	*neuter*
nom.	is (he)	ea (she)	id (it)
gen.	ēius (of him, his)	ēius (of her, her)	ēius (of it, its)
dat.	eī (to, for him)	eī (to, for her)	eī (to, for it)
acc.	eum (him)	eam (her)	id (it)
abl.	eō (by, with him)	eā (by, with her)	eō (by, with it)

Plural

nom.	eī (they)	eae (they)	ea (they)
gen.	eōrum (of them, their)	eārum (of them, their)	eōrum (of them, their)
dat.	eīs (to, for them)	eīs (to, for them)	eīs (to, for them)
acc.	eōs (them)	eās (them)	ea (them)
abl.	eīs (by, with them)	eīs (by, with them)	eīs (by, with them)

The preposition cum (with) does not precede the ablative of the first and second person personal pronoun. Instead, it is appended to it:

>   Pax vōbīscum.

>   Peace be with you.

Traditional greeting at the Catholic Mass

LII. Special uses of the third-person pronoun [GLG 308]

96. As an adjective, the third person pronoun may be translated as 'that' in the singular or 'those' in the plural.

>   tū id aurum nōn surripuistī?

>   You didn't steal that gold?

Plautus, *The Pot of Gold* 772

97. If a pronoun stands for a thing, translate using 'it' in English.

>   classem comparāvit eīque Dātim praefēcit.

>   He prepared a fleet and put Datis in charge of it.

Nepos, *Miltiades* 4. 1

98. Is, ea, id may also mean 'the following'.

>   in ipsīs moenibus, ea erunt principia.

>   For these particular walls, the principles will be the following:

Vitruvius 1. 4. 1

EXERCISES

A. Vocabulary

ā or ab (*prep. with abl.*)	from, by
adiciō, adicere, adiēcī, adiectum	add to, throw to
apud (*prep. with acc.*)	at, among, with
Aventīnum, Aventīnī, n.	the Aventine (one of Rome's seven hills)
cīvitās, cīvitātis, f.	state
condō, condere, condidī, conditum	establish, hide
contrā (*adverb or prep. with acc.*)	against, in reply

dīmicō, dīmicāre, dīmicāvī, dīmicātum	fight
ē or ex (*prep. with abl.*)	out of
fīlia, fīliae, f.	daughter
Iāniculum, Iāniculī, n.	the Janiculum (hill on the right bank of the Tiber)
imperium, imperī, n.	command, rule, power
Latīnī, Latīnōrum, m. (*plural*)	the Latins (who lived in Latium, the area in which Rome is situated)
mare, maris, n.	sea
mīlliārium, mīlliārī, n.	milestone
mōns, mōntis, m.	mountain
nepōs, nepōtis, m.	grandson, descendant
ōstium, ōstiī, n.	entrance
Rōma, Rōmae, f.	Rome
sextus-decimus, -a, -um	sixteenth
suprā (*adverb or prep. with acc.*)	above
suscipiō, suscipere, suscēpī, susceptum	take up, undertake
Tiberis, Tiberis, m.	the Tiber river (which runs through Rome)
urbs, urbis, f.	city

B. Translations

The Roman historian Eutropius wrote *A Brief History of Rome* in the fourth century, a text which served well into the nineteenth century as a standard guide to the history of the Empire. Like other epitomizing historians of the Late Roman period, Eutropius preferred concision to content. The paragraph below tells of Ancus Marcius (Ancus Marcius, Ancī Marcī, m., traditionally dated 640-617 BC), the fourth king of Rome and grandson of Numa Pompilius (Numa Pompilius, Numae Pompilī, m., traditionally dated 715-673 BC), the second king.

Ancus Marcius, Numae ex fīliā nepōs, suscēpit imperium. contrā Latīnōs dīmicāvit. Aventīnum mōntem cīvitātī adiēcit et Iāniculum. apud ōstium Tiberis cīvitātem suprā mare sextō-decimō mīlliāriō ab urbe Rōmā condidit.

Eutropius 1. 5. 1-2

Eutropius went on to describe the achievements of Tarquin the Elder or Prīscus Tarquinius (Prīscus Tarquinius, Prīscī Tarquinī, m., traditionally dated 616-579 BC), successor to Ancus Marcius as king. The following paragraph in English is based on this account. Additional vocabulary to assist the translation appears below.

Then Tarquin the Elder took power. He doubled the number of senators. He built a circus at Rome and established the Roman games. He also conquered the Sabines. He made the walls and sewers. In the thirty-eighth year of his rule, the sons of Ancus Marcius killed him.

Eutropius 1. 6. 1-2

Additional vocabulary

aedificō, aedificāre, aedificāvī, aedificātum	build
annus, annī, m.	year
circus, circī, m.	circle, circus
cloāca, cloācae, f.	sewer
duplicō, duplicāre, duplicāvī, duplicātum	double
etiam	even, also
fīlius, fīlī, m.	son
īnstituō, īnstituere, īnstituī, īnstitūtum	establish, decide, prepare
lūdus, lūdī, m.	game
mūrus, mūrī, m.	wall
numerus, numerī, m.	number
occīdō, occīdere, occīdī, occīsum	kill
Rōmānus, -a, -um	Roman
Sabīnī, Sabīnōrum, m. (*plural*)	Sabines, a people of central Italy, north of Latium
senātor, senātōris, m.	senator
trīcēsimus-octāvus, -a, -um	thirty-eighth
vincō, vincere, vīcī, victum	conquer

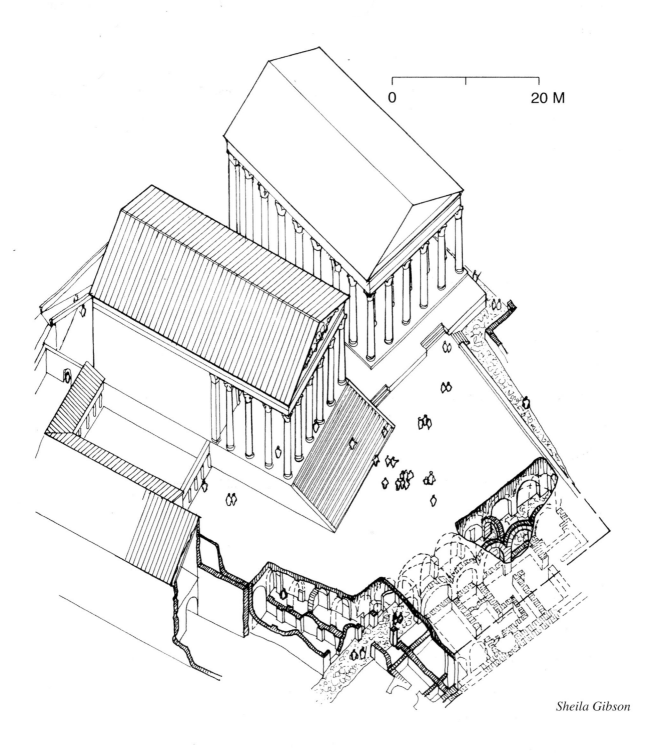

Sheila Gibson

Fig. 14. Temples of the Great Mother (Magna Mater) and Victory on the Palatine in Rome, ca. AD 200.

Sheila Gibson

Fig. 15. The temple of Antoninus and Faustina in the Roman Forum, begun in AD 141 by
Antoninus to honour his wife Faustina.

Fig. 16. The church of San Lorenzo in Miranda in the temple of Antoninus and Faustina in the Roman Forum.

Sheila Gibson

Fig. 17. The eastern façade of the temple of Roma and Venus on the Via Sacra in Rome. Originally constructed in the second century AD, the temple was rebuilt by the emperor Maxentius after a fire in AD 307. There are colonnaded porticoes of Egyptian grey granite along the sides.

Chapter 5

Demonstratives and intensifiers
Special adjectives
The passive voice for all tenses in the indicative

Once when I was staying hīc,
Bathing with my cousin Dick,
As I knew he could not swim
I stood sadly watching him,
For, I thought, he's sure to sink
If he goes much further hinc,
And without amazing luck
He can hardly scramble hūc.
"Nāte, Dick," I cried, "this way."
But the prig retorted, "Nay!
'Nāte' is the plural, 'nā'
Must be what you meant to say."
"Nā!" I cried, he answered "No!"
But he feathered far too low.
"Nā!" said I, "for nisi nābis
Moriendō poenās dābis."
But he answered, "No! No! No!
'Nābis' should be 'naverō!'"
"Nā," I cried, "ad lapis hoc!"
Thinking he deserved a shock.
Then the waters swallowed him
(As I said, he could not swim).

Anonymous, perhaps Cyril Alington (1872-1955),
'The Scholar Who Could Not Swim' in *Cautionary Canticles*

Some adjectives, such as the demonstratives and intensifiers, are irregular in the genitive and dative. Although a minority amongst adjectives, they are important and not to be relegated to the fringes of grammatical society. Passive constructions are also important. Although we are rightly told to prefer the active to the passive and to enter into 'the active work of life,' passivity still has its uses.

LIII. Demonstratives [GLG 103-104, 305-307, 310]

99. Demonstrative adjectives (this, that, these, those) add emphasis to nouns, and like other adjectives, they must agree with the nouns they modify in case, number, and gender. The demonstratives are:

HIC, HAEC, HOC

this; this, near to the speaker; this of mine; these (in plural)

	singular				**plural**		
	masc.	*fem.*	*neut.*		*masc.*	*fem.*	*neut.*
nom.	hic	haec	hoc		hī	hae	haec
gen.	hūius	hūius	hūius		hōrum	hārum	hōrum
dat.	huīc	huīc	huīc		hīs	hīs	hīs
acc.	hunc	hanc	hoc		hōs	hās	haec
abl.	hōc	hāc	hōc		hīs	hīs	hīs

ILLE, ILLA, ILLUD

that; that at a distance; that distinguished; those (in plural)

nom.	ille	illa	illud		illī	illae	illa
gen.	illīus	illīus	illīus		illōrum	illārum	illōrum
dat.	illī	illī	illī		illīs	illīs	illīs
acc.	illum	illam	illud		illōs	illās	illa
abl.	illō	illā	illō		illīs	illīs	illīs

Hic may sometimes mean 'the latter'; ille may mean 'the former.'

ISTE, ISTA, ISTUD

that of yours; that I was talking to you about

nom.	iste	ista	istud		istī	istae	ista
gen.	istīus	istīus	istīus		istōrum	istārum	istōrum
dat.	istī	istī	istī		istīs	istīs	istīs
acc.	istum	istam	istud		istōs	istās	ista
abl.	istō	istā	istō		istīs	istīs	istīs

ĪDEM, EADEM, IDEM [IS + DEM]

the same

	singular			plural		
	masc.	*fem.*	*neut.*	*masc.*	*fem.*	*neut.*
nom.	īdem	eadem	idem	īdem (eidem)	eaedem	eadem
gen.	ēiusdem	ēiusdem	ēiusdem	eōrundem	eārundem	eōrundem
dat.	eīdem	eīdem	eīdem	īsdem (eīsdem)	īsdem (eīsdem)	īsdem (eīsdem)
acc.	eundem	eandem	idem	eōsdem	eāsdem	eadem
abl.	eōdem	eādem	eōdem	īsdem (eīsdem)	īsdem (eīsdem)	īsdem (eīsdem)

Notice that -dem is uninflected, while, sound changes apart, the prefix, based on is, ea, id declines regularly.

LIV. Demonstrative adverbs [GLG 91, 307]

100. A demonstrative adverb, sometimes known as a deictic, denotes or asks about a relative position. Note the lengths of the vowels for different demonstrative adverbs.

eō	to that place
eōdem	to the same place
hīc	here
hinc	hence
hūc	hither
ibi	in that place
ubi	where
illīc	there
illinc	thence, from that place
illō	to that place
illūc	thither, to that place
inde	from that place
unde	whence
istīc	there where you are
istinc	from that place where you are
istūc	to that place where you are
quō	whither

LV. Intensifying adjectives [GLG 103, 311]

101. An intensifying adjective emphasises the particular or distinctive nature of the word to which it refers.

It translates as 'himself,' 'herself,' 'itself,' or 'themselves.'

		IPSE, IPSA, IPSUM					
		himself, herself, itself, themselves					
		singular			**plural**		
	masc.	*fem.*	*neut.*		*masc.*	*fem.*	*neut.*
nom.	ipse	ipsa	ipsum		ipsī	ipsae	ipsa
gen.	ipsīus	ipsīus	ipsīus		ipsōrum	ipsārum	ipsōrum
dat.	ipsī	ipsī	ipsī		ipsīs	ipsīs	ipsīs
acc.	ipsum	ipsam	ipsum		ipsōs	ipsās	ipsa
abl.	ipsō	ipsā	ipsō		ipsīs	ipsīs	ipsīs

Ipse may sometimes be translated as 'even' or 'very.'

LVI. Adjectives with -īus in the genitive and -ī in the dative [GLG 76]

102. Other adjectives use -īus in the genitive singular and -ī in the dative singular:

alius, -a, -ud (using the gen. alterīus)	another, other
alius ... alius ✗	one ... other (some ... others, *in plural*) ✗
alter, altera, alterum	other (of two)
neuter, neutra, neutrum	neither
nūllus, -a, -um	not any
sōlus, -a, -um	alone
tōtus, -a, -um	whole
ūllus, -a, um	any
ūnus, -a, -um	one
uter, utra, utrum	either, whichever of two

In other words, these words decline in the same way that the demonstratives decline.

THIRD CONJUGATION (-IŌ) IMPERFECT PASSIVE

capiō, capere (stem: cape-, shifts to capi-)

1st	capiēbar	I was being taken	capiēbāmur	we were being taken
2d	capiēbāris	you were being taken	capiēbāminī	you were being taken
3d	capiēbātur	he, she, it was being taken	capiēbantur	they were being taken

FOURTH CONJUGATION IMPERFECT PASSIVE

audiō, audīre (stem: audi-; note the short i)

1st	audiēbar	I was being heard	audiēbāmur	we were being heard
2d	audiēbāris	you were being heard	audiēbāminī	you were being heard
3d	audiēbātur	he, she, it was being heard	audiēbantur	they were being heard

LX. The formation of the future tense, passive, for first and second conjugation verbs [GLG 122-127]

106. Verbs in the first and second conjugations form the future tense in the passive by adding the personal endings shown below to the stem. These endings are essentially -bo, -be, -bi, or -bu with the passive personal endings.

FIRST CONJUGATION FUTURE PASSIVE

amō, amāre (stem: amā-)

	singular		plural		
1st	amābor	I shall be loved	amābimur	we shall be loved
2d	amāberis	you will be loved	amābiminī	you will be loved
3d	amābitur	he, she, it will be loved	amābuntur	they will be loved

SECOND CONJUGATION FUTURE PASSIVE

moneō, monēre (stem: monē-)

1st	monēbor	I shall be warned	monēbimur	we shall be warned
2d	monēberis	you will be warned	monēbiminī	you will be warned
3d	monēbitur	he, she, it will be warned	monēbuntur	they will be warned

LIX. The formation of the imperfect tense, passive voice [GLG 122-127]

105. To form the imperfect in the passive voice:

(a)   add -ba- to the stem, or if the verb is in the fourth conjugation, add -ēba-;

(b)   add the personal endings used to form the present passive.

Remember that verbs in the third conjugation with first principal parts ending in -iō will look like fourth conjugation verbs in the imperfect, and thus will use -i-, rather than -e- in the verbal stem, and -ēba-, and not simply -ba-.

FIRST CONJUGATION IMPERFECT PASSIVE

amō, amāre (stem: amā-)

	singular			**plural**	
1st	amā**bar**	I was being loved		amā**bāmur**	we were being loved
2d	amā**bāris**	you were being loved		amā**bāminī**	you were being loved
3d	amā**bātur**	he, she, it was being loved		amā**bantur**	they were being loved

---

SECOND CONJUGATION IMPERFECT PASSIVE

moneō, monēre (stem: monē-)

1st	monē**bar**	I was being warned		monē**bāmur**	we were being warned
2d	monē**bāris**	you were being warned		monē**bāminī**	you were being warned
3d	monē**batur**	he, she, it was being warned		monē**bantur**	they were being warned

---

THIRD CONJUGATION IMPERFECT PASSIVE

regō, regere (stem: rege-)

1st	regē**bar**	I was being ruled		regē**bāmur**	we were being ruled
2d	regē**bāris**	you were being ruled		regē**bāminī**	you were being ruled
3d	regē**bātur**	he, she, it was being ruled		regē**bantur**	they were being ruled

SECOND CONJUGATION PRESENT PASSIVE

moneō, monēre (stem: monē-)

1st	moneor	I am being warned	monēmur	we are being warned
2d	monēris	you are being warned	monēminī	you are being warned
3d	monētur	he, she, it is being warned	monentur	they are being warned

THIRD CONJUGATION PRESENT PASSIVE

regō, regere (stem: rege-, shifts to regi-; reguntur in the third person plural)

1st	regor	I am being ruled	regimur	we are being ruled
2d	regeris	you are being ruled	regiminī	you are being ruled
3d	regitur	he, she, it is being ruled	reguntur	they are being ruled

THIRD CONJUGATION (-IŌ) PRESENT PASSIVE

capiō, capere (stem: cape-, shifts to capi-; capiuntur in the third person plural)

1st	capior	I am being taken	capimur	we are being taken
2d	caperis	you are being taken	capiminī	you are being taken
3d	capitur	he, she, it is being taken	capiuntur	they are being taken

FOURTH CONJUGATION PRESENT PASSIVE

audiō, audīre (stem: audī-; audīuntur in the third person plural)

1st	audior	I am being heard	audīmur	we are being heard
2d	audīris	you are being heard	audīminī	you are being heard
3d	audītur	he, she, it is being heard	audīuntur	they are being heard

LVII. Alius [GLG 221, 319, 482]

103. A common idiom in Latin concerns the repetition of the word alius, a repetition usually in different cases:

fallācia

alia aliam trūdit.

One lie follows on the heels of another.

Terence, *The Lady of Andros* 778-779

This construction is actually an abbreviation. The unabbreviated form of the above is:

Alia fallācia aliam fallāciam trūdit; alia fallācia aliam fallāciam trūdit.

When alius is repeated in two different cases within a sentence, the translation is 'one (or some) ... one (or some); another (or others) ... another (or others).' The literal translation, therefore, becomes

One lie follows on the heels of one lie; another lie follows on the heels of another.

LVIII. The formation of the present tense, passive voice [GLG 122-127]

104. In the passive, the present tense is conjugated by adding -r to the first principal part for the first person singular, and then adding the endings shown below to the verbal stem for the other forms. But:

(a)   as with the active forms, the -e in the verbal stem of the third conjugation verbs shifts to an -i, except for the second-person singular;

(b)   the third-person plural form of the third conjugation, however, drops the -e of the stem and adds -untur;

(c)   fourth conjugation verbs also add -untur to the stem, not simply -ntur, to form the third-person plural form of the present tense;

(d)   third conjugation verbs that have the first principal part ending in -iō are essentially conjugated as if they were fourth conjugation verbs, except for the second-person singular form.

FIRST CONJUGATION PRESENT PASSIVE

amō, amāre (stem: amā-)

	singular		plural	
1st	amo**r**	I am being loved	amā**mur**	we are being loved
2d	amā**ris**	you are being loved	amā**minī**	you are being loved
3d	amā**tur**	he, she, it is being loved	ama**ntur**	they are being loved

LXI. The formation of the future tense for verbs in the third and fourth conjugations, passive voice [GLG 122-127]

107. To form the future passive of verbs in the third and fourth conjugations:

(a)   drop the active endings of the future active, and

(b)   replace these with the passive personal endings.

Note that, unlike the second person singular in the present passive, the second person singular in the future passive has a long e. Remember too that -iō verbs in the third conjugation will essentially resemble fourth conjugation verbs in the future passive.

THIRD CONJUGATION FUTURE PASSIVE

regō, regere (stem: rege-)

	singular			**plural**	
1st	reg**ar**	I shall be ruled		reg**ēmur**	we shall be ruled
2d	reg**ēris**	you will be ruled		reg**ēminī**	you will be ruled
3d	reg**ētur**	he, she, it will be ruled		reg**entur**	they will be ruled

---

THIRD CONJUGATION (-IŌ) FUTURE PASSIVE

capiō, capere (stem: cape-, shifts to capi-)

1st	capi**ar**	I shall be taken		capi**ēmur**	we shall be taken
2d	capi**ēris**	you will be taken		capi**ēminī**	you will be taken
3d	capi**ētur**	he, she, it will be taken		capi**entur**	they will be taken

---

FOURTH CONJUGATION FUTURE PASSIVE

audiō, audīre (stem: audi-)

1st	audi**ar**	I shall be heard		audi**ēmur**	we shall be heard
2d	audi**ēris**	you will be heard		audi**ēminī**	you will be heard
3d	audi**ētur**	he, she, it will be heard		audi**entur**	they will be heard

LXII. The formation of the perfect tense, passive voice [GLG 122-127]

108. To form the passive of the perfect tense, use the fourth principal part, and combine it with the relevant form of the present tense of the verb esse. The fourth principal part must agree in gender and number with the word that it modifies.

FIRST CONJUGATION PERFECT PASSIVE

amō, amāre, amāvī, amātum (fourth principal part: amātus, -a, -um)

singular		plural	
1st amātus, -a, -um **sum**	I was loved, have been loved	amātī, -ae, -a **sumus**	we were loved, etc.
2d amātus, -a, -um **es**	you were loved, etc.	amātī, -ae, -a **estis**	you were loved, etc.
3d amātus, -a, -um **est**	he, she, it was loved, etc.	amātī, -ae, -a **sunt**	they were loved, etc.

SECOND CONJUGATION PERFECT PASSIVE

moneō, monēre, monuī, monitum (fourth principal part: monitus, -a, -um)

1st monitus, -a, -um **sum**	I was warned, etc.	monitī, -ae, -a **sumus**	we were warned, etc.
2d monitus, -a, -um **es**	you were warned, etc.	monitī, -ae, -a **estis**	you were warned, etc.
3d monitus, -a, -um **est**	he, she, it was warned, etc.	monitī, -ae, -a **sunt**	they were warned, etc.

THIRD CONJUGATION PERFECT PASSIVE

regō, regere, rēxī, rēctum (fourth principal part: rēctus, -a, -um)

1st rēctus, -a, um **sum**	I was ruled, etc.	rēctī, -ae, -a **sumus**	we were ruled, etc.
2d rēctus, -a, -um **es**	you were ruled, etc.	rēctī, -ae, -a **estis**	you were ruled, etc.
3d rēctus, -a, -um **est**	he, she, it was ruled, etc.	rēctī, -ae, -a **sunt**	they were ruled, etc.

THIRD CONJUGATION (-IŌ) PERFECT PASSIVE

capiō, capere, cēpī, captum (fourth principal part: captus, -a, -um)

1st captus, -a, -um **sum**	I was taken, etc.	captī, -ae, -a **sumus**	we were taken, etc.
2d captus, -a, -um **es**	you were taken, etc.	captī, -ae, -a **estis**	you were taken, etc.
3d captus, -a, -um **est**	he, she, it was taken, etc.	captī, -ae, -a **sunt**	they were taken, etc.

FOURTH CONJUGATION PERFECT PASSIVE

audiō, audīre, audīvī, audītum (fourth principal part: audītus, -a, -um)

1st	audītus, -a, -um **sum**	I was heard, etc.	audītī, -ae, -a **sumus**	we were heard, etc.
2d	audītus, -a, -um **es**	you were heard, etc.	audītī, -ae, -a **estis**	you were heard, etc.
3d	audītus, -a, -um **est**	he, she, it was heard, etc.	audītī, -ae, -a **sunt**	they have been heard, etc.

LXIII. The formation of the pluperfect tense, passive voice [GLG 122-127]

109. To form the pluperfect tense in the passive, use the fourth principal part, together with the imperfect of the verb esse as a second word. The fourth principal part must agree with the word it modifies.

FIRST CONJUGATION PLUPERFECT PASSIVE

amō, amāre, amāvī, amātum (fourth principal part: amātus, -a, -um)

singular **plural**

1st	amātus, -a, -um **eram**	I had been loved	amātī, -ae, -a **erāmus**	we had been loved
2d	amātus, -a, -um **erās**	you had been loved	amātī, -ae, -a **erātis**	you had been loved
3d	amātus, -a, -um **erat**	he, she, it had been loved	amātī, -ae, -a **erant**	they had been loved

SECOND CONJUGATION PLUPERFECT PASSIVE

moneō, monēre, monuī, monitum (fourth principal part: monitus, -a, -um)

1st	monitus, -a, -um **eram**	I had been warned	monitī, -ae, -a **erāmus**	we had been warned
2d	monitus, -a, -um **erās**	you had been warned	monitī, -ae, -a **erātis**	you had been warned
3d	monitus, -a, -um **erat**	he, she, it had been warned	monitī, -ae, -a **erant**	they had been warned

THIRD CONJUGATION PLUPERFECT PASSIVE

regō, regere, rēxī, rēctum (fourth principal part: rēctus, -a, -um)

1st	rēctus, -a, -um **eram**	I had been ruled	rēctī, -ae, -a **erāmus**	we had been ruled
2d	rēctus, -a, -um **erās**	you had been ruled	rēctī, -ae, -a **erātis**	you had been ruled
3d	rēctus, -a, -um **erat**	he, she, it had been ruled	rēctī, -ae, -a **erant**	they had been ruled

THIRD CONJUGATION (-IŌ) PLUPERFECT PASSIVE

capiō, capere, cēpī, captum (fourth principal part: captus, -a, -um)

1st	captus, -a, -um **eram**	I had been taken	captī, -ae, -a **erāmus**	we had been taken
2d	captus, -a, -um **erās**	you had been taken	captī, -ae, -a **erātis**	you had been taken
3d	captus, -a, -um **erat**	he, she, it had been taken	captī, -ae, -a **erant**	they had been taken

FOURTH CONJUGATION PLUPERFECT PASSIVE

audiō, audīre, audīvī, audītum (fourth principal part: audītus, -a, -um)

1st	audītus, -a, -um **eram**	I had been heard	audītī, -ae, -a **erāmus**	we had been heard
2d	audītus, -a, -um **erās**	you had been heard	audītī, -ae, -a **erātis**	you had been heard
3d	audītus, -a, -um **erat**	he, she, it had been heard	audītī, -ae, -a **erant**	they had been heard

LXIV. The formation of the future perfect tense, passive voice [GLG 122-127]

110. To form the future perfect tense in the passive, take the fourth principal part, and combine this with the relevant form of the future tense of the verb esse. The fourth principal part must agree with the word that it modifies.

FIRST CONJUGATION FUTURE PERFECT PASSIVE

amō, amāre, amāvī, amātum (fourth principal part: amātus, -a, -um)

singular			**plural**		
1st	amātus, -a, -um **erō**	I shall have been loved	amātī, -ae, -a **erimus**	we shall have been loved
2d	amātus, -a, -um **eris**	you will have been loved	amātī, -ae, -a **eritis**	you will have been loved
3d	amātus, -a, -um **erit**	he, she, it will have been loved	amātī, -ae, -a **erunt**	they will have been loved

SECOND CONJUGATION FUTURE PERFECT PASSIVE

moneō, monēre, monuī, monitum (fourth principal part: monitus, -a, -um)

1st	monitus, -a, -um **erō**	I shall have been warned	monitī, -ae, -a **erimus**	we shall have been warned
2d	monitus, -a, -um **eris**	you will have been warned	monitī, -ae, -a **eritis**	you will have been warned
3d	monitus, -a, -um **erit**	he, she, it will have been warned	monitī, -ae, -a **erunt**	they will have been warned

THIRD CONJUGATION FUTURE PERFECT PASSIVE

regō, regere, rēxī, rēctum (fourth principal part: rēctus, -a, -um)

1st	rēctus, -a, -um **erō**	I shall have been ruled	rēctī, -ae, -a **erimus**	we shall have been ruled
2d	rēctus, -a, -um **eris**	you will have been ruled	rēctī, -ae, -a **eritis**	you will have been ruled
3d	rēctus, -a, -um **erit**	he, she, it will have been ruled	rēctī, -ae, -a **erunt**	they will have been ruled

THIRD CONJUGATION (-IŌ) FUTURE PERFECT PASSIVE

capiō, capere, cēpī, captum (fourth principal part: captus, -a, -um)

1st	captus, -a, -um **erō**	I shall have been taken	captī, -ae, -a **erimus**	we shall have been taken
2d	captus, -a, -um **eris**	you will have been taken	captī, -ae, -a **eritis**	you will have been taken
3d	captus, -a, -um **erit**	he, she, it will have been taken	captī, -ae, -a **erunt**	taken they will have been taken

FOURTH CONJUGATION FUTURE PERFECT PASSIVE

audiō, audīre, audīvī, audītum (fourth principal part: audītus, -a, -um)

1st	audītus, -a, -um **erō**	I shall have been heard	audītī, -ae, -a **erimus**	we shall have been heard
2d	audītus, -a, -um **eris**	you will have been heard	audītī, -ae, -a **eritis**	you will have been heard
3d	audītus, -a, -um **erit**	he, she, it will have been heard	audītī, -ae, -a **erunt**	heard they will have been heard

EXERCISES

A. Vocabulary

accēdō, accēdere, accessī, accessum	go to
accipiō, accipere, accēpī, acceptum	receive
annus, annī, m.	year
auxilium, auxilī, n.	help
contendō, contendere, contendī, contentum	hasten, march, struggle
cupiō, cupere, cupīvī, cupītum	desire
dux, ducis, m.	leader
ēiciō, ēicere, ēiēcī, ēiectum	cast out
exercitus, exercitūs, m.	army
expellō, expellere, expulī, expulsum	drive out, expel
flētus, flētūs, m.	weeping
īrātus, -a, -um	enraged, angry
māter, mātris, f.	mother
octāvus-decimus, -a, -um	eighteenth
oppūgnō, oppūgnāre, oppūgnāvī, oppūgnātum	attack
postquam	after
precātiō, precātiōnis, f.	prayer
quīntus, -a, -um	fifth
removeō, removēre, remōvī, remōtum	move back, withdraw
rēx, rēgis, m.	king
Rōmānus, -a, -um	Roman
saepe	often
superātus, -a, -um	overcome, vanquished
usque	all the way, all the time
uxor, uxōris, f.	wife
veniō, venīre, vēnī, ventum	come
vincō, vincere, vīcī, vīctum	conquer

B. Translations

Eutropius summarises one of the most famous stories of early Rome: the tale of the Roman general Coriolanus (Coriolānus, Coriolānī, m.), the name or cognomen given to Gnaeus Marcius (Gnaeus Marcius, Gnaeī Marcī, m.; Eutropius gives him the praenomen Quintus). In 493 BC, he had captured Corioli (Coriolī, Coriolōrum, m. plural), a town in Latium, from the Volsci (Volscī, Volscōrum, m. plural), a nearby people in the south. Accused of tyrranical behaviour, Coriolanus later deserted to the Volsci and then marched on Rome. Only the entreaties of his wife Volumnia (Volumnia, Volumniae, f.) and his mother Veturia (Vetūria, Vetūriae, f.) prevented him from taking the city. These events form the basis of Shakespeare's *Coriolanus*.

Octāvō-decimō annō postquam rēgēs ēiectī erant, ex urbe Quīntus Marcius, dux Rōmānus, expulsus est. Ille Coriolōs cēperat, Volscōrum cīvitātem. Ad ipsōs Volscōs contendit īrātus, et auxilia contrā Rōmānōs accēpit. Rōmānōs saepe vīcit; usque ad quīntum mīlliārium urbis accēssit. Oppūgnāre etiam patriam cupiēbat, sed ad eum māter Vetūria et uxor Volumnia ex urbe vēnerant. eārum flētū et precātiōne superātus, remōvit exercitum.

Eutropius 1. 15. 1-2

After telling of Coriolānus, Eutropius recounts another famous story: the tale of L. (Lucius) Quintius Cincinnātus (Cincinnātus, Cincinnātī, m.) who preferred quiet obscurity to supreme power.

In the next year, when the Roman army was besieged around Mons Algidus at the twelfth milestone from the city, Lucius Quintius Cincinnatus was made dictator. When that man was found, he was ploughing his field. He wiped off his sweat, received the toga praetexta, and after the enemy was slaughtered, freed the army. He then went back home to his field.

Eutropius 1. 17. 1-2

Additional vocabulary

ager, agrī, m.	field
arō, arāre, arāvī, arātum	plough
caedō, caedere, cecīdī, caesum	cut, kill
colō, colere, coluī, cultum	cultivate, inhabit, worship

dētergeō, dētergēre, dētersī, dētersum	wipe off
dictātor, dictātōris, m.	dictator, an extraordinary Roman magistrate, elected in emergencies
domus, domūs (§ 28 for the forms)	home
duodecimus, -a, -um	twelfth
hostis, hostis, m. or f.	enemy (of the state)
inveniō, invenīre, invēnī, inventum	find
līberō, līberāre, līberāvī, līberātum	free
Mōns Algidus, Mōntis Algidī, m.	a mountain near Rome
obsideō, obsidēre, obsēdī, obsessum	besiege, occupy
revenio, revenīre, revēnī, —	return
sūdor, sūdōris, m.	sweat
toga praetexta, togae praetextae, f.	toga of magistrates and free-born children, bordered with purple

Fig. 18. The site of the Circus Maximus in Rome, used for chariot races, and remains of the Domus Augustana.

Sheila Gibson

Fig. 19. The Basilica of Maxentius or Basilica Nova on the Via Sacra in Rome, showing its coffered ceiling, supported by marble columns set on a marble floor. Maxentius began construction in AD 306, and Constantine finished it in 313.

Chapter 6

The imperative mood
Participles and the ablative absolute
Gerunds and gerundives
Active and passive periphrastic constructions

> 'Cavē, Gaberbocchum moneō tibi, nāte, cavendum
> (Unguibus ille rapit. Dentibus ille necat.)
> Et fuge Jubbubum, quō nōn īnfestior āles,
> Et Bandersnatcham, quae fremit usque, cavē.'

> Hassard H. Dodgson (Lewis Carroll's uncle), 'Gaberbocchus' in S. D. Collingwood,
> *Lewis Carroll Picture Book* (1899)

For the most part, the constructions outlined in the chapter heading are sheep in wolves' clothing and less horrific than they appear. They are simply jargon for more verbal and adjectival forms.

LXV. The imperative mood [GLG 112, 130, 266–275]

111. The imperative mood expresses direct commands.

(a)　The singular active imperative is formed by taking the second principal part and eliminating the -re.

(b)　The plural active imperative is formed by adding -te to the singular imperative for verbs of the first, second, and fourth conjugations. For verbs of the third conjugation, eliminate the -e of the singular imperative, and replace with -ite.

ACTIVE IMPERATIVE

FIRST CONJUGATION: **amō, amāre (stem: amā-)**

amā!	Love! *(singular)*	amāte!	(You all) love! *(plural)*

SECOND CONJUGATION: **moneō, monēre (stem: monē-)**

monē!	Warn!	monēte!	(You all) warn!

THIRD CONJUGATION: **regō, regere (stem: rege-)**

rege!	Rule!	regite!	(You all) rule!

THIRD CONJUGATION (-IŌ): **capiō, capere (stem: cape-)**

cape!	Take!	capite!	(You all) take!

FOURTH CONJUGATION: **audiō, audīre (stem: audī-)**

audī!	Hear!	audīte!	(You all) hear!

---

petite et dabitur vōbīs: quaerite et inveniētis: pulsāte et aperiētur vōbīs.

Ask, and it will be given to you. Seek, and you will find. Knock, and it will be opened to you.

Matthew 7: 7

112. The following irregular imperatives are common:

> Dīc, dīcite, from dīcō (say)
>
> Dūc, dūcite, from dūcō (lead)
>
> Es, este, from esse (be); note also estō, estōte.
>
> Fac, facite, from faciō (do, make)
>
> Fer, ferte, from ferō (bear)
>
> Mementō, mementōte, from meminī (remember)

113. The negative imperative is expressed in the following ways:

(a) nōlī (sing.) or nōlīte (plural), from the irregular verb nōlle, with the infinitive.

> nōlī verberāre lapidem.
>
> Don't strike a stone!

Plautus, *Curculiō* 197

(b) nē with the present or perfect subjunctive.

> nē requīrās.
>
> Don't look for it.

Cicero, *On Old Age* 10. 33

(c) cavē or cavēte (beware) and a subjunctive verb with or without nē.

> cavē festīnēs.
>
> Mind you don't hurry.

Cicero, *Letters to His Friends* 16. 12. 6

(d) nē with the imperative.

> tū nē cēde malīs.
>
> You, do not yield to evils.

Virgil, *Aeneid* 6. 95

(e) the imperative of a verb meaning 'to cease' or 'stop,' followed by the infinitive.

> Dēsine mēque tuīs incendere tēque querēlīs.
>
> Stop enflaming me and yourself with those complaints of yours.

Virgil, *Aeneid* 4. 360

Constructions (a) and (b) are normal in prose; (c), (d), and (e) are found primarily in poetry and comedy.

LXVI. Participles [GLG 80, 82, 121–129, 437–438, 536–537, 664–670]

114. A participle is a verbal adjective, that is, an adjective that derives from a verb. In the proverb

Let sleeping dogs lie

the word 'sleeping' is an English participle, since it modifies 'dogs,' but comes from the verb 'to sleep'.

Latin participles exist in the following forms and tenses: the present active (but not the passive); the perfect passive (but not the active); the future active and passive. As adjectives, they must agree with nouns they modify in case, number, and gender.

(a)   The present active participle adds -ns to the verbal stem in the nominative singular and -nt- elsewhere. The participle is then declined as if it were a third-declension i-stem noun. The present participle is translated using the -ing form of the English verb or the formula 'while _____ing.'

PRESENT ACTIVE PARTICIPLES
FIRST CONJUGATION: **amāns, amantis (loving, while loving)**

	singular		**plural**	
	masc./fem.	*neut.*	*masc./fem.*	*neut.*
nom.	amāns	amāns	amantēs	amantia
gen.	amantis	amantis	amantium	amantium
dat.	amantī	amantī	amantibus	amantibus
acc.	amantem	amāns	amantēs	amantia
abl.	amante (ī)	amante (ī)	amantibus	amantibus

Similarly:

SECOND CONJUGATION:	monēns, monentis, etc.	(while) warning
THIRD CONJUGATION:	regēns, regentis, etc.	(while) ruling
THIRD CONJUGATION (-IŌ);	capiēns, capientis, etc.	(while) taking
FOURTH CONJUGATION:	audiēns, audientis, etc.	(while) hearing

Note that the present participle tends to take an -e in the ablative singular if the participle is used as a substantive and an -ī when used as an adjective. Fourth conjugation verbs use -ēns in the nominative singular and -entis in the genitive. Third conjugation verbs with -iō in the first principal part are treated essentially as if they were fourth conjugation verbs.

(b) The perfect passive participle is the last principal part of the verb. It is translated using the formula, 'having been _____.' The participle declines using first and second declension endings.

PERFECT PASSIVE PARTICIPLES

FIRST CONJUGATION:	amātus, -a, -um	having been loved
SECOND CONJUGATION:	monītus, -a, -um	having been warned
THIRD CONJUGATION:	rectus, -a, -um	having been ruled
THIRD CONJUGATION (-IŌ)|;	captus, -a, -um	having been taken
FOURTH CONJUGATION;	audītus, -a, -um	having been heard

(c) To form the future active participle, take the fourth principle part, drop the ending -us, -a, -um, and substitute, -ūrus, -ūra, -ūrum. These decline using first and second declension adjective endings. Translate using the formula 'about to _____' or 'going to _____.'

FUTURE ACTIVE PARTICIPLES

FIRST CONJUGATION:	amātūrus, -a, -um	about to love
SECOND CONJUGATION:	monītūrus, -a, -um	about to warn
THIRD CONJUGATION:	rectūrus, -a, -um	about to rule
THIRD CONJUGATION (-IŌ):	captūrus, -a, -um	about to take
FOURTH CONJUGATION:	audītūrus, -a, -um	about to hear

(d) The future passive participle, also called the gerundive, is formed by

(i) taking the present stem, adding -nd- , and

(ii) then adding the endings of a first and second declension adjective. For the fourth conjugation and for -iō verbs of the third declension, drop the -ō of the first principal part, and add -end- before the endings of a first and second declension adjective. Translate using the formula '_____ing.' The gerundive may also be translated in English with the formula 'to be _____ed.'

FUTURE PASSIVE PARTICIPLES (GERUNDIVES)

FIRST CONJUGATION:	amandus, -a, -um	loving, to be loved
SECOND CONJUGATION:	monendus, -a, -um	warning, to be warned
THIRD CONJUGATION:	regendus, -a, -um	ruling, to be ruled
THIRD CONJUGATION (-IŌ);	capiendus, -a, -um	taking, to be taken
FOURTH CONJUGATION:	audiendus, -a, -um	hearing, to be heard

---

115. The translation of the participle depends upon the relationship between the tense of the participle and the tense of the main verb.

(a) The present participle expresses action which occurs at exactly the same time as the action of the main verb.

> M. Catōnem vīdī in bibliothēcā sedentem.

> I saw Marcus Cato sitting in the library.

> *Cicero, On Ends* 3. 2. 7

(b) The perfect participle expresses action which has happened before the time of the main verb.

> T. Manlius Gallum caesum spoliāvit.

> Titus Manlius despoiled a slain Gaul.

> *Livy* 6. 42. 5

(c) The future participle expresses action which will happen after the time of the main verb.

> moritūrī tē salūtāmus.

> We, about to die, salute you.

> *said to be the traditional greeting of gladiators to Caesar*
> *at the Roman games*

(d) On the gerundive, see § 121–122.

116. After translating the Latin literally (which may be called putting the Latin into the 'choctaw'), the participial phrase may be smoothed out by adding 'when,' 'since,' 'although,' 'because,' or 'after.'

> Dionysius quidem tyrannus Syrācūsīs expulsus Corinthī puerōs docēbat.

> In fact, after he was driven out as tyrant from Syracuse, Dionysius used to teach boys at Corinth.

> *Cicero, Tusculan Disputations* 3. 12. 27

When English uses a participle, the participle is usually placed next to the noun or pronoun that the participle describes. Otherwise, we may get into trouble with the sense — as in the advertisement 'For sale, automobile by elderly lady, only slightly used ....' In Latin, there is a case ending on the participle, showing what noun or pronoun is described, and so it is not necessary to put the participle next to the word described.

In fact, Latin very much prefers this word order: the noun or pronoun described, followed by any adverbs, prepositional phrases, objects of participle, etc. (*i.e.*, any words that are to be taken with the participle), followed by the participle itself. Thus, English says: 'Caesar was wounded while leading his men out of the camp,' or, in somewhat less natural order, 'Caesar, while leading his men out of the camp, was wounded.' Latin prefers this order:

Caesar his-men out-of-the-camp while leading was wounded.

The whole participial expression forms a pocket, with the noun (or pronoun) described at one end, the participle at the other, and all other related words inside. But English prefers to go directly to the participle after the noun or pronoun is translated, and then return to the contents of the pocket. To put it another way: if you are translating from Latin to English, to sight a participle is to sight a friend, since you know that the words that come in its train will make good sense in relation to it.

LXVII. The active periphrastic construction [GLG 247]

117. The future active participle is often combined with any of the forms of the verb esse to form the active periphrastic construction. The participle must agree in gender, number, and case with the word it modifies.

dēditōs ūltimīs cruciātibus adfectūrī fuērunt.

They were going to put those who had surrendered to the ultimate tortures.

Livy 21. 44. 4

LXVIII. The ablative absolute [GLG 409–440]

118. An absolute is an adverbial subordinate clause grammatically unrelated to or unconnected with the rest of the sentence. Thus, the first sentence below has an absolute construction, but the second does not.

Caesar commanding, the Romans kept fighting bravely.

Commanding the Romans, Caesar kept fighting bravely.

In the second sentence, 'commanding' modifies the main subject (Caesar); a grammatical connection therefore exists between the two parts of the sentence.

119. An ablative absolute consists of two words in the ablative case, often set off from the rest of the sentence by commas. These words usually describe the background against which the action of the main part of the sentence may be understood. For this reason, the ablative absolute may be called an ablative of attendant circumstance. Usually, the first word is a noun, the second a participle.

(a) Translate the noun first.

(b) Translate the participle literally, after the noun.

(c) After rendered into the choctaw, smooth out the translation using 'when,' 'since,' 'after,' 'because,' or 'although.'

> hīs rēbus cōgnitīs, Caesar Gallōrum animōs verbīs cōnfīrmāvit.

> After he had learnt about these matters (these matters having been learnt), Caesar strengthened
> the courage of the Gauls with his words.

> Caesar, *Gallic War* 1. 33. 1

The lack of a past participle active is especially troublesome when turning English into Latin. To get around this problem, use a subordinate clause: for 'having heard this, he returned,' write 'cum hoc audīvisset, redīvit.' Otherwise, rewrite the English sentence using a perfect passive participle and the ablative absolute construction: 'hōc audītō, redīvit.' Since transitive verbs alone have a personal passive construction, the ablative of the perfect passive participle of an intransitive verb cannot be used in the ablative absolute construction. 'Caesar having been persuaded' must accordingly be rendered 'Caesarī cum persuāsum esset.'

120. If there is no participle, and the ablative absolute simply consists of two nouns, supply the English word 'being.'

> is, M. Messālā M. Pīsōne cōnsulibus, coniūrātiōnem nōbilitātis fēcit.

> He, M. Messala and M. Piso being consuls, contrived a conspiracy of nobles.

> Caesar, *Gallic War* 1. 2. 1

LXIX. Gerundives [GLG 115, 425–433]

121. Often, what in English would be the direct object of a gerundive seems to be attracted to the case of the gerundive itself. In reality, the gerundive as an adjective is simply agreeing with the word it modifies in case, number, and gender.

> nōn est plācandī spēs mihi nūlla deī.

> I have not a little hope of pleasing god (*literally* no hope of the god to be pleased).

> Ovid, *Tristia* 5. 8. 22

122. Note also the following common constructions using the gerundive:

(a)   With the ablatives causā or grātiā to express purpose. Translate using 'for the sake of.'

Menapiī lēgātōs ad eum pācis petendae causā mittunt.

The Menapii send legates to him for the sake of asking for peace.

Caesar, Gallic War 6. 6. 2

Note that causā and grātiā appear after the genitive governed.

(b)   The prepostion ad with an accusative gerundive after it expresses purpose.

lēgātī ad dēdendās urbēs vēnērunt.

Ambassadors arrived to surrender their cities.

Livy 37. 44. 4

(c)   The passive periphrastic construction expresses obligation or necessity. See § 124.

LXX. Gerunds [GLG 112, 425–433]

123. A gerund, like an infinitive, is a verbal noun. The gerund uses the same endings as the neuter singular gerundive.

(a)   The gerund never appears in the nominative; use an infinitive instead.

incipere multōst quam impetrāre facilius.

It is easier by far to begin than to win through.

Plautus, The Little Carthaginian 974

(b)   The gerund in a genitive construction may be translated 'of _____ing.'

postrēmō dissimulandī causā aut expūrgandī in senātum vēnit.

Afterwards, for the sake of dissimulating or of clearing himself, he came into the Senate.

Sallust, Catilinarian Conspiracy 31. 5

(c)   The gerund often appears in the ablative without a preposition and is translated following the rules

for translating such an ablative.

hominis autem mēns discendō alitur et cōgitandō.

But the mind of man is nourished by learning and thinking.

Cicero, On Duties 1. 30. 105

(d)   The gerund in a construction using the dative may be translated 'for _____ing.'

est autem ūtilis bitūmināta aut nitrōsa bibendō atque pūrgātiōnibus.

But waters with bitumen and soda are useful for drinking and for purges.

Pliny, *Natural History* 31. 32. 59

The basic differences between a gerund and a gerundive are these:

The gerund is a noun, the gerundive an adjective.

The gerund is active, the gerundive passive.

The gerund is in the neuter gender, the gerundive in all genders.

The gerund is used only in the singular, the gerundive in both numbers.

The gerund has no nominative case. The gerundive has all cases.

LXXI. The passive periphrastic construction [GLG 251, 355]

124. The gerundive with a form of esse expresses necessity or obligation. This is known as the passive periphrastic construction. Translate as follows:

(a)   regard the gerundive as if it were a passive infinitive: e. g., to be seen, to be carried, to be taught;

(b)   if the form of esse is present, include 'has' or 'have' or 'must.' If the form of esse is past, include 'had.' If the form of esse is future, include 'will have;'

(c)   finally, translate the subject of the gerundive.

If there is a dative in the construction, it will be a dative of agent.

haec praecipuē colenda est nōbīs, haec semper adhibenda.

These we must especially cultivate; these we must always bring to bear. (i.e., These have to be cultivated especially by us; these have to be brought to bear always.)

Cicero, *On the Orator* 2. 35. 148

If the gerundive belongs to a verb which usually takes a dative case, then this dative is translated normally, and agency is expressed by ā or ab and the ablative.

cīvibus ā vōbīs cōnsulendum.

You must consult the citizens.

Cicero, *On Pompey's Command* 2. 6

In indirect statement, esse is often omitted. On indirect statement, see § 128–133.

> Caesar statuit exspectāndam classem.

> Caesar decided that he had to wait for the fleet.

Caesar, *Gallic War* 3. 14. 1

125. The passive periphrastic construction allows a deponent verb to have a passive translation.

> quod fuit illīs cōnandum atque efficiendum.

> This ought to have been attempted by them and carried out.

Caesar, *Civil War* 1. 65. 5

EXERCISES

A. Vocabulary

agō, agere, ēgī, āctum	do, drive, discuss
cōnsul, cōnsulis, m.	consul
corrumpō, corrumpere, corrūpī, corruptum	destroy, adulterate
damnō, damnāre, damnāvī, damnātum	condemn
decem (*indeclinable*)	ten
decemvir, decemvirī, m.	magistrate in a commission of ten
duo, -ae, -o	two
habeō, habēre, habuī, habitum	have, hold, consider
mīles, mīlitis, m. or f.	soldier
mīlitō, mīlitāre, mīlitāvī, mīlitātum	be a soldier, serve as a soldier
moveō, movēre, mōvī, mōtum	move
nōminō, nōmināre, nōmināvī, nōminātum	name
occīdō, occīdere, occīdī, occīsum	kill
pater, patris, m.	father
potestās, potestātis, f.	power
prīmus, -a, -um	first
prō (*prep. with abl.*)	for, in front of, instead of
quīdam, quaedam, quoddam (*gen. cūiusdam*)	a, one, a certain, some
reveniō, revenīre, revēnī, —	return

secundus, -a, -um	second, favourable
stuprum, stuprī, n.	defilement
sustineō, sustinēre, sustinuī, sustentum	withstand, hold up, endure
tollō, tollere, sustulī, sublātum	raise, remove, put out of the way
trecentēsimus (-a, -um) et alter (altera, alterum)	three hundred and second
tumultus, tumultūs, m.	uprising
ūnus, -a, -um	one
virgō, virginis, f.	maiden

B. Translations

Eutropius continues his first book of Roman history with the story of Ap. (Appius) Claudius (Appius Claudius, Appī Claudī, m.), consul in 451 BC, with a nature as corrupt as his family was distinguished. The story below tells of his seduction of the daughter of Lucius Virginius (Virgīnius, Virgīnī, m.).

Annō trecentēsimō et alterō ab urbe conditā, prō duōbus cōnsulibus decem factī sunt, summam potestātem habentēs, decemvirī nōminātī. sed postquam prīmō annō bene ēgērunt, secundō ūnus ex hīs, Ap. Claudius, Virgīnī cūiusdam contrā Latīnōs mīlitantis fīliam virginem corrūpit; eam pater occīdit, quod stuprum ā decemvirō nōn sustinēbat, et reveniēns ad mīlitēs mōvit tumultum. sublāta est ē decemvirīs potestās ipsīque damnātī sunt.

Eutropius 1. 18. 1–2

Eutropius concludes his first book with some final examples of Rome's military prowess:

In the three hundred and fifteenth year after the founding of the city, the Fidenates revolted against the Romans. The Veientes and Tolumnius, their king, kept providing help to them, the Volsci fighting in addition. But with Mamercus Aemilius as dictator and L. Quintius Cincinnatus as master of the cavalry, having been conquered, they lost their king as well. Fidenae was captured and razed.

Eutropius 1. 19. 1–2

Additional vocabulary

eques, equitis, m.	horseman; cavalry (plural)
excīdō, excīdere, excīdī, excīsum	raze, demolish
Fīdēnae, Fīdēnārum, f. plural	a town in Italy
Fīdenātēs, Fīdenātum	Fidenates, an Italian tribe
magister, magistrī, m.	master
perdō, perdere, perdidī, perditum	destroy, lose
rebellō, rebellāre, rebellāvī, rebellātum	revolt
Tolumnius, -ī, m.	Tolumnius, king of the Veientes
trecentēsimus et quīntus-decimus, -a, -um	three hundred and fifteenth
Vēientēs, Vēientium, m. plural	inhabitants of Veii in Etruria
Volscī, Volscōrum, m. plural	a people in the south of Latium

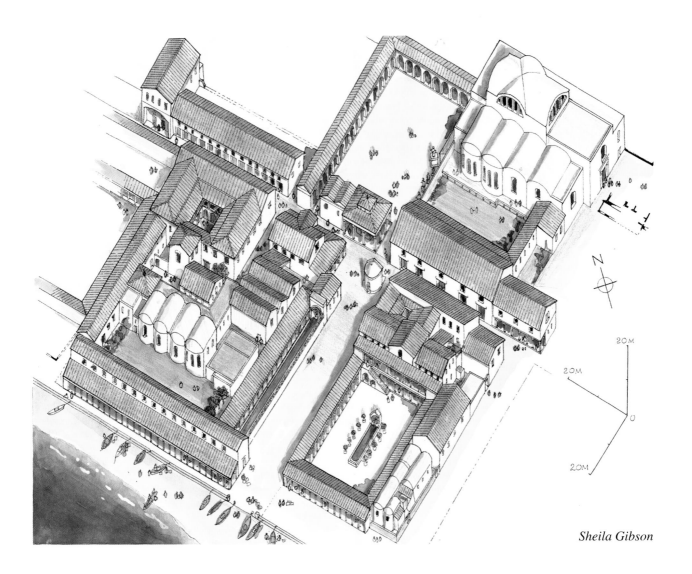

Sheila Gibson

Fig. 20. The site of Vicus Laurentium Augustanorum (Castelporziano) in Italy, a seaside settlement 6 km south of Ostia.

Sheila Gibson

Fig. 21. Two small temples at Vicus Laurentium Augustanorum (Castelporziano) in Italy, a seaside town 6 km south of Ostia. The statues along the side stand in front a baths building.

Chapter 7

Infinitives and indirect speech
Miscellaneous notes on verbs
Relative pronouns
Reflexive pronouns

In gīrum īmus noctēs, et cōnsūmimur īgnī.
— a palindrome on Roman moths

A principal theme of this chapter is subordination. If, as some say, the tense system — and not the wheel — is the most momentous invention in human history (since tenses made it easier to lie), then subordinate clauses are probably the invention most crucial after that, because they impose order on sequences of thought.

LXXII. The infinitive [GLG 115, 279–283, 423–424, 647]

126. An infinitive is a verbal noun. In essence, it is the 'base' form of a verb, introduced by the word 'to.' The only tenses of the infinitive that exist in Latin are described below:

(a)   The present active infinitive is simply the second principal part of the verb.

PRESENT ACTIVE INFINITIVE

FIRST CONJUGATION:	amāre	to love
SECOND CONJUGATION:	monēre	to warn
THIRD CONJUGATION:	regere	to rule
THIRD CONJUGATION (-IŌ):	capere	to take
FOURTH CONJUGATION:	audīre	to hear

To express a rapid sequence of events, the present infinitive is often used instead of the third person active imperfect indicative. Its subject, when expressed, is in the nominative case. This is called the historical infinitive. It may be translated by supplying the third person imperfect indicative of the verb concerned.

lacrimās interdum vix tenēre.

He was barely in between times holding back tears.

Cicero, *Verrine Orations* 2. 4. 18. 39

(b)   The present passive infinitive is formed by taking the present stem and adding -rī, except in the third conjugation. The third conjugation present passive infinitive is formed by substituting an -ī for the -ere of the second principal part.

PRESENT PASSIVE INFINITIVE

FIRST CONJUGATION:	amārī	to be loved
SECOND CONJUGATION:	monērī	to be warned
THIRD CONJUGATION:	regī	to be ruled
THIRD CONJUGATION (-IŌ):	capī	to be taken
FOURTH CONJUGATION:	audīrī	to be heard

(c)   To form the perfect active infinitive, take the third principal part of the verb, drop the -ī and add -isse.

PERFECT ACTIVE INFINITIVE

FIRST CONJUGATION:	amāvisse	to have loved
SECOND CONJUGATION:	monuisse	to have warned
THIRD CONJUGATION:	rēxisse	to have ruled
THIRD CONJUGATION (-IŌ):	cēpisse	to have taken
FOURTH CONJUGATION:	audīvisse	to have heard

(d)   The perfect passive infinitive is the perfect passive participle with esse as a second word.

PERFECT PASSIVE INFINITIVE

FIRST CONJUGATION:	amātus, -a, -um esse	to have been loved
SECOND CONJUGATION:	monitus, -a, -um esse	to have been warned
THIRD CONJUGATION:	rēctus, -a, -um esse	to have been ruled
THIRD CONJUGATION (-IŌ):	captus, -a, -um esse	to have been taken
FOURTH CONJUGATION:	audītus, -a, -um esse	to have been heard

In practice, the perfect passive infinitive appears with the fourth principal part in the accusative.

(e)   The future active infinitive is the future active participle with esse as a second word.

FUTURE ACTIVE INFINITIVE

FIRST CONJUGATION:	amātūrus, -a, -um esse	to be about to love
SECOND CONJUGATION:	monitūrus, -a, -um esse	to be about to warn
THIRD CONJUGATION:	rēctūrus, -a, -um esse	to be about to rule
THIRD CONJUGATION (-IŌ):	captūrus, -a, -um esse	to be about to take
FOURTH CONJUGATION:	audītūrus, -a, -um esse	to be about to hear

---

In practice, the future active infinitive is seen with the fourth principal part in the accusative.

(f)   The future passive infinitive is the supine (fourth principle part) in -um with, as a second word, īrī (the passive infinitive of eō, to go). This infinitive is rarely seen.

FUTURE PASSIVE INFINITIVE

FIRST CONJUGATION:	amātum īrī	to be about to be loved
SECOND CONJUGATION:	monitum īrī	to be about to be warned
THIRD CONJUGATION:	rēctum īrī	to be about to be ruled
THIRD CONJUGATION (-IŌ):	captum īrī	to be about to be taken
FOURTH CONJUGATION:	audītum īrī	to be about to be heard

(g)   The perfect passive infinitive and the future active infinitive are frequently written without esse.

127. Several verbs require a present infinitive to complete their meanings.

audeō, audēre, ausus sum	dare
coepī, coepisse, coeptum	begin
cōnor, cōnārī, cōnātus sum	try
cōnstituō, cōnstituere, cōnstituī, cōnstitūtum	establish, decide
contendō, contendere, contendī, contentum	hasten, march, struggle
cupiō, cupere, cupīvī, cupītum	desire
dēbeō, dēbēre, dēbuī, dēbitum	owe, ought
dubitō, dubitāre, dubitāvī, dubitātum	hesitate (*with infinitive*); doubt (*with subjunctive*)

incipiō, incipere, incēpī, inceptum	begin, undertake
īnstituō, īnstituere, īnstituī, īnstitūtum	establish, decide, prepare
licet, licēre, licuit or licitum est	it is permitted
mālō, mālle, māluī, —	prefer
nōlō, nōlle, nōluī, —	be unwilling
parō, parāre, parāvī, parātum	prepare, get
possum, posse, potuī, —	be able, can
properō, properāre, properāvī, properātum	hasten
sōleō, sōlēre, sōlitus sum	be accustomed
studeō, studēre, studuī, —	be eager for, be devoted to
temptō, temptāre, temptāvī, temptātum	try
videor, vidērī, vīsus sum	seem, seem best, be seen
volō, velle, voluī, —	wish

This type of infinitive is known as a complementary infinitive. Thus:

> ēmorī cupiō.

> I want to drop dead.

Terence, *The Self-Tormentor* 971

Some verbs require an accusative before the infinitive.

cōgō, cōgere, coēgī, coāctum	force, collect
iubeō, iubēre, iussī, iūssum	order
oportet, oportēre, oportuit, —	it is necessary
patior, patī, passus sum	allow, suffer
prohibeō, prohibēre, prohibuī, prohibitum	keep ... away, prevent
vetō, vetāre, vetuī, vetitum	forbid

LXXIII. Indirect speech [GLG 508, 527–535, 648–663]

128. Indirect speech is also known as indirect discourse or indirect statement (ōrātiō oblīqua in Latin). In this construction, the wording of what has been said or thought is reported and not quoted directly. The following, for example, is in direct speech:

> Time will teach Man and the Devil: 'Your intellects are not vast.'

The poet Lord Byron (1788–1824) reports this statement in indirect discourse as follows:

But time, which brings all beings to their level,

And sharp Adversity, will teach at last

Man, — and, as we would hope, — perhaps the devil,

That neither of their intellects are vast.

Lord Byron, *Don Juan*, Canto 4.2

129. Unlike English, Latin does not use the word 'that' in indirect statement. Instead, the subject of what was the direct quotation is put into the accusative case, and what was the main verb becomes an infinitive. Verbs which take this accusative and infinitive construction are verbs of mental action. They convey information or indicate the receipt or possession of information (and so may be called 'head and tel.' verbs): saying, hearing, thinking, believing, knowing, telling, feeling, hoping, realising, and the like.

Every infinitive in indirect statement must have a subject in the accusative case, even though the subject may not be expressed in English (*e.g.* The sentence 'he claims to be mad' is really 'he claims himself to be mad.'). The third person pronouns (he, she, it, they) must be translated by the reflexive pronouns whenever the subject of the main verb is the same subject of the infinitive.

The following common verbs take the indirect statement construction, using the accusative and infinitive:

audiō, audīre, audīvī, audītum	hear
cōgnōscō, cōgnōscere, cōgnōvī, cōgnītum	learn; know (*in perf.*)
comperiō, comperīre, comperī, compertum	find out
dīcō, dīcere, dīxī, dictum	say, tell, speak
exīstimō, exīstimāre, exīstimāvī, exīstimātum	think, suppose, believe
intellegō, intellegere, intellēxī, intellēctum	learn, perceive, know
nūntiō, nūntiāre, nūntiāvī, nūntiātum	report, announce, declare
putō, putāre, putāvī, putātum	think
reperiō, reperīre, repperī, repertum	find, discover, ascertain
respondeō, respondēre, respondī, respōnsum	reply, answer
sciō, scīre, scīvī, scītum	know, know how
sentiō, sentīre, sēnsī, sēnsum	discern, think, feel, sense, realize, see

The following verbs will often have a future infinitive following the accusative:

     polliceor, pollicērī, pollicitus sum   promise

     spērō, spērāre, spērāvī, spērātum   hope, expect

Note also the expressions certiōrem facere (to inform) and certior fīērī (to be informed).

     To translate an accusative and infinitive construction, you may use the word 'that.'

     Thalēs aquam dīxit esse initium rērum.

     Thales said that water was the origin of matter. (*i.e.*, Thales said water to be the origin of matter.)

Cicero, On the Nature of Gods 1. 10. 25

The part of an infinitive that is a participial form must agree with the accusative subject.

130. Sometimes a verb of the senses should be supplied by the reader, particularly when an accusative and infinitive construction follows a colon.

     redditur respōnsum: immātūram rem agī.

     A response was given: [they said that] the matter was being done prematurely.

Livy 2. 45. 8

131. If the time of the verb in the noun clause and the time of the verb in the main clause are exactly the same, then a present infinitive is used.

     vītae summa brevis spem nōs vetat incohāre longam.

     Life's brief tenure forbids that we build up great hope.

Horace, Odes 1. 4. 15

132. If the time of the verb in the noun clause expresses action before the action of the verb in the main clause, then a perfect infinitive is used.

     salvum tē advēnisse gaudeō.

     I rejoice that you have arrived safely.

Terence, Phormio 286

133. If the time of the verb in the noun clause expresses action after the action of the verb in the main clause, then a future infinitive is used.

     inter sē coniūrant nihil āctūrōs (esse).

     They swore among themselves that they would do nothing.

Caesar, Gallic War 3. 8. 3

LXXIV. Fore and negō [GLG 248, 447]

134. Fore is the future infinitive of esse and may substitute for futūrus, -a, -um esse.

> omnium labōrum fīnem fore exīstimābant.

> They kept thinking it would prove the end of all their troubles.

Caesar, Civil War 1. 68. 3

135. Often, fore is followed by ut and the subjunctive in a result clause. The present passive subjunctive is used if the main verb is in a primary tense, and the imperfect passive subjunctive is used if the main verb is in a secondary tense. See § 190–194.

> spērō fore ut contingat id nōbīs.

> I hope that it may so turn out for us.

Cicero, Tusculan Disputations 1. 34. 82

136. The future passive in indirect statement can be expressed in two ways:

(1) supine in -um with īrī as a second word.

> cum intereā rūmor vēnit datum īrī gladiātōrēs, populus convolat.

> When meanwhile a rumour came that a gladiatorial show was going to be given, people flew in.

Terence, The Mother-in-Law 39–40

(2) fore ut followed by a passive subjunctive.

> spērābat fore ut Caesaris mīlitēs exanimārentur.

> He was hoping that Caesar's soldiers would be out of breath.

Caesar, Civil War 3. 92. 3

137. Negō is usually substituted for dīcō ... nōn ('say ... not ...'). Translate with 'not' next to the infinitive.

> assem sēsē negat datūrum.

> He says that he will not give a penny.

Cicero, In Defence of P. Quinctius 5. 19

LXXV. The iterative form [GLG 191]

138. The verbal suffix -tō or -itō gives iterative or frequentative force to a word and implies habitual or repeated action. The iterative form of the verb is created either from the verbal base (*e.g.*, agitō, agitāre, put in constant or violent motion) or else from the perfect passive participle (*e.g.*, ductitō, ductitāre, to make a practice of leading off). Some are denominatives, that is, words derived from noun-stems (*e.g.*, nōbilitō, nōbilitāre, to make known generally).

LXXVI. Ut and the indicative [GLG 561–565]

139. The conjunction ut, when it governs a verb in the indicative mood, is translated 'as,' 'when,' or 'how.'

> sed Pompēius, ut equitātum suum pulsum vīdit, aciē excessit.

> But when Pompeius saw his own cavalry beaten, he left the battleline.

> Caesar, *Civil War* 3. 94. 5

LXXVII. Prefixes [GLG 200]

140. A few prefixes alter the force of verbs other than verbs of motion.

(a) Per- and con- add emphasis and are often translated 'thoroughly' or 'very': perficiō, cōnficiō (complete, finish, *i.e.*, do thoroughly).

(b) In- may negate a word: īnfirmō (deprive of strength, weaken).

LXXVIII. Postquam, ubi, and cum prīmum [GLG 561–565]

141. Postquam (after), ubi (when), and cum prīmum (as soon as) are used with the indicative mood. The perfect tense is usually used with postquam and cum prīmum.

> eō postquam Caesar pervēnit, obsidēs, arma, servōs poposcit.

> After Caesar arrived there, he demanded hostages, arms, slaves.

> Caesar, *Gallic War* 1. 27. 3

LXXIX. Compound verbs [GLG 200]

142. When a verb looks unfamiliar, break it down to its root word and a prefix:

> importō: im- (in) and portō (carry). Therefore: 'I carry in;'

> referō: re- (back) and ferō (bear, carry, say). Therefore: 'I bear back.'

143. The compound often alters its spelling to make pronunciation easier.

> afferō (from ad and ferō, bring to)

> assūmō (from ad and sumō, take to oneself)

> commisceō (from cum and misceō, mix together)

importō (from in and portō, bring in)

irrumpō (from in and rumpō, break in)

LXXX. Abbreviated forms [GLG 131]

144. The -v- and the vowel following it are often dropped in the perfect system (*e.g.*, amāsse for amāvisse; portārunt for portāvērunt).

LXXXI. Defective verbs [GLG 175]

145. Certain verbs cannot be conjugated in the present, imperfect, or future tense and only use the perfect system. But they may be translated in the present, imperfect, or future tense despite using a perfect, pluperfect, or future perfect form.

coepī, coepisse, coeptum	begin
meminī, meminisse, —	remember
ōdī, ōdisse, ōsum	hate

Thus:

ōdī	I hate
ōderam	I used to hate
ōderō	I shall hate.

LXXXII. The supine expressing purpose [GLG 434–435]

146. The supine, ending in -um, may be used to express purpose after verbs of motion.

Spectātum veniunt.

They come in order to watch.

Ovid, *The Art of Love* 1. 99

LXXXIII. Relative pronouns [GLG 105, 610–637]

147.   A relative pronoun (who, which, etc.) connects two sentences together, with one sentence becoming the main clause, the other a subordinate clause:

I know the man + The man broke the bank at Monte Carlo =

I know the man who broke the bank at Monte Carlo.

In a way, a relative clause is a phrase that modifies a noun. The word in the main clause to which the relative pronoun refers is called the antecedent of the relative pronoun. In Latin, the relative pronoun agrees in gender and number with the antecedent, but the case of the relative pronoun depends upon how it is used in the subordinate clause. Thus:

> M. Octāvus cum eīs, quās habēbat, nāvibus Salōnās pervēnit.

> Marcus Octavus arrived at Salonae with the ships which he was commanding.

Caesar, Civil War 3. 9. 1

In this instance, the relative pronoun quās is in the accusative, because it is the direct object of habēbat. The feminine plural is used because its antecedent, nāvibus, is also feminine and in the plural.

148. The relative pronouns are:

<hr>

RELATIVE PRONOUNS

	singular			**plural**		
	masc.	*fem.*	*neut.*	*masc.*	*fem.*	*neut.*
nom.	quī	quae	quod	quī	quae	quae
gen.	cūius	cūius	cūius	quōrum	quārum	quōrum
dat.	cuī	cuī	cuī	quibus	quibus	quibus
acc.	quem	quam	quod	quōs	quās	quae
abl.	quō	quā	quō	quibus	quibus	quibus

They are translated as follows:

nom.	who, which, that
gen.	whose
dat	to whom, for whom
acc.	whom, which, that
abl.	by, with, etc. whom, which

<hr>

As with the first and second person personal pronouns, the preposition cum (with) is appended to the ablative: *e.g.*, quibuscum.

149. A relative pronoun may also act as a substitute for the personal pronoun. Translate as if the pronoun were hīc, haec, hōc.

hī loca capere īnstituunt. quod ubi Crassus animadvertit nōn cunctandum exīstimāvit.

These men decided to take up positions. When Crassus noticed this, he thought that he ought not to delay.

Caesar, *Gallic War* 3. 23. 7

LXXXIV. The relative clause of purpose [GLG 630]

150. A relative pronoun may be used in a clause to express purpose after verbs that express the action of sending. This is known as the relative clause of purpose.

immittēbantur illī canēs quī investīgābant omnia.

The dogs were being sent in to track everything down.

Cicero, *Verrine Orations* 2. 4. 21. 47

LXXXV. Reflexive pronouns [GLG 218, 309]

151. As the term suggests, reflexive pronouns take the place of other nouns and refer back to the subject of a sentence. In the following sentence, the direct object 'yourself' is a reflexive pronoun that refers back to the subject 'you':

Sir, you have but two topics, yourself and me, and I am sick of both.

Samuel Johnson (1709–1784), reported in Boswell's *Life of Johnson*, annō 1776

The first and second person reflexive pronouns resemble the first and second person personal pronouns, except, of course, that there is no nominative reflexive pronoun in any person, since a nominative cannot refer back to itself.

nunc ad mē redeō.

I now get back to myself.

Horace, *Satires* 1. 6. 45

152. Some verbs augment their meanings when they are conjugated together with the reflexive pronoun. The reflexive pronoun must be in the accusative case and must be in the same person as the subject of the verb:

mē trādō   I surrender

tē trādis   You surrender

153. The third person reflexive pronouns are as follows:

THIRD PERSON REFLEXIVE PRONOUNS		
	singular	**plural**
nom.	–	–
gen.	suī	suī
dat.	sibi	sibi
acc.	sē (or sēsē)	sē (or sēsē)
abl.	sē (or sēsē)	sē (or sēsē)

These always refer to the subject of the clause. Thus, if the subject is male, for example, sē will mean 'himself;' if the subject is female, sē will mean 'herself;' and if the subject is plural (male or female), sē will mean 'themselves.' When dealing with reflexives, one should always refer back to the subject.

> omne animal sē dīligit.

> Every animal loves itself.

> > Cicero, *On Ends* 5. 9. 24

The ablative is appended to the preposition cum (with): *i.e.*, sēcum

154. Remember that is, ea, id, unlike the third-person reflexive pronouns, refer to someone else. Thus, the first sentence below describes the killing of others, the second suicide.

> tantam eōrum multitūdinem nostrī interfēcērunt.

> Our men killed such a great multitude of them.

> > Caesar, *Gallic War* 2. 11. 6

> noctū ad ūnum omnēs, dēspērātā salūte, sē ipsī interficiunt.

> At night, to a man, every single one kills himself, having despaired of safety.

> > Caesar, *Gallic War* 5. 37. 6

LXXXVI. The reflexive adjective [GLG 102, 309]

155. Like a reflexive pronoun, a reflexive adjective refers back to the subject of the sentence in which it appears. As an adjective, it modifies a noun. In the following sentence, the reflexive adjective 'my own' modifies 'foot':

> I will not pull the thorn out of your foot and put it into my own foot.

> > An English proverb

156. Like any other adjective, a Latin reflexive adjective will agree with the noun it modifies in case, number, and gender. The first and second person reflexive adjectives are meus, -a, -um (my own) and tuus, -a, -um (your own) in the singular, and noster, nostra, nostrum (our own) and vester, vestra, vestrum (your own) in the plural. These decline like first and second declension adjectives.

The third person reflexive adjective is suus, -a, -um. Translate as 'his own,' 'her own,' 'its own,' or 'their own,' depending upon the subject of the sentence.

> canis lymphārum in speculō vīdit simulācrum suum.

> A dog saw its own image in the reflection of the waters.

Phaedrus 1. 4. 2–3

EXERCISES

A. Vocabulary

Achillēs, Achillis, m.	Achilles, Greek warrior and hero in the Trojan War
adversus, -a, -um	facing, opposite, unfavourable
capiō, capere, cēpī, captum	take; form (a plan or conspiracy)
castra, castrōrum, n. plural	camp
committō, committere, commīsī, commissum	commit, entrust; begin (a contest)
dīcō, dīcere, dīxī, dictum	say, call
dīmittō, dīmittere, dīmīsī, dīmissum	send away
dominus, dominī, m.	master
dūcō, dūcere, dūxī, ductum	lead, consider
elephantus, elephantī, m.	elephant, ivory
expavēscō, expavēscere, expāvī, —	fear greatly
explōrātor, explōrātōris, m.	scout
genus, generis, n.	race, kind, offspring
iaceō, iacēre, iacuī, —	lie
incōgnitus, -a, -um	unknown
Ītalia, Ītaliae, f.	Italy
iubeō, iubēre, iussī, iūssum	order
mittō, mittere, mīsī, missum	send, let go

mortuus, -a, -um	dead
orbis, orbis, f.	circle, world
orīgō, orīginis, f.	beginning, origin
ostendō, ostendere, ostendī, ostentum	show
pūgna, pūgnae, f.	fight
tālis, tāle	such
tōtus, -a, -um	all, the whole
trahō, trahere, trāxī, tractum	draw, drag, trace
videō, vidēre, vīdī, vīsum	see
vulnus, vulneris, n.	wound

B. Translations

Eutropius' second book describes the war against the expansionist Greek king Pyrrhus (Pyrrhus, Pyrrhī, m.) of Epirus (Ēpīrus, Ēpīrī, m.) (280–275 BC). Never before had the Romans encountered an enemy from across the seas, and P. (Publius) Valerius Laevinus (Valērius Laevīnus, Valērī Laevīnī, m.) was initially despatched against him.

   Pyrrhus, Ēpīrī rēx, quī ex genere Achillis orīginem trahēbat, mox ad Ītaliam vēnit. missus est contrā eum cōnsul P. Valērius Laevīnus quī iussit explōrātōrēs Pyrrhī captōs per castra dūcī, ostendī omnem exercitum tumque dīmittī. commissā mox pūgnā, elephantōrum auxiliō vīcit Pyrrhus, quōs incōgnitōs Rōmanī expāvērunt. Ubi Rōmānōs adversō vulnere mortuōs iacēre vīdit, dīxit sē tālēs mīlitēs habentem tōtīus orbis dominum fore.

Eutropius 2. 11. 1-3

Eutropius continues with the story of a plot conceived by a doctor against Pyrrhus. The story is also told by the polymath Aulus Gellius who quotes the actual letter sent to Pyrrhus by the Roman consul Gaius Fabricius (Fabricius, Fabricī, m.).

   The doctor of Pyrrhus went to Fabricius at night, promising that he would kill Pyrrhus with poison. Him Fabricius ordered to be bound and led back to Pyrrhus, saying: 'It does not please us to fight by means of bribes or rewards or tricks.' Then the king said: 'That is Fabricius, who turns away from honour with more difficulty than the sun turns aside from its course.'

Eutropius 2. 14. 2–3 with Aulus Gellius 3. 8. 8

Additional vocabulary

āvertō, āvertere, āvertī, āversum	turn away
cursus, cursūs, m.	course
difficilis, difficile	difficult
dolus, dolī, m.	trickery, treachery
honestās, honestātis, f.	honour, good
medicus, medicī, m.	doctor
placeō, placēre, placuī, — (*with dative*)	please
praemium, praemiī, n.	reward, prize
pretium, pretī, n.	price, bribe, reward
prōmittō, prōmittere, prōmīsī, prōmissum	send forth, promise
redūco, redūcere, redūxī, reductum	lead back
sōl, sōlis, m.	sun
venēnum, venēnī, n.	poison
vinciō, vincīre, vinxī, vinctum	bind

Fig. 22a. Frieze in the Villa of the Mysteries at Pompeii.

Fig. 22b. Detail of the frieze in the Villa of the Mysteries at Pompeii, with the movement depicted in three-dimensions across the corner of the room.

Sheila Gibson

Fig. 23. The 'Grotte di Catullo,' named after the famous poet, whose family owned the villa. The villa was built in the early second century AD on the peninsula of Sirmio. The central block is 180 by 105 m.

Chapter 8

Deponents and semi-deponents
Further miscellaneous notes on verbs
Interrogatives and indefinite pronouns
The subjunctive and its morphology

Instruction sore long time I bore,
And cramming was in vain,
Till Heaven did please my woes to ease
With water on the brain.

Charles Kingsley (1819–1875), *The Water-Babies*

This chapter concludes the survey of the indicative with questions and uncertainties: in other words, interrogatives and indefinites. Indefinition is also inherent in the subjunctive mood, which specialises in hypotheticals. It is not surprising then that some subjunctive forms recall the future tense, since by definition, what will be cannot be known.

LXXXVII. Deponent verbs [GLG 113, 128, 163–166]

157. Deponent verbs have translations in the active voice, although they appear passive in form. Thus:

cōnor	I am trying
cōnābar	I was trying
cōnātus sum	I tried

158. The following are the most common deponents:

arbitror, arbitrārī, arbitrātus sum	think
cōnor, cōnārī, cōnātus sum	try
ēgredior, ēgredī, ēgressus sum	go out
fateor, fatērī, fassus sum	confess
hortor, hortārī, hortātus sum	urge
loquor, loquī, locūtus sum	speak
mōlior, mōlīrī, mōlītus sum	build, undertake
morior, morī, mortuus sum	die

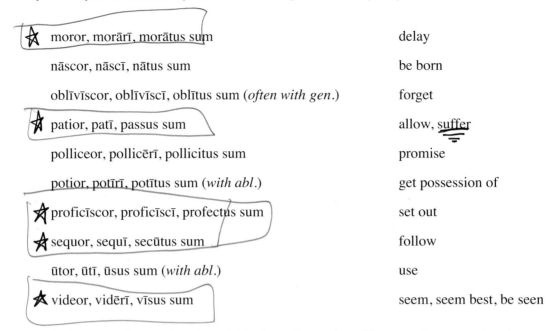

moror, morārī, morātus sum	delay
nāscor, nāscī, nātus sum	be born
oblīvīscor, oblīvīscī, oblītus sum (*often with gen.*)	forget
patior, patī, passus sum	allow, suffer
polliceor, pollicērī, pollicitus sum	promise
potior, potīrī, potītus sum (*with abl.*)	get possession of
proficīscor, proficīscī, profectus sum	set out
sequor, sequī, secūtus sum	follow
ūtor, ūtī, ūsus sum (*with abl.*)	use
videor, vidērī, vīsus sum	seem, seem best, be seen

159. Certain forms of deponent verbs exist in the active voice. These are the present active participle, the future active participle, and the future active infinitive. They are to be translated in the active.

loquēns	speaking
locūtūrus	about to speak
locūtūrus esse	to be about to speak

LXXXVIII. Semi-deponent verbs [GLG 167]

160. A semi-deponent is regular in the present, imperfect, and future tenses. But in the perfect, pluperfect, and future perfect, it is passive in form and active in meaning. A semi-deponent verb only has three principle parts, since a perfect active principle part does not exist. These are the most common semi-deponents:

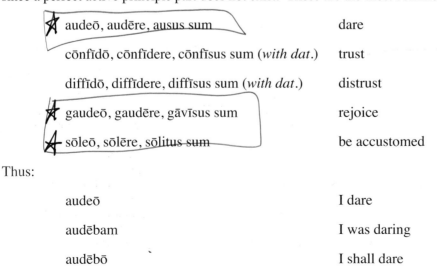

audeō, audēre, ausus sum	dare
cōnfīdō, cōnfīdere, cōnfīsus sum (*with dat.*)	trust
diffīdō, diffīdere, diffīsus sum (*with dat.*)	distrust
gaudeō, gaudēre, gāvīsus sum	rejoice
sōleō, sōlēre, sōlitus sum	be accustomed

Thus:

audeō	I dare
audēbam	I was daring
audēbō	I shall dare

ausus sum	I dared
ausus eram	I had dared
ausus erō	I shall have dared

LXXXIX. The passive imperative [GLG 121]

161. The passive imperative (*e.g.*, Be gone!) is more often formed from deponent verbs than regular ones.

(a) In form, the singular passive imperative resembles the present active infinitive; here, however, there is in fact the alternate second person passive personal ending.

SINGULAR PASSIVE IMPERATIVES

FIRST CONJUGATION:	amāre	Be loved!
SECOND CONJUGATION:	monēre	Be warned!
THIRD CONJUGATION:	regere	Be ruled!
THIRD CONJUGATION (-IŌ):	capere	Be taken!
FOURTH CONJUGATION:	audīre	Be heard!
FIRST CONJUGATION DEPONENT:	cōnāre	Try!

(b) The plural passive imperative substitutes the second person plural passive personal ending (-minī) for the ending -re. A third declension verb will shift the vowel of the verbal stem from -e to -i.

PLURAL PASSIVE IMPERATIVES

FIRST CONJUGATION:	amāminī	(You all) be loved!
SECOND CONJUGATION:	monēminī	(You all) be warned!
THIRD CONJUGATION:	regiminī	(You all) be ruled!
THIRD CONJUGATION (-IŌ):	capiminī	(You all) be taken!
FOURTH CONJUGATION:	audīminī	(You all) be heard!
FIRST CONJUGATION DEPONENT:	cōnāminī	(You all) try!

XC. Ablatives after verbs [GLG 407]

162. Five verbs commonly require the ablative case to complete their meanings. These are:

fruor, fruī, frūctus (or fruitūrus) sum	enjoy
fungor, fungī, fūnctus sum	perform
potior, potīrī, potītus sum	get possession of
ūtor, ūtī, ūsus sum	use
vescor, vescī, —	eat

XCI. Prohibeō, vetō, and the infinitive [GLG 423, 532]

163. Prohibeō and vetō are followed by an infinitive and translated 'prevent ... from.'

prohibentur adīre ad fīliōs.

They are prevented from approaching their sons.

Cicero, *Verrine Orations* 2. 5. 45. 117

XCII. Interrogatives [GLG 106, 450–457, 467]

164. An interrogative is a word that indicates a question is asked (*e.g.*, 'who,' 'what,' 'where,' 'when,' 'how,' 'why'). Direct questions may be introduced by an interrogative particle, an interrogative pronoun, an interrogative adjective, or an interrogative adverb.

165. An interrogative particle is left untranslated; it is simply a word or an attachment (called an enclitic) to the end of a word, indicating a question is being asked. The interrogative particles are:

(1)   -ne, which expects no particular answer and is attached to the first word of the question or, in rarer

instances, to an important word near the beginning;

omnisne pecūnia dissolūta est?

Was all the money paid?

Cicero, *Verrine Orations* 2. 3. 77. 180

(2)   nōnne expects an affirmative answer and is the first word of a question;

nōnne meministī?

Do you not remember?

Cicero, *On Ends* 2. 3. 10

(3)   num expects a negative answer and is the first word of a question.

> num immemorēs discipulī?

> Pupils aren't forgetful, are they?

Terence, *Woman of Andros* 477

If a question begins with an interrogative pronoun, adjective, or adverb, a particle is not needed.

166. As a type of pronoun, the interrogative pronoun ('who,' 'what,' 'to whom,' etc.) replaces a noun and has the following forms:

INTERROGATIVE PRONOUNS

	singular		plural		
	masc./fem.	*neut.*	*masc.*	*fem.*	*neut.*
nom.	quis	quid	quī	quae	quae
gen.	cūius	cūius	quōrum	quārum	quōrum
dat.	cuī	cuī	quibus	quibus	quibus
acc.	quem	quid	quōs	quās	quae
abl.	quō	quō	quibus	quibus	quibus

Note that the plural forms resemble those for the relative pronoun. Translations are:

nom.	who? what?
gen.	whose? of what?
dat.	to whom? to what?; for whom? for what?
acc.	whom? what?
abl.	by whom? by what?, for whom? for what?, with whom? with what?

---

167. As the term suggests, an interrogative adjective modifies a noun:

> What child is this, who laid to rest

> On Mary's lap is sleeping?

William Dix (1837–1865), 'The Manger Throne'

In the example above, the interrogative adjective 'what' modifies 'child.'

In Latin, the interrogative adjective has the same forms as the relative pronoun, but the alternate form qua is sometimes found for the feminine singular quae. As with all adjectives, the interrogative adjective must agree with the word it modifies in case, number, and gender:

quō id iūre fēcistī?

By what legal right did you do this?

Cicero, *Verrine Orations* 2. 3. 49. 118

Translate the interrogative adjective as 'what' or 'which'.

168. Other interrogative adjectives are:

quālis, quāle	what kind of, as
quantus, -a, -um	how great, how much
quot	how many
uter, utra, utrum	which (of two)

169. The interrogative adverbs in Latin (with some ancillary meanings) are:

cūr	why
quam ob rem	why, therefore
quandō	when, since
quārē	why, therefore
quem ad modum	how, as
quō	where (to what place)
quō tempōre	when
quōmodo	how, as
quotiēns	how often
quousque	how long
ubi	when, where
unde	from where

Num in indirect questions does not imply an answer in the negative, but rather simply 'whether.'

XCIII. Indefinite pronouns [GLG 107, 313–319]

170. Indefinite pronouns identify persons or objects not certainly known to the listener. The most common indefinite pronouns are as follows:

aliquis, aliquid (gen., alicūius, dat., alicuī, etc.)   someone, something

quīdam, quaedam, quoddam (gen. cūiusdam, dat. cuīdam, etc.)   a certain

quisquam, quicquam (gen., cūiusquam, dat., cuīquam, etc.)   anyone, anything

quisque, quaeque, quidque (gen., cūiusque, dat., cuīque, etc.)   each, everyone

quisquis, quidquid (quicquid) (gen., cūiuscūius, dat., cuīcuī, etc.)   whoever, whatever

XCIV. After sī, nisi, num, and nē [GLG 107, 315, 371]

171. After sī, nisi, num, and nē, the indefinite aliquis ('anyone,' 'someone') shortens to quis; quid is short for aliquid ('anything,' 'something').

> numquam, sī quid mihi crēdis, amāvī
>
> hunc hominem.
>
> If you believe anything of me: never have I loved this man.

Juvenal 10. 68–69

172. Sometimes quid introduces a partitive genitive.

> quid portās novī?
>
> What news do you bring?

Seneca, *Thyestes* 626

173. The adjective quī, quae (qua), quod may translate as the adjective 'any.'

> Sī quī rēx, sī qua cīvitās, sī qua nātiō fēcisset aliquid in cīvēs Rōmānōs ēius modī,
>
> nōnne pūblicē vindicārēmus?
>
> If any king, if any state, if any nation had done anything of this sort against Roman citizens,
>
> should we not take public vengeance?

Cicero, *Verrine Orations* 2. 5. 58. 149

XCV. The subjunctive mood [GLG 255–256]

174. Unlike the indicative mood which expresses facts, the subjunctive mood is used in sentences that express ideas, especially probable or possible ones,. The subjunctive mood has only four tenses: the present, imperfect, perfect, and pluperfect. It is only possible to translate a subjunctive form when one knows why the subjunctive is used within a sentence. The remaining sections of this chapter therefore concentrate on morphology, with syntax considered later.

XCVI. Formation of the present subjunctive, active and passive
[GLG 120–129]

175. To form the present subjunctive of regular verbs:

(a)   drop the -re from the second principal part of the verb; then

(b)   change the final vowel of the verbal stem to

   -e for the first conjugation,

   -ea for the second conjugation,

   -a for the third conjugation, and

   -ia for the fourth conjugation.

Verbs in the third conjugation with -iō in the first principal part use -ia in the present subjunctive.

(c)   Finally, add the personal endings for the active or passive voices as required.

FIRST CONJUGATION PRESENT SUBJUNCTIVE

amō, amāre (subjunctive stem: ame-)

	ACTIVE		PASSIVE	
	singular	**plural**	**singular**	**plural**
1st	amem	amēmus	amer	amēmur
2d	amēs	amētis	amēris	amēminī
3d	amet	ament	amētur	amentur

The present subjunctive of dō in its early Latin form – duim, duis, duit, etc. — is sometimes encountered.

SECOND CONJUGATION PRESENT SUBJUNCTIVE

moneō, monēre (subjunctive stem: monea-)

1st	moneam	moneāmus	monear	moneāmur
2d	moneās	moneātis	moneāris	moneāminī
3d	moneat	moneant	moneātur	moneantur

THIRD CONJUGATION PRESENT SUBJUNCTIVE

regō, regere (subjunctive stem: rega-)

1st	regam	regāmus	regar	regāmur
2d	regās	regātis	regāris	regāminī
3d	regat	regant	regātur	regantur

THIRD CONJUGATION (-IŌ) PRESENT SUBJUNCTIVE

capiō, capere (subjunctive stem: capia-)

1st	capiam	capiāmus	capiar	capiāmur
2d	capiās	capiātis	capiāris	capiāminī
3d	capiat	capiant	capiātur	capiantur

FOURTH CONJUGATION PRESENT SUBJUNCTIVE

audiō, audīre (subjunctive stem: audia-)

1st	audiam	audiāmus	audiar	audiāmur
2d	audiās	audiātis	audiāris	audiāminī
3d	audiat	audiant	audiātur	audiantur

XCVII. The present subjunctive of esse [GLG 116]

176. As one would anticipate, the present subjunctive of esse is irregular:

PRESENT SUBJUNCTIVE OF ESSE

	singular	plural
1st	sim	sīmus
2d	sīs	sītis
3d	sit	sint

XCVIII. Formation of the imperfect subjunctive, active and passive [GLG 120–129]

177. The imperfect subjunctive of regular verbs is formed by adding the personal endings, active or passive as necessary, to the second principal part.

FIRST CONJUGATION IMPERFECT SUBJUNCTIVE

amō, amāre (stem: amāre-)

	ACTIVE		PASSIVE	
	singular	**plural**	**singular**	**plural**
1st	amārem	amārēmus	amārer	amārēmur
2d	amārēs	amārētis	amārēris	amārēminī
3d	amāret	amārent	amārētur	amārentur

SECOND CONJUGATION IMPERFECT SUBJUNCTIVE

moneō, monēre (stem: monēre-)

1st	monērem	monērēmus	monērer	monērēmur
2d	monērēs	monērētis	monērēris	monērēminī
3d	monēret	monērent	monērētur	monērentur

THIRD CONJUGATION IMPERFECT SUBJUNCTIVE

regō, regere (stem: regere-)

1st	regerem	regerēmus	regerer	regerēmur
2d	regerēs	regerētis	regerēris	regerēminī
3d	regeret	regerent	regerētur	regerentur

THIRD CONJUGATION (-IŌ) IMPERFECT SUBJUNCTIVE

capiō, capere (stem: capere-)

1st	caperem	caperēmus	caperer	caperēmur
2d	caperēs	caperētis	capereris	caperēminī
3d	caperet	caperent	caperētur	caperentur

FOURTH CONJUGATION IMPERFECT SUBJUNCTIVE

audiō, audīre (stem: audīre-)

1st	audīrem	audīrēmus	audīrer	audīrēmur
2d	audīrēs	audīrētis	audīrēris	audīrēminī
3d	audīret	audīrent	audīrētur	audīrentur

XCIX. The imperfect subjunctive of esse [GLG 116]

178. From the above, it follows that the imperfect subjunctive of esse is as follows:

IMPERFECT SUBJUNCTIVE OF ESSE

1st	essem	essēmus
2d	essēs	essētis
3d	esset	essent

C. Formation of the perfect subjunctive, active and passive [GLG 120–129]

179. To form the perfect active subjunctive:

(a)   drop the -ī of the third principal part; then

(b)   add -eri and the personal endings to the perfect active stem.

To form the perfect passive subjunctive:

(a)   append the present subjunctive of esse to the fourth principal part as a second word;

(b)   remember that the fourth principal part must agree in case, number, and gender with the word it modifies.

FIRST CONJUGATION PERFECT SUBJUNCTIVE

amō, amāre, amāvī, amātum

(perfect active stem: amāv-; fourth principal part: amātus, -a, -um)

	ACTIVE		PASSIVE	
	singular	plural	singular	plural
1st	amāverim	amāverīmus	amātus, -a, -um sim	amātī, -ae, -a sīmus
2d	amāverīs	amāverītis	amātus, -a, -um sīs	amātī, -ae, -a sītis
3d	amāverit	amāverint	amātus, -a, -um sit	amātī, -ae, -a sint

SECOND CONJUGATION PERFECT SUBJUNCTIVE

moneō, monēre, monuī, monitum

(perfect active stem: monu-; fourth principal part: monitus, -a, -um)

1st	monuerim	monuerīmus	monitus, -a, -um sim	monitī, -ae, -a sīmus
2d	monuerīs	monuerītis	monitus, -a, -um sīs	monitī, -ae, -a sītis
3d	monuerit	monuerint	monitus, -a, -um sit	monitī, -ae, -a sint

THIRD CONJUGATION PERFECT SUBJUNCTIVE

regō, regere, rēxī, rēctum

(perfect active stem: rēx-; fourth principal part: rēctus, -a, -um)

1st	rēxerim	rēxerīmus	rēctus, -a, -um sim	rēctī, -ae, -a sīmus
2d	rēxerīs	rēxerītis	rēctus, -a, -um sīs	rēctī, -ae, -a sītis
3d	rēxerit	rēxerint	rēctus, -a, -um sit	rēctī, -ae, -a sint

THIRD CONJUGATION (-IŌ) PERFECT SUBJUNCTIVE

capiō, capere, cēpī, captum

(perfect active stem: cēp-; fourth principal part: captus, -a, -um)

1st	cēperim	cēperīmus	captus, -a, -um sim	captī, -ae, -a sīmus
2d	cēperīs	cēperītis	captus, -a, -um sīs	captī, -ae, -a sītis
3d	cēperit	cēperint	captus, -a, -um sit	captī, -ae, -a sint

FOURTH CONJUGATION PERFECT SUBJUNCTIVE

audiō, audīre, audīvī, audītum

(perfect active stem: audīv-; fourth principal part: audītus, -a, um)

1st	audīverim	audīverīmus	audītus, -a, -um sim	audītī, -ae, -a sīmus
2d	audīverīs	audīverītis	audītus, -a, -um sīs	audītī, -ae, -a sītis
3d	audīverit	audīverint	audītus, -a, -um sit	audītī, -ae, -a sint

---

CI. The perfect subjunctive of esse [GLG 116]

180. From the above, the perfect subjunctive of esse is as follows:

PERFECT SUBJUNCTIVE OF ESSE

	singular	plural
1st	fuerim	fuerīmus
2d	fuerīs	fuerītis
3d	fuerit	fuerint

CII. Formation of the pluperfect subjunctive, active and passive
[GLG 120–129]

181. To form the pluperfect active subjunctive:

   (a) drop the -ī of the third principal part; then

   (b) add -isse to the perfect active stem; then

   (c) add the personal endings in the active.

To form the pluperfect passive:

   (a) append the imperfect subjunctive of esse to the fourth principal part;

   (b) remember that the fourth principal part must agree with the word it modifies in case,

   number, and gender.

FIRST CONJUGATION PLUPERFECT SUBJUNCTIVE

amō, amāre, amāvī, amātum

(perfect active stem: amāv-; fourth principal part: amātus, -a, -um)

	ACTIVE		PASSIVE	
	singular	plural	singular	plural
1st	amāvissem	amāvissēmus	amātus, -a, -um essem	amātī, -ae, -a essēmus
2d	amāvissēs	amāvissētis	amātus, -a, -um essēs	amātī, -ae, -a essētis
3d	amāvisset	amāvissent	amātus, -a, -um esset	amātī, -ae, -a essent

SECOND CONJUGATION PLUPERFECT SUBJUNCTIVE

moneō, monēre, monuī, monitum

(perfect active stem: monu-; fourth principal part: monitus, -a, -um)

1st	monuissem	monuissēmus	monitus, -a, -um essem	monitī, -ae, -a essēmus
2d	monuissēs	monuissētis	monitus, -a, -um essēs	monitī, -ae, -a essētis
3d	monuisset	monuissent	monitus, -a, -um esset	monitī, -ae, -a essent

THIRD CONJUGATION PLUPERFECT SUBJUNCTIVE

regō, regere, rēxī, rēctum

(perfect stem: rēx-; fourth principal part: rēctus, -a, -um)

1st	rēxissem	rēxissēmus	rēctus, -a, -um essem	rēctī, -ae, -a essēmus
2d	rēxissēs	rēxissētis	rēctus, -a, -um essēs	rēctī, -ae, -a essētis
3d	rēxisset	rēxissent	rēctus, -a, -um esset	rēctī, -ae, -a essent

THIRD CONJUGATION (-IŌ) PLUPERFECT SUBJUNCTIVE

capiō, capere, cēpī, captum

(perfect active stem: cēp-; fourth principal part: captus, -a, -um)

1st	cēpissem	cēpissēmus	captus, -a, -um essem	captī, -ae, -a essēmus
2d	cēpissēs	cēpissētis	captus, -a, -um essēs	captī, -ae, -a essētis
3d	cēpisset	cēpissent	captus, -a, -um esset	captī, -ae, -a essent

---

FOURTH CONJUGATION PLUPERFECT SUBJUNCTIVE

audiō, audīre, audīvī, audītum

(perfect active stem: audīv-; fourth principal part: audītus, -a, -um)

1st	audīvissem	audīvissēmus	audītus, -a, -um essem	audītī, -ae, -a essēmus
2d	audīvissēs	audīvissētis	audītus, -a, -um essēs	audītī, -ae, -a essētis
3d	audīvisset	audīvissent	audītus, -a, -um esset	audītī, -ae, -a essent

---

CIII. The pluperfect subjunctive of esse [GLG 116]

182. The pluperfect of esse is as follows:

PLUPERFECT SUBJUNCTIVE OF ESSE

	singular	**plural**
1st	fuissem	fuissēmus
2d	fuissēs	fuissētis
3d	fuisset	fuissent

EXERCISES

A. Vocabulary

adsideō, adsidēre, adsēdī, —	sit by or near, besiege
arx, arcis, f.	citadel
atque (*before vowels or h*); ac (*before consonants*)	and (*a closer connective than* et);
	as, than (*after words of likeness or difference*)
~~cibārius, -a, -um~~	of food
cōpiōsus, -a, -um	plentiful
dēfēnsor, dēfēnsōris, m.	protector
diēs, diēī, m. or f.	day
~~Hispānia, Hispāniae, f.~~	Spain

interrogō, interrogāre, interrogāvī, interrogātum	ask, question
iūs, iūris, n.	justice, right, duty
~~iūs dīcere~~	administer justice
locus, locī, m.	place
(*in the nom. plural*: locī, single places; loca, regions)	
manus, manūs, f.	hand, band of men
moenia, moenium, n. plural	walls
mūniō, mūnīre, mūnīvī, mūnītum	fortify
oppidum, oppidī, n.	town
~~perendiē~~	on the day after tomorrow
procul	at a distance, far
prōtendō, prōtendere, prōtendī, prōtentum	stretch out
rēs, reī, f.	thing, matter, occurrence
sedeō, sedēre, sēdī, sessum	sit
sistō, sistere, stitī, statum	stop, set
situs, situs, m.	position, situation
stō, stāre, stetī, statum	stand
~~tertius, -a, -um~~	third
~~vadimōnium, vadimōnī, n.~~	security, bail
validus, -a, -um	strong
vīsō, vīsere, vīsī, vīsum	see, visit

B. Translations

Aulus Gellius is known for a collection of miscellaneous information called *The Attic Nights*, a text that would remain influential through the Renaissance and afterward. Gellius recounts the following two stories about the Punic Wars, a series of three wars in which Rome fought with Carthage in the course of the third and second centuries BC. The first tale tells of the military acumen of Publius Scipio Africanus (Scīpiō, Scīpiōnis, m.) who led Rome to victory in the Second Punic War.

Scīpiō adsidēbat oppūgnābatque oppidum in Hispāniā, sitū, moenibus, dēfēnsōribus validum et mūnītum, rē etiam cibāriā cōpiōsum, nūllaque ēius potiundī spēs erat, et quōdam diē iūs in castrīs sedēns dīcēbat, atque ex eō locō id oppidum procul vīsēbatur. Tum ē mīlitibus, quī in iūre apud eum stābant, interrogāvit aliquis: 'in quem diem locumque vadimōnium prōmittī iubēs?' et Scīpiō, manum ad ipsam oppidī quod obsidēbātur arcem prōtendēns, 'perendiē,' inquit, 'sēsē sistete illō in locō.' atque ita factum; diē tertiō, oppidum captum est eōdemque diē in arce ēius oppidī iūs dīxit.

Aulus Gellius 6. 1. 8–11

The next story describes the fortitude of the Roman general Atilius Regulus (Rēgulus, Rēgulī, m.). Regulus had been captured by the Carthaginians in the first Punic War, but decided to submit to torture, rather than return to Rome as part of a prisoner-exchange.

In a certain dark and deep dungeon, they shut Rēgulus up, and a long time afterwards, when the sun seemed most blazing, they led him out suddenly. Having placed him opposite, facing the rays of the sun, they confined him there, forcing him to direct his eyes on the sky. He was deprived of sleep for a long time and died.

Aulus Gellius 7. 4. 3–4

Additional vocabulary

ārdēns, ārdentis	blazing, fiery
āter, ātra, ātrum	black, dark
caelum, caelī, n.	sky, heaven
claudō, claudere, clausī, clausum	close, shut in
cōgō, cōgere, coēgī, coāctum	force, collect
contineō, continēre, continuī, contentum	hold in, confine
diū	for a long time
ictus, ictūs, m.	blow, ray (of the sun)
intendō, intendere, intendī, intentum	stretch, direct
oppōnō, oppōnere, opposuī, oppositum	place against, before
post	afterwards (*adv.*); after, behind (*prep. with acc.*)
profundus, -a, -um	deep
repente	suddenly
somnus, somnī, m.	sleep
tenebrae, tenebrārum, f. plural	darkness, dungeon

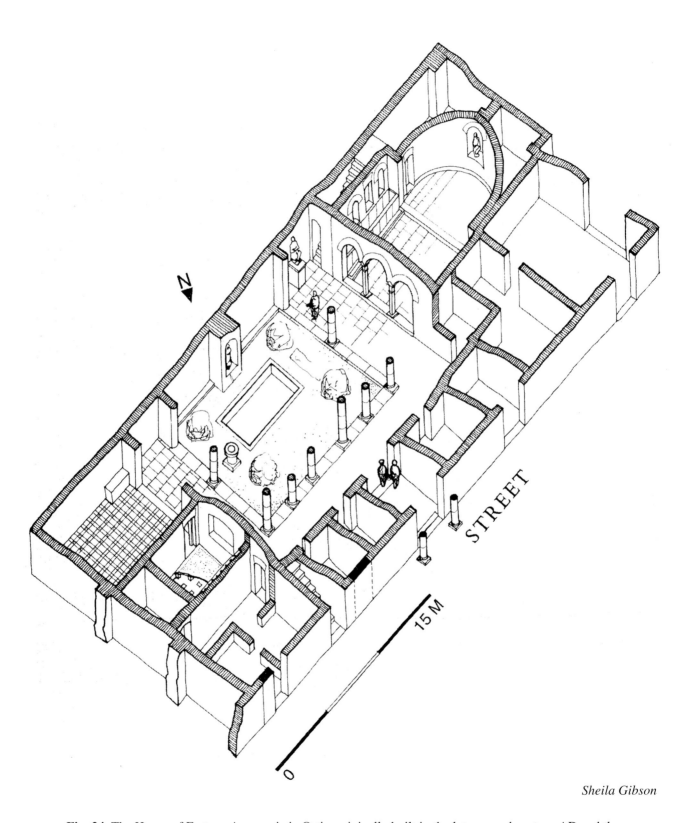

N

STREET

15 M

0

Sheila Gibson

Fig. 24. The House of Fortuna Annonaria in Ostia, originally built in the late second century AD and then remodelled in the fourth century. The rooms were configured around a central courtyard and fountain.

Fig. 25. Wall-painting in the House of the Labyrinth in Pompeii, depicting baroque architecture in the first century BC.

Sheila Gibson

Fig. 26. An insula block at Ostia, originally from the second or third century AD. There is a cookhouse on the ground floor. Similar constructions remain in use today.

Chapter 9

The subjunctive used independently
The subjunctive in subordinate clauses
Sequence of tenses

What is there more that I can say
Of Jam? Why, nothing more to-day.
The Jam's before me, thick and sweet:
What's writing, when a man can eat?
And as Erigena has said
(An author far too little read),
Jam hōra adest ut mangiam.
And that is all I know of Jam.

Hilaire Belloc (1870–1953), 'On Jam'

There is an English subjunctive, even if the rules regarding it are apparent more in the breach than the observance. But we still say, for example, 'Be that as it may' or 'I wish I were ....' The Latin subjunctive is more frequently used.

CIV. Subjunctives in independent clauses [GLG 257–265]

183. In independent or main clauses, the Latin subjunctive may appear as

(a)   a hortatory subjunctive, in which the present subjunctive forms a mild or polite command. If negative, the subjunctive will be introduced by nē. Only the present subjunctive is used in this construction. Translate using 'let' or 'may.' This type of subjunctive is also known as the jussive subjunctive.

amēmus patriam.

Let us love the fatherland.

Cicero, *In Defence of Sestius* 68. 143

(b)   an optative, in which a wish relating to the future is expressed by the present or perfect subjunctive with or without utinam at the beginning. Wishes hopeless in present time use utinam and the imperfect subjunctive; wishes hopeless in past time use utinam with the pluperfect subjunctive. The negative is normally utinam nē.

sed utinam revīvīscat frāter.

How I wish my brother would come back to life.

Aulus Gellius 10. 6. 2

Illud utinam nē vērē scrīberem.

Would that what I am writing were not true.

Cicero, *Letters to His Friends* 5. 17. 3

(c)   a potential subjunctive expressing a possibility; the negative is nōn.

crēderēs vīctōs.

You would have thought them beaten.

Livy 2. 43. 9

(d)   a deliberative subjunctive, in which questions and exclamations imply doubt, indignation, the impossibility of an act, obligation, or impropriety. The present subjunctive refers to present time, the imperfect to past time. The negative is nōn.

quid agam nunc?

What should I do now?

Cicero, *Letters to Atticus* 10. 12. 1

CV. Subjunctives in dependent or subordinate clauses [GLG 543–588]

184. The subjunctive is most often found in dependent or subordinate clauses. The term subjunctive, in fact, comes from the Latin sub (under) and iungere (to join), precisely because subjunctive constructions usually appear in what were once called subjoined clauses, now more commonly called subordinate clauses. In these instances, the subjunctive is used in:

(a)   purpose clauses;

(b)   indirect command;

(c)   result clauses;

(d)   fear clauses;

(e)   cum-clauses;

(f)   indirect question.

CVI. Purpose clauses [GLG 543–549]

185. A purpose clause answers the question 'why?':

> From his brimstone bed at break of day
>
> A walking the Devil is gone,
>
> To look at his little snug farm of the World,
>
> And see how his stock went on.

Robert Southey (1774–1843), 'The Devil's Walk'

In the example above, the main clause is 'The Devil is gone a walking', and the purpose clause is 'to look at his little snug farm ....'

186. In Latin, a positive purpose clause is introduced by ut. A negative purpose clause uses nē. Translate using 'in order to,' 'in order that,' 'so that,' or 'to' in the positive. In the negative, try 'in order that ... not,' 'so that ... not,' or 'to avoid ....'

The present tense of the subjunctive is used in the purpose clause if the main verb is in a primary tense (the present, future, or future perfect tense). The English auxiliary verb 'may' best helps to translate the present subjunctive.

> ēsse oportet ut vīvās, nōn vīvere ut edās.
>
> You must eat in order that you may live, not live in order that you may eat.

[Cicero], *To Herrennius* 4. 28. 39

The imperfect tense of the subjunctive is used in the purpose clause if the main verb is in a secondary tense (the imperfect, perfect, or pluperfect).

> nē tōnsōrī collum committeret, tondēre fīliās suās docuit.
>
> In order that he need not entrust his neck to a barber, he taught his own daughters to use a razor.

Cicero, *Tusculan Disputations* 5. 20. 58

187. Instead of ut,

(a) the relative pronoun can be used. The relative pronoun frequently expresses purpose.

> serit arborēs, quae alterī saeclō prōsint.
>
> He plants trees to be of use to the next generation.

Cicero, *Tusculan Disputations* 1. 14. 31

(b) quō used with a comparative adjective or adverb may also express purpose.

> castella commūnit, quō facilius prohibēre possit.

> He fortifies the ramparts, so that he may more easily hold them back.

> Caesar, *Gallic War* 1. 8. 2

Quōminus (*i.e.,* 'that thereby the less') is often seen in this construction, with verbs of preventing or refusing.

> nōn dēterret sapientem mors quōminus reī pūblicae cōnsulat.

> Death is no excuse for taking less of an interest in the republic.

> Cicero, *Tusculan Disputations* 1. 38. 91

CVII. Indirect command [GLG 547]

188. The indirect command is a variant of the purpose clause. Ut is used in a positive indirect command, nē in the negative. Since the construction of the indirect command is identical to that of the purpose clause, only the present or imperfect subjunctive is used.

> ōrant ut sibi parcat.

> They beg him to spare their lives.

> Caesar, *Gallic War* 6. 9. 7

189. Any verb used to give an order, however mildly, belongs to the Great Ordering Family and follows the rules for indirect command. The main types of verbs are:

(a)   These verbs take the accusative before the ut-clause:

addūcō, addūcere, addūxī, adductum	influence
admoneō, admonēre, admonuī, admonitum	warn, advise
cohortor, cohortārī, cohortātus sum	urge
cūrō, cūrāre, cūrāvī, cūrātum	provide for, take care
hortor, hortārī, hortātus sum	urge
moneō, monēre, monuī, monitum	warn, advise
★ rogō, rogāre, rogāvī, rogātum	ask

Q. Navium prīmōrēsque aliōs centuriōnum hortātur ut cohortem hostium invādant.

He urges Quintus Navius and the other leaders of the centurions to attack the cohort of the enemy.

> Livy 26. 5. 12

(b)   These verbs take the dative before the ut-clause:

★ imperō, imperāre, imperāvī, imperātum   order

★ mandō, mandāre, mandāvī, mandātum   order, entrust

permittō, permittere, permīsī, permissum   permit, entrust

★ persuādeō, persuādēre, persuāsī, persuāsum   persuade

suādeō, suādēre, suāsī, suāsum   advise

suīsque imperāvit nē quod omnīnō tēlum in hostēs rēicerent.

He ordered his own men not to throw back any weapon at all against the enemy.

Caesar, *Gallic War* 1. 46. 2

(c)   These verbs take ā or ab and the ablative before the ut-clause:

impetrō, impetrāre, impetrāvī, impetrātum   gain one's request

ōrō, ōrāre, ōrāvī, ōrātum   beg

★ petō, petere, petīvī, petītum   seek, attack, ask

poscō, poscere, poposcī, —   demand

postulō, postulāre, postulāvī, postulātum   demand

petō ā tē, ut mihi īgnōscās.

I am asking you to pardon me.

Cicero, *Against Vatinius* 3. 7

(d)   This verb takes no personal object:

prōvideō, prōvidēre, prōvīdī, prōvīsum   foresee, take care

prōvidē, nē quid eī dēsit.

Take care that she wants for nothing.

Cicero, *Letters to Atticus* 11. 3. 3

Note, however, that these three verbs do not take the indirect command construction and use instead the accusative followed by an infinitive:

iubeō, iubēre, iussī, iūssum   order

patior, patī, passus sum   allow, suffer

vetō, vetāre, vetuī, vetitum   forbid

līctōrēs ad eum accēdere cōnsul iussit.

The consul commanded the lictors to approach him.

Livy 24. 9. 1

These verbs may take either an ut-clause or an infinitive after them.

cupiō, cupere, cupīvī, cupītum   desire

permittō, permittere, permīsī, permissum   permit, entrust

volō, velle, voluī, —   wish

Cupiō is never used with ut in Classical Latin prose.

CVIII. Result clauses [GLG 552]

190. Sentences may express the expected or actual result of a particular situation:

The world is so full

of a number of things,

I'm sure we should all

be as happy as kings.

Robert Louis Stevenson (1850–1894), 'Happy Thought' in *A Child's Garden of Verses*

The first two lines of the quatrain comprise the main clause, and the last two lines make up the result clause.

Such a sentence requires the subjunctive in Latin. The clause illustrating a result is always introduced by the conjunction ut and expressed by the subjunctive mood. Translate using 'so (or such) ... that.'

nēmō adeō ferus est, ut nōn mītēscere possit.

There is no one so fierce that he cannot be tamed.

Horace, *Epistles* 1. 1. 39

191. The following words are common if there is any negative in the result clause:

ut ... nēmō   no one, nobody

ut ... nihil   nothing

ut ... nōn   not

ut ... nūllus, -a, -um   no, not any

ut ... numquam   never

exercituī quidem omnī tantus incessit dolor ut nēmō aut tribūnī aut centuriōnis imperium dēsīderāret.

So great a sorrow had fallen on all the army, that no one waited for the command of either the tribune or centurion.

Caesar, *Civil War* 3. 74. 2

192. Result clauses are usually introduced in the main clause by such adverbs as

✗	adeō	so far (often omitted in translation)
✗	ita	thus, so
✗	sīc	thus, so
✗	tam	so

Ita and sīc modify only verbs; tam modifies adjectives and adverbs; adeō modifies verbs, adjectives, and adverbs.

> ita mē gessī nē tibi pudōrī essem.

> I so carried myself as not to give you cause for embarrasment.

> Livy 40. 15. 6

193. The following words may also introduce result clauses:

✗	tālis, tāle	such
✗	tantus, -a, -um	so great, so much
✗	tot (undeclinable)	so many

> tantum ā vāllō prīma aciēs aberat, utī (ut) nē tēlō adicī posset.

> The first battle line was so great a distance from the wall that no weapon could be thrown.

> Caesar, *Civil War* 3. 55

194. The tense of the Latin subjunctive will generally be the same as the tense of the English verb.

CIX. Indirect result clauses and relative clauses of characteristic [GLG 553, 631]

195. Two other constructions using the subjunctive are related to result clauses.

(a) Indirect result clauses are sometimes known as noun clauses of result. They occur after certain

verbs of doing, accomplishing, or happening:

accēdit, accēdere, accessit	added to this the fact (that)
accidit, accidere, accidit	it happens (that)
efficiō, efficere, effēcī, effectum	accomplish, bring it about (that)
ēvenit, ēvenīre, ēvēnit	the result is (that)
faciō, facere, fēcī, factum	do, make
fit, fiērī, factum est	it happens (that)

Thus, the subjunctive is used after phrases such as accidit ut (it happened that), fiēbat ut (it happened that), or efficere ut (to bring it about that). The tense of the subjunctive in English and in Latin will be the same.

efficiam profectō ut intellegātis.

I shall certainly make sure that you understand.

Cicero, In Defence of Cluentius 3. 7

(b) Clauses with their verbs in the subjunctive mood and introduced by the relative pronoun are sometimed called relative clauses of characteristic. These clauses tell not what thing, but rather what kind of thing is meant. They are often introduced by an expression of the following nature:

is est quī	he is the (sort of) man to
nēmō est quī	there is no one who
nihil est quod	there is nothing which
quis est quī	who is there who
sunt quī	there are people who
ūnus est quī	he is the only one who

CX. Fear clauses [GLG 550]

196. English sentences that express a fear that something should happen use what are called fear-clauses:

When I have fears that I may cease to be....

John Keats (1795–1821), 'When I have fears'

The phrase 'that I may cease to be' is a fear-clause.

In Latin, these clauses are governed by verbs that express fear such as timeō or vereor. They are introduced by ut, if there is a negative in the clause, and nē, if the clause is affirmative. Thus:

(a) nē and the subjunctive are used if one is afraid that something will happen;

(b) ut and the subjunctive are used if one is afraid it will not happen.

The verb of the fear clause is in the subjunctive mood, usually present, if the main indicative verb is in a primary tense (present, future, or future perfect), or imperfect, if the main verb is in a secondary tense (perfect, pluperfect, imperfect).

timeō nē nihil tibi praeter lacrimās queam reddere.

I fear that I can render you nothing but tears.

Cicero, In Defence of Cn. Plancius 42. 101

CXI. Cum-clauses [GLG 578–588]

197. When cum is followed by the subjunctive mood, translate it as 'when,' 'since,' 'because,' 'although,' or 'after.' If tamen (nevertheless) appears in the main clause, translate cum as 'although.' The tense of the subjunctive follows the rules for the sequence of tenses given below, § 200–205.

(a) When translated as 'since,' the cum-clause is called a causal clause. Any tense of the subjunctive is possible.

(b) When translated as 'although,' the clause is called a concessive clause. Any tense of the subjunctive is possible.

(c) A temporal or circumstantial cum-clause takes 'when' as a translation and states a time. When the cum-clause has no influence over the action of the main clause, then the indicative mood is used.

> iam dīlūcēscēbat cum sīgnum cōnsul dedit.

> Daylight was already beginning to grow when the consul gave the signal.

> Livy 36. 24. 6

When the circumstances described in the cum-clause have affected the actions described in the main clause, then the subjunctive mood is used. In this latter instance, the imperfect and pluperfect subjunctives are usually the tenses found.

> cum in iūs dūcī dēbitōrem vīdissent, undique convolābant.

> Once they had seen a debtor being hauled off to court, they flew to his assistance from every side.

> Livy 2. 27. 8

CXII Indirect question [GLG 467]

198. An indirect question is a subordinate clause introduced by an interrogative word. The following are direct questions:

> What are we? What may we be?

Analogous indirect questions would be:

> We know what we are, but know not what we may be.

> Shakespeare (d. 1616), *Hamlet* 5. 42

The clause depends upon a main verb which suggests or asks a question, such as verbs of knowing, telling, showing, asking, wondering, enquiring, etc (§ 129 on 'head and tel.' verbs).

The actual indirect question is introduced by an interrogative pronoun, adjective, or adverb and has its verb in the subjunctive mood.

In Latin, the tense of the subjunctive will follow the rules for the sequence of tenses (§ 200-205).

ipse docet quid agam.

He himself teaches what I shall do.

Ovid, Metamorphoses 4. 428

199. In an indirect question, -ne or num may mean 'whether.'

speculārī dīligentissimē coepī num Ascyltos vēnisset.

I began to check very carefully whether Ascyltos had come along.

Petronius 92. 2

CXIII. The sequence of tenses [GLG 509–519]

200. The relationship between the tense of the verb in the main clause and the tense of the subjunctive in the subordinate clause determines what is called the sequence of tenses.

201. The primary tenses of the indicative are the present, future, and future perfect tenses, as well as the perfect tense when it is translated in English using the auxiliary verb 'has' or 'have.'

The secondary (or historic) tenses of the indicative are the imperfect and pluperfect tenses, as well as the perfect tense when it is translated in English as the simple past. (*i.e.*, without 'have' or 'has').

202. The primary tenses of the subjunctive are the present and the perfect tenses, and the secondary tenses are the imperfect and pluperfect tenses.

203. Only primary tenses of the subjunctive may be used after a primary tense of the indicative. Only secondary tenses of the subjunctive may be used after a secondary tense of the indicative.

204. In general (for exceptions to these rules can seem very frequent), the sequence of tenses is as follows, if the verb of the main clause is in a primary tense:

(a)   if the action of the subordinate clause is going on at exactly the same time as the time of the main verb, then the present subjunctive is used in the subordinate clause.

suīsque ut idem faciant imperat.

He commands his own forces to do likewise.

Caesar, Gallic War 5. 37. 1

(b)   if the action of the subordinate clause expresses time before the time of the main verb, then the

perfect subjunctive is used.

>   nōn is es ut tē pudor umquam ā turpitūdine revocārit.

>   You are not one such that shame has ever called you from the brink of immorality.

>   Cicero, *Catilinarian Orations* 1. 9. 22

(c)   if the action of the subordinate clause expresses time after the time of the main verb, then the future

active participle with the present subjunctive of sum is used.

>   deinde dē imperātōris fide quaerunt rectēne sē illī commissūrī sint.

>   Then from the oath of the general, they ask whether they will commit themselves rightly.

>   Caesar, *Civil War* 1. 74. 2

205.   The sequence of tenses is as follows, if the verb of the main clause is in a secondary tense:

(a)   if the action of the subordinate clause is going on at exactly the same time as the time of the main

verb, then the imperfect subjunctive is used.

>   veniēbat ad cēnam ut satiāret dēsīderia nātūrae.

>   He used to come to dinner to satisfy the cravings of nature.

>   Cicero, *On Ends* 2. 8. 25

(b)   if the action of the subordinate clause takes place before the action of the main verb, then the

pluperfect subjunctive is used.

>   cum id animadvertisset, cōpiās suās omnēs prō castrīs īnstrūxit.

>   After he had noticed this, he drew up all his troops in front of the camp.

>   Caesar, *Alexandrian War* 74. 1

(c)   if the verb of the subordinate clause expresses action happening after the action of the main verb,

then the future active participle with the imperfect subjunctive of sum is used.

>   anteā dubitābam ventūraene essent.

>   Before, I wasn't certain whether they would come.

>   Cicero, *Letters to His Friends* 2. 17. 5

EXERCISES

A. Vocabulary

admoveō, admovēre, admōvī, admōtum	move to, apply to
alūmen, alūminis, n.	alum
ārdeō, ārdēre, ārsī, ārsum	burn, love, be eager
Attica, Atticae, f.	Attica (in Greece)
cōpia, cōpiae, f.	abundance, supply; forces, resources (*plural*)
dēfendō, dēfendere, dēfendī, dēfensum	defend
diū	for a long time
Graecī, Graecōrum, m.	Greeks (*plural*)
grātia, grātiae, f.	influence, gratitude;
	for the sake of (*in abl. sing., after a gen.*)
incendō, incendere, incendī, incensum	set on fire, arouse
interpōnō, interpōnere, interposuī, interpositum	put between, interpose
līgneus, -a, -um	wooden
līgnum, līgnī, n.	wood
māteria, māteriae, f.	material, matter
numquam	never
oblinō, oblinere, oblēvī, oblitum	daub, smear
praefectus, praefectī, m.	prefect
prōpūgnō, prōpūgnāre, prōpūgnāvī, prōpūgnātum	defend, fight for
satis	enough, sufficiently
scrībō, scrībere, scrīpsī, scrīptum	write
struō, struere, strūxī, strūctum	build, arrange
subdō, subdere, subdidī, subditum	put under
submoveō, submovēre, submōvī, submōtum	move up, drive off
succendō, succendere, succendī, succēnsum	kindle from below
tempus, temporis, n.	time; temple (of the head)
terra, terrae, f.	land
turris, turris, f. (turrem / turrim *in acc.*; turre / turrī *in abl.*)	tower

[handwritten:] For Tuesday!!

B. Translations

L. (Lucius) Cornelius Sulla Felix (Sulla, Sullae, m.), a conservative and cruel dictator, was also one of Rome's most able generals in the first century BC. He successfully prosecuted a war overseas against King Mithridates of Pontus, the region about the Black Sea (Mithridātēs, Mithridātī, m.; Pontus, Pontī, m.). As with the war against Pyrrhus, different campaigns accrued legendary status. Aulus Gellius recounts the following two stories about the protagonists. The first tells of Sulla's battle with Archelaus (Archelāus, Archelāī, m.), prefect of Mithridates at the Piraeus harbour (Pīraeus, Pīraeī, m.) in Athens. The second tells of Mithridates' attempts to protect himself against poisoning.

scrīptum est, cum oppūgnāret L. Sulla in terrā Atticā Pīraeum et contrā eum Archelāus rēgis Mithridātī praefectus ex eō oppidō prōpūgnāret, turrim līgneam dēfendendī grātiā strūctam nōn ārsisse, quod alūmine ab Archelāō oblita fuisset. Cum Sulla cōnātus esset tempōre māgnō, ēdūxit cōpiās, ut Archelāī turrim ūnam quam ille interposuit līgneam incenderet. Vēnit, accessit, līgna subdidit, submōvit Graecōs, īgnem admōvit; satis sunt diū cōnātī. ita Archelāus omnem māteriam oblēverat alūmine ut numquam incensūra esset. quod Sulla atque mīlitēs mīrābantur, et postquam nōn succendit, redūxit cōpiās.

Aulus Gellius 15. 1. 6–7

It was written that Mithridates, that king of Pontus, was accustomed to drink the blood of ducks with drugs which expelled poisons, and that the king himself, by the constant use of such remedies, was on his guard against secret treachery. Later, after he had fled into the farthest part of his kingdom, having been conquered in battle, and had decided to die, having tried in vain the most violent poisons, he transfixed himself with his own sword.

Aulus Gellius 17. 16. 2–5

Additional vocabulary

adsiduus, -a, -um	constant
anas, anatis, f.	duck
caveō, cavēre, cāvī, cautum	beware, be on guard against (*with ā or ab and the abl.*)
clandestīnus, -a, um	secret, hidden
dēcernō, dēcernere, dēcrēvī, dēcrētum	decide, decree

expellō, expellere, expulī, expulsum	drive out, expel
frūstrā	in vain
fugiō, fugere, fūgī, —	flee, avoid
gladius, gladī, m.	sword
hauriō, haurīre, hausī, haustum	draw, drink, exhaust
īnsidiae, īnsidiārum, f. plural	ambush, treachery
medicāmentum, medicāmentī, n.	drug, remedy
sanguis, sanguinis, m.	blood
trānsigō, trānsigere, trānsēgī, trānsāctum	pierce through, transfix
ūsus, ūsūs, m.	use, experience
venēnum, venēnī, n.	poison
violēns, violentis	violent

Fig. 27. Maison Carée at Nîmes (ancient Nemausus) in France, built ca. AD 1-10. The temple was built during the

lifetime of Augustus, and shows the influence of metropolitan Roman architecture on the provinces.

Fig. 28. The Pont du Gard, an aqueduct constructed over the river Gardon, bringing water to Nîmes in France, erected in the late first century BC.

Chapter 10

Irregular verbs
Miscellanous notes on the subjunctive
Impersonal verbs
Conditionals

Īte. Missa est.
The Mass is ended. Go in peace.

The ending of the Latin Mass and its traditional translation

In all languages, there are words and phrases that fall outside the rules of grammar. No one says 'Woe is I' rather than 'Woe is me,' despite the need for a predicate nominative after the verb 'to be,' and no one questions that the past tense of 'eat' is 'ate,' rather than 'eated'. Similarly, Latin irregular verbs and impersonal constructions should be accepted for what they are and simply memorized.

CXIV. Ferō, fīō, mālō, nōlō, and volō [GLG 171, 173, 174, 261]

206. The irregularities of the following lie primarily in the present tense:

ferō, ferre, tulī, lātum	bear, carry, say
fīō, fierī, factus sum	be made, be done
mālō, mālle, māluī, —	prefer
nōlō, nōlle, nōluī, —	be unwilling
volō, velle, voluī, —	wish

Other tenses are essentially regular in formation, once one knows the principal parts. Below, only the irregular forms that exist for each verb are noted.

FERŌ, FERRE, TULĪ, LĀTUM

bear, carry, say

PRESENT INDICATIVE		ACTIVE		PASSIVE	
		singular	**plural**	**singular**	**plural**
1st		ferō	ferimus	feror	ferimur
2d		fers	fertis	ferris	feriminī
3d		fert	ferunt	fertur	feruntur

IMPERFECT INDICATIVE	ferēbam, etc.	ferēbar, etc.	
FUTURE INDICATIVE	feram, etc.	ferar, etc.	
PRESENT INFINITIVE	ferre	ferrī	
IMPERATIVE	fer	ferte	ferre	feriminī

FĪŌ, FIERĪ, FACTUS SUM

be, be made, be done

PRESENT INDICATIVE		IMPERFECT INDICATIVE		FUTURE INDICATIVE	
singular	**plural**	**singular**	**plural**	**singular**	**plural**
1st fīō	fīmus	fīēbam	fīēbamus	fīam	fīēmus
2d fīs	fītis	fīēbas	fīēbatis	fīēs	fīētis
3d fit	fīunt	fīēbat	fīēbant	fīet	fīent

PRESENT SUBJUNCTIVE		IMPERFECT SUBJUNCTIVE	
1st fīam	fīāmus	fīerem	fīerēmus
2d fīās	fīātis	fīerēs	fīerētis
3d fīat	fīant	fīeret	fīerent

IMPERATIVE

fī   fīte

MĀLŌ, MĀLLE, MĀLUĪ, —

prefer

PRESENT INDICATIVE

	singular	plural
1st	mālō	mālumus
2d	māvis	māvultis
3d	māvult	mālunt

IMPERFECT INDICATIVE   mālēbam, etc.

FUTURE INDICATIVE   mālam, etc.

PRESENT SUBJUNCTIVE

	singular	plural
1st	mālim	mālīmus
2d	mālīs	mālītis
3d	mālit	mālint

NŌLŌ, NŌLLE, NŌLUĪ, —

be unwilling

PRESENT INDICATIVE

	singular	plural
1st	nōlō	nōlumus
2d	nōn vīs	nōn vultis
3d	nōn vult	nōlunt

IMPERFECT INDICATIVE   nōlēbam, etc.

FUTURE INDICATIVE   nōlam, etc.

PRESENT SUBJUNCTIVE

	singular	plural
1st	nōlim	nōlīmus
2d	nōlīs	nōlītis
3d	nōlit	nōlint

VOLŌ, VELLE, VOLUĪ, —

wish

PRESENT INDICATIVE

	singular	plural
1st	volō	volumus
2d	vīs	vultis
3d	vult	volunt

IMPERFECT INDICATIVE   volēbam, etc.

FUTURE INDICATIVE   volam, etc.

PRESENT SUBJUNCTIVE

	singular	plural
1st	velim	velīmus
2d	velīs	velītis
3d	velit	velint

To express a wish with an adverse consequence, vellem and mallem may be used with the imperfect or pluperfect subjunctive:

vellem mē ad cēnam invitāssēs.

If only you had invited me to dinner!

Cicero, *Letters to his Friends* 12. 4. 1

CXV. Edō, eō, possum, and sum [GLG 116, 119, 169, 172]

207. The following irregular verbs are also commonly found:

EDŌ, ĒSSE, ĒDĪ, ĒSUM or ESSUM
eat

PRESENT INDICATIVE	singular	plural
1st	edō	edimus
2d	edis, edēs	estis, ēstis
3d	edit, ēst	edunt

In the present passive, the only irregularity is in the third person, for which both editur and ēstur are attested.

IMPERFECT INDICATIVE	edēbam, etc.	
FUTURE INDICATIVE	edam, etc.	
PRESENT SUBJUNCTIVE	edam, etc.	
IMPERFECT SUBJUNCTIVE	ēssem, etc.	
IMPERATIVE	ēs	ēste

EŌ, ĪRE, ĪVĪ or IĪ, ITUM
go

	PRESENT INDICATIVE		IMPERFECT INDICATIVE		FUTURE INDICATIVE	
	singular	plural	singular	plural	singular	plural
1st	eō	īmus	ībam	ībāmus	ībō	ībimus
2d	īs	ītis	ības	ībātis	ībis	ībitis
3d	it	eunt	ībat	ībant	ībit	ībunt

PRESENT SUBJUNCTIVE

	singular	plural			
1st	eam	eāmus	PRESENT PARTICIPLE	iēns, euntis (gen.)	
2d	eās	eātis	GERUND	eundī (gen. sing.)	
3d	eat	eant	IMPERATIVE	ī	īte

POSSUM, POSSE, POTUĪ, —

be able, can

See the paradigm on esse below. The present system of possum is identical to the present system of sum, but with the prefix pot-. The t of pot- becomes s in front of another s (*e.g.*, possumus, but poterāmus). In the perfect forms, when t encounters f, the f drops away (*e.g.*, potuī, not potfuī).

SUM, ESSE, FUĪ, FUTŪRUM

be

	PRESENT INDICATIVE		IMPERFECT INDICATIVE		FUTURE INDICATIVE	
	singular	**plural**	**singular**	**plural**	**singular**	**plural**
1st	sum	sumus	eram	erāmus	erō	erimus
2d	es	estis	erās	erātis	eris	eritis
3d	est	sunt	erat	erant	erit	erunt

	PRESENT SUBJUNCTIVE					
1st	sim	sīmus				
2d	sīs	sītis			IMPERATIVE	
3d	sit	sint			es	este

CXVI. Further notes on the subjunctive [GLG 229, 554-556, 571-572, 577, 650]

208. To express anticipation, the subjunctive mood may be used in a clause introduced by a word meaning 'before' or 'until'.

> hunc celeriter, priusquam ab adversāriīs sentiātur, commūnit.

> This he swiftly fortifies, before it should be noticed by the enemy.

Caesar, Civil War 1. 54. 4

209. Note, however, that antequam and priusquam are often written as two words, the ante- or the prius- being in the main clause and the -quam being in the subordinate clause. Translate as if the whole word were where -quam is.

> ante autem vidēmus fulgōrem quam sonum audīmus.

> But we see the flash before we hear the sound.

> > Seneca, *Natural Questions* 2. 12. 6

210. A subordinate clause inside the indirect discourse construction will have its verb in the subjunctive mood, but the translation is not affected. The subject of the clause will be in the nominative. The tense of the subjunctive will conform to the rules for the sequence of tenses (§ 200-205)

> Socrates dīcere solēbat omnēs in eō quod scīrent satis esse ēloquentēs.

> Socrates used to say that everyone was eloquent enough in what he knew.

> > Cicero, *On the Orator* 1. 14. 63

211. The word quīn is followed by the subjunctive.

(a)   Quīn following a negative expression of doubt is translated 'that'. The tense of the subjunctive follows the rule for the sequence of tenses (§ 200-205)

> nec dubitārī dēbet quīn fuerint ante Homērum poētae.

> Nor should one doubt that there were poets before Homer.

> > Cicero, *Brutus* 18. 71

(b)   Quīn following a negative expression of hindering or preventing is translated 'from _____ing'.

> nec sē tenuit quīn contrā suum doctōrem librum ēderet.

> Nor did he restrain himself from publishing a book against his own teacher.

> > Cicero, *Academica* 2. 4. 12

(c)   After a negative expression with esse, quīn is translated 'who ... not' or 'that/which ... not'.

> Nēmō est tam fortis quīn reī novitāte perturbētur.

> There is no one so brave who is not perturbed by the novelty of the situation.

> > Caesar, *Gallic War* 6. 39. 3

(d)   Quīn may follow absum (and any of its forms) or possum facere (and any of its forms):

> Facere nōn possum quīn cotidiē ad tē mittam litterās.

> I cannot help but send you a daily letter.

> > Cicero, *Letters to Atticus* 12. 27. 2

212. Dum is used as follows:

(a) When dum is followed by the indicative, it means 'while'. Even if the indicative verb is in the

present tense, translate the verb as past in English.

> Haec super arvōrum cultū pecorumque canēbam
>
> et super arboribus, Caesar dum māgnus ad altum
>
> fulminat Euphrātēn.
>
> I was singing of these: the care of the fields, and of cattle, and of trees,
>
> while great Caesar thundered near deep Euphrates.

Virgil, *Georgics* 4. 559-561

(b) When dum is followed by the subjunctive, however, it means 'until'.

> rūsticus exspectat dum dēfluat amnis.
>
> A country bumpkin waits until the river shall run dry.

Horace, *Epistles* 1. 2. 42

CXVII. Impersonal verbs [GLG 208]

213. An impersonal verb is one that does not have a specific person or thing for its subject:

fulget	it shines
fulgurat	it lightens
fulminat	it thunders, it lightens
ningit	it snows
pluit	it rains
tonat	it thunders

Other common impersonal expressions are:

accidit, accidere, accidit	it happens (*with ut and the subjunctive*)
ēvenit, ēvenīre, ēvēnit	the result is (*with ut and the subjunctive*)
fit, fierī, factum est	it happens (*with ut and the subjunctive*)
licet, licēre, licuit	it is permitted (*with dat. and present inf.*)
necesse est, esse, fuit	it is necessary (*with ut and subjunctive*)
oportet, oportēre, oportuit	it is necessary (*with accus. and present inf.*)

Licet and oportet may also be used with the subjunctive without ut. Licet introduces a concession ('granted that ....'). Oportet expresses a requirement ('require it that ....').

Note such impersonal expressions in the second conjugation as:

mē miseret	I pity (*with gen.*)
mē oportet	I ought (it is necessary for me to ....)
mē paenitet	I repent (*with gen.*)
mē piget	I am disgusted
mē pudet	I am ashamed

214. Latin sometimes uses an impersonal passive to express a general statement. The verbs thus used are normally intransitive verbs. Avoid literal translation into English; try to supply a subject.

ventum erat ad līmen.

They had come to the threshhold.

Virgil, Aeneid 6. 45

215. Verbs which require the dative are used impersonally in the passive:

Sed tamen satis fiet ā nōbīs, neque parcētur labōrī.

But nevertheless, we will satisfy you, nor will we stint in our labour.

Cicero, Letters to Atticus 2. 14. 2

CXVIII. Conditional sentences [GLG 589-602]

216. A conditional sentence consists of an 'if'-clause (or sī-clause), known as the protasis, and a 'then'-clause, known as the apodosis:

If it were done when 'tis done, then 'twere well

It were done quickly.

Shakespeare (d. 1616), Macbeth 1. 6. 7

Sīn possesses an adversative sense: 'but if'; 'if however'.

(a)   In Latin, if the verb in a condition is in the indicative mood, then the verb is translated normally.

This is known as the simple conditional.

sī occīdī, rēctē fēcī.

If I killed him, I did rightly.

Quintilian 4. 5. 13

(b)   If there is a present subjunctive in both parts of a condition, use 'should ... would' in translation. This is known as the future less vivid conditional. The condition here represents future time, and there is the implication that it is possible for the condition to be fulfilled, but that the fulfilment is not probable.

hanc ego viam, sī aut asperam atque arduam aut plēnam esse perīculōrum aut

īnsidiārum negem, mentiar.

If I should deny that this path is either rough and arduous or full of dangers and

traps, I would be lying.

Cicero, *In Defence of Sestius* 46. 100

(c)   The future more vivid construction, on the other hand, uses the future or future perfect indicative tenses in both the protasis and the apodosis, suggesting that fulfilment is likely.

sīc scrībes aliquid, sī vacābis.

So then, you will write something, if you will get the time.

Cicero, *Letters to Atticus* 12. 38. 2

(d)   If there is an imperfect subjunctive in both parts of a condition, use 'were ... would' in translation. This is known as a present contrary-to-fact conditional. The condition here represents present time, and it is implied that the fulfillment of the condition is impossible.

sīc sapientia nōn expeterētur, sī nihil efficeret.

Thus wisdom would not be pursued, if it were to achieve nothing.

Cicero, *On Ends* 1. 13. 42

(e)   If there is a pluperfect subjunctive in both parts of a condition, translate using the formula 'had ... would have'. The condition here represents past time and that the fulfillment of the condition is impossible. This is known as a past contrary-to-fact conditional.

Illud sī scīvissem, ad id meās litterās accommodāvissem.

If I had known that, I would have adapted my letter to it.

Cicero, *Letters to His Friends* 4. 15. 1

EXERCISES

A. Vocabulary

carcer, carceris, m.	prison
cōnsulō, cōnsulere, cōnsuluī, cōnsultum	consult; take thought for (*with dat.*)
cōnsurgō, cōnsurgere, cōnsurrēxī, cōnsurrēctum	rise together
dēsistō, dēsistere, dēstitī, dēstitum	cease
X ē rēpūblicā	for the good of the state
eximō, eximere, exēmī, exēmptum	take away
invidia, invidiae, f.	ill-will, envy, hatred
longus, -a, -um	long
ōrātiō, ōrātiōnis, f.	speech
perficiō, perficere, perfēcī, perfectum	do, make, accomplish
prehendō, prehendere, prehendī, prehensum	grasp, seize
prōsequor, prōsequī, prōsecūtus sum	follow, honour
quisquis, quicquid	whoever, whatever
quoad	while, until, as far as
quoniam	since
sententia, sententiae, f.	opinion, plan
ūtor, ūtī, ūsus sum (*with abl.*)	use
viātor, viātōris, m.	traveller, court-officer

B. Translations

C. (Gāius) Julius Caesar (Caesar, Caesaris, m.) is perhaps the most famous Roman of all. Brilliant and ambitious, he came to power in Rome in 48 BC, but concealed the ruthlessness of his dictatorship beneath a republican veneer. The following story from Aulus Gellius, telling of Caesar's rivalry with the conservative senator Marcus (M.) Catō (Cato, Catōnis, m.), is illustrative of Caesar's character.

C. Caesar cōnsul M. Catōnem sententiam rogāvit. Catō rem, quae cōnsulēbātur, quoniam nōn ē rēpūblicā vidēbātur, perficī nōlēbat. Ēius reī dūcendae grātiā longā ōrātiōne ūtēbātur eximēbatque dīcendō diem. Erat enim iūs senātōrī, ut sententiam rogātus dīceret ante quicquid vellet aliae reī et quoad vellet. Caesar cōnsul viātōrem vocāvit eumque, cum fīnem nōn faceret, prehendī loquentem et in carcerem dūcī iūssit. Senātus cōnsurrēxit et prōsequēbātur Catōnem in carcerem. Hāc invidiā factā, Caesar dēstitit et dimittī Catōnem iussit.

Aulus Gellius 4. 10. 8

Julius Caesar was assassinated in 44 BC. After a period of civil strife culminating in the Battle of Actium in 31 BC against the forces of Marcus Antonius (Antōnius, Antōnī, m.) — better known as Mark Anthony — and Queen Cleopatra of Egypt, Octavian (Octāviānus, Octāviānī, m.) assumed power as Julius Caesar's adopted son. Macrobius records the following anecdote about Octavian, later called Augustus. The story is said to have taken place after the Battle of Actium.

Among those congratulating Caesar was a man holding a raven whom he had trained to say the following: Hail, Caesar, Victor and General. Caesar, amazed, bought this dutiful bird. The associate of this man, to whom nothing of that liberality had come, asserted to Caesar that he also had another raven, which the associate asked that he be compelled to bring. Having been brought, the raven expressed the words which it had learnt: Hail, Anthony, Victor and General. Not irritated at all, Caesar considered it would be suffi- cient, if he were to order the man to divide the largesse with his comrade.

Macrobius, *Saturnālia* 2. 4. 29-30

Additional vocabulary

adferō, adferre, attulī, adlātum	bring
adfirmō, adfirmāre, adfirmāvī, adfirmātum	assert
aveō, avēre, —, —	hail
avis, avis, f.	bird
corvus, corvī, m.	raven
dīvidō, dīvidere, dīvīsī, dīvīsum	divide
dōnātīvum, dōnātīvī, n.	largess
ēmō, ēmere, ēmī, ēmptum	buy
exasperō, exasperāre, exasperāvī, exasperātum	irritate
exprimō, exprimere, expressī, expressum	express, squeeze out
grātulor, grātulārī, grātulātus sum	congratulate, rejoice (*often with dat.*)
īnstituō, īnstituere, īnstituī, īnstitūtum	train, establish, decide, prepare
līberālitās, līberālitātis, f.	liberality
officiōsus, -a, -um	dutiful
socius, socī, m.	comrade, ally
verbum, verbī, n.	word
vīctor, vīctōris, m.	victor

Fig. 29. The Arch of Constantine in Rome, completed in AD 315.

Fig. 30. Porphyry sculptures of the Tetrarchs, Venice.

GRAMMATICAL APPENDICES

AN INTRODUCTION TO DACTYLIC HEXAMETER
NUMBERS
THE ROMAN CALENDAR
WORDS READILY CONFUSED
POINTS FOR REVIEW
WORD ORDER
SOME MULTIPLE CHOICE QUESTIONS

Oft in the stilly night,
When the mind is fumbling fuzzily,
I brood about how little I know,
And know that little so muzzily.
Ere slumber's chains have bound me,
I think it would suit me nicely,
If I knew one tenth of the little I know,
But knew that tenth precisely.

...

Gently my eyelids close;
I'd rather be good than clever;
And I'd rather have my facts all wrong
Than have no facts whatever.

Ogden Nash (1902–1971), 'Who Did Which? or Who Indeed?'

GRAMMATICAL APPENDIX 1

AN INTRODUCTION TO DACTYLIC HEXAMETER

Down in a deep, dark dell sat an old cow munching a beanstalk.

Traditional school mnemonic for the rhythm of a dactylic hexameter line

A. Basic metrics [GLG 729–754]

217. The basis of Latin poetry is syllabic quantity, rather than stress as in English poetry. A syllable is long if it contains a long vowel or a diphthong. In this instance, the syllable is said to be 'long by nature.' If a short vowel is followed by two consonants, then that syllable is also said to be long. In that case, the syllable is 'long by position.'

Note also the following special circumstances:

(a)   x (= ks) and z (= ds) are considered double consonants;

(b)   qu (= kw) is considered a single consonant;

(c)   h is not considered a consonant and does not affect length;

(d)   y is a vowel;

(e)   i can be both a vowel and a consonant.

218. If two consonants follow a short vowel, and the first consonant is b, c, d, f, g, p, or t with the second consonant l or r, then that syllable may remain short. It need not be long by position, and in such cases, the syllable is said to have been rendered common. The mnemonic for this rule is as follows:

*F*resh *p*eanuts *b*ust *t*he *d*arn *c*ow's *g*uts before l or r render a syllable common.

219. The last syllable in a line of verse is the anceps (meaning 'double–headed') syllable, which the poet and the reader may treat as either long or short.

220. Scanning verse entails marking the quantity of each syllable above the vowel sound. Long syllables are designated by ⁻ above the vowel; short syllables have ˘ above the vowel. The anceps syllable is marked with ˣ above the vowel.

221. Elision is the suppression of a syllable at the end of a word. It takes place when a word ending with a vowel has immediately after it another word beginning with a vowel or h.

Elision also takes place when a word beginning with a vowel or h follows a word ending with a vowel and m after it. In this instance, the final syllable of the word with the vowel and m is dropped. In the example below, the syllables that are not pronounced are enclosed within brackets.

mōnstr(um) horrend(um), īnfōrm(e), ingēns, cuī lūmen adēmptum

a terrifying monster, hideous, huge, with a burnt-out eye

Virgil, Aeneid 3. 658

The elided vowel is reversed if the second word is es or est. When this happens, the e of es or est is dropped.

222. The term foot refers to an established set of long and short syllables by means of which rhythmic movement is created. When scanning verse, one foot is separated from another by the symbol I.

223. Ictus is the recurring rhythmic beat in a line of verse. Accent is the normal prose stress of a word. The coincidence of these two items is not necessary in Latin verse, and it is often the clash between ictus and accent that gives Latin poetry (or any musical composition) its sense of movement and power. Coincidence of ictus and accent is more common in English verse.

224. A caesura or 'cutting' is a metrical pause or phrase-break. The caesura must come at the end of a word. In scanning verse, the caesura is indicated by a double vertical line: ‖.

B. Dactylic hexameter [GLG 783–785, 796]

225. Dactylic hexameter is based on

(a) the rhythm ‾ ˘ ˘ (a long syllable followed by two short syllables), known as a dactyl, and

(b) the rhythm ‾ ‾ (two long syllables), known as a spondee.

226. A line of dactylic hexameter verse essentially uses the following metrical pattern

‾ ˘ ˘ | ‾ ˘ ˘ | ‾ ˘ ˘ | ‾ ˘ ˘ | ‾ ˘ ˘ | ‾ ˣ

with ˣ representing either a long or short syllable.

But each of the first five dactyls may be replaced with a spondee, in order to vary the rhythm. The fifth foot normally has a dactyl, although very occasionally, a spondee will take its place.

227. The caesura generally occurs in the middle of the third foot of the verse.

Ārmă vĭI rūmquĕ că I nō ‖ Trōi I aē quī I prīmŭs ăb I ōriš....

I sing of arms and the man who first from the shores of Troy....

Virgil, Aeneid 1. 1

C. Some poetic constructions [GLG 131, 212, 218, 338, 423, 436, 438, 725]

228. The common alternate form of the third person plural perfect is -ēre, rather than -ērunt.

> incubuēre marī.

> They fell upon the sea.

Virgil, Aeneid 1. 84

The accusative ending -īs may substitute for -ēs in the third declension.

> prōspicit errantīs.

> He observes them wandering.

Virgil, Aeneid 1. 185

229. The infinitive may be used to express purpose more often than in prose.

> tum celerāre fugam patriāque excēdere suādet.

> Then he persuades her to hasten her flight and leave her native land.

Virgil, Aeneid 1. 357

Often the future participle is used.

> haec in nostrōs fabricāta est māchina mūrōs,

> īnspectūra domōs ventūraque dēsuper urbī.

> This contrivance has been built against our walls, to look into our homes and swoop

> down upon our city.

Virgil, Aeneid 2. 46–47

230. The supine in -ū, used after certain adjectives as an ablative of specification, is very often seen in poetry, but also appears in prose.

> terque ipsa solō (mīrābile dictū)

> ēmicuit.

> The very object flashed three times from the ground (wondrous to relate!).

Virgil, Aeneid 2. 174–175

231. The passive verbal endings may represent the middle voice: that is, the verb will be passive in form, but reflexive or active in sense. Thus, the middle voice uses the same endings as the passive, but as with deponents, verbs that are in the middle are translated actively. The middle voice may also have a reflexive sense if it expresses an action done on behalf of the subject.

trīstior et lacrimīs oculōs suffūsa nitentīs

adloquitur Venus.

Saddened and with her eyes suffused with glistening tears, Venus addressed him.

Virgil, *Aeneid* 1. 228–229

D. More poetic usage [GLG 29, 33, 65, 337–338, 354, 374, 385, 392]

232. Note the Virgilian use of the neuter plural of an adjective or participle with a genitive.

obsēdēre aliī tēlīs angusta viārum.

Others have besieged the narrow streets (i.e., the narrows of the streets) with their weapons.

Virgil, *Aeneid* 2. 332

233. The genitive singular of a first declension noun sometimes takes the archaic ending -āī, rather than -ae.

aulāī mediō lībābant pōcula Bacchī.

In the middle of the hall, they were pouring libations of wine.

Virgil, *Aeneid* 3. 354

234. The genitive may be used with an adjective to limit the extent of that adjective.

... dīves opum studiīsque asperrima bellī...

... rich in resources and in its zeal for war overly harsh...

Virgil, *Aeneid* 1. 14

235. The short form of the second declension genitive plural is -um, instead of -ōrum (*e.g.*, superum, for superōrum).

... multum ille et terrīs iactātus et altō

vī superum.

Much was that man tossed on land and sea by the power of the gods.

Virgil, *Aeneid* 1. 3–4

236. A dative may express 'motion-toward.'

it clāmor caelō.

A cry goes up to heaven.

Virgil, *Aeneid* 5. 451

237. A dative of agent, usual with the gerundive in prose, may take the place of an ablative of agent.

neque cernitur ūllī.

Nor is he seen by anyone.

Virgil, *Aeneid* 1. 440

238. An accusative of 'motion-toward' may omit the preposition.

> Ītaliam fātō profugus Lāvīniaque vēnit
>
> lītora.
>
> He came to Italy and the Lavinian shores, exiled by fate.
>
> Virgil, *Aeneid* 1. 2–3

239. An accusative of respect is more commonly seen than an ablative of respect and usually refers to a part of the body.

> Ecce manūs iuvenem intereā post terga revinctum
>
> pāstōrēs māgnō ad rēgem clāmōre trahēbant.
>
> Behold, shepherds in the meanwhile were dragging with a great shout a young man,
>
> his hands bound behind his back, to the king.
>
> Virgil, *Aeneid* 2. 57–58

240. Greek accusative forms may be used for Greek names or Greek words used in poetry. Note the Greek form of the first declension accusative singular: *e.g.*, Aenēan (Aenēās), Orontēn (Orontēs). The Greek form of the third declension accusative singular is found in such forms as: āēra (āēr), aethera (aethēr), Anthea (Antheus), Lāocoōnta (Lāocoōn).

241. The ablative of location may be found without a preposition.

> Crēta Iovis māgnī mediō iacet īnsula pontō.
>
> Crete, the island of great Jupiter, lies in the midst of the sea.
>
> Virgil, *Aeneid* 3. 104

E. Figures of poetic speech [GLG 671–700]

242. *Alliteration* is the use of words beginning with the same consonant to evoke the sense of the passage. The following refers to sea-serpents:

> fit sonitus spūmante sālō.
>
> A sound emerges from the foaming sea.
>
> Virgil, *Aeneid* 2. 209–211

243. An *anachronism* wrongly attributes something to a time it did not exist. In the example below, the reference to theatres is an anachronism, since these did not exist in the time of Dido and Aeneas.

           ... hīc alta theātrī

fundāmenta locant aliī.

Here, others lay deep foundations for a theatre.

Virgil, Aeneid 1. 427–428

244. *Anaphora* is the repetition of the same word at the beginning of successive phrases.

    classibus hīc locus, hīc aciē certāre solēbant.

This was where the fleet lay, this was where they used to strive in battle.

Virgil, Aeneid 2. 30

245. *Anastrophe* is the placing of a preposition after the word it governs.

    namque vidēbat, utī bellantēs Pergama circum

    hāc fugerent Grāī.

For he was seeing how here the warring Greeks were in flight around Troy.

Virgil, Aeneid 1. 466–467

246. *Aposiopesis* means, in Greek, a 'silencing-off.' It is the abandonment of a statement uncompleted, usually for a threatening or suspenseful effect.

    quōs ego —! sed mōtōs praestat compōnere flūctūs.

Whom I —! But I had best calm these troubled seas.

Virgil, Aeneid 1. 135

247. An *apostrophe* is the direct address of a person, animal, object, or personified force.

    dī patriī, quōrum semper sub nūmine Trōia est ....

Gods of our ancestors, under whose protection Troy lies forever ....

Virgil, Aeneid 9. 247

248. *Asyndeton* is the omission of a connective where a conjunction such as 'and' might have been used. Where the conjunction 'but' is omitted, the use is called adversative asyndeton.

    nāvem in cōnspectū nūllam, trēs lītore cervōs

    prōspicit errantīs.

There is no ship in sight, but he observes three deer wandering along the shore.

Virgil, Aeneid 1. 184–185

249. *Chiasmus* refers to word order in which the order or syntax of the first part of a phrase or sentence is reversed in the second part.

> lūctantīs ventōs tempestātēsque sonōrās
>
> imperiō premit.
>
> He oppresses with his power the contending winds and the sounding storms.

Virgil, Aeneid 1. 53–54

250. *Hendiadys* is the use of two nouns connected by 'and' instead of a noun and an adjective or a noun and a genitive. The two nouns express one idea.

> hōc metuēns, mōlemque et mōntīs īnsuper altōs
>
> imposuit.
>
> Fearing this, he piled tall, massive mountains on top of them.

Virgil, Aeneid 1. 61–62

251. *Hyperbole* is gross exaggeration for effect.

> tēcta fremunt, resonat māgnīs plangōribus aethēr.
>
> The rooftops ring, the sky resounds with great wailing.

Virgil, Aeneid 4. 668

252. *Hysteron proteron* is the reversal of the logical order of time.

> moriāmur et in media arma ruāmus.
>
> Let us die, and let us rush into the midst of battle.

Virgil, Aeneid 2. 353

253. *Irony* is the use of words where the opposite of the literal sense is intended.

> māgnum et memorābile nōmen,
>
> ūna dolō dīvum sī fēmina vīcta duōrum est.
>
> There is great and memorable renown, when a lone woman is undone by
>
> the trickery of two gods.

Virgil, Aeneid 4. 94–95

Irony often takes the special form known as *dramatic irony*, where the full import of a speaker's words is known only to the audience or the reader.

254. *Litotes* is the expression of a positive by means of a negative.

> haud aliter puppēsque tuae pūbēsque tuōrum
>
> aut portum tenet aut plēnō subit ōstia vēlō.
>
> Not otherwise will your ships and your men reach harbour and enter its mouth with full sail.

Virgil, Aeneid 1. 399

255. *Metaphor* is the application of a word which is literally appropriate to one object or activity to another object or activity in order to suggest a resemblance between them.

īnfēlīx Dīdō longumque bibēbat amōrem.

And unhappy Dido was drinking deep draughts of love.

Virgil, Aeneid 1. 749

256. *Metonymy* is the use of one noun for a related noun which it suggests.

implentur veteris Bacchī pīnguisque ferīnae.

They take their fill of old wine and rich meat.

Virgil, Aeneid 1. 215

257. *Onomatopoeia* is the fitting of the sound of a word to its sense.

curvīsque immūgiit Aetna cavernīs.

Aetna bellowed in its curved caverns.

Virgil, Aeneid 3. 674

258. *Prolepsis* is the use of an epithet before the action makes it logically appropriate.

incute vim ventīs submersāsque obrue puppīs.

Strike force into the winds, and overwhelm and sink their ships (literally, overwhelm

their sunken ships).

Virgil, Aeneid 1. 69

259. A *simile* is a comparison usually introduced by qualis or velut.

quālis apēs aestāte novā per flōrea rūra

exercet sub sōle labor ....

As bees in the new summer through a countryside filled with flowers ply their trade beneath the sun ....

Virgil, Aeneid 1. 430-431

260. *Synchysis* is interlocked word order, where the modifier of one pair comes between the parts of the other.

aspera tum positīs mītēscunt saecula bellīs.

Then, once war has been put aside, the harsh ages will grow milder.

Virgil, Aeneid 1. 291

261. *Tmesis* refers to the cutting of a word into two parts.

et multō nebulae circum dea fūdit amictū.

And the goddess poured round them a thick covering of cloud.

Virgil, Aeneid 1. 412

262. *Zeugma* is the use of a verb with a pair (or more) of nouns or expressions to only one of which it is
strictly applicable in sense.

iūra magistrātūsque legunt sānctumque senātum.

They adopt laws and choose magistrates and revered senate.

Virgil, Aeneid 1. 426

Grammatical appendix 2

Numbers

A. Cardinals, ordinals, and Roman numerals

	CARDINAL	ORDINAL	ROMAN NUMERAL
1	ūnus, -a, -um	prīmus, -a, -um	I
2	duo, duae, duo	alter or secundus, -a, -um	II
3	trēs, trēs, tria	tertius, -a, -um	III
4	quattuor	quārtus, -a, -um	IV or IIII
5	quīnque	quīntus, -a, -um	V
6	sex	sextus, -a, -um	VI
7	septem	septimus, -a, -um	VII
8	octō	octāvus, -a, -um	VIII

9	novem	nōnus, -a, -um	IX or VIIII
10	decem	decimus, -a, -um	X
11	ūndecim	ūndecimus, -a, -um	XI
12	duodecim	duodecimus, -a, -um	XII
13	tredecim	tertius decimus, -a, -um	XIII
14	quattuordecim	quārtus decimus, -a, -um	XIV or XIIII
15	quīndecim	quīntus decimus, -a, -um	XV
16	sēdecim	sextus decimus, -a, -um	XVI
17	septendecim	septimus decimus, -a, -um	XVII
18	duodēvīgintī	duodēvicēsimus, -a, -um	XVIII
19	ūndēvīgintī	ūndēvīcēsimus, -a, -um	XIX or XVIIII
20	vīgintī	vīcēsimus, -a, -um	XX
21	ūnus et vīgintī or vīgintī ūnus	vīcēsimus prīmus, -a, -um	XXI
22	duo et vīgintī or vīgintī duo	vīcēsimus secundus, -a, -um	XXII
30	trīgintā	trīcēsimus, -a, -um	XXX
40	quadrāgintā	quadrāgēsimus, -a, -um	XL or XXXX
41	quadrāgintā ūnus or ūnus et quadrāgintā	quadrāgēsimus prīmus, -a, -um	XLI
50	quīnquāgintā	quīnquāgēsimus, -a, -um	L
60	sexāgintā	sexāgēsimus, -a, -um	LX
70	septuāgintā	septuāgēsimus, -a, -um	LXX
80	octōgintā	octōgēsimus, -a, -um	LXXX
90	nōnāgintā	nōnāgēsimus, -a, -um	XC or LXXXX
100	centum	centēsimus, -a, -um	C
101	centum et ūnus	centēsimus prīmus, -a, -um	CI
200	ducentī, -ae, -a	ducentēsimus, -a, -um	CC
300	trecentī	trecentēsimus, -a, -um	CCC
400	quadringentī	quadringentēsimus, -a, -um	CD or CCCC
500	quīngentī	quīngentēsimus, -a, -um	D
600	sēscentī	sēscentēsimus, -a, -um	DC
1000	mīlle	mīllēsimus, -a, -um	M
2000	duo mīlia	bis mīllēsimus, -a, -um	MM

B. The declension of numbers

Only ūnus, duo, and trēs decline. All others are indeclinable. For obvious reasons, ūnus, -a, -um exists only in the singular, while duo, -ae, -o and trēs, -ia exist only in the plural.

ŪNUS, ŪNA, ŪNUM

one

	masculine	*feminine*	*neuter*
nom.	ūnus	ūna	ūnum
gen.	ūnīus	ūnīus	ūnīus
dat.	ūnī	ūnī	ūnī
accus.	ūnum	ūnam	ūnum
abl.	ūnō	ūnā	ūnō

DUO, DUAE, DUO

two

	masculine	*feminine*	*neuter*
nom.	duo	duae	duo
gen.	duōrum	duārum	duōrum
dat.	duōbus	duābus	duōbus
accus.	duōs	duās	duō
abl.	duōbus	duābus	duōbus

TRĒS, TRIA

three

nom.	trēs	trēs	tria
gen.	trium	trium	trium
dat.	tribus	tribus	tribus
acc.	trēs	trēs	tria
abl.	tribus	tribus	tribus.

Note: Cardinal numbers and quīdam, paucī, and multī when used as nouns take ex with the ablative, not a partitive genitive. Mīlia, however, is always followed by a genitive.

GRAMMATICAL APPENDIX 3

THE ROMAN CALENDAR

In March, July, October, May
The Ides are on the fifteenth day,
The Nones the seventh; but all besides
Have two days less for Nones and Ides.

Traditional school mnemonic for the reckoning points of the Roman month

A. Months (adjectives)

mēnsis, mēnsis, m.	month (from metior, metīrī, mēnsus - to measure)
Iānuārius, -a, -um	January
Februārius, -a, -um	February
Mārtius, -a, -um	March
Aprīlis, -e	April
Māius, -a, -um	May
Iūnius, -a, -um	June
Iūlius, -a, -um (Quīntīlis, -e)	July
Augustus, -a, -um (Sextīlis, -e)	August
September, Septembris, Septembre	September
Octōber, Octōbris, Octōbre	October
November, Novembris, Novembre	November
December, Decembris, Decembre	December

B. Days (nouns)

Kalendae, Kalendārum, f.	Kalends (1st of the month)
Nōnae, Nōnārum, f.	Nones (5th of the month; but in March, May, July, October, the 7th; the term refers to the ninth day before the Ides; note also Nōna, -ae, f. - a goddess presiding over the ninth month of a woman's pregnancy, also regarded as one of the Fates.)
Īdūs, Īduum, f.	Ides (13th of the month; but in March, May, July, October, the 15th)

C. The reckoning of days

Days were always reckoned from the Kalends, Nones, and Ides, working backwards from these and counting *internally* (*e.g.*, the third day before the 15th is the 13th).

Examples:

1 November	Kalendīs Novembribus (ablative)
31 October	prīdiē Kalendās Novembrēs (accusative)
30 October	diē tertiō ante Kalendās Novembrēs
	ante diem tertium Kalendās Novembrēs
	a. d. III Kal. Nov.
27 October	ante diem VI Kalendās Novembrēs
	a. d. VI Kal. Nov.
21 October	ante diem XII Kalendās Novembrēs
	a. d. XII Kal. Nov.
25 December	a. d. VIII Kal. Ian.
15 March	Īdibus Mārtiīs
14 March	prīdiē Īd. Mārt.
13 March	a. d. III Īd. Mārt.
5 October	a. d. III Nōn. Oct. (Nōnās Octōbrēs)

D. The seasons (annī tempus)

autumnus, autumnī, m.	autumn	autumnus, -a, -um	autumnal
hiem(p)s, hiemis, f.	winter	hiemālis, -e	of winter
vēr, vēris, n.	spring	vernālis, -e	of spring
aestās, aestātis, f.	summer	aestīvus, -a, -um	of summer

GRAMMATICAL APPENDIX 4

WORDS READILY CONFUSED

'If so then,' cried the Squire, 'answer me directly to what I propose: Whether do you judge the
analytical investigation of the first part of my enthymeme deficient secundum quoad,
or quoad minus and give me your reasons too; give me your reasons,
I say, directly.' — 'I protest,' cried Moses, 'I don't rightly comprehend the force of your reasoning.'

Oliver Goldsmith (1730–1774), *The Vicar of Wakefield*

A. Words in Latin with similar spelling

ā, ab (*with abl.*)	from, away from
ad (*with acc.*)	to, toward
ācer, ācris, ācre	sharp, pointed, piercing
acer, aceris, n.	maple tree
aeger, aegra, aegrum	sick, ill
ager, agrī, m.	field, farm
agger, aggeris, m.	mound, heap, rampart
āēr, āeris, m.	air, atmosphere
aes, aeris, n.	copper
aestās, aestātis, f.	summer
aestus, aestūs, m.	heat
aetās, aetātis, f.	age
agō, agere, ēgī, āctum	do, drive, discuss
augeō, augēre, auxī, auctum	increase
anima, animae, f.	soul, spirit
animal, animālis, n.	animal
animus, animī, m.	spirit, courage (*in plural*)

āra, ārae, f.	altar
aura, arae, f.	breeze, air
aureus, aurea, aureum	golden
auris, auris, f.	ear
aurum, aurī, n.	gold
audeō, audēre, ausus sum	dare
audiō, audīre, audīvī, audītum	hear
bellum, bellī, n.	war
bellus, bella, bellum	handsome
cadō, cadere, cecidī, cāsum	fall
caedō, caedere, cecīdī, caesum	cut, kill
cēdō, cēdere, cessī, cessum	go, yield
cedo (*plural* cette)	gimme (give me – *a colloquial imperative*)
cāneō, cānēre, canuī, —	be grey, hoary
canis, canis, m. or f.	dog
canō, canere, cecinī, —	sing
capiō, capere, cēpī, captum	seize, take, capture
cupiō, cupere, cupīvī, cupītum	desire, want
carō, carnis, f.	flesh
cārus, cāra, cārum	dear
carrus, carrī, m.	wagon, cart
cīvis, cīvis, m. or f.	citizen
cīvitās, cīvitātis, f.	citizenship, state
clāva, clāvae, f.	branch
clāvis, clāvis, f.	key
clāvus, clāvī, m.	nail; purple stripe (for senators or equitēs)

coma, comae, f.	hair
comes, comitis, m. or f.	companion
cōmis, cōme	kind, obliging
comedō, comedōnis, m.	glutton, gormandizer
cōmoedus, cōmoedī, m.	comic actor, comedian
concilium, concilī, n.	council, gathering
cōnsilium, cōnsilī, n.	advice, plan, wisdom, counsel
cōnsul, cōnsulis, m.	consul
cōnsulō, cōnsulere, cōnsuluī, cōnsultum	consider, reflect, deliberate
cōnsistō, cōnsistere, cōnstitī, cōnstitum	stop, stand, make a stand
cōnstat (*impersonal*)	it is agreed
cōnstituō, cōnstituere, cōnstituī, cōnstitūtum	decide
deinde	then, next
dēmum	finally
dēligō, dēligāre, dēligāvī, dēligātum	bind
dēligō, dēligere, dēlēgī, dēlēctum	choose
dīligō, dīligere, dīlēxī, dīlēctum	love, cherish
deus, deī, m.	god
diēs, diēī, m. or f.	day
dicō, dicāre, dicāvi, dicātum	make known, dedicate
dīcō, dīcere, dīxī, dictum	say, talk, mention
diffīdō, diffīdere, diffīsus sum	distrust
diffindō, diffindere, diffidī, diffissum	cleave, divide
dīves, dīvitis	rich
dīvitiae, dīvitiārum, f. (*plural*)	riches

doleo, dolēre, doluī, dolitūrus	grieve
dolor, dolōris, m.	pain, sorrow
dolus, dolī, m.	treachery
ēdō, ēdere, ēdidī, ēditum	eject, emit; bring forth
edō, ēsse, ēdī, ēsum	eat
ēducō, ēducāre, ēducāvī, ēducātum	educate
ēdūcō, ēdūcere, ēdūxī, ēductum	lead out
faciō, facere, fēcī, factum	do, make
falx, falcis, f.	sickle, scythe
fax, facis, f.	torch
fāma, fāmae, f.	report, fame
famēs, famis, f.	hunger
fātum, fātī, n.	fate
for, fārī, fātus sum	speak
fera, ferae, f.	wild beast
ferē	nearly
feriō, ferīre, —, —	strike, flog
ferō, ferre, tulī, lātum	bear, carry, endure
ferreus, -a, -um	iron (*adj.*)
ferrum, ferrī, n.	iron, iron implement, sword
ferus, fera, ferum	wild, savage
fretum, fretī, n.	strait, channel
frētus, frēta, frētum	relying on, trusting to (*with dat. or abl.*)
foedus, foederis, n.	treaty, pact
foedus, foeda, foedum	foul, dirty

fōrte	by chance
fortis, forte	brave, strong
fugiō, fugere, fūgī, —	flee
fugō, fugāre, fugāvī, fugātum	put to flight
fūmus, fūmī, m.	smoke
fūnis, fūnis, m.	rope
fūnus, fūneris, n.	death, destruction
gener, generī, m.	son-in-law
gēns, gentis, f.	nation, race
genū, genūs, n.	knee
genus, generis, n.	kind, class
habeō, habēre, habuī, habitum	have, hold, consider
habitō, habitāre, habitāvī, habitātum	live, dwell
haereō, haerēre, haesī, haesum	cling, cling to, stand fast, be perplexed
hauriō, haurīre, hausī, haustum	draw, drink, exhaust
hīc	here (in this place)
hinc	from this place
hūc	to this place
iaceō, iacēre, iacuī,	lie down
iaciō, iacere, iēcī, iactum	throw, hurl
iactō, iactāre, iactāvī, iactātum	throw (sē iactāre show off)
in (*with abl.*)	in, on
in (*with acc.*)	into
interdum	sometimes
intereā	meanwhile
interim	meanwhile

lābor, lābī, lapsus sum	slide, slip, glide
labor, labōris, m.	labour, toil, exertion
labōrō, labōrāre, labōrāvī, labōrātum	strive, be hard pressed
lateō, latēre, latuī, —	lie hidden
lātus, lāta, lātum	wide, broad
lātus, lāta, lātum	*perf. pass. participle of ferō*
latus, latēris, n.	side
lepōs, lepōris, m.	charm, grace
lepus, leporis, m.	a hare (also a term of endearment)
lēvis, lēve	smooth, smoothed
levis, leve	light
līber, lībera, līberum	free
liber, librī, m.	book
līberī, līberōrum, m. (*plural*)	children
līberō, līberāre, līberāvī, līberātum	free
lībērtās, lībērtātis, f.	freedom
lībērtus, lībērtī, m.	freedman
lūctus, lūctūs, m.	sorrow
lūcus, lūcī, m.	grove
lūx, lūcis, f.	light
mālō, mālle, māluī, —	prefer
malus, mala, malum	bad
mālum, mālī, n.	apple
mālus, mālī, m.	ship's mast
maneō, manēre, mānsī, mānsum	remain
moneō, monēre, monuī, monitum	warn

mēns, mentis, f.	mind
mēnsa, mēnsae, f.	table
mēnsis, mēnsis, m.	month
mercēs, mercēdis, f.	hire, pay
merx, mercis, f.	goods, merchandise
miser, misera, miserum	wretched, sad
mittō, mittere, mīsī, missum	send
mora, morae, f.	delay
morbus, morbī, m.	illness, disease
morior, morī, mortuus sum	die
moror, morārī, morātus sum	delay
mors, mortis, f.	death
mōs, mōris, m.	custom, habit, manner
mulceō, mulcēre, mulsī, mulsum	stroke, touch lightly
mulgeō, mulgēre, —, —	milk
nancīscor, nancīscī, nactus sum	obtain, get
nāscor, nāscī, nātus sum	be born
natō, natāre, natāvi, natātum	swim
niteō, nitēre, nituī, —	shine, glisten
nītor, nītī, nīsus or nīxus sum	bear upon
nōmen, nōminis, n.	name
nūmen, nūminis, n.	divine will
numquam	never
nunc	now
obses, obsidis, m. or f.	hostage
obsideō, obsidēre, obsēdī, obsessum	besiege
obsidiō, obsidiōnis, f.	siege

occidō, occidere, occidī, occāsum	fall down, fall
occīdō, occīdere, occīdī, occīsum	beat, smash, crush
ōmen, ōminis, n.	omen
omnīnō	wholly; at all (*with a negative*)
omnis, omne	every, all
onerō, onerāre, onerāvī, onerātum	load
onus, oneris, n.	burden
opera, operae, f.	effort
operiō, operīre, operuī, opertus	cover
opperior, opperīrī, oppertus	wait for
ops, opis, f.	power, ability
opus, operis, n.	work
opus est (*with abl.*)	there is need of
ōra, ōrae, f.	shore
ōrō, ōrare, ōrāvī, ōrātum	pray
ōs, ōris, n.	mouth, face
os, ossis, n.	bone
pār, pāris	equal, like
pars, partis, f.	part, direction, side
parcō, parcere, pepercī, parsum	be sparing, spare (*with dat.*)
pāreō, pārēre, pāruī, —	be visible; obey (*with dat.*)
pariō, parere, peperī, partum	give birth to
parō, parāre, parāvī, parātum	provide, prepare
pateō, patēre, patuī, —	lie open
patior, patī, passus sum	suffer, allow, endure
potior, potīrī, potītus sum	gain possession of
pater, patris	father
patria, patriae	fatherland
patrius, -a, -um	of a father, native

petō, petere, petīvī, petītum	seek, attack, ask
putō, putāre, putāvī, putātum	think
pila, pilae, f.	ball
pīla, pīlae, f.	pillar
pīlum, pīlī, n.	javelin
pilus, pilī, m.	a hair
placeō, placēre, placuī, placitum	please
plācō, plācāre, plācāvī, plācātum	soothe, reconcile
plāga, plāgae, f.	blow, wound
plaga, plagae, f.	region, quarter
pōnō, pōnere, posuī, positum	put, put down
possum, posse, potuī, —	be able, can
pōns, pōntis, m.	bridge
pontus, pontī, m.	sea
porta, portae, f.	gate
portō, portāre, portāvī, portātum	carry
portus, portūs, m.	harbour
populus, populī, m.	people
pōpulus, pōpulī, f.	poplar
praeda, praedae, f.	booty
praedō, praedōnis, m.	robber, pirate
praedor, praedārī, praedātus sum	plunder
prōdeō, prōdīre, prōdīvī, prōditum	go forth
prōdō, prōdere, prōdidī, prōditum	betray, hand down
prōsum, prōdesse, prōfuī, —	benefit (*with dat.*)

quaerō, quaerere, quaesīvī, quaesītum	seek, ask
queror, querī, questus sum	complain
quālis, quāle	of what kind? of what sort?
quam	how?
quantus, quanta, quantum	how large, how great
quī, quae, quod	*the relative pronoun*
quī, quae, quod	*the interrogative adjective*
quis, quis, quid	*the interrogative pronoun*
quot	how many
quīdam, quaedam, quoddam	a certian
quidem	indeed (*often not translated*)
rāmus, rāmī, m.	branch
rēmus, rēmī, m.	oar
sāl, sālis, m.	salt
saltem	at least
saltus, saltūs, m.	woodland, pasture
salūs, salūtis, f.	safety
sānō, sānāre, sānāvī, sānātum	cure, heal
sānus, sāna, sānum	sound, healthy
sonus, sonī, m.	sound
serviō, servīre, servīvī, servītum	serve
servō, servāre, servāvī, servātum	save, guard
sōl, sōlis, m.	sun
sōleō, sōlēre, sōlitus sum	be accustomed
solum, solī, n.	ground
sōlus, sōla, sōlum	alone
solvō, solvere, solvī, solūtum	loosen, set sail, perform

spērō, spērāre, spērāvī, spērātum	hope
spīrō, spīrāre, spīrāvī, spīrātum	breathe
tālis, tāle	of such a kind, of such a sort
tam	so
tantus, tanta, tantum	so large, so great
tempestās, tempestātis, f.	storm
tempus, tempōris, n.	time, temple
tot	so many
tōtus, tōta, tōtum	whole
tūtus, tūta, tūtum	safe
umquam	ever
numquam	never
unda, undae, f.	wave
unde	from where, whence
vadō, vadere, —, —	go
vadum, vadī, n.	ford, shoal, sea
vallis, vallis, f.	valley
vāllum, vāllī, n.	rampart
veneror, venerārī, venerātus sum	worship
veniō, venīre, vēnī, ventum	come
vēnor, vēnārī, vēnātus sum	hunt
vēr, vēris, n.	spring
vēritās, vēritātis, f.	truth
vērō	indeed (*often not translated*)
vērum (*adv.*)	but
vērus, -a, -um	true
vir, virī, m.	man
vīs, —, f.	force, violence; strength (*in plural*)

Vesta, Vestae, f.	Vesta, goddess of the hearth
vestis, vestis, f.	garment
vetō, vetāre, vetuī, vetitus	forbid
via, viae, f.	road, way
vīta, vītae, f.	life
vītō, vītāre, vītāvī, vītātum	avoid
vitta, vittae, f.	garland, filet
vinciō, vincīre, vinxī, vinctum	bind
vincō, vincere, vīcī, vīctum	conquer
vīctus, vīctūs, m.	food, way of life
vīvō, vīvere, vīxī, —	live
virga, virgae, f.	rod
virgō, virginis, f.	maiden, girl
volō, volāre, volāvī, volātum	fly
volō, velle, voluī, —	wish, want

B. Words in English with ambiguous meanings and their equivalents in Latin

army

> aciēs, aciēī, f. – line of battle
>
> āgmen, āgminis, n. – army in marching orders
>
> exercitus, exercitūs, m. – *general term*

ask

- *If someone is asking for or demanding a thing (rather than an action), the simplest procedure is to use petō and ā or ab with an accusative. (e.g., hastam ab eō petīvī.)*

- *If the asking involves wanting information and indirect question is involved, better use quaerō with ā or ab and the ablative. (e.g., quaesīvī ā Cicerōne quid cōniūrātī fēcissent.)*

- *If the asking involves wanting information and an 'about' phrase is involved (i.e., to ask about...), better use interrogō with an accusative. (e.g., Cicerōnem dē cōniūrātīs interrogāvī.)*

- *If the information asked for is represented by a neuter pronoun or adjective, or is someone's opinion, use a double accusative after rogō. (e.g., multa eum rogāvī.)*

blood

    cruor, cruōris, m. – gore

    sanguis, sanguinis, m. – *general term*

but

    at – *strongly adversative, oppositional*

    autem – *weakest adversative, generally following an emphatic word or two or more closely connected words*

    sed – *corrective, often after a negative clause*

    tamen – *after a conditional or concessive word*

country

    patria, patriae, f. – fatherland

    regiō, regiōnis, f. – a tract of country

    rūs, rūris, n. – countryside

enemy

    adversārius, adversārī, m. – opponent *in any sense*

    hostis, hostis, m. – public enemy, enemy of the state

    inimīcus, inimīcī, m. – personal enemy

field

    ager, agrī, m. – agricultural land

    campus, campī, m. – open country

fault

    culpa, culpae, f. – blame, guilt

    vitium, vitiī, n. – blemish, vice

feast

    cēna, cēnae, f. – principal meal of the day

    convīvium, convīvī, n. – social meal, meal in the company of one's friends

    epulae, epulārum, f. plural – banquet

    epulum, epulī, n. – sumptuous meal

hope

    optō, optāre, optāvī, optātum – hope against hope

    spērō, spērāre, spērāvī, spērātum – hope with reasonable probability

inhabit

    habitō, habitāre, habitāvī, habitātum – *with regard to individuals*

    incolō, incolere, incoluī, – *with regard to peoples or a community*

inhabitant

> cīvis, cīvis, m. or f. – citizen

> incola, incolae, m. or f. – native, foreign resident

kill

> interficiō, interficere, interfēcī, interfectum – *general term*

> interimō, interimere, interēmī, interēmptum – cut life short

> necō, necāre, necāvī, necātum – kill arbitrarily

> occīdō, occīdere, occīdī, occīsum – strike down

> percutiō, percutere, percussī, percussum – transfix, beat

> trucīdō, trucīdāre, trūcīdāvī, trūcīdātum – massacre

know

> cōgnōscō, cōgnōscere, cōgnōvī, cōgnitum – ascertain

> nōvī (*perfect of* nōscō) – become acquainted with

> sciō, scīre, scīvī, scītum – know something as a fact

letter

> epistula, epistulae, f. – *the object itself*

> litterae, litterārum, f. plural – communications, *contents of the letter*

long

> diū – *with reference to time*

> longē –*with reference to distance*

make a speech

> ōrātiōnem facere – compose a speech

> ōrātiōnem habere – deliver a speech

man

> homō, hominis, m. – human being

> vir, virī, m. – male person

marry

> in mātrimōnium dūcere – *when a man is the subject, in the active voice*

> nūbō, nūbere, nūpsī, nūptum – *when a woman is the subject, literally meaning 'to take the veil'.*

master

> dominus, dominī, m. – owner

> magister, magistrī, m. – overseer

nation

> gēns, gentis, f. – race

nātiō, nātiōnis, f. – tribe, *a subdivision of gēns*

populus, populī, m. – people as an organised community

opinion

opīniō, opīniōnis, f. – impression, belief

sententia, sententiae, f. – *opinion held after mature deliberation*

or

aut – *contrasts a real or important difference*

vel – *makes a minor contrast*

persuade

For the sentence 'I persuade you to do this,' one would use the Great Ordering Family, because pressure is being brought on someone to do something. But for 'I persuade you that this is false,' one would use the acc. and inf. of indirect discourse, because I have merely succeeded in getting across a bit of information.

play

canō, canere, cecinī, — – *with reference to an instrument*

lūdō, lūdere, lūsī, lūsum – *with reference to a game*

pretend

dissimulō, dissimulāre, dissimulāvī, dissimulātum – *representing something true as false*

simulō, simulāre, simulāvī, simulātum – *representing something false as true*

reign

imperō, imperāre, imperāvī, imperātum – act as emperor, general

rēgnō, rēgnāre, rēgnāvī, rēgnātum – act as king

show

mōnstrō, mōnstrāre, mōnstrāvī, mōnstrātum – point out

ostendō, ostendere, ostendī, ostentum – display

soul

anima, animae, f. – life common to all animals

animus, animī, m. – rational soul of man

speak

dīcō, dīcere, dīxī, dictum – *used with regard to formal expression*

loquor, loquī, locūtus sum – *more general term*

troops

cōpiae, cōpiārum, f. – *military force in the aggregate*

mīlitēs, mīlitum, m. – *with regard to the individual soldiers*

uncle

> avunculus, avunculī, m. – maternal uncle
>
> patruus, patruī, m. – paternal uncle

wall

> moenia, moenium, n. plural – city walls
>
> mūrus, mūrī, m. – *general term*
>
> pariēs, parietis, m. – wall of a house or building

wander

> errō, errāre, errāvī, errātum – *of involuntary or ignorant roaming*
>
> vagor, vagārī, vagātus sum – roam on purpose

where

> quō – *motion implied*
>
> ubi – *no motion implied*

wretch

> miser, miserī, m. – *with regard to outward circumstances*
>
> perditus, perditī, m. – *with regard to inner depravity*

POINTS FOR REVIEW:
>SYNOPSES
>SUMMARY OF THE QUANTITIES OF FINAL SYLLABLES
>CASE USAGE
>WAYS OF EXPRESSING PURPOSE

Amō, amās, I love a lass,
As cedar tall and slender;
Sweet cowslip's grace
Is her nominative case,
And she's of the feminine gender.

John O'Keefe (1747–1833), *Agreeable Surprises* 2. 2

A. Synopses

A synopsis in grammar is an exercise listing all forms of a particular verb in the indicative and the subjunctive for a given person, together with all infinitives, participles, and imperatives. It is useful as a way to become familiar with the different verb forms. The forms may be written out as one speaks and sees the forms — and the hand will remember, no less than the eye or ear.

The following are examples of synopses.

EXAMPLE 1: SYNOPSIS OF AMŌ

Principal parts: **amō, amāre, amāvī, amātum (love)**

Person: **first person plural**

INDICATIVE

	ACTIVE	PASSIVE
PRESENT	amāmus	amāmur
IMPERFECT	amābāmus	amābāmur
FUTURE	amābimus	amābimur
PERFECT	amāvimus	amātī, -ae, -a sumus
PLUPERFECT	amāverāmus	amātī, -ae, -a erāmus
FUTURE PERFECT	amāverimus	amātī, -ae, -a erimus

SUBJUNCTIVE

	ACTIVE	PASSIVE
PRESENT	amēmus	amēmur
IMPERFECT	amārēmus	amārēmur
FUTURE	— — — — —	— — — — —
PERFECT	amaverīmus	amātī, -ae, -a sīmus
PLUPERFECT	amāvissēmus	amātī, -ae, -a essēmus
FUTURE PERFECT	— — — — —	— — — — —

PARTICIPLES

	ACTIVE	PASSIVE
PRESENT	amāns, amantis	— — — — —
PERFECT	— — — — —	amātus, -a, -um
FUTURE	amātūrus, -a, -um	amandus, -a, -um

INFINITIVES

	ACTIVE	PASSIVE
PRESENT	amāre	amārī
PERFECT	amāvisse	amātus, -a, -um esse
FUTURE	amātūrus, -a, -um esse	amātum īrī

IMPERATIVES

	ACTIVE	PASSIVE
SINGULAR	amā	amāre
PLURAL	amāte	amāminī

EXAMPLE 2: SYNOPSIS OF TOLLŌ

Principal parts: **tollō, tollere, sustulī, sublātum (raise, remove, put out of the way)**

Person: **third person singular**

INDICATIVE

	ACTIVE	PASSIVE
PRESENT	tollit	tollitur
IMPERFECT	tollēbat	tollēbātur
FUTURE	tollet	tollētur
PERFECT	sustulit	sublātus, -a, -um est
PLUPERFECT	sustulerat	sublātus, -a, -um erat
FUTURE PERFECT	sustulerit	sublātus, -a, -um erit

SUBJUNCTIVE

	ACTIVE	PASSIVE
PRESENT	tollat	tollātur
IMPERFECT	tolleret	tollerētur
FUTURE	— — — — —	— — — — —
PERFECT	sustulerit	sublātus, -a, -um sit
PLUPERFECT	sustulisset	sublātus, -a, -um esset
FUTURE PERFECT	— — — — —	— — — — —

PARTICIPLES

	ACTIVE	PASSIVE
PRESENT	tollēns, tollentis	— — — — —
PERFECT	— — — — —	sublātus, -a, -um
FUTURE	sublātūrus, -a, -um	tollendus, -a, -um

INFINITIVES

	ACTIVE	PASSIVE
PRESENT	tollere	tollī
PERFECT	sustulisse	sublātus, -a, -um esse
FUTURE	sublātūrus, -a, -um esse	sublātum īrī

IMPERATIVES

	ACTIVE	PASSIVE
SINGULAR	tolle	tollere
PLURAL	tollite	tolliminī

B. Quantity of final syllables

ā   long in abl. sing. 1st declension (portā)

    long in stem 1st conjugation (amā-)

a   short in nom. sing. 1st declension (porta)

    short in neuters (tempora)

-am   short in acc. sing. 1st declension (portam)

-ās   long in acc. plu. 1st declension (portās)

-ē   long in abl. sing. 5th declension (diē)

    long in stem of 2d conjugation (monē-)

    long in adverbs (but short in bene, male, saepe) (pulchrē)

-e   short in abl. sing. 3d declension (mīlite)

    short in neut. 3d declension adjs. (forte)

    short in the verbal ending -re (tenēre)

-em   short in acc. sing. 3d declension (mīlitem)

-ēs   long in nom. and acc. plu. 3d declension (mīlitēs)

-ī   long always (fortī, audī)

-i   usually (but not always) short in mihi, tibi, sibi, ibi, ubi

-īs   long in dat. and abl. plu. 1st and 2d declensions (portīs, puerīs)

    long in acc. plu. 3d declension i-stems (navīs)

-ō   long in dat. and abl. sing. 2d decl. (puerō)

    long (but occasionally short) in verb endings (amō)

-ōs   long in acc. plu. 2d declension (puerōs)

-ū   long always (dictū)

-um   short always (puerum)

-ūs   long in gen. sing., nom. and acc. plu. 4th declension (exercitūs)

-us   short in nom. sing. 2d and 4th declensions (fīlius, exercitus)

C. Case usage

1. Nominative

    a.   predicate § 41–2

    b.   subject § 8

2. Genitive

    a.   descriptive § 50

    b.   measurement § 50

    c.   objective § 50

    d.   partitive § 50

    e.   poetic limiting genitive § 234

    f.   possessive § 8

    g.   with causā or grātiā § 122

    h.   with particular adjectives § 50

    i.   with particular verbs § 50

3. Dative

    a.   after compound verbs § 53

    b.   agency with the gerundive or in poetry § 52, 124, 237

    c.   double dative § 54

        i. dative of reference § 54

        ii. dative of purpose § 52

    d.   indirect object § 8, 51

    e.   poetic dative of place to § 236

    f.   possession § 52

    g.   with particular adjectives § 56

    h.   with 17 'sacred' verbs § 55

4. Accusative

    a.   accusative subject of infinitive § 129

    b.   adverbial accusative § 62

    c.   cognate accusative § 78

    d.   direct object § 8

    e.   double accusative § 78

    f.   duration of time § 79

    g.   exclamatory § 81

    h.   extent of space § 79

    i.   place to which ('motion-toward') with prepositions § 80, 81

    j.   place to which without a preposition ('motion-toward') § 80, 238

    k.   poetic accusative of part of body affected (Greek accusative) § 239

5. Ablative

    a.   ablative absolute § 118–20

    b.   accompaniment § 8, 84

    c.   after certain verbs § 162

    d.   agency § 83, 124

    e.   attendant circumstance § 119

    f.   cause § 87

    g.   comparison § 74

    h.   degree of difference § 74

    i.   description or quality § 87

    j.   manner § 87

    k.   means or instrument § 8, 87

    l.   place-from-which with prepositions § 85, 87

    m. place-from-which without a preposition § 85, 87

    n.   place-where (location) with prepositions § 86

    o.   place-where (location) without a preposition § 241

    p.   respect or specification § 61, 87, 230

    q.   separation § 85

    r.   source § 85

    s.   time when or time within which § 87

6. Locative

    a.   naming towns and small islands § 89

    b.   domī, humī, rūrī § 89

7. Vocative

    a.   direct address § 88

D. Ways of expressing purpose

    a.   ad plus the accusative gerund or gerundive § 122

    b.   double dative § 52, 54

    c.   future participle § 229

    d.   genitive of gerund or gerundive with causā § 122

    e.   genitive of gerund or gerundive with grātiā § 122

    f.   infinitive (poetry) § 229

    g.   quī plus the present or imperfect subjunctive § 187

    h.   quō plus a comparative with the present or imperfect subjunctive § 187

    i.   supine in -um (accusative) after verbs of motion § 146

    j.   ut or nē with the present or imperfect subjunctive § 185–6

GRAMMATICAL APPENDIX 6

WORD ORDER

I know I mar my cause with words.

Gerard Manley Hopkins (1844–1859), 'A Voice from the World'

The following rules generally apply to the translation of English into Latin:

1. The main verb of a clause should appear at the end of its clause, not necessarily at the end of the sentence if the sentence consists of several clauses.

2. In indirect discourse, the head and tel. verb appears before the infinitive, unless the sentence is very short.

3. A complementary infinitive should precede the verb it completes.

4. An adverb precedes the word it modifies.

5. In an ablative absolute, the noun should begin the construction, and the participle (or other ablative element) should end it.

6. If, in English, the expressed subject is in a subordinate clause, and the subject of the main verb is only implied, take the expressed subject out of the subordinate clause, and translate it with the main verb.

7. An adjective should follow the noun it modifies. But hic, ille, is, adjectives of quantity, and possessive adjectives usually stand before their nouns. If the noun is modified by two adjectives, put one before the noun, and the other after it.

Grammatical appendix 7

Some multiple choice questions

Say, lad, have you things to do?
Quick, then, while your day's at prime ....

A. E. Housman (1859–1936), *A Shropshire Lad* XXIV

Choose the best translation for each sentence.

1. I begged him to defend himself and his property.

    a. eum ōrāvī ut sē suaque dēfenderet.

    b. eum ōrāvī ut eum ēiusque dēfenderet.

    c. sē ōrāvī ut sē suaque dēfenderet.

    d. sē orāvī ut eum ēiusque dēfenderet.

2. If he does this, his friends will rejoice.

    a. sī id facit, amīcī suī gaudēbunt.

    b. sī id facit, amīcī ēius gaudēbunt.

    c. sī id fēcerit, amīcī ēius gaudēbunt.

    d. sī id fēcerit, amīcī suī gaudēbunt.

3. Nor did they accept anything else.

    a. neque quid aliud adsecūtī sunt.

    b. neque aliquid aliud adsecūtī sunt.

    c. neque quicquam aliud adsecūtī sunt.

    d. neque quoddam aliud adsecūtī sunt.

4. I asked if anyone knew this.

    a. rogāvī sī aliquis hoc scīret.

    b. rogāvī sī quisquam hoc scīret.

    c. rogāvī sī quis hoc scīret.

    d. rogāvī sī quīdam hoc scīret.

5. I ask these men their opinion.

    a. hīs sententiam rogō.

    b. sententiam hōrum rogō.

    c. hōs sententiam rogō.

    d. ab illīs virīs sententiam rogō.

6. Therefore do not hesitate ...

    a. quārē nē dubitās ...

    b. quārē nōlīte dubitāre ...

    c. quārē nōlītis dubitāre ...

    d. quārē nōn dubitētis ...

7. Suffer the little ones to come unto me (two possibilities).

    a. parcite parvulīs ut ad mē eant.

    b. patiminī parvulōs ad mē venīre.

    c. patiminī parvulōs ut ad mē veniant.

    d. parite parvulōs ut ad mē veniant.

    e. pārēte parvulīs ut ad mē veniant.

    f. sinite parvulōs ad mē venīre.

8. That concerned me.

    a. id mihi rettulit.

    b. id mea rēfert.

    c. id mea interfuit.

    d. id mē cūrābat.

9. We are prevented from leaving (two possibilities).

    a. tenēmur quīn discēdāmus.

    b. tenēmur quī discēdere volumus.

    c. tenēmur nē discēdāmus.

    d. tenēmur quod discēdēmus.

    e. tenēmur quōminus discēdāmus.

10. If the boy should be good, he would be praised.

    a. sī puer est bonus, laudātur.

    b. sī puer fuerit bonus, laudābitur.

    c. sī puer sit bonus, laudētur.

    d. sī puer esset bonus, laudārētur.

11. Would that I hadn't been born!

    a. utinam nē nātus essem!

    b. utinam nē nāscerer!

    c. utinam nē nāscar!

    d. utinam nē nātus sim!

12. I regret having done this.

    a. hōc factō id paenitet.

    b. paenitet mē haec fēcisse.

    c. quod factum est mihi paenitet.

    d. mē paenitet haec facere.

13. quemvīs alium patī possem.

    a. I would be able to endure a certain other man.

    b. Although I could endure another man.

    c. I would be able to endure any other man whatsoever.

    d. Another man whom you wish I could endure.

14. mīlitēs imperātōrī pārent.

    a. The soldiers are preparing for their general.

    b. They obey the general's soldiers.

    c. The soldiers obey the general.

    d. They prepare the soldiers for the general.

15. patriae hīs rēbus nocētur.

    a. He is pleased by these affairs of the state.

    b. He is harmed by these affairs of the state.

    c. The country is harmed by these things.

    d. He envies the state because of these things.s

16. urbī satis praesidī est.

    a. In the city, there is enough protection.

    b. The city's supplies are in the garrison's hands.

    c. The city's garrison is sufficient.

    d. The city has sufficient garrison.

17. amāntissimus patriae erat.

    a. He was very patriotic.

    b. He was the greatest lover in the country.

    c. He was very fond of his father.

    d. His father had a very great lover.

18. oblīvīscere caedis et incendiōrum.

    a. To remember laughter and burning

    b. Forget slaughter and burning!

    c. Remember slaughter and burning!

    d. You cut off your remembrance of the burning also.

19. omnia perīcula parvī dūcenda sunt.

    a. The boys must be led into all dangers.

    b. All the boy's dangers must be faced.

    c. All dangers should be considered of little importance.

    d. You must consider the boy's dangers to be small.

20. cōgnōveram Caesarem flūmen trānsisse.

    a. I had known that Caesar had crossed the river.

    b. I knew that Caesar was crossing the river.

    c. I knew that Caesar had crossed the river.

    d. I learned that Caesar had crossed the river.

21. ōderint dum metuant.

    a. They will have hated while they are afraid.

    b. They may have hated until they feared.

    c. Let them hate provided that they fear.

    d. They hated only while they feared.

22. ēloquar an sileam?

    a. I will speak out and (then) keep silent.

    b. Am I to speak out and keep silent?

    c. Shall I speak or keep silent?

    d. Let me speak out, and I will keep silent.

23. dīcit illās gentēs veritās esse nē Caesar venīret.

    a. He says that those tribes feared that Caesar had come.

    b. He says that those tribes feared that Caesar would come.

    c. He says that those tribes feared that Caesar would not come.

    d. He says that those tribes feared that Caesar had not come.

24. dīxī quid factūrus esset.

    a. I said that he would do anything.

    b. I told what he intended to do.

    c. I told what he had done.

    d. I told what he would have done.

25. explōrātōrēs speculandī causā mīsit.

    a. The spying scouts were sent for a reason.

    b. He sent spying scouts in his cause.

    c. Because of spying, he sent scouts.

    d. He sent scouts to spy.

26. utinam tibi istam mentem dī duint.

    a. For thus the gods gave you that intention.

    b. O gods, may you give me that intention.

    c. Would that the gods would give you that intention.

    d. For so the gods would give you that intention.

27. Vellem hōs sēcum ēdūceret.

    a. I would like those he led out with him.

    b. I would that he were taking these men out with him.

    c. I would like him to take these as his help.

    d. I would that he had taken these men out with him.

28. equitātum suīs auxiliō mīsit.

    a. He sent the cavalry to his auxiliaries.

    b. He sent the cavalry as his auxiliaries.

    c. He sent help to his men to fight as cavalry.

    d. He sent the cavalry to aid his men.

29. hoc facere non potes ut mihi nōn noceās.

    a. You cannot be doing this to harm me.

    b. You cannot be doing this in order not to harm me.

    c. You cannot do this without harming me.

    d. You cannot do this, as you do me no harm.

30. accēdēbat ut nihil saxa timērent.

    a. Added to this was the fact that rocks should fear nothing.

    b. In addition, no one feared the rocks.

    c. In addition, rocks should fear nothing.

    d. Added to this was the fact that they did not fear the rocks at all.

31. cōnsul videt nē quid rēs pūblica dētrīmentī capiat.

    a. The consul sees that the state is suffering no harm.

    b. The consul sees to it that the state may suffer no harm.

    c. The consul takes such care that the state suffers no harm.

    d. The consul does not see what harm the state is suffering.

32. nāves tenēbantur quōminus in eundem portum venīrent.

    a. The ships were prevented from reaching the same harbour.

    b. The ships were led back because they came to the same harbour.

    c. They held back the ships from reaching the same harbour.

    d. The ships were held back less, in order that they could reach the same harbour.

33. verērī videntur ut habeam satis praesidī.

    a. They seem to fear that I may have sufficient protection.

    b. They seem to be feared, as I have sufficient protection.

    c. They fear to see how I may have sufficient protection.

    d. They seem to fear that I may not have sufficient protection.

34. nōn verentur nē id facere nōn possit.

    a. They fear that he will be unable to do this.

    b. They do not fear that he will be able to do this.

    c. They do not fear that he will be unable to do this.

    d. They fear that he may be able to do this.

35. dubitās, Catilīna, abīre?

    a. Do you doubt that he is leaving, Catiline?

    b. Do you leave in doubt, Catiline?

    c. Do you doubt that Catiline is leaving?

    d. Do you hesitate to go away, Catiline?

36. ūnus erat quī addūcī nōn posset.

    a. This was one who could not lead.

    b. One is that man who cannot be led.

    c. There is (always) one man who cannot be persuaded.

    d. He was the only one who could not be persuaded.

37. nōn erit idōneus quī ad bellum Asiāticum mittātur.

    a. He who is being sent to the war in Asia will not be suitable.

    b. He will not be suitable since he was sent to the war in Asia.

    c. He will not be a suitable man to be sent to the war in Asia.

    d. It will not be suitable to send Asiaticus to the war.

38. hoc accidit tum cum fōrtūnās multī āmīsērunt.

    a. This happened then, since many people had lost their fortunes.

    b. This, then, was an accident, since many people had lost their fortunes.

    c. Although many people had lost their fortunes, this was an accident.

    d. This happened at the time when many people had lost their fortunes.

39. ille cum Galliae tum Britanniae magnam partem obtinuit.

    a. He possessed a large part, first of Gaul, and then of Britain.

    b. He then possessed a large part of Britain with Gaul.

    c. He possessed a large part not only of Gaul, but of Britain.

    d. When he was in Gaul, he received a large share of Britain.

40. dum canit quīdam exiit.

    a. Someone went out until he should sing.

    b. A certain man will come out, provided that he sings.

    c. While he is singing, someone leaves.

    d. While he was singing, someone left.

41. exspectāvit dum reliquae nāvēs eō convenīrent.

    a. He waited while the other ships assembled there.

    b. He waited as long as the other ships were assembling there.

    c. He waited until the other ships should assemble there.

    d. He has agreed to wait provided that the other ships assemble there.

42. pāx facta est priusquam proelium commīsērunt.

    a. Peace was made before they began battle.

    b. Peace was made before the battle should be begun.

    c. Peace was made until they should start battle.

    d. Peace was made formerly, but they started a battle.

43. pāx facta est priusquam proelium committerent.

    a. Peace was made before they began battle.

    b. Peace was made before the battle should be begun.

    c. Peace was made until they should start battle.

    d. Peace was made formerly, but they started a battle.

44. Caesar questus est quod bellum ūltrō sibi fēcissent.

    a. Caesar complained because they had voluntarily made war among themselves.

    b. Caesar complained because they had voluntarily made war on him.

    c. Caesar asked what war they had voluntarily waged among themselves.

    d. Caesar inquired because they might voluntarily have waged war among themselves.

45. sīn autem servīre meae laudī māvis ...

    a. But allow me to add to my glory, Mavis, ...

    b. But if you prefer to add to my praise ...

    c. But allow that you prefer to add to my praise ...

    d. But if to add to the praise of my Mavis ...

46. quid tandem tabernīs incēnsīs futūrum fuit?

    a. What, pray, was the future of the burned shops?

    b. What, pray, would have been in the burned shops?

    c. What, pray, would have happened, if the shops had been burned?

    d. Finally, was anything going to happen to the burned shops?

47. mihi imperāvit ut sī servus essem.

    a. He orders me to be his slave.

    b. He gave me orders, and so I was his slave.

    c. He ordered me to be his slave.

    d. He ordered me (about) as if I were his slave.

48. licet ille fortis sit, tamen sē dēdet.

    a. Brave though he be, still he will surrender.

    b. He is permitted to be brave; yet he surrenders.

    c. He grants that he is brave; yet he will surrender.

    d. Although it pleases him to be brave, yet he will surrender.

49. vīsum est Caesarī in Galliam contendere.

    a. He was seen hastening into Gaul to Caesar.

    b. It seemed he was hastening into Gaul to Caesar.

    c. Caesar seemed to be hastening into Gaul.

    d. It seemed best to Caesar to hasten into Gaul.

50. interficiātur oportet.

    a. Let him be put to death as he deserves.

    b. He ought to be put to death.

    c. It is permitted for him to be killed.

    d. It is shameful that he should be killed.

51. eum interficī oportet.

    a. He ought to be put to death.

    b. It is fitting to kill him.

    c. It is permitted for him to kill.

    d. It suits him to be killed.

52. mihi venīre licuit.

    a. He may come to me.

    b. I might have come.

    c. I am allowed to come.

    d. He could have come to me.

53. negat sē posse iter dare.

    a. He refuses to grant him a passage.

    b. He denies granting a passage to him.

    c. He says he cannot grant a passage.

    d. He says he cannot grant him a passage.

54. dīxit fore ut posset.

    a. He said that he was able to come.

    b. He said that he would be able.

    c. He easily said that he could.

    d. He said that he was able to speak.

55. hoc optimum factū putābant.

    a. After this had happened, they thought very hard.

    b. They thought that this excellent thing had been done.

    c. They thought that this was the best thing to do.

    d. After doing this excellent thing, they took thought.

56. hōs ad Caesarem mittunt rogātum auxilium.

    a. They asked for help and sent these men to Caesar.

    b. They sent these men to Casear, as the help he had asked for.

    c. This help they sent to Caesar as asked.

    d. They sent these men to Caesar to ask for help.

57. ut prīmum loquī posse coepī.

        a. So that I would be able to speak first.

        b. So that I began to be able to speak first.

        c. When I began to be able to speak first.

        d. As soon as I began to be able to speak.

58. ut hoc prōfectō vērum est!

        a. As I set out, this is true!

        b. I assure you that this is true!

        c. Assuredly, this is true!

        d. I profess that this is the truth!

        e. Assuredly, how true this is!

59. Match the left column to its appropriate translation.

    a. cōnsulis pessimē   i. By the consul's worst action.

    b. cōnsilium cōnsulis   ii. The consul's is worst.

    c. concilium cōnsulum   iii. You give very bad advice.

    d. senātūs cōnsultum   iv. The meeting of the consuls.

                           v. The consuls' appeasement.

                        vi. It is the plan which you advise.

                      vii. After consulting the senate.

                    viii. A senatorial plan.

                        ix. The consuls' plan.

                         x. A senatorial decree.

                      xi. A consul's plan.

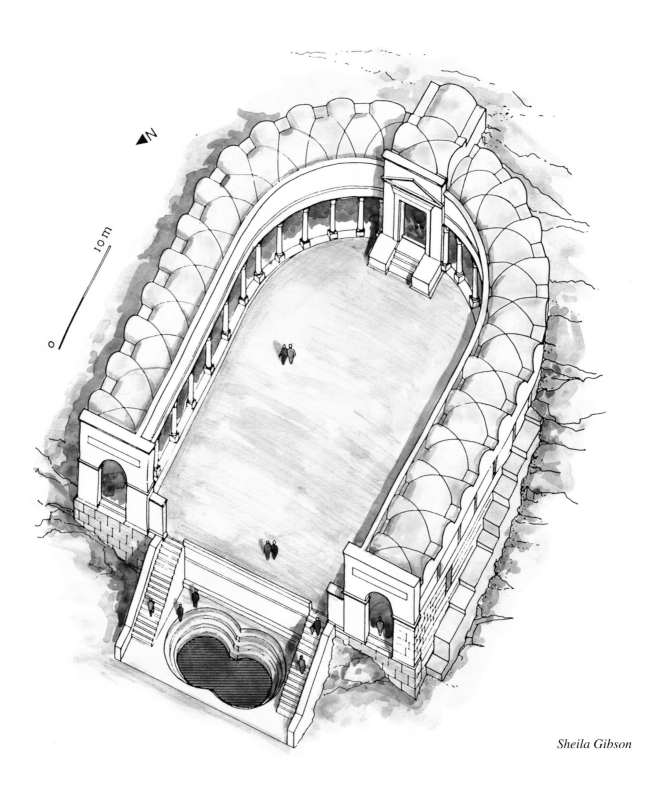

Sheila Gibson

Fig. 31. The Sanctuary of the Nymphs near Zaghouan, the source of the aqueduct that supplied Carthage. It dates to around the second century AD.

PART TWO:

Readings from Livy

The Latin authors which the form were doing were Livy and Virgil, and when either of these were on the next day's programme, most of the Sixth considered that they were justified in taking a night off. They relied on their ability to translate both authors at sight and without previous acquaintance.

P. G. Wodehouse (1881–1975), 'The Manoeuvres of Charteris' in *Tales of St Austin's*

INTRODUCTORY NOTE

Livy claimed to have read all Greek and Latin annals. The claim may even be true, although it smacks of the defensive pride which drove Lawrence of Arabia to claim that he had read all the books in the Oxford Union Library.

R. M. Ogilvie, *A Commentary on Livy Books 1-5* (1965), 5

The readings that follow are taken from a history of Rome written by the Augustan writer Titus Livius, more commonly known as Livy (ca. 59 BC–AD 17). Livy recorded Roman history from its foundation and is one of the principal sources for much of what we know – or think we know – about early Rome. By no means, however, may the work of Livy be called a primary source. He had access to private records and state archives, but these are unlikely to have dated as far back as the eighth century BC, and claims and traditions regarding Roman ancestry often depended on political and propagandistic context.

The texts that follow have not been simplified or adapted. Because of the violence described, some of what Livy writes may worry those concerned to keep boys and girls 'unspotted from the world'. But to omit or mollify the content of these episodes would be to do disservice to a great writer. Livy's history, in other words, is not for children.

Sheila Gibson

Fig. 32. Shops along the sea front at Carthage, dating mainly to the early fifth century AD. The shops are on two levels, with porticoes along the bottom. There are balconies above.

ESCAPE FROM TROY:

The arrival of Aeneas in Italy

> *O Muse! relate me the facts, if you happen to know 'em*
> *Concerning the hero of this astonishing poem;*
> *Explain why the queen of the gods was so terribly eager*
> *So clever and pious a man at each step to beleaguer; –*
> *Why with wrath she pursued him, – with shipwreck and tempest and thunder:*
> *Do they cultivate such reprehensible morals up yonder?*

> Thomas Worth, *A free and independent translation of the* Aeneid *of Virgil ...*
> *Designed for the use of families, schools, and colleges, and especially for students in Virgil,*
> *into whose hands this volume may be put without the least danger of its being used as a pony* (1870)

The most famous account of the wanderings of the Trojan hero after the fall of Troy is the *Aeneid*, composed by Virgil in the first century BC, during the reign of Augustus. Livy, a contemporary of Virgil, records a variant account. Here, he describes the wandering of Aeneas (Aenēās, Aenēae, m.; dat. Aenēae, acc. Aenēan, abl. Aenēā) and his beleaguered army of Trojan warriors (Trōiānī, Trōiānōrum, m.), who finally land in an area of Italy ruled by King Latinus (Latīnus, Latīnī, m.), presumably around the twelfth century BC.

Vocabulary

ager, agrī, m.	field
brevis, breve	short
error, errōris, m.	wandering, error
fidēs, fideī, f.	faith, belief; *that which creates faith or belief:*
	loyalty, promise, protection, evidence, fulfilment
foedus, foederis, n.	treaty
nāvis, nāvis, f.	ship
nōmen, nōminis, n.	name
pāx, pācis, f.	peace
quaerō, quaerere, quaesīvī, quaesītum	look for, enquire
teneō, tenēre, tenuī, —	hold

Ibi ēgressī, Trōiānī, ut quibus ab immēnsō prope errōre nihil praeter arma et nāvēs superesset, cum praedam ex agrīs agerent, Latīnus rēx Aborīginēsque, quī tum ea tenēbant loca, ad arcendam vim advenārum, armātī ex urbe atque agrīs concurrunt.[1] Duplex inde fāma est.[2] Aliī proeliō vīctum Latīnum pācem cum Aeneā, deinde adfīnitātem iūnxisse trādunt.[3] Aliī, cum īnstrūctae aciēs cōnstitissent, priusquam sīgna canerent, prōcessisse Latīnum inter prīmōrēs, ducemque advenārum ēvocāvisse ad conloquium.[4]

Percontātum deinde quī mortālēs essent, unde aut quō cāsū profectī domō, quidve quaerentēs in agrum Laurentem exīvissent.[5] Postquam audīerit multitūdinem Trōiānōs esse, ducem Aenēan, fīlium Anchīsae et

---

[1] **ibi** – there (*i.e.*, Italy); **Trōiānī** is the subject of the cum-clause (*i. e.*, the straightforward word order would be 'cum Trōiānī praedam ex agrīs agerent, etc.'); **ut** – explanatory ('since') with a subjunctive verb, the approximate equivalent of a causal cum-clause with the subjunctive; **quibus** – the third person plural relative pronoun used instead of the equivalent personal pronoun; **immēnsus, -a, -um** – immeasurable; **prope** – nearly (*adverbial*); as an adverb, it qualifies **immēnsō**; **praeter** (*with acc.*) – except for; **arma, armōrum**, n. pl. – arms; **supersum, superesse, superfuī, superfutūrum** – remain, survive; **praeda, praedae**, f. – booty; **Aborīginēs, Aborīginum**, m. pl. – native inhabitants; **arceō, arcēre, arcuī, —** – hinder; **advena, advenae**, m. – newcomer; **armō, armāre, armāvī, armātum** – arm; **concurrō, concurrere, concurrī, concursum** – run together.

[2] **duplex, duplicis** – double, of two sorts; **inde** – then; from that point; **fāma, fāmae**, f. – story, rumour.

[3] **aliī ... aliī** – some ... others; the main verb is **trādunt** at the end of the sentence, used here as a verb of mental action ('pass on the tradition that ...'); **proelium, proeliī**, n. – battle; **adfīnitās, adfīnitātis**, f. – connection by marriage; **iungō, iungere, iūnxī, iūnctum** – enter into (usually the verb means 'join' or 'join together'); **trādō, trādere, trādidī, trāditum** – pass on.

[4] This and the following sentences are in indirect speech with a verb of speech understood; **īnstruō, īnstruere, īnstrūxī, īnstrūctum** – draw up; **aciēs, aciēī**, f. – line of battle; **cōnsistō, cōnsistere, cōnstitī, cōnstitum** – stop, stand, make a stand; **sīgnum, sīgnī**, n. – sign, standard; **signa** – acc. with **canerent**; understand the subject as 'trumpeters' or other such; **canō, canere, cecinī, —** – sound, sing; **prōcēdō, prōcēdere, prōcessī, —** – proceed; **prīmōris, prīmōre** – chief; **ēvocō, ēvocāre, ēvocāvī, ēvocātum** – call out; **conloquium, conloquī**, n. – conference.

[5] **percontor, percontārī, percontātus sum** – enquire; **unde** – from where; **aut** – or; **cāsus, cāsūs**, m. – event, misfortune, chance; **quō cāsū** – abl. of cause; **-ve** – or (*enclitic*); **Laurēns, Laurentis** – of or belonging to Laurentium, a coastal town in Latium.

Veneris, cremātā patriā, domō profugōs, sēdem condendaeque urbī locum quaerere, et nōbilitātem admīrātum

gentis virīque et animum vel bellō vel pācī parātum,[6] dextrā datā, fidem futūrae amīcitiae sānxisse.[7]

Inde foedus ictum inter ducēs. Inter exercitūs salūtātiōnem factam.[8] Aenēan apud Latīnum fuisse in hos-

pitiō.[9] Ibi Latīnum apud penātēs deōs domesticum pūblicō adiūnxisse foedus, fīliā Aenēae in mātrimōnium

datā.[10]

Ea rēs utique Trōiānīs spem adfirmat tandem stabilī certāque sēde fīniendī errōris.[11] Oppidum condunt.

Aenēās ab nōmine uxōris Lāvīnium appellat.[12] Brevī stirpis quoque virīlis ex novō mātrimōniō fuit, cuī

Ascānium parentēs dīxēre nōmen.[13]

Livy 1. 1. 5–11

---

[6] **multitūdō, multitūdinis**, f. – multitude; after its initial use as an infinitive with indirect statement, **esse** needs to be
supplied again for each of the descriptive clauses for which there is no infinitive **Anchīsēs, Anchīsae**, m. – Anchises
(father of Aeneas); **Venus, Veneris**, f. – Venus; **cremō, cremāre, cremāvī, cremātum** – consume by fire; **profugus,
profugī**, m. – exile; **sēdēs, sēdis**, f. – seat, abode; **condendaeque urbī** – dative of purpose; **nōbilitās, nobilitātis**, f. –
nobility; **gēns, gentis**, f. – race; **bellum, bellī**, n. – war; **vel ... vel** – either ... or; **parō, parāre, parāvī, parātum** –
prepare.

[7] **dexter, dextra, dextrum** – right; **dextrā = dextrā manū**; **amīcitia, amīcitiae**, f. – friendship; **futūrae amīcitiae** –
objective gen.; **sanciō, sancīre, sānxī, sānctum** – confirm.

[8] **inde** – then; **īciō, īcere, īcī, ictum** – strike; **salūtātiō, salūtātiōnis**, f. – greeting, saluting.

[9] **hospitium, hospitī**, n. – hospitality.

[10] **penātēs, penātium**, m. – guardian deities of the household; **domesticus, -a, -um** – domestic; **pūblicus, -a, -um** –
public; understand the word foedus again; **adiungō, -ere, adiūnxi, adiūnctum** – join; **mātrimōnium, mātrimōnī**, n.
– marriage.

[11] **utique** – at any rate; **adfirmō, adfirmāre, adfirmāvī, adfirmātum** – strengthen; **tandem** – at last; **stabilis, stabile**
– stable; **certus, -a, -um** – certain, fixed; **sēde** – abl. of means; **fīniō, fīnīre, fīnīvī, fīnītum** – put an end to; **fīniendī
errōris** is an objective genitive depending on **spem**.

[12] **appellō, appellāre, appellāvī, appellātum** – call

[13] **brevī = brevī tempore**; **stirpis, stirpis**, m. – offspring; **quoque** – also; **virīlis, -e** - male, **novus, -a, -um** – new;
parēns, parentis, m. and f. – parent; **dīxēre = dīxērunt**; **nōmen dīcere** – give the name; according to Virgil, Ascanius
was the son of Aeneas and his first wife, Creusa.

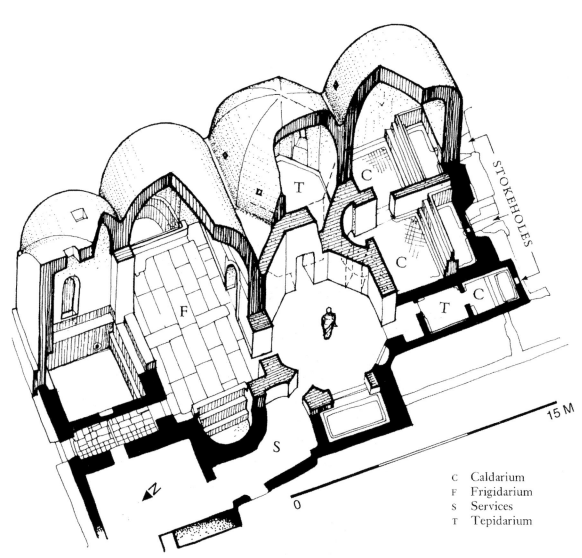

STOKEHOLES

C

C

C

T

C

T

F

S

Z

15 M

0

C Caldarium
F Frigidarium
S Services
T Tepidarium

Sheila Gibson

Fig. 33. The Hunting Baths at Lepcis Magna in modern Libya, dating to the late second or early third century AD. The baths had three types of rooms for the visitors: the tepidarium (warm room), the caldarium (hot room), and the frigidarium (an unheated room).

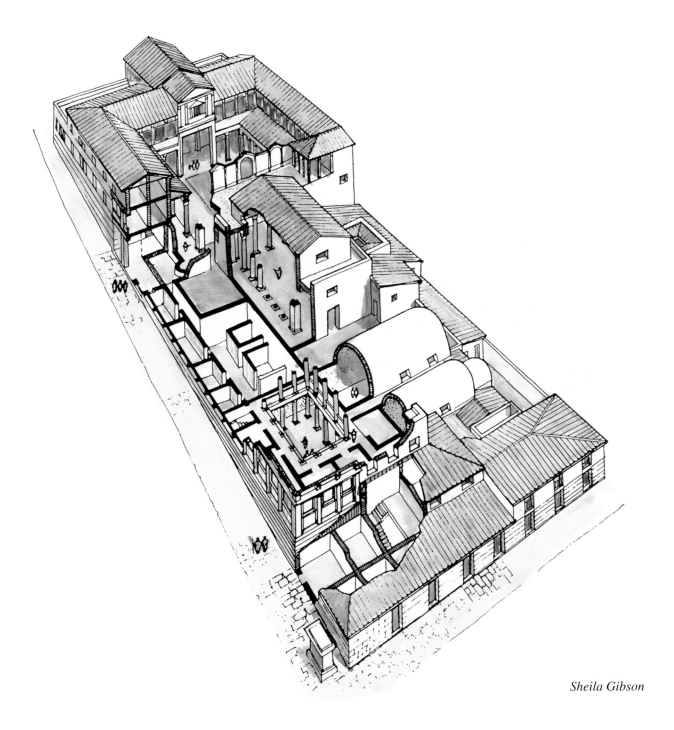

Sheila Gibson

Fig. 34. The 'Palazzo delle Colonne,' a wealthy private residence in Ptolemais in modern Libya, built in the first century BC or the first century AD. There are also shops along the north street frontage.

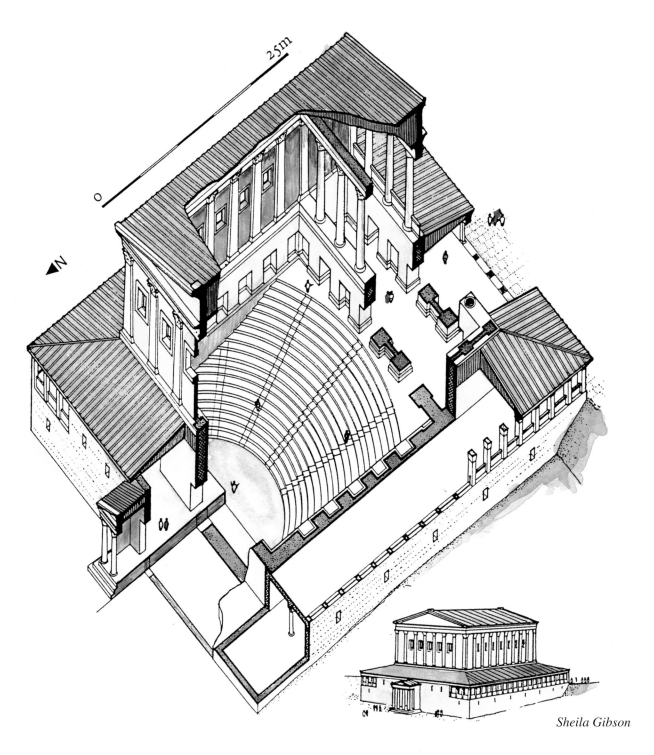

Sheila Gibson

Fig. 35. The Odeum of Agrippa, built around 15 BC in the agora in Athens. The building seated about 1,000 spectators. M. V. Agrippa (ca. 64 – ca. 12 BC) had been a lifelong friend of Augustus and a successful military commander, who used his accumulated wealth to improve the sewage system of Rome. He also made architectural benefactions around the empire.

ROMULUS AND REMUS:

The wolf and the shepherd

*Her princes in the midst thereof are like wolves ravening the prey, to shed blood,
and to destroy souls, to get dishonest gain.*

Ezekiel 22: 27

The image of a wolf suckling Romulus (Rōmulus, -ī, m.) and Remus (Remus, -ī, m.) is one of the best known in Roman history, depicted in art that ranges from the famous bronze in the Capitoline Museum (though the statues of the babies are Renaissance work) to a painting by Jackson Pollock (in which the wolf – and the children too, if any – is, predictably enough, difficult to find). The tale belongs to the realm of legend. The theme of the doomed child, exposed to the elements but miraculously saved, who returns home to cause a ruler trouble, is common in folklore and apparent in stories of such figures as Perseus, Oedipus, Cyrus the Great, and Moses.

Vocabulary

aqua, aquae, f.	water
expōnō, expōnere, exposuī, expositum	expose, put forth
legō, legere, lēgī, lēctum	collect, choose, read, skim along
magister, magistrī, m.	master
putō, putāre, putāvī, putātum	think
rēgnum, rēgnī, n.	rule, kingdom
reor, rērī, ratus sum	think
sacerdōs, sacerdōtis, m. and f.	priest
scelus, sceleris, n.	crime
voluntās, voluntātis, f.	will, good will, consent

Proca deinde regnat.[1] Is Numitōrem atque Amūlium prōcreat.[2] Numitōrī, quī stirpis māximus erat, rēgnum vetustum Silviae gentis lēgat.[3]

Plūs tamen vīs potuit quam voluntās patris aut verēcundia aetātis.[4] Pulsō frātre, Amūlius rēgnat.[5] Addit scelerī scelus. Stirpem frātris virīlem interimit.[6] Frātris fīliae Reae Silviae, per speciem honōris, cum Vestālem eam lēgisset, perpetuā virginitāte spem partūs adimit.[7]

Sed dēbēbātur (ut opīnor) fātīs tantae orīgō urbis māximīque secundum deōrum opēs imperī principium.[8] Vī compressa, Vestālis, cum geminum partum ēdidisset, seu ita rata seu quia deus auctor culpae honestior erat,

---

[1] **Proca, Procae**, m. – king of Alba Longa, into which region Ascanius had migrated after his father's death; **rēgnō, rēgnāre, rēgnāvī, rēgnātum** – rule.

[2] **Numitor, Numitōris**, m. – brother of Amulius, grandfather of Romulus and Remus; **Amūlius, Amūlī**, m. – Alban king after Proca; **prōcreō, prōcreāre, prōcreāvī, prōcreatum** – breed, beget.

[3] **stirpis, stirpis**, m. and f. – offspring; **māximus = māximus nātū** ('greatest by birth;' i. e., the eldest); **vetustus, -a, -um** – ancient; **Silvius, -a, -um** – belonging to the Silvian kings of Alba Longa; **gēns, gentis**, f. – race, nation, family; **lēgō, lēgāre, lēgāvī, lēgātum** – bequeath.

[4] **potuit – possum** here means 'to be powerful', taken with **plūs** (more); **patris,** together with **aetatis**, are objective genitives; **verēcundia, verēcundiae**, f. – reverence; **aetās, aetātis**, f. – age.

[5] **pellō, pellere, pepulī, pulsum** – drive, rout; **frāter, frātris**, m. – brother.

[6] **virīlis, virīle** – male; **interimō, interimere, interēmī, interēmptum** – kill.

[7] **fratris** – gen. dependent on **fīliae** which is in apposition to **Reae Silviae** (dat. of reference or a so-called dat. of disadvantage); **Rea Silvia, Reae Silviae**, f. – daughter of Numitor; mother of Romulus and Remus; **per** – 'on the pretext of' (rather than simply 'through'); **speciēs, speciēī**, f. – appearance; **honor, honōris**, m. – honour; **Vestālis, Vestālis**, f. – a Vestal priestess (who was not allowed to marry); **perpetuus, -a, -um** – continuous, everlasting; **virginitās, virginitātis**, f. – virginity; **partus, partūs**, m. – birth, offspring; **adimō, adimere, adēmī, adēmptum** – take away.

[8] **dēbēbatur** is in the singular, even though it has two subjects **orīgō** and **principium**, since these are closely related ideas; **opīnor, opīnārī, opīnātus sum** – suppose; **fātum, fātī**, n. – destiny; fate; **tantae urbis** as a gen. phrase is dependent on **orīgō, orīginis**, f. – origin; **māximus, -a, -um** - means 'richest' in this context; the gen. phrase **māximī imperī** is dependent on **principium**; **secundum** – (*prep. with acc.*) following after; **opēs, opum**, f. – wealth, resources; **principium, principī**, n. – beginning.

Mārtem incertae stirpis patrem nūncupat.[9]

Sed nec dī nec hominēs aut ipsam aut stirpem ā crūdēlitāte rēgiā vindicant.[10] Sacerdōs vīncta in custōdiam dātur.[11] Puerōs in prōfluentem aquam mittī iubet.[12]

Fōrte quādam dīvīnitus, super rīpās Tiberis effūsus lēnibus stāgnīs; nec adīrī usquam ad iūstī cursum poterat amnis.[13]   Et posse, quamvis languidā, mergī aquā īnfantēs spem ferentibus dābat.[14]   Ita velut dēfūnctī rēgis imperiō, in proximā adluviē ubi nunc fīcus Rūmīnālis est — Rōmulārem vocātam ferunt — puerōs expōnunt.[15] Vastae tum in hīs locīs sōlitūdinēs erant.[16]

---

[9]   **comprimō, comprimere, compressī, compressum** – repress, suppress; **geminus, -a, -um** – twin; **ēdō, ēdere, ēdidī, ēditum** – give out; **seu ... seu** – whether ... or; **quia** – because; **auctor, auctōris**, m. – author, founder; **culpa, culpae**, f. – fault, blame; **honestus, -a, -um** – honourable; Livy, in other words, claims that Rea Silvia may have said that Mars was the father of her children, because this was better than claiming the children were illegitimate ; **Mārs, Mārtis**, m. – Mars, god of agriculture, pasture, and war; **incertus, -a, -um** – uncertain; **esse** is the implied infinitive of the indirect statement with the main verb **nūncupō, nūncupāre, nūncupāvī, nūncupātum** – announce publicly.

[10]   **dī = deī**; **ipsam** refers to Rea Silvia; **crūdēlitās, crūdēlitātis**, f. – cruelty; **rēgius, -a, -um** – royal; **vindicō, vindicāre, vindicāvī, vindicātum** – rescue.

[11]   **vinciō, vincīre, vinxī, vīnctum** – bind; **custōdia, custōdiae**, f. – prison.

[12]   **prōfluō, prōfluere, prōfluxī, prōfluxum** – flow; the understood subject of **iubet** is Amulius.

[13]   **fōrs, fōrtis**, f. – chance; **dīvīnitus** – by divine providence; **rīpa, rīpae**, f. – bank; **Tiberis** is nominative; **effundō, effundere, effūdī, effūsum** – pour out; **effūsus = effūsus est**; **lēnis, lēne** – gentle; **stāgnum, stāgnī**, n. – pool of standing water; **lēnibus stāgnīs** – abl. of means; **adeō, adīre, adīvī, adītum** – go to; approach; **usquam** – at any place; **iūstus, -a, -um** – regular; in theory, **ad iūstī cursum** should read **ad iūstum cursum** ('near its regular course'), but the epithet has been transferred from the course itself to the river, which is the presumed genitive noun which **iūstī** would modify; **cursus, cursūs**, m. – course; **amnis, amnis**, m. – current (of a river or stream).

[14]   The assumed subject of the main verb **dābat** is the fact of the Tiber having overflowed; **quamvīs** – although; the adverb qualifies **languidā**; **languidus, -a, -um** – sluggish; **mergō, mergere, mērsī, mērsum** – overwhelm; **īnfāns, īnfantis** – young; **ferentibus** – the dat. pres. act. participle should be taken with **spem** and the direct objects of **ferentibus** are Romulus and Remus (**īnfantēs**): 'hope to those carrying the children that ...'

[15]   **velut** – just as if; **dēfungor, dēfungī, dēfūnctus sum** – discharge (*with abl.*); **adluviēs, adluviēī**, f. – pool of water; **fīcus, fīcī**, f. – fig-tree; **Rūmīnālis, Rūmīnāle** – of Rumina, a Roman goddess of nursing; **Rōmulāris, Rōmulāre** – of Romulus; **ferunt** – 'they say' (rather than 'bear' or 'carry'); understand **eam**, referring to the fig-tree, as the subject of the indirect statement; **vocō, vocāre, vocāvī, vocātum** – call.

[16]   **vastus, -a, -um** – huge, desolate; **sōlitūdō, sōlitūdinis**, f. – desert.

Tenet fāma, cum fluitantem alveum, quō expositī erant puerī, tenuis in siccō aqua dēstituisset, lupam sitientem, ex mōntibus quī circā sunt, ad puerīlem vāgītum cursum flēxisse;[17] eam submissās īnfantibus adeō mītem praebuisse mammās ut linguā lambentem puerōs magister rēgiī pecoris invēnerit.[18]

Faustulō fuisse nōmen ferunt;[19] ab eō, ad stabula, Lārentiae uxōrī ēducandōs datōs.[20] Sunt quī Lārentiam, vulgātō corpore, 'lupam' inter pāstōrēs vocātam putent;[21] inde locum fābulae ac mīrāculō datum.[22]

Livy 1. 3. 9 – 4. 7

---

[17] **fāma, famae**, f. – rumour; **fluitō, fluitāre, fluitāvī, fluitātum** – float; iterative of **fluō**; **alveus, alveī**, m. – basket, container; **quō** – where; **tenuis, tenue** – shallow; **siccus, -a, -um** – dry (land); **dēstituō, dēstituere, dēstituī, dēstitūtum** – abandon; **lupa, lupae**, f. – wolf; **sitiō, sitīre**, —, — – thirst; **puerīlis, puerīle** – childish, boyish; **vāgītus, vāgītūs**, m. – crying; **cursus, -ūs**, m. – course; **flectō, flectere, flēxī, flexum** – bend.

[18] The text is still in indirect statement; **submittō, submittere, submīsī, submissum** – lower; **mītis, mīte** – gentle; **adeō mītem** is adverbial ('so gently'); **praebeō, praebēre, praebuī, praebitum** – offer; **mamma, mammae**, f. – teat; **ut** introduces a result clause; **lingua, linguae**, f. – tongue; **lambō, lambere**, —, — – lick; the participle **lambentem** is understood to refer to the wolf, the direct object of **invēnerit**; **pecus, pecoris**, n. – herd; **inveniō, invenīre, invēnī, inventum** – find.

[19] The dat. of possession **eō** needs to be understood with **nōmen**; **Faustulus, Faustulī**, m. – Faustulus (the name of the master of the royal flock); the dat. is used in parallel with the understood **eō**; for **ferunt**, see above, n. 15 ('they say …')

[20] Understand **ferunt** again as the main verb of the indirect statement; understand the boys (**puerōs**) as the subject of the indirect statement; **stabulum, stabulī**, n. – quarters; **Lārentia, Lārentiae**, f. – Larentia (wife of Faustulus); **ēducō, ēducāre, ēducāvī, ēducātum** – educate; the gerundive expresses purpose; **datōs = datōs esse**.

[21] **vulgō, vulgāre, vulgāvī, vulgātum** – make general or common; the ablative absolute suggests causality: 'because she had been generous with her personal favours'; **vocātam = vocātam esse**.

[22] The indirect statement construction continues; **inde** – then; **locus, locī**, m. – 'grounds' (*i.e.*, 'reason,' rather than 'place') **fābula, fābulae**, f. – tale; **mīrāculum, mīrāculī**, n. – wonder; **datum = datum esse**.

Fig. 36. Theatre of Ephesus in Turkey, enlarged in the second half of the first century AD.

Fig. 37. The façade of the Library of Celsus at Ephesus in Turkey, ca. AD 117-120, which is an example of Roman baroque architecture.

Romulus and Remulus:

The birth of Rome

Any labour I do wants time.

An anagram of the proverb 'Rome was not built in a day'

After Romulus and Remus had grown up, they learnt the truth of their birth and restored Numitor to the kingship of Alba Longa. They then decided to build the city which became Rome, founded, according to tradition, in 753 BC.

Vocabulary

aetās, aetātis, f.	age
cadō, cadere, cecidī, casum	fall
certāmen, certāminis, n.	conflict, struggle
cupīdō, cupīdinis, f.	desire
facilis, facile	easy
facile	easily
interveniō, intervenīre, intervēnī, interventum	intrude upon (*with dat.*)
īra, īrae, f.	anger, angry impulse
multitūdō, multitūdinis, f.	multitude
nūntiō, nūntiāre, nūntiāvī, nūntiātum	report
principium, principī, n.	beginning

Ita, Numitōrī Albānā rē permissā, Rōmulum Remumque cupīdō cēpit in iīs locīs ubi expositī ubique ēducātī erant urbis condendae.[1]   Et supererat multitūdō Albānōrum Latīnōrumque.[2]   Ad id pāstōrēs quoque accesserant, quī omnēs facile spem facerent parvam Albam, parvum Lāvīnium prae eā urbe quae conderētur fore.[3]

Intervēnit deinde hīs cōgitātiōnibus avītum malum: rēgnī cupīdō; atque inde foedum certāmen coortum ā satis mītī principiō.[4]   Quoniam geminī essent nec aetātis verēcundiā discrīmen facere posset, ut dī, quōrum tūtēlae ea loca essent, auguriīs legerent quī nōmen novae urbī daret, quī conditam imperiō regeret, Palātium Rōmulus, Remus Aventīnum, ad inaugurandum, templa capiunt.[5]

---

[1]   **Albānus, -a, -um** – of Alba Longa; **Albānā rē = Albānā rē pūblicā**; **permittō, permittere, permīsī, permissum** – entrust; **iīs locīs** – the third person personal pronoun in this instance acts as the equivalent of **illīs**; **ēducō, ēducāre, ēducāvī, ēducātum** – educate; **urbis condendae** = objective gen. with **cupīdō**.

[2]   **supersum, superesse, superfuī, superfutūrum** – to be in superabundance; *i.e.*, there was such a surge in population that a move to a new city had to be contemplated; **Albānī, Albānōrum**, m. – inhabitants of Alba Longa; **Latīnī, Latīnōrum**, m. – inhabitants of Latium

[3]   **id** refers to the fact of the superfluity in population; **pāstor, pāstōris**, m. – herdsman; **accēdō, accēdere, accessī, accessum** – to be added; **quoque** – also; **quī** introduces what is essentially a clause of result (*i.e.*, there were so many herdsmen that expectations for a larger city grew); **spem facere** – to raise the expectation; **parvus, -a, -um** – small; **Alba, Albae**, f. – Alba Longa, mother city of Rome, built by Ascanius; **Lāvīnium, Lāvīnī**, n. – Lavinium, city in Latium founded by Aeneas; **prae** (*prep. with abl.*) – in comparison with.

[4]   **cōgitātiō, cōgitātiōnis**, f. – plan, design; **avītus, -a, -um** – ancestral; **rēgnī** – objective gen. with **cupīdō**; **foedus, -a, -um** – foul; **coorior, coorīrī, coortus sum** – arise suddenly; **coortum = coortum est**; **satis** – enough (*adv.* taken with **mītī**); **mītis, mīte** – gentle.

[5]   **quoniam** introduces a causal clause as if it were a cum-clause with the subjunctive; the subject of the clause is contained in **posset**, which is used impersonally; **geminī, geminōrum**, m. – twins; **aetātis** = objective gen.; **verēcundia, verēcundiae**, f. – respect; **discrīmen, discrīminis**, n. – difference; **ut** introduces a purpose clause with the subjunctive, dependent on the main verb **capiunt**; **dī = deī**; **tūtēla, tūtēlae**, f. – protection (gen. of possession dependent on **ea loca** with the relative pronoun **quōrum**: 'under whose protection'); **ea** is the equivalent of **illa**; **augurium, auguriī**, n. – bird-omen; **conditam = conditam urbem**; **imperium, imperī**, n. – power; **Palātium, Palātiī**, n. – Palatine hill, one of the seven hills of Rome; **Aventīnum, Aventīnī**, n. – Aventine, one of the seven hills of Rome; **ad** + gerund expresses purpose; **inaugurō, inaugurāre, inaugurāvī, inaugurātum** – take an augury in; **templum, templī**, n. – 'an open place for observation,' a special meaning with reference to auguries; normally the word means 'temple;' the neuter plural **templa** is used in apposition (loosely) with **Palātium** and **Aventīnum**.

Priōrī Remō augurium vēnisse fertur: sex vulturēs; iamque nūntiātō auguriō, cum duplex numerus Rōmulō sē ostendisset, utrumque rēgem sua multitūdō cōnsalūtāverat:[6] tempore illī praeceptō, at hī numerō avium rēgnum trahēbant.[7]

Inde, cum altercātiōne congressī, certāmine īrārum ad caedem vertuntur.[8]   Ibi in turbā ictus, Remus cecidit.[9]   Vulgātior fāma est lūdibriō frātris Remum novōs trānsiluisse mūrōs; inde ab īrātō Rōmulō, cum verbīs quoque increpitans adiēcisset, 'sīc deinde, quīcumque alius trānsiliet moenia mea,' interfectum.[10]   Ita sōlus potītus imperiō Rōmulus;[11] condita urbs conditōris nōmine appellāta.[12]

Livy 1. 6. 3 – 7. 3

---

[6]   **priōrī** (first) modifies **Remō**; birds appear to Remus before they appear to Romulus; **fertur** – 'it is said;' **sex** – six; **vultur, vulturis**, m. – vulture; **duplex, duplicis** – double; **numerus, numerī**, m. – number; **ostendō, ostendere, ostendī, ostentum** – show; **sua multitūdō** – 'his own crowd;' the reflexive adjective refers to Romulus and Remus in turn; **cōnsalūtō, cōnsalūtāre, cōnsalūtāvī, cōnsalūtātum** – hail.

[7]   **illī ... hī** – the former ... the latter (taken with ablatives of means); **praecipiō, praecipere, praecēpī, praeceptum** – receive in advance; anticipate; **avis, avis**, f. – bird; **trahō, trahere, traxī, tractum** – to lay claim to (rather than the more common meaning of 'draw' or 'drag').

[8]   **altercātiō, altercātiōnis**, f. – dispute; **congredior, congredī, congressus sum** – meet; **congressī = congressī essent; certāmine** is an ablative of separation; **caedēs, caedis**, f. – slaughter; **vertō, vertere, vertī, versum** – turn.

[9]   **turba, turbae**, f. – crowd; **īciō, īcere, īcī, ictum** – strike.

[10]   **vulgātus, -a, -um** – common; **fāma, fāmae**, f. – rumour; **lūdibrium, lūdibrī**, n. – mockery (perhaps a dat. of purpose with the objective gen. **frātris**); **frāter, frātris**, m. – brother, **novus, -a, -um** – new; **quīcumque alius** – 'whoever else;' **trānsiliō, trānsilīre, trānsiluī, —** – leap; **īrātus, -a, -um** – angry; **increpitō, increpitāre, —, —** – frequentative of **increpō, increpāre, increpuī, increpitum** (chide, harass); **adiciō, adicere, adiēcī, adiectum** – 'added to the offence'; **sīc deinde** – add a main verb such as **'pereat'** ('may he perish'); **interficiō, interficere, interfēcī, interfectum** – kill; **interfectum = interfectum esse.**

[11]   **potītus = potītus est** (*with abl.*).

[12]   **conditōr, conditōris**, m. – founder; **appellō, appellāre, appellāvī, appellātum** – call; **appellāta = appellāta est.**

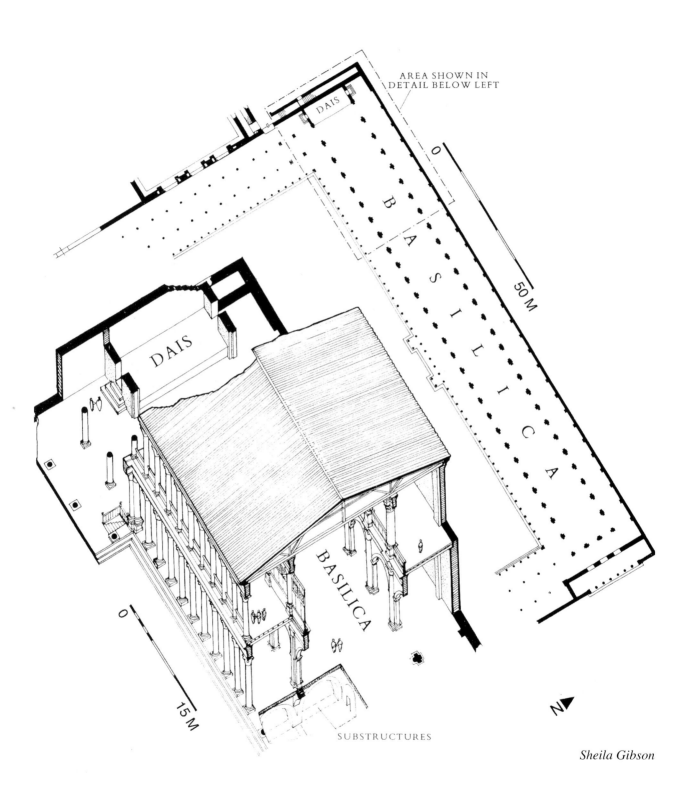

AREA SHOWN IN
DETAIL BELOW LEFT

DAIS

DAIS

B A S I L I C A

0

50 M

BASILICA

0

15 M

SUBSTRUCTURES

N

Sheila Gibson

Fig. 38. The agora at Smyrna in Turkey, mid-second century AD. This is a detail of the two-storeyed basilica to the north.

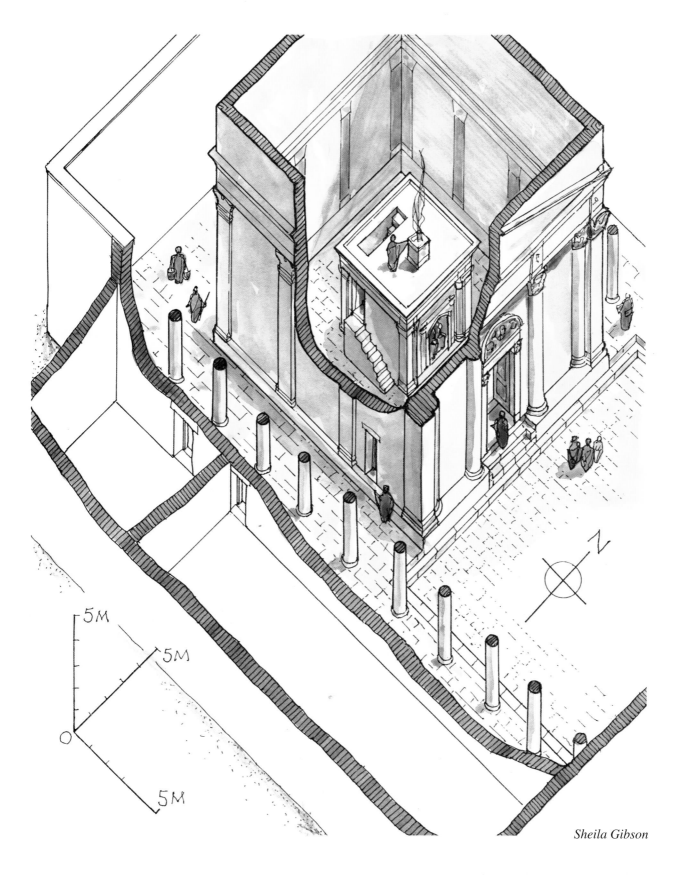

Sheila Gibson

Fig. 39. Detail of the temple complex at Khirbet et-Tannur in Jordan, built ca. 100–125 AD, showing the enclosure

surrounding the altar platform where burnt offerings were made. The name 'Khirbet' means 'ruins'.

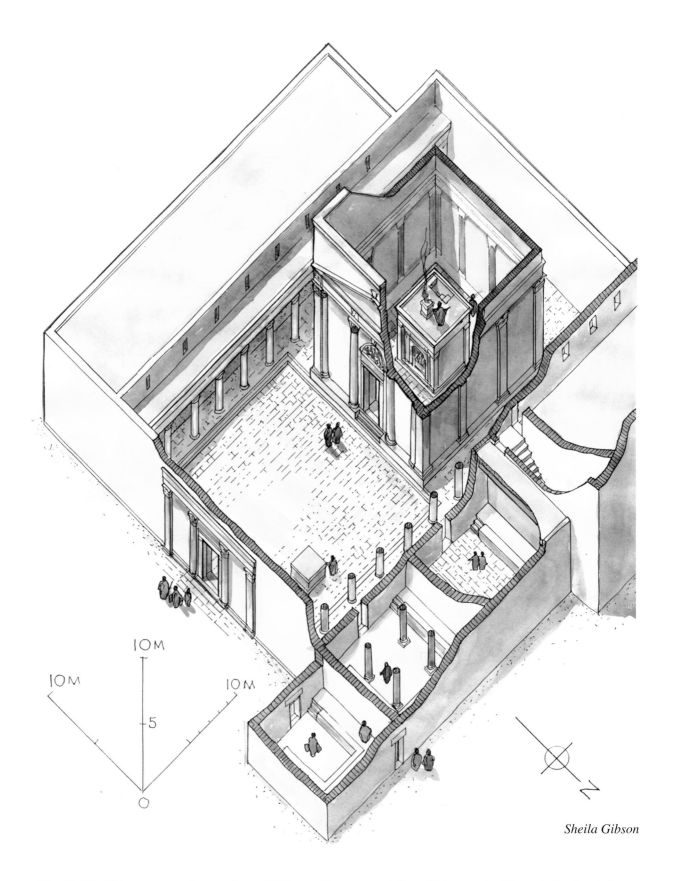

Sheila Gibson

10M

10M   10M

5

O

N

Fig. 40. The Nabataean temple complex at Khirbet et-Tannur on a hilltop 70 km north of Petra in Jordan, built ca. AD 100–125. Around the courtyard are dining rooms with benches for reclining during banquets.

THE RAPE OF LUCRETIA:

A drinking party and its aftermath

She lived with too much grace to be
Of our crude humanity.
For even our shame's refined
By her purity of mind.
Now place the wreath about her head
And let the sentinels of the dead
Guard the grave where our Lucretia lies.

Ronald Duncan (1914–1982), *The Rape of Lucretia*, scene 2 (with music by Benjamin Britten, 1913–1976)

After Romulus, a succession of kings ruled Rome over the next two and a half centuries. The last was Tarquinius Superbus or Tarquin the Proud (Tarquinius, -ī, m., Superbus, -ī, m.), forced by the citizenry to leave the city in 509 BC, angered over the rape of the matron Lucretia (Lucrētia, -ae, f.) by his son Sextus (Sextus, -ī, m.). Lucretia became a paradigm for the virtues appropriate to Roman women, and her story has resonated through the centuries, most notably in Shakespeare's *Rape of Lucrece*.

Vocabulary

adventus, adventūs, m.	arrival
convīvium, convīvī, n.	dinner
dormiō, dormīre, dormīvī, dormītum	sleep
ingenium, ingenī, n.	character, talent
modus, modī, m.	manner, measure, limit
paucī, -ae, -a	few
pergō, pergere, perrēxī, perrēctum	continue, proceed
stringō, stringere, strinxī, strictum	draw tight, draw (a sword), touch, trim
terō, terere, trīvī, trītum	spend, wear out
verbum, verbī, n.	word

Rēgiī quidem iuvenēs interdum ōtium convīviīs cōmissātiōnibusque inter sē terēbant.[1] Fōrte, pōtantibus hīs

apud Sextum Tarquinium, ubi et Collātīnus cēnābat Tarquinius, Ēgeriī fīlius, incidit dē uxōribus mentiō.[2]

Suam quisque laudāre mīrīs modīs.[3] Inde, certāmine accēnsō, Collātīnus negat verbīs opus esse; paucīs id

quidem hōrīs posse scīrī: quantum cēterīs praestet Lucrētia sua.[4]

'Quīn, sī vigor iuventae inest, cōnscendimus equōs invīsimusque praesentēs nostrārum ingenia?[5] Id

cuīque spectātissimum sit: quod necopīnātō virī adventū occurrerit oculīs.'[6]

Incaluerant vīnō.[7] 'Age sānē!' omnēs.[8] Citātīs equīs, āvolant Rōmam.[9] Quō cum prīmīs sē intendentibus

tenebrīs pervēnissent, pergunt inde Collātiam, ubi Lucrētiam haudquāquam ut rēgiās nurūs, quās in convīviō

---

[1] **iuvenis, iuvenis**, m. – young man; **interdum** – now and then; **ōtium, ōtī**, n. – leisure; **cōmissātiō, cōmissātiōnis**, f. – revelling.

[2] **pōtō, pōtāre, pōtāvī, pōtātum** – drink; **apud** – with; at the house of (*prep. with acc.*) ; **et** – 'also,' rather than 'and;' **Collātīnus, Collātīnī**, m. – Collatinus, a member of the Tarquin family (Tarquinius); he is the husband of Lucretia and son of Egerius; **cēnō, cēnāre, cēnāvī, cēnātum** – dine; **incidō, incidere, incidī, — —** – fall, happen, occur; **mentiō, mentiōnis**, f. – mention.

[3] **suam = suam uxōrem; quisque, quidque** – each, everyone; **laudāre** is a historical infinitive; translate as if it were a past tense; **id** is essentially the equivalent of **hōc** and refers to the fact of Lucretia'a preeminence in virtue over other wives; **mīrus, -a, -um** – wonderful.

[4] **accendō, accendere, accendī, accēnsum** – set on fire, arouse; **negō, negāre, negāvī, negātum** – deny; **opus esse** – the infinitive of the indirect statement has an impersonal subject ('there is need'); **hōra, hōrae**, f. – hour; **sciō, scīre, scīvī, scītum** – know; **quantus, -a, -um** – how much; **cēterī, -ae, -a** – the other, the rest of; **cēterīs = cēterīs uxōribus; praestō, praestāre, praestitī, praestitum** – excel (with dat.).

[5] **quīn = quidne** (why ... not?); **vigor, vigōris**, m. – vigour; **iuventa, iuventae**, f. – youth; **īnsum, īnesse, īnfuī, īnfutūrum** – be in; **inest** requires **nōbīs** (us) to complete the sense of the phrase; **cōnscendō, cōnscendere, cōnscendī, cōnscēnsum** – climb up; **equus, equī**, m. – horse; **invīsō, invīsere, invīsī, invīsum** – investigate; see; **praesēns, praesentis** – present (*i. e.*, those who are present at the dinner); **nostrārum = nostrārum uxōrum**.

[6] **spectātus, -a, -um** – examined; **spectātissimum** – 'the decisive proof;' **quod** – that which; what; **necopīnātus, –a, -um** – unexpected; **occurrō, occurrere, occurī, occursum** – meet (*with dat.*); **oculus, oculī**, m. – eye.

[7] **incalēscō, incalēscere, incaluī, — —** – grow hot; **vīnum, vīnī**, n. – wine.

[8] **sānē** – certainly; the expression **age sānē** must mean approximately 'away then' or 'do it then'; supply a main verb with **omnēs** such as **dīxērunt**.

[9] **citō, citāre, citāvī, citātum** – hurry; **āvolō, āvolāre, āvolāvī, āvolātum** – fly away.

lusūque cum aequālibus vīderant tempus terentēs, sed, nocte sērā, dēditam lānae inter lūcubrantēs ancillās in mediō aedium sēdentem inveniunt.[10]

Muliebris certāminis laus penes Lucrētiam fuit.[11]   Adveniēns vir Tarquiniīque exceptī benīgnē.[12]   Vīctor marītus cōmiter invītat rēgiōs iuvenēs.[13]

Ibi Sextum Tarquinium mala libīdō Lucrētiae per vim stuprandae capit;[14] cum forma tum spectāta castitas incitat.[15]   Et tum quidem ab nocturnō iuvenālī lūdō in castra redeunt.[16]

---

[10]   **quō = eō** (there, to that place); **sē** is the direct object of the participle **intendentibus; intendō, intendere, intendī, intentum** – stretch over; **tenebrae, tenebrārum**, f. – shadows, darkness; **perveniō, pervenīre, pervēnī, perventum** – arrive; **Collātia, Collātiae**, f. – Collatia, a town thirteen miles east of Rome; **haudquāquam** – not at all; **nurus, nurūs**, f. – daughter-in-law; **lusus, lusūs**, m. – gaming; **aequālis, aequāle** – equal in age (presumably, here the word refers to those of equivalent social status); **nox, noctis**, f. – night; **sērus, -a, -um** – late; **dēdō, dēdere, dēdidi, dēditum** – surrender; **lāna, lānae**, f. – wool; spinning; **lūcubrō, lūcubrāre, lūcubrāvī, lūcubrātum** – work by lamplight; **ancilla, ancillae**, f. – slave-girl, servant; **medius, -a, -um** – middle; **aedis, aedis**, f. – house.

[11]   **muliebris, muliebre** – about women; **laus, laudis**, f. – praise, glory; **penes** – in the house of (*with acc.*).

[12]   **adveniō, advenīre, advēnī, adventum** – arrive; **excipiō, excipere, excēpī, exceptum** – receive; **exceptī = exceptī sunt; benīgnus, -a, -um** – kind-hearted.

[13]   **vīctor, vīctōris**, m. – victor; the word is in apposition with **marītus, marītī**, m. – husband; **cōmis, cōme** – courteous, affable; **invītō, invītāre, invītāvī, invītātum** – invite.

[14]   **libīdō, libīdinis**, f. – desire, passion; **stuprō, stuprāre, stuprāvī, stuprātum** – debauch, ravish; **stuprandae** – objective gen. with **libīdō.**

[15]   **cum ... tum** – not only ... but also; **castitās, castitātis**, f. – purity; **incitō, incitāre, incitāvī, incitātum** – rouse.

[16]   **nocturnus, -a, -um** – nocturnal; **iuvenālis, iuvenāle** – youthful; **lūdus, lūdī**, m. – game; **redeō, redīre, redīvī, reditum** – go back.

Paucīs interiectīs diēbus, Sextus Tarquinius, īnsciō Collātīnō, cum comite ūnō Collātiam vēnit.[17]   Ubi exceptus benīgnē ab īgnārīs cōnsilī, cum post cēnam in hospitāle cubiculum dēductus esset, amōre ārdēns, postquam satis tūta circā, sōpītīque omnēs vidēbantur, strictō gladiō, ad dormientem Lucrētiam vēnit, sinistrāque manū mulieris pectore oppressō: 'Tace, Lucrētia,' inquit.[18] 'Sextus Tarquinius sum. Ferrum in manū est.[19] Moriēre, sī ēmīseris vōcem.'[20]

Livy 1. 57. 5 – 58. 2

---

[17] **intericiō, intericere, interiēcī, interiectum** – intervene; **īnscius, -a, -um** – not knowing; **īnsciō Collātīnō** – abl. of attendant circumstance; **comes, comitis**, m. or f. – companion.

[18] **excipiō, excipere, excēpī, exceptum** – receive; **exceptus = exceptus erat**; **īgnārus, -a, -um** – ignorant (of); **cōnsilium, cōnsilī**, n. – plan; **cēna, cēnae**, f. – dinner; **hospitālis, hospitāle** – relating to a guest; **cubiculum, cubiculī**, n. – bed-chamber; **dēdūcō, dēdūcere, dēdūxī, dēductum** – lead away; **amor, amōris**, m. – love; **satis** – enough (*adv.* with **tūta**); **tūtus, -a, um** – safe, protected; **circā** – around; the verb **vidēbantur** (seem) from the end of the clause must be used here to complete the sense; **sōpiō, sōpīre, sōpīvī, sōpītum** – put to sleep; **gladius, gladī**, m. – sword; **sinister, sinistra, sinistrum** – left; **mulier, mulieris**, f. – woman; **pectus, pectoris**, n. – breast; **opprimō, opprimere, oppressī, oppressum** – overwhelm; **taceō, tacēre, tacuī, tacitum** – be silent; **inquit** – he says (*third sing. of a defective verb*).

[19] **ferrum, ferrī**, n. – iron, weapon.

[20] The sentence is a future more vivid conditional; the **-re** ending is an alternate second person passive ending for **–ris**; **ēmittō, ēmittere, ēmīsī, ēmissum** – send forth; **vōx, vōcis**, f. – 'sound,' rather than the more usual 'voice.'

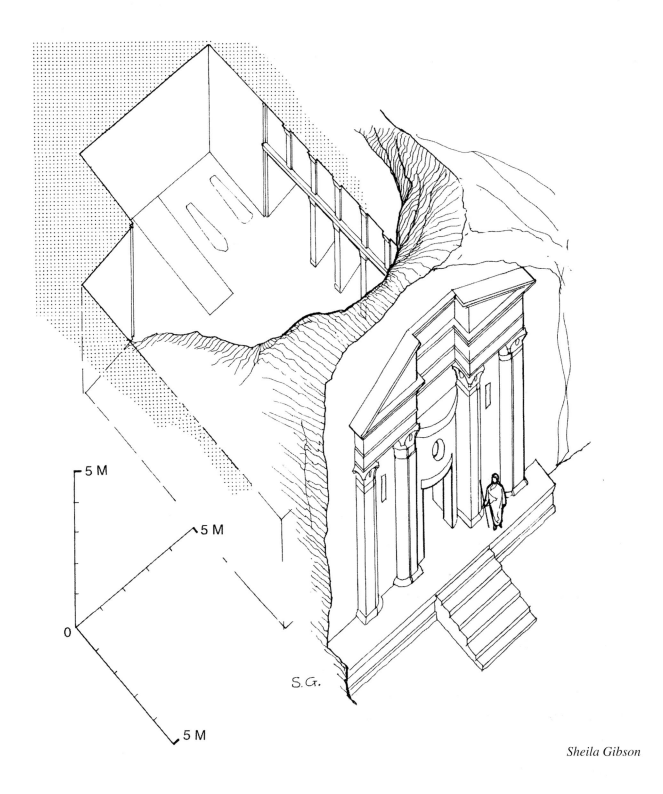

5 M

5 M

0

5 M

S.G.

Sheila Gibson

Fig. 41. The rock-cut Tomb of the Broken Pediment at Petra in Jordan, carved ca. first century AD.

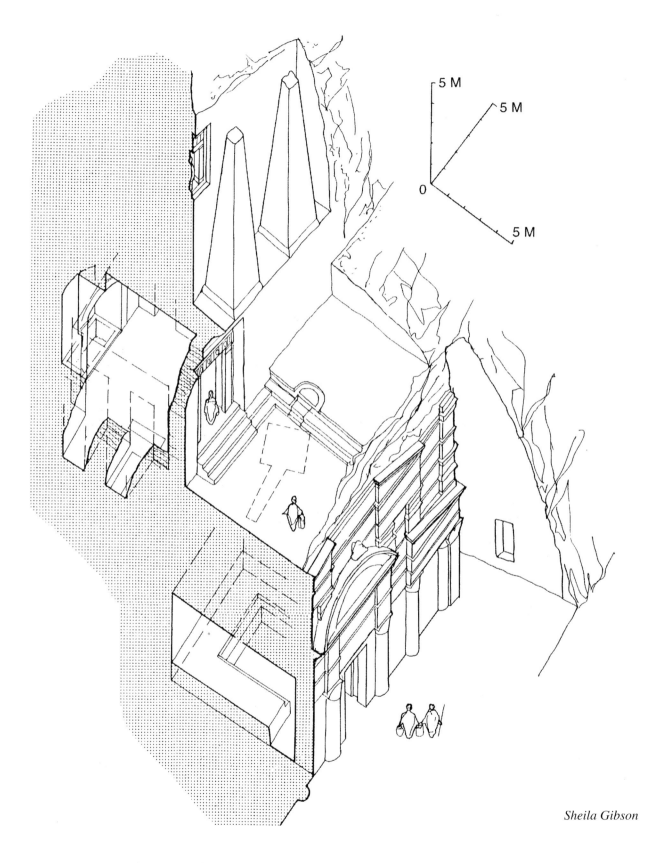

Sheila Gibson

Fig. 42. The Obelisk Tomb, with the Bab el Siq Triclinium for funeral banquets below, carved out of the rock at Petra in Jordan, in ca. the first century AD.

Sheila Gibson

Fig. 43. Detail of the altar platform at Khirbet et-Tannur in Jordan, which was enlarged ca. AD 200.
The colours provide an indication of how it would have looked with the original paint.

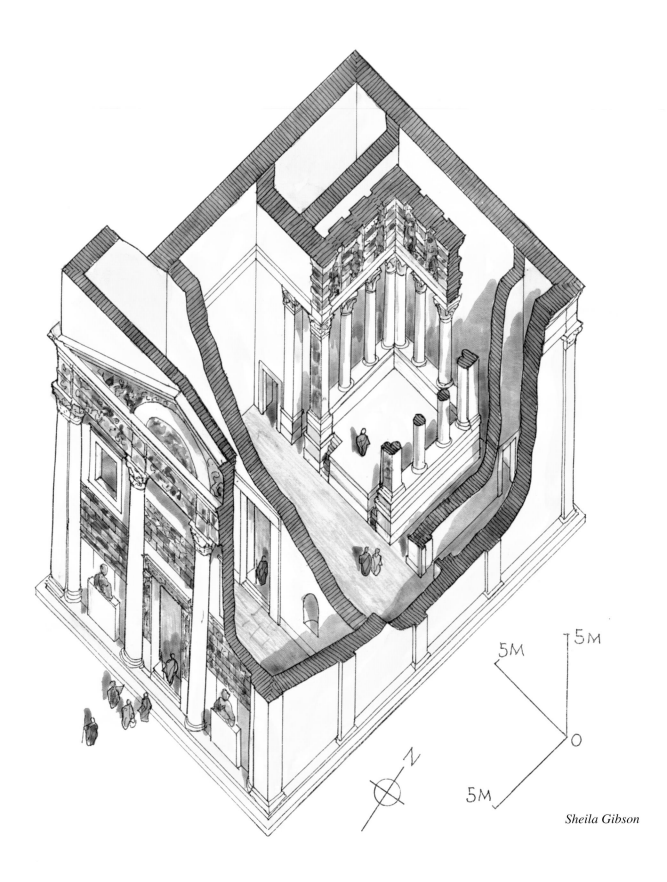

5M

5M

5M

0

N

Sheila Gibson

Fig. 44. The brightly painted Nabataean temple at Khirbet edh-Dharieh, 70 km north of Petra in Jordan. It was

built ca. AD 100 by the same architect and sculptors who had built nearby Khirbet et-Tannur.

THE RAPE OF LUCRETIA:
A call for help

Imagine here as one in dead of night
From forth dull sleep by dreadful fancy waking,
That thinks she hath beheld some ghastly sprite
Whose grim aspect sets every joint a-shaking.
What terror 'tis! But she in worser taking,
From sleep disturbed, heedfully doth view
The sight which makes supposèd terror true.

W. Shakespeare (d. 1616), *The Rape of Lucrece* 449–455

Lucretia succumbs to her ordeal and then summons her family.

Vocabulary

absolvō, absolvere, absolvī, absolūtum	acquit (*with abl.*); loosen
cōgō, cōgere, coēgī, coāctum	force, collect
hostis, hostis, m. and f.	enemy
mēns, mentis, f.	mind, intention
mulier, mulieris, f.	woman
nox, noctis, f.	night
nūntius, nūntī, m.	message, messenger
ops, opis, f.	help, aid; wealth, resources (*in plural*)
somnus, somnī, m.	sleep
vīvō, vīvere, vīxī, —	live

Cum pavida ex somnō mulier nūllam opem, prope mortem imminentem vidēret, tum Tarquinius fatērī amōrem, ōrāre, miscēre precibus minās, versāre in omnēs partēs muliebrem animum.[1]   Ubi obstinātam vidēbat et nē mortis quidem metū inclīnārī, addit ad metum dēdecus.[2]   Cum mortuā iugulātum servum nūdum positūrum ait, ut in sordidō adulteriō necāta dīcātur.[3]

Quō terrōre cum vīcisset obstinātam pudīcitiam velut vīctrīx libīdō, profectusque inde Tarquinius, ferōx expūgnātō decore muliebrī, esset, Lucrētia maesta tantō malō nūntium Rōmam eundem ad patrem Ardeamque ad virum mittit, ut cum singulīs fidēlibus amīcīs veniant;[4] ita factō mātūrātōque opus esse;[5] rem atrōcem incidisse.[6]

---

[1]   The verbs in the main clause are historical infinitives; **pavidus, -a, -um** – trembling, fearful; **prope** – nearly (*adverbial*); the word is to be taken with **imminentem; immineō, imminēre**, —, — – overhang; **fateor, fatērī, fassus sum** – confess; **ōrō, ōrāre, ōrāvī, ōrātum** – beg; **misceō, miscēre, miscuī, mīxtum** – mix, confuse; **prex, precis**, f. – prayer; **minae, minārum**, f. – threats; **versō, versāre, versāvī, versātum** – turn, ponder; **pars, partis**, f. – part, direction, side; **muliebris, muliebre** – womanly.

[2]   **obstinō, obstināre, obstināvī, obstinātum** – resolute; obstinate; **nē ... quidem** – not even; **metus, metūs**, m. – fear; **inclīnō, inclīnāre, inclīnāvī, inclīnātum** – bend, turn; **addō. addere, addidī, additum** – add; **dēdecus, dēdecoris**, n. – disgrace.

[3]   **mortuus, -a, -um** – dead; **iugulō, iugulāre, iugulāvī, iugulātum** – cut by the throat; **servus, servī**, m. – slave; **nūdus, -a, -um** – naked; **pōnō, pōnere, posuī, positum** – put, put down; **positūrum = positūrum esse**; **ait** – he says; **sordidus, -a, -um** – sordid; **adulterium, adulterī**, n. – adultery; **necō, necāre, necāvī, necātum** – kill; **necāta = necāta esse**.

[4]   **quō = hōc**; **terror, terrōris**, m. – fear; **pudīcitia, pudīcitiae**, f. – chastity, modesty; **velut** – just as; **vīctrīx, vīctrīcis**, f. – conqueror; the noun is in appposition to **libīdō, libīdinis**, f. – desire, passion; **ferōx, ferōcis** – headstrong; haughty; the ablative phrase after **ferōx** is dependent upon the adjective, explaining in what respect Tarquin has become haughty; **profectusque ... esset** is still part of the cum-clause; **expūgnō, expūgnāre, expūgnāvī, expūgnātum** – take by storm; **decus, decoris**, n. – beauty, glory; **maestus, -a, -um** – sad; **Ardea, Ardeae**, f. – Ardea, a town near Rome; **singulī, -ae, -a** – single; **fidēlis, fidēle** – trusty.

[5]   **mātūrō, mātūrāre, mātūrāvī, mātūrātum** – hasten; the participles **factō** and **mātūrātō** are the equivalents of nouns: 'action' and 'haste'; **opus esse** and **incidisse** are infinitives in indirect statement

[6]   **atrōx, atrōcis** – cruel, violent; **incidō, incidere, incidī, incāsum** – happen.

Spurius Lucrētius cum Publiō Valēriō, Volēsī fīliō, Collātīnus cum Luciō Iūniō Brūtō venit, cum quō fōrte Rōmam rediēns ab nūntiō uxōris erat conventus.[7] Lucrētiam sedentem maestam in cubiculō inveniunt.[8]

Adventū suōrum lacrimae obortae; quaerentīque virō 'Satin salvē?' 'Minimē,' inquit;[9] 'quid enim salvī est, mulierī āmissā pudīcitiā?[10] Vestīgia virī aliēnī, Collātīne, in lectō sunt tuō.[11] Cēterum corpus est tantum violātum; animus insōns.[12] Mors testis erit.[13] Sed date dexterās fidemque haud impūne adulterō fore.[14] Sextus est Tarquinius, quī hostis prō hospite, priōre nocte, vī armātus, mihi – sibique sī vōs virī estis – pestiferum hinc abstulit gaudium.'[15]

---

[7] **Spurius Lucrētius** (father of Lucretia), **Publius Valērius, Volēsius, Lucius Iūnius Brūtus** – all masculine second declension nouns; **fōrte** – by chance; **redeō, redīre, redīvī, redītum** – go back; **conveniō, convenīre, convēnī, conventum** – meet.

[8] **cubiculum, cubiculī**, n. – bed-chamber; **inveniō, invenīre, invēnī, inventum** – find.

[9] **suōrum** must refer to Lucretia's family, and not to the actual subject of the sentence; **lacrima, lacrimae**, f. – tear; **oborior, oborīrī, obortus sum** – arise; **obortae = obortae sunt**; **satin = satisne**; understand a verb such as **agis** with the question; **salvus, -a, -um** – safe; **inquit** – she said.

[10] **enim** – for, indeed; **salvī** is a partitive gen., here the equivalent of the noun **salūs** ('health'); **āmittō, āmittere, āmīsī, āmissum** – send away, lose.

[11] **vestīgium, vestīgī**, n. – trace; **aliēnus, -a, -um** – another; **lectus, lectī**, m. – bed.

[12] **cēterum** – for the rest (*adv.*); **tantum** – only; **violō, violāre, violāvī, violātum** – harm; **īnsōns, īnsōntis** – innocent; understand **est** as the verb.

[13] **testis, testis**, m. and f. – witness.

[14] **dext(e)rās** (right) = **dexterās manūs; fīdem** here means a 'pledge;' **haud** – not; **impūne** – without punishment; **adulter, adulterī**, m. – adulterer.

[15] **hospes, hospitis**, m. – host, guest; **prō** – instead of (*prep. with abl.*); **armō, armāre, armāvī, armātum** – arm; **sibi** refers to Sextus: the offence will be destructive of him as well, hopes Lucretia; **pestifer, pestifera, pestiferum** – pestilential (with reference to **mihi sibique**); **hinc** – from here; **auferō, auferre, abstulī, ablātum** – carry off; **gaudium, gaudiī**, n. – joy, pleasure.

Dant ōrdine omnēs fidem.[16] Cōnsōlantur aegram animī āvertendō noxam ab coāctā in auctōrem dēlictī: mentem peccāre, nōn corpus, et unde cōnsilium āfuerit, culpam abesse.[17]

'Vōs,' inquit, 'vīderitis quid illī dēbeātur. Ego mē etsī peccātō absolvō, suppliciō nōn līberō;[18] nec ūlla deinde impudīca Lucrētiae exemplō vīvet.'[19] Cultrum, quem sub veste abditum habēbat, eum in corde dēfīgit; prōlapsaque in vulnus moribunda cecidit.[20] Conclāmat vir paterque.[21]

Livy 1. 58. 3–12

---

[16] The subject of the sentence is **omnēs**; **ōrdō, ōrdinis**, m. – line, order (**ōrdine**, usually 'regularly' or 'properly,' must mean here 'one after the other.')

[17] **cōnsolor, cōnsōlārī, cōnsōlātus sum** – console; **aeger, aegra, aegrum** – sick; **animī** is a locative; **āvertō, āvertere, āvertī, āversum** – turn away; **noxa, noxae**, f. – fault, hurt; **auctor, auctōris**, m. and f. – author, founder; **dēlictum, dēlictī**, n. – offence; the infinitives **peccāre** and **abesse** are used because the indirect statement construction is assumed; **peccō, peccāre, peccāvī, peccātum** – sin; Lucretia's family means that the state of mind determines whether or not there is fault; **cōnsilium, cōnsilī**, n. – intent; **absum, abesse, āfuī, āfutūrum** – be absent, be distant; **culpa, culpae**, f. – fault, blame.

[18] **etsī** – although; **peccātum, peccāti**, n. – fault; **supplicium, supplicī**, n. – punishment; **līberō, līberāre, līberāvī, līberātum** – free (*with abl. of separation*).

[19] The subject of the statement after **nec** is **ulla impudīca (fēmina)**; **impudīcus, -a, -um** – shameless; the genitive **Lucrētiae** is to be taken with **exemplum, exemplī**, n. – precedent, example, warning; in other words: for all posterity, shamed women will understand that, following Lucretia's example, they must kill themselves.

[20] **culter, cultrī**, m. – knife; **vestis, vestis**, f. – garment; **abdō, abdere, abdidī, abditum** – hide; **cor, cordis**, n. – heart; **dēfīgō, dēfīgere, dēfīxī, dēfīxum** – fix firmly; **prōlābor, prōlābī, prōlapsus sum** – slip forwards; **vulnus, vulneris**, n. – wound; **moribundus, -a, -um** – dying.

[21] **conclāmō, conclāmāre, conclāmāvī, conclāmātum** – cry aloud; the singular verb is used with a plural subject, emphasising the closeness of connection between father and husband; **conclāmāre** is also the regular Latin verb used to bewail the dead at a funeral.

Fig. 45. Temple of Hathor at Dendara in southern Egypt. After Cleopatra died in 30 BC, the Romans
ruled Egypt, but still built some temples in the local Egyptian style.

Sheila Gibson

10M

10M

10M

0

Fig. 46. The temple of Augustus at Philae in Egypt, erected in 13/12 BC, the year Augustus became pontifex maximus. In front is the arch of the emperor Diocletian.

HORATIUS AT THE BRIDGE:
Lars Porsenna attacks

Then out spake brave Horatius,
The Captain of the Gate:
'To every man upon this earth
Death cometh soon or late.
And how can man die better
Than facing fearful odds,
For the ashes of his fathers,
And the temples of his Gods ....'

Thomas Babington Macaulay (1800-1859), 'Horatius' in *Lays of Ancient Rome*

Banished, Tarquin the Proud fled to King Lars Porsenna of the Etruscans (Lars, Lartis, m.; Porsenna, Porsennae, m.), whom he convinced to march on Rome. Despite the historical veneer of Livy's account, this march must still be accounted legend, a cultural touchstone to which Romans could refer. The episode of Horatius at the bridge was most famously reworked by the English historian and essayist Thomas Babington Macaulay in a collection of narrative poems, *Lays of Ancient Rome* (1842).

Vocabulary

adsum, adesse, adfuī, adfutūrum	be present, help
excipiō, excipere, excēpī, exceptum	catch, receive, follow, exempt
impetus, impetūs, m.	attack
paene	almost
pōnō, pōnere, posuī, positum	put, put down
pōns, pōntis, m.	bridge
praesidium, praesidī, n.	guard, protection
quisque, quidque	each, everyone; everything
relinquō, relinquere, relīquī, relictum	leave
testor, testārī, testātus sum	declare, make known

Cum hostēs adessent, prō sē quisque in urbem ex agrīs dēmigrant.[1] Urbem ipsam saepiunt praesidiīs.[2] Alia mūrīs, alia Tiberī obiectō vidēbantur tūta.[3] Pōns sublicius iter paene hostibus dedit, nī ūnus vir fuisset, Horātius Coclēs;[4] id mūnīmentum illō diē fōrtūna urbis Rōmānae habuit.[5]

Quī, positus fōrte in statiōne pōntis, cum captum repentīnō impetū Iāniculum atque inde citātōs dēcurrere hostēs vīdisset trepidamque turbam suōrum arma ōrdinēsque relinquere, reprehēnsāns singulōs, obsistēns obtestānsque deum et hominum fidem, testābātur nēquīquam, dēsertō praesidiō, eōs fugere;[6] sī trānsitum pōntem ā tergō reliquissent, iam plūs hostium in Palātiō Capitōliōque quam in Iāniculō fore.[7]

Itaque monēre, praedīcere ut pōntem ferrō, īgnī, quācumque vī possint, interrumpant:[8] sē impetum hostium, quantum corpore ūnō posset obsistī, exceptūrum.[9]

---

[1] **prō** – for; on behalf of (*prep. with abl.*); **dēmigrō, dēmigrāre, dēmigrāvī, dēmigrātum** – go away; despite the plural form of **dēmigrant**, the subject of the verb is **quisque** since a plurality of people is implied.

[2] **saepiō, saepīre, saepsī, saeptum** – fence in.

[3] **alia ... alia** – some ... others; neuter plural here: 'some (sections) ... other (sections)'; **Tiberī** – the abl. form of **Tiberis; obiciō, obicere, obiēcī, obiectum** – cast in the way; **tūtus, -a, -um** – protected, safe.

[4] **sublicius, -a, -um** – resting upon piles (*i.e.*, built entirely of wood); this bridge would have been the only way across the Tiber at the time; **iter, itineris**, n. – way, journey; **paene** – nearly (*adv.* to be taken with **dedit**); **nī = nisi** (if ... not, unless); **coclēs, coclitis**, m. – a person blind in one eye.

[5] **id** is the direct object of **habuit** and refers to the fact of Horatius' presence at the bridge; in essence, **id = eum**, which has been attracted to the case of **mūnīmentum, mūnīmentī**, n. – defence, protection (in appposition to **id**).

[6] **quī = ille; fōrte** – by chance; **statiō, statiōnis**, f. – post, station; **repentīnus, -a, -um** – sudden; **Iāniculum, Iāniculī**, n. – Janiculum, a hill of Rome on the right bank of the Tiber; **citātus** – at full speed; **dēcurrō, dēcurrere, dēcucurrī, dēcursum** – run down; **trepidus, -a, -um** – trembling, anxious; **turba, turbae**, f. – crowd; **arma, armōrum**, n. pl. – arms; **ōrdō, ōrdinis**, m. – line, order; **reprehēnsō, reprehēnsāre**, —, — – hold back repeatedly; **singulī, -ae, -a** – single, one at a time; **obsistō, obsistere, obstitī, obstitum** – oppose; **obtestor, obtestārī, obtestātus sum** – call as a witness; **deum = deōrum; nēquīquam** – in vain (adv. to be taken inside the indirect statement with **fugere**, not with **testābātur**); **dēserō, dēserere, dēseruī, dēsertum** – abandon; **fugiō, fugere, fūgī**, — – flee, avoid.

[7] **trānsitum** – perfect passive participle of **trānseō** (cross); **tergum, tergī**, n. – back; **Palātium, Palātiī**, n. – Palatine, one of the seven hills of Rome; **Capitōlium, Capitōliī**, n. – Capitol hill, including the temple of Jupiter.

[8] The main verbs are historical infinitives followed by indirect command; **praedīcō, praedīcere, praedīxī, praedictum** – advise, warn, predict; **ferrum, ferrī**, n. – iron, weapon; **quācumque vī** – 'with whatever force'; **interrumpō, interrumpere, interrūpī, interruptum** – break, sever.

[9] **sē = Horatius; quantus, -a, -um** – so much as (normally **tantus ... quantus** – so much ... as); **quantum** is an adverbial acc. of extent.

Vādit inde in prīmum aditum pontis; īnsīgnisque inter cōnspecta cēdentium pūgnae terga, obversīs comminus ad ineundum proelium armīs, ipsō mīrāculō audāciae obstupefacit hostēs.[10]

Livy 2. 10. 1– 5

---

[10] **vādō, vādere**, —, — – go; **aditus, aditūs**, m. – approach; **īnsīgnis, īnsīgne** – conspicuous; **inter** (among) governs **terga**, which is modified by the perfect passive participle of **cōnspiciō, cōnspicere, cōnspexī, cōnspectum** – catch sight of; **cēdō, cēdere, cēssī, cessum** – yield (*with dat.*); **cēdentium** must be understood as modifying a word such as **eōrum** and governing the dative of **pūgna, pūgnae**, f. – fight; **obvertō, obvertere, obvertī, obversum** – turn forwards; **comminus** – hand to hand (*adv.*); **mīrāculum, mīrāculī**, n. – wonder, marvel; **audācia, audāciae**, f. – boldness; **obstupefaciō, obstupefacere, obstupefēcī, obstupefactum** – astonish.

Fig. 47. The temple of Augustus at Philae in Egypt in 13/12 BC. It had red granite columns and black stone capitals.

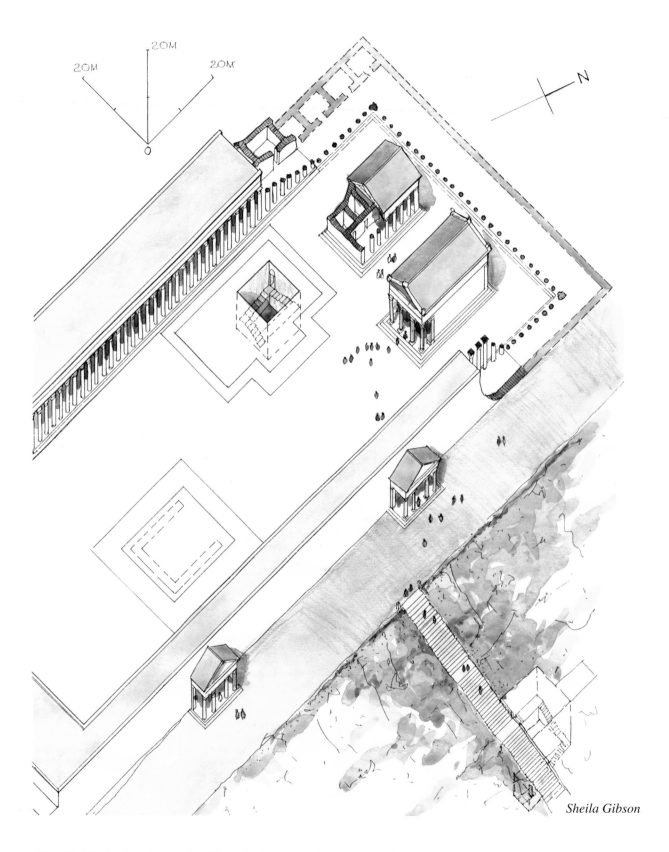

20M
20M
20M
0

N

Sheila Gibson

Fig. 48. The Ptolemaic temple of Serapis, known as the Serapeum, in Alexandria in Egypt, built by Ptolemy III Euergetes I (246–221 BC). The cult statue stood in the temple building. There were underground passages with stairs leading down. Along the side of the complex was a colonnade containing rooms for studying.

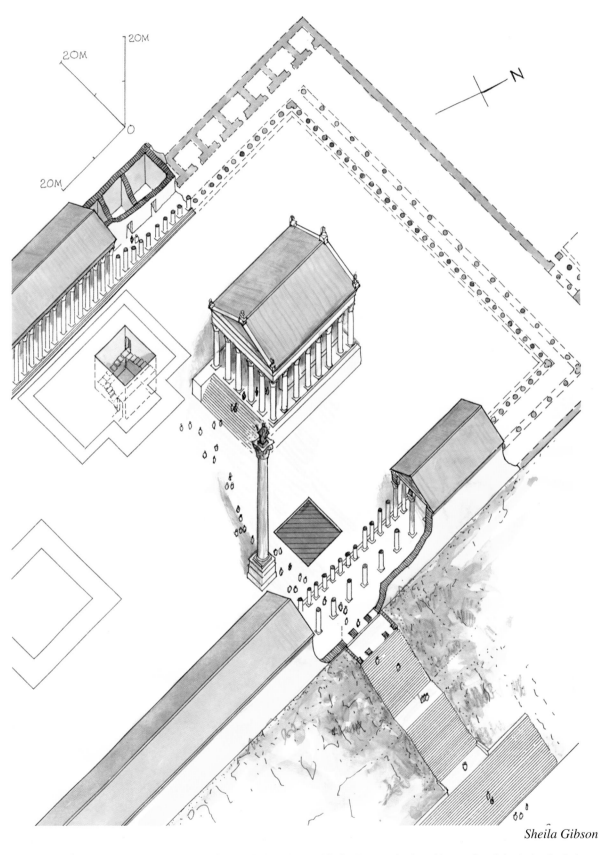

20M

20M

20M

N

Sheila Gibson

Fig. 49. The Roman Serapeum or temple of Serapis in Alexandria in Egypt, depicted here after Diocletian's Column, commonly called 'Pompey's Pillar,' was erected in AD 298.

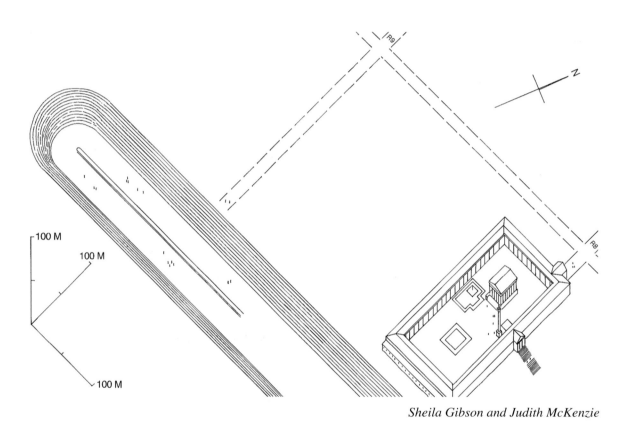

100 M

100 M

100 M

Sheila Gibson and Judith McKenzie

Fig. 50. The race-track, known as the Lageion, in Alexandria in Egypt, next to the temple of Serapis complex in ca. AD 300. The Lageion was about the same size as the Circus Maximus in Rome.

Reading 7

Horatius at the Bridge:

Into the deep

To Horatius, who kept his Bridge to himself.

Dedication in *Aces Made Easy* (1934), a guide to playing bridge,
by W. D. H. McCullough and Fougasse (the cartoonist Kenneth Bird, 1887–1965)

With the help of two others, Horatius fends off the Etruscan army.

Vocabulary

cēdō, cēdere, cessī, cessum	go, yield (*sometimes with dat.*)
cunctor, cunctārī, cunctātus sum	delay
flūmen, flūminis, n.	river
ingēns, ingentis	huge, dreadful
oculus, oculī, m.	eye
pars, partis, f.	part, direction, side
perficiō, perficere, perfēcī, perfectum	do, make, complete, accomplish
perīculum, perīculī, n.	danger
pudor, pudōris, m.	shame, modesty
singulī, -ae, -a	single, one at a time

Duōs tamen cum eō pudor tenuit, Spurium Larcium ac Tītum Herminium, ambōs clārōs genere factīsque.[1]
Cum hīs, prīmam perīculī procellam et quod tumultuōsissimum pūgnae erat parumper sustinuit.[2] Deinde
eōs quoque ipsōs, exiguā parte pōntis relictā, revocantibus quī rescindēbant, cēdere in tūtum coēgit.[3]

Circumferēns inde trucēs mināciter oculōs ad procerēs Etruscōrum, nunc singulōs prōvocāre, nunc
increpāre omnēs: servitia rēgum superbōrum, suae lībertātis immemorēs, aliēnam oppūgnātum venīre.[4]
Cunctātī aliquamdiū sunt, dum alius alium, ut proelium incipiant, circumspectant.[5] Pudor deinde com-
mōvit aciem; et, clāmōre sublātō, undique in ūnum hostem tēla cōniciunt.[6]

Quae cum in obiectō cuncta scūtō haesissent, neque ille minus obstinātus ingentī pōntem obtinēret

---

[1] **ac = atque; ambō, -ae, -ō** – both; **clārus, -a, -um** – clear, bright, famous; **clārōs** is followed by ablatives of respect;
genus, generis, n. – family; **factum, factī**, n. – deed

[2] **Cum hīs** – abl. of accompaniment; **procella, procellae**, f. – storm; **quod** – what; the entire relative clause is one of
the direct objects (along with **procellam**) of **sustinuit**; **tumultuōsus, -a, -um** – tumultuous, disquieting; **pūgna,
pūgnae**, f. – fight; **parumper** – for a little while; **sustineō, sustinēre, sustinuī, sustentum** – stop, withstand.

[3] **eōs** = Larcius and Herminius; **quoque** – also; **exiguus, -a, -um** – small; **revocantibus ... rescindēbant** is an abl.
absolute = **revocantibus eīs quī rescindēbant**; **revocō, revocāre, revocāvī, revocātum** – call back; **rescindō,
rescindere, rescidī, rescissum** – cut down; **tūtum, tūtī**, n. – safety.

[4] **circumferō, circumferre, circumtulī, circumlātum** – direct about; **trux, trucis** – savage; **mināx, minācis** –
threatening; **procer, proceris**, m. – noble; **Etruscī, Etruscōrum**, m. – Etruscans; **nunc** – now; **prōvocāre** and
increpāre are historical infinitives; **prōvocō, prōvocāre, prōvocāvī, prōvocātum** – call forth; **increpō, increpāre,
increpuī, increpitum** – address angrily; **servitia ... venīre** – indirect statement; **servitium, servitī**, n. – a body of
slaves; **superbus, -a, -um** – proud; **lībertās, lībertātis**, f. – freedom; **immemor, immemoris** – unmindful; **aliēnus, -
a, -um** – another; **aliēnam** needs to be understood with a word such as **terram** (land); **veniō** with the supine
oppūgnātum (attack) expresses purpose.

[5] **aliquamdiū** – for some considerable time; **proelium, proelī**, n. – battle; **incipiō, incipere, incēpī, inceptum** –
begin; **circumspectō, circumspectāre, circumspectāvī, circumspectātum** – look around.

[6] **commoveō, commovēre, commōvī, commōtum** – set in motion; **aciēs, aciēī**, f. – line of battle; **clāmor, clāmōris**,
m. – shout; **undique** – from all sides, on all sides; **tēlum, tēlī**, n. – weapon; **cōniciō, cōnicere, cōniēcī, cōniectum** –
throw, throw together.

gradū, iam impetū cōnābantur dētrūdere virum, cum simul fragor ruptī pōntis, simul clāmor Rōmānōrum, alacritāte perfectī operis sublātus, pavōre subitō impetum sustinuit.[7]

Tum Coclēs 'Tiberīne pater,' inquit, 'tē sānctē precor, haec arma et hunc mīlitem propitiō flūmine accipiās'[8] Ita sīc armātus in Tiberim dēsiluit, multīsque superincidentibus tēlīs, incolumis ad suōs trānāvit, rem ausus plūs fāmae habitūram ad posterōs quam fideī.[9]

Grāta ergā tantam virtūtem cīvitās fuit.[10] Statua in comitiō posita.[11] Agrī quantum ūnō diē circumarāvit datum.[12]

Livy 2. 10. 6–1

---

[7] **quae = tēla; obiciō, obicere, obiēcī, obiectum** – throw against, expose; **cunctus, -a, -um** – all, the whole; **scūtum, scūtī**, m. – shield; **haereō, haerēre, haesī, haesūrum** – cling, cling to; **obstinō, obstināre, obstināvī, obstinātum** – be persistent, **resolve; obtineō, obtinēre, obtinuī, obtentum** – hold; **gradus, gradūs**, m. – step; **dētrūdō, dētrūdere, dētrūsī, dētrūsum** – dislodge; **simul ... simul** – both ... and; **fragor, fragōris**, m. – crashing; **rumpō, rumpere, rūpī, ruptum** – break; **alacritās, alacritātis**, f. – joy; **opus, operis**, n. – work; **pavor, pavōris**, m. – panic; **subitus, -a, -um** – sudden; **sustineō, -ēre, sustinuī, sustentum** – withstand, hold up.

[8] **Tiberīnus, -a, -um** – of the Tiber; **inquit** – he says; **sānctus, -a, -um** – pious, solemn; **sānctē** is presumably an adverb with **precor, precārī, precātus sum** – pray; the subsequent indirect command drops **ut; arma, armōrum**, n. – arms; **propitius, -a, -um** – favourable.

[9] **armō, armāre, armāvī, armātum** – arm; **dēsiliō, dēsilīre, dēsiluī, — —** – jump down; **superincidō, superincidere, —, —** – fall on top of; **incolumis, incolume** – safe; **suōs = suōs populōs; trānō, trānāre, trānāvī, trānātum** – swim; **fāma, fāmae**, f. – legend, fame, rumour; **posterī, posterōrum**, m. pl. – future generations; **fidēs** has the sense of 'credibility' here.

[10] **grātus, -a, -um** – grateful; **ergā** (*prep. with accus.*) – toward; **virtus, virtūtis**, f. – courage, virtue; **cīvitās, cīvitātis**, f. – state.

[11] **statua, statuae**, f. – statue; **comitium, comitī**, n. – place of assembly; **posita = posita est**.

[12] **agrī** is a partitive gen. dependent on **quantum** – how much; **circumarō, circumarāre, circumarāvī, circumarātum** – plough around; **datum = datum est**.

Fig. 51. Some of about twenty teaching rooms in the city centre of Alexandria, Egypt, ca. the sixth century AD.

MUCIUS SCAEVOLA:

An assassination attempt

Fōrte dux fel flat in gutture.
By chance, the leader inhales poison in his throat – or
Forty ducks fell flat in gutter.

A traditional example of school humour using 'false' Latin; here, unusually,
the grammar is passable in both English and Latin.

Aside from the odd allusion or painting (by Rubens or van Dyck, for example), the story of Gaius Mucius Scaevola (Gāius, -ī, m.; Mūcius, -a, -um; Scaevola, -ae, m.) is not much treated in later art or literature, presumably because the legend is so perplexing. As the Etruscans continued to besiege Rome, Gaius Mucius determined to assassinate Lars Porsenna in a night raid. The plot failed; the king's scribe was killed instead; and Mucius was captured. Determined to trick Porsenna into believing all Romans were as resolved as he to win over the Etruscans, Mucius held his right hand over a flame with apparent equanimity, an illustration of Roman resoluteness in the face of adversity. So impressed was Porsenna that he arranged a truce, and forever after, Gaius Mucius was known as 'Scaevola' or 'Lefty.' The story has all the hallmarks of an event or practice imperfectly understood. The hand over the flame suggests a ritual, and the sacrifice of a king-substitute to assure future peace is a form of religious scapegoatism known elsewhere.

Vocabulary

adulēscēns, adulēscentis	young
audāx, audācis	bold
cōnsistō, cōnsistere, cōnstitī, cōnstitum	stop, stand, make a stand
cōnstituō, cōnstituere, cōnstituī, cōnstitūtum	establish, decide
custōs, custōdis, m. and f.	guard
fōrte	by chance
fortis, forte	brave
iuvō, iuvāre, iūvī, iūtum	help
metuō, metuere, metuī,—	fear
populus, populī, m.	people
trahō, trahere, trāxī, tractum	draw, draw down, drag

Obsidiō erat nihilō minus, et frūmentī cum summā cāritāte inopia, sedendōque expūgnātūrum sē urbem spem Porsenna habēbat, cum Gāius Mūcius, adulēscēns nōbilis — cuī indīgnum vidēbatur populum Rōmānum servientem, cum sub rēgibus esset, nūllō bellō nec ab hostibus ūllīs obsessum esse, līberum eundem populum ab eīsdem Etruscīs obsidērī, quōrum saepe exercitūs fūderit — itaque, māgnō audācīque aliquō facinore eam indīgnitātem vindicandam ratus, prīmō suā sponte penetrāre in hostium castra cōnstituit.[1] Dein metuēns nē sī cōnsulum iniūssū et īgnārīs omnibus īret, fōrte dēprehensus ā custōdibus Rōmānīs retraherētur ut trānsfuga, fōrtūnā tum urbis crīmen adfirmante, senātum adit.[2]

'Trānsīre Tiberim,' inquit, 'patrēs, et intrāre, sī possim, castra hostium volō,[3] nōn praedō nec populātiōnum in vicem ultor.[4] Māius — sī dī iuvant — in animō est facinus.'

---

[1]   **obsidiō, obsidiōnis,** f. – siege; **nihilō minus** – no less; **frūmentum, frūmentī,** n. – grain; the gen. is dependent on **inopia; cāritās, cāritātis,** f. – dearness, expense; **inopia, inopiae,** f. – lack; *i.e.,* since there was a shortage, what grain could be had was very expensive; **sedeō, sedēre, sēdī, sessum** – keep the field; **expūgnō, expūgnāre, expūgnāvī, expūgnātum** – take by assault, storm; **nōbilis, nōbile** – noble; **indīgnus, -a, -um** – unworthy; **serviō, servīre, servīvī, servītum** – to be a slave; **servientem** is contrasted with **līberum** later on; **bellum, bellī,** n. – war; **obsideō, obsidēre, obsēdī, obsessum** – besiege, occupy; **līber, lībera, līberum** – free; **fundō, fundere, fūdī, fūsum** – defeat, pour; **itaque** – accordingly, and so; **aliquis, aliqua, aliquid** – some; **facinus, facinoris,** n. – deed, crime; **indīgnitās, indīgnitātis,** f. – indignity; **vindicō, vindicāre, vindicāvī, vindicātum** – punish, avenge; **vindicandam = vindicandam esse; suā sponte** – of his own accord; **penetrō, penetrāre, penetrāvī, penetrātum** – penetrate.

[2]   **dein = deinde; cōnsulum** is a gen. plural dependent on **iniūssū** – without an order (*adv.*); **īgnārus, -a, -um** – ignorant; **īgnārīs omnibus** – abl. absolute; understand the participle as 'being;' **dēprehendō, dēprehendere, dēprehendī, dēprehēnsum** – arrest; **retrahō, retrahere, retraxī, retractum** – drag back; **ut** – as; **trānsfuga, trānsfugae,** m. and f. – deserter; **fōrtūna, fōrtūnae,** f. – fortune; **crīmen, crīminis,** n. – charge, crime; **adfirmō, adfirmāre, adfirmāvī, adfirmātum** – confirm; **fōrtūnā ... adfirmante** – a causal abl. absolute; Livy means that the circumstances of the city were such that any strange behaviour was liable to be interpreted as treason: 'the circumstances of the city at the time lending credence to the charge'; **adeō, adīre, adīvī, aditum** – go to.

[3]   **trānseō, trānsīre, trānsīvī, trānsitum** – go across; **inquam, inquis, inquit** – he says; **intrō, intrāre, intrāvī, intrātum** – go into.

[4]   **praedō, praedōnis,** m. – plunderer; **populātiō, populātiōnis,** f. – devastation; **in vicem** – in turn; **ultor, ultōris,** m. – avenger.

Adprobant patrēs.[5] Abditō intrā vestem ferrō proficīscitur.[6] Ubi eō vēnit, in cōnfertissimā turbā prope rēgium tribūnal cōnstitit.[7] Ibi cum stīpendium mīlitibus fōrte darētur, et scrība cum rēge sedēns parī ferē ōrnātū multa ageret, eumque milites vulgō adīrent, timēns scīscitārī uter Porsenna esset, nē īgnōrandō rēgem sēmet ipse aperīret quis esset — quō temere traxit fōrtūna facinus — scrībam prō rēge obtruncat.[8]

Livy 2. 12. 1–7

---

[5] **adprobō, adprobāre, adprobāvī, adprobātum** – approve.

[6] **abdō, abdere, abdidī, abditum** – hide; **intrā** – inside (*with accus.*); **vestis, vestis**, f. – garment, covering; **ferrum, ferrī**, n. – iron, weapon.

[7] **eō** – there; **cōnfertus, -a, -um** – crowded together; **turba, turbae**, f. – crowd; **prope** – near (*with accus.*); **rēgius, -a, -um** – royal; **tribūnal, tribūnālis**, n. – platform.

[8] **stīpendium, stīpendī**, n. – wage; **scrība ... ageret** continues the cum-clause; **scrība, scrībae**, m. – secretary; **pār, paris** – equal, like; **ferē** – about, generally; **ōrnātus, ōrnātūs**, m. – dress, equipment; **vulgō** – openly, in a crowd (*adv.*); **timeō, timēre, timuī, — —** – fear; **scīscitor, scīscitārī, scīscitātus sum** – enquire repeatedly; **īgnōrō, īgnōrāre, īgnōrāvī, īgnōrātum** – not know; **rēgem** – direct object of **īgnōrandō**; **sēmet = sē** (*strengthened form*); **aperiō, aperīre, aperuī, apertum** – expose, open, reveal; the indirect question **quis esset** expands and explains **sēmet** as the direct object of **aperīret**; **quō** refers to Mucius' inability to identify the king properly; **temere** – by accident; **traxit** here must mean approximately 'dragged down'; **obtruncō, obtruncāre, obtruncāvī, obtruncātum** – cut down.

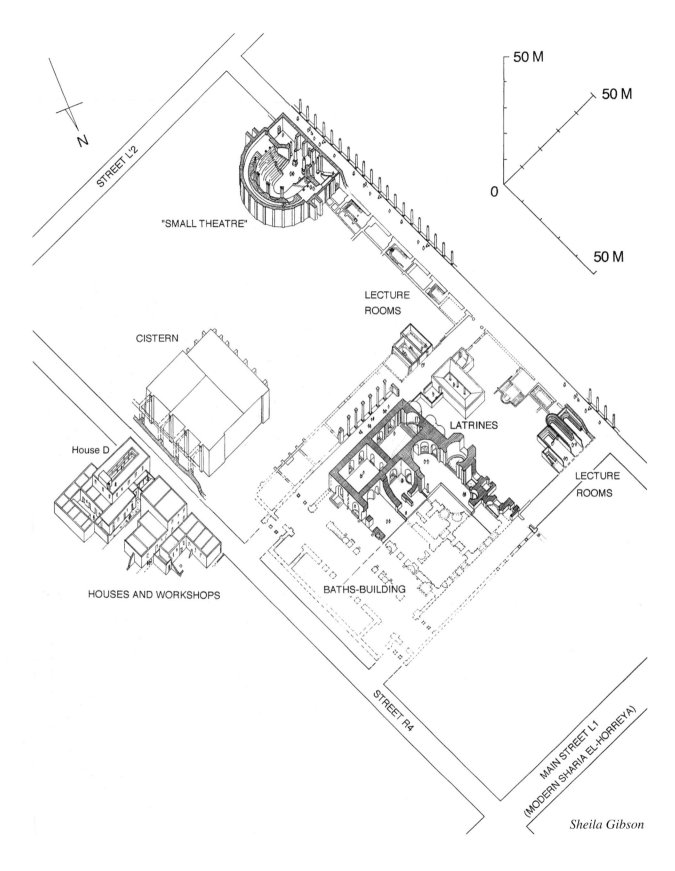

N

STREET L'2

50 M

50 M

0

50 M

"SMALL THEATRE"

LECTURE
ROOMS

CISTERN

House D

LATRINES

LECTURE
ROOMS

HOUSES AND WORKSHOPS

BATHS-BUILDING

STREET R4

MAIN STREET L1
(MODERN SHARIA EL-HORREYA)

Sheila Gibson

Fig. 52. The city-block at Kom el-Dikka in the centre of Alexandria in Egypt as it would have appeared in the sixth century AD, with the baths building, the lecture rooms of the educational complex, and the 'small theatre'.

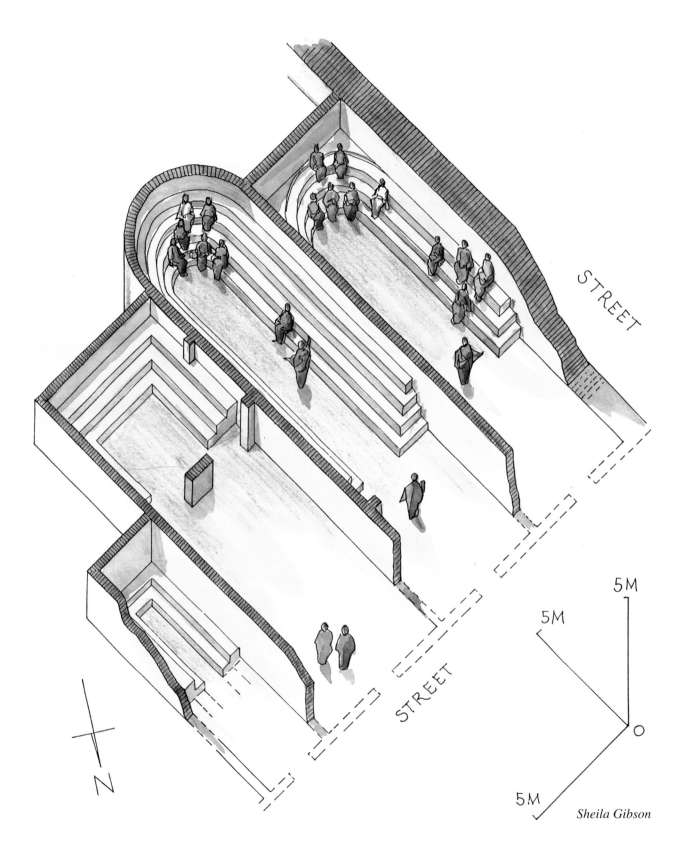

Fig. 53. Teaching rooms from the educational complex in the city centre of Alexandria in Egypt. They were in use from the fifth to the seventh centuries AD. The complex was the successor of the Ptolemaic Museum.

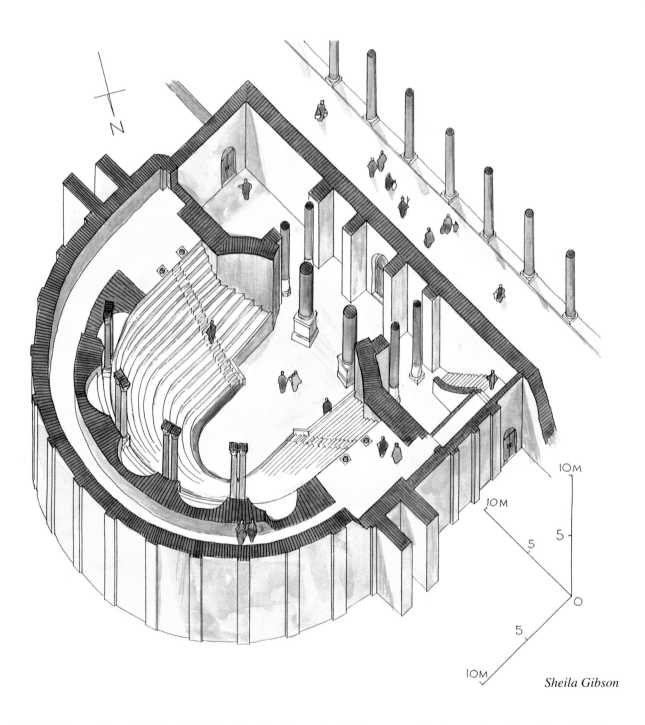

Sheila Gibson

Fig. 54. The small roofed 'theatre' of the educational complex in the centre of ancient and modern Alexandria in Egypt. It might have been used as a concert hall or lecture theatre in the fifth and sixth centuries AD.

MUCIUS SCAEVOLA:

A desperate ruse

Swore he to Lars Porsenna:
'My hand upon this flame
Is merely one of all the sum
Of Romans, much the same,
Who neither flinch when fighting,
Nor flee whate'er the cost,
Who prefer to die with honour
Than to live, the battle lost....'

T. A. Seyer, *Had Macaulay written 'Scaevola'* (2004)

Mucius Scaevola is brought before Lars Porsenna for interrogation and torture.

Vocabulary

decus, decoris, n.	beauty, glory
faciō, facere, fēcī, factum	do, make
gerō, gerere, gessī, gestum	carry, carry on, wear
iuventūs, iuventūtis, f.	young people
petō, petere, petīvī, petītum	seek, attack, ask
stō, stāre, stetī, statum	stand
vādō, vādere, —, —	go
via, viae, f.	way
virtūs, virtūtis, f.	courage, virtue
vocō, vocāre, vocāvī, vocātum	call

Vādentem inde quā per trepidam turbam cruentō mucrōne sibi ipse fēcerat viam, cum, concursū ad clāmōrem factō, comprehēnsum rēgiī satellitēs retrāxissent, ante tribūnal rēgis dēstitūtus, tum quoque inter tantās fōrtūnae minās, metuendus magis quam metuēns, 'Rōmānus sum,' inquit, 'cīvis; Gāium Mūcium vocant.[1] Hostis hostem occīdere voluī, nec ad mortem minus animī est quam fuit ad caedem.[2] Et facere et patī fortia Rōmānum est.[3] Nec ūnus in tē ego hōs animōs gessī. Longus post mē ōrdō est idem petentium decus.[4] Proinde in hōc discrīmen — sī iuvat — accingere, ut in singulās hōrās capite dīmicēs tuō, ferrum hostemque in vestibulō habeās rēgiae.[5] Hoc tibi, iuventūs Rōmāna, indīcimus bellum.[6] Nūllam aciem, nūllum proelium timueris.[7] Ūnī tibi et cum singulīs rēs erit.'

---

[1] **vādentem** refers to Mucius; **inde quā** – 'there where;' **trepidus, -a, -um** – trembling, anxious; **turba, turbae**, f. – crowd; **cruentus, -a, -um** – bloody; **mucrō, mucrōnis**, m. – sword; **concursus, concursūs**, m. – throng, crowd; **clāmor, clāmōris**, m. – shout; **comprehendō, comprehendere, comprehendī, comprehēnsum** – seize firmly; **rēgius, -a, -um** – royal; **satelles, satellitis**, m. – bodyguard; **retrahō, retrahere, retrāxī, retractum** – drag back; **tribūnal, tribūnālis**, n. – platform; **dēstituō, dēstituere, dēstituī, dēstitūtum** – set apart; **tum quoque** – 'even so;' **fōrtūna, fōrtūnae**, f. – fortune; **minae, minārum**, f. – threats; **metuō, -ere, metuī, —** – fear; **metuendus ... metuēns** – *i.e.*, despite having been captured, Mucius inspired more fear than he experienced himself; **inquit** – he says; **cīvis, cīvis**, m. or f. – citizen; for **vocant**, understand the additional direct object **mē**.

[2] **hostis** is in apposition with the subject of **voluī; occīdō, occīdere, occīdī, occīsum** – kill; **caedēs, caedis**, f. – slaughter, murder.

[3] **facere** and **patī** are the subjects; the infinitives take the direct object **fortia** ('brave deeds'); **Rōmānum** ('a Roman characteristic') a predicate nominative with **est**.

[4] **ōrdō, ōrdinis**, m. – line, order.

[5] **proinde** – in like manner; **discrīmen, discrīminis**, n. – crisis, difference; **accingō, accingere, accinxī, accinctum** – prepare, make ready for; **accingere** – passive imperative followed by the indirect command construction; **singulī, -ae, -a** – single, one at a time; **hōra, hōrae**, f. – hour; **capite** – normally Latin would have had **dē capite** with **dīmicēs** (fight), but Livy has omitted the preposition; **ferrum, ferrī**, n. – iron, weapon; **vestibulum, vestibulī**, n. – fore-court; **rēgia, rēgiae**, f. – palace.

[6] **iuventūs Rōmāna** is in apposition with the subject of **indīcimus; indīcō, indīcere, indīxī, indictum** – proclaim; **bellum, bellī**, n. – war.

[7] **aciēs, aciēī**, f. – line of battle; **proelium, proeliī**, n. – battle; **timeō, timēre, timuī, —** – fear; the perfect subjunctive is used to express prohibition.

Cum rēx, simul īrā īnfēnsus perīculōque conterritus, circumdarī īgnēs minitābundus iubēret nisi exprōmeret properē quās īnsidiārum sibi minās per ambāgēs iaceret, 'Ēn tibi,' inquit, 'ut sentiās quam vīle corpus sit eīs quī māgnam glōriam vident;' dextramque accēnsō ad sacrificium foculō inicit.[8]

Quam cum velut aliēnātō ab sēnsū torrēret animō, prope attonitus mīrāculō rēx — cum ab sēde suā prōsiluisset āmovērīque ab altāribus iuvenem iussisset — 'Tu vērō abī,' inquit, 'in tē magis quam in mē hostīlia ausus.[9] Iubērem mācte virtūte esse, sī prō meā patriā ista virtūs stāret.[10] Nunc, iūre bellī, līberum tē, intāctum inviolātumque hinc dīmittō.'[11]

---

[8] **simul** – at the same time; **īnfēnsus, -a, -um** – hostile; **conterreō, conterrēre, conterruī, conterritus** – frighten completely; **circumdō, circumdāre, circumdedī, circumdātum** – give around; **minitābundus, -a, -um** – threatening; **exprōmō, exprōmere, exprōmpsī, exprōmptum** – disclose; **nisi** – if … not; **properē** – hastily; **quās** is an interrogative adjective modifying **minās** (threats); **īnsidiae, īnsidiārum**, f. pl. – ambush, treachery; **sibi** refers to Porsenna; **ambāgēs, ambāgis**, f. – roundabout way; **iaciō, iacere, iēcī, iactum** – let drop, hint; **ēn** – see; **tibi** as a reflexive pronoun should be taken with **sentiās** ('see for yourself'); **quam** is an adverb ('how', 'in what way'); **vīlis, vīle** – cheap; **corpus** is a predicate nom. with **est**; **glōria, glōriae**, f. – glory; **dexter, dextra, dextrum** – right, favourable; **accendō, accendere, accendī, accēnsum** – set on fire; **sacrificium, sacrificī**, n. – sacrifice; apparently, a fire had been lit by the Etruscans preparatory to a sacrifice; **foculus, foculī**, m. – brazier; **iniciō, inicere, iniēcī, iniectum** – cast in.

[9] **quam** = **manum dextram**; **velut** – just as if; **aliēnātō ab sēnsū animō** – abl. of description; **aliēnō, aliēnāre, aliēnāvī, aliēnātum** – alienate; **sēnsus, -ūs**, m. – feeling, sense; **torreō, torrēre, torruī, tostum** – roast; **prope** – nearly (*adv.* taken with **attonitus**); **attonō, attonāre, attonuī, attonitum** – stun; **mīrāculum, mīrāculī**, n. – wonder; **sēdēs, sēdis**, f. – seat, abode; **prōsiliō, prōsilīre, prōsiluī,** — – leap forth; **āmoveō, āmovēre, āmōvī, āmōtum** – put away; **altāria, altārium**, n. pl. – altar; **iuvenis, iuvenis** – young man; **vērō** – indeed (*often not translated*); **abeō, abīre, abīvī, abitūrum** – go away; **hostīlis, hostīle** – hostile.

[10] **iubērem** is an imperfect subjunctive in the apodosis of a future less vivid construction, with **tē** as an understood direct object; **mācte** (*indecl.*) **esse** – be honoured for (*with abl.*); **patria, patriae**, f. – fatherland.

[11] **nunc** – now; **līber, lībera, līberum** – free; **intāctus, -a, -um** – uninjured; **inviolātus, -a, -um** – unhurt.

Tunc Mūcius, quasi remūnerāns meritum, 'Quandō quidem,' inquit, 'est apud tē virtūtī honōs, ut beneficiō tuleris ā mē quod mīnīs nequistī: trecentī coniūrāvimus prīncipēs iuventūtis Rōmānae, ut in tē hāc viā
grassārēmur.¹² Mea prīma sors fuit;¹³ cēterī, ut cūiusque ceciderit prīmī, quoad tē opportūnum fōrtūna
dederit, suō quisque tempōre aderunt.'¹⁴

Mūcium dīmissum, cuī posteā Scaevolae ā clāde dextrae manūs cognōmen inditum, lēgātī ā Porsennā
Rōmam secūtī sunt.¹⁵

Livy 2. 12. 8–13. 1

---

¹² **tunc = tum**; **quasi** – just as if; **remūneror, remūnerārī, remūnerātus sum** – repay; **meritum, meritī**, n. – service;
quandō – since; **virtūtī** = dat. of reference; **honōs (honor), honōris**, m. – honour; **ut ...** – a purpose clause; the main
verb on which the **ut**-clause depends, however, is unexpressed; understand the sentence to run along the lines of the
following: 'in order that you gain information, (I will tell you as follows:) ...'; **beneficium, beneficī**, n. – favour;
beneficiō is a dat. of purpose; **nequeō, nequīre, nequīvī, — —** – be unable; **nequistī = nequīvistī**; **quod ... nequistī** as
a phrase is the direct object of **tuleris**; **trecentī, -ae, -a** – three hundred; **trecentī** modifies **prīnceps, prīncipis**, m.
(leader) and the phrase is in apposition with the subject of **coniūrō, coniūrāre, coniūrāvī, coniūrātum** – swear
together; **grassor, grassārī, grassātus sum** – proceed against.

¹³ **prīmus, -a, -um** – first; **sors, sortis**, f. – lot (as in a lottery).

¹⁴ **cēterī, -ae, -a** – the others, rest of; **ut ... prīmī** – understand **sors** (lot) as the noun governing the genitives **cūiusque**
and **prīmī**: 'as the lot of each one takes its ranking as the first lot;' **quoad** – until; **opportūnus, -a, -um** – exposed
(understand the adj. with the infinitive **esse**); **fōrtūna, fōrtūnae**, f. – fortune; the phrase **suō quisque tempōre** is in
apposition to **cēterī**.

¹⁵ **clādēs, clādis**, f. – damage; **cognōmen, cognōminis**, n. – name; **indō, indere, indidī, inditum** – place upon;
lēgātus, lēgātī, m. – ambassador, lieutenant; **lēgātī** should be taken with **ā Porsennā**.

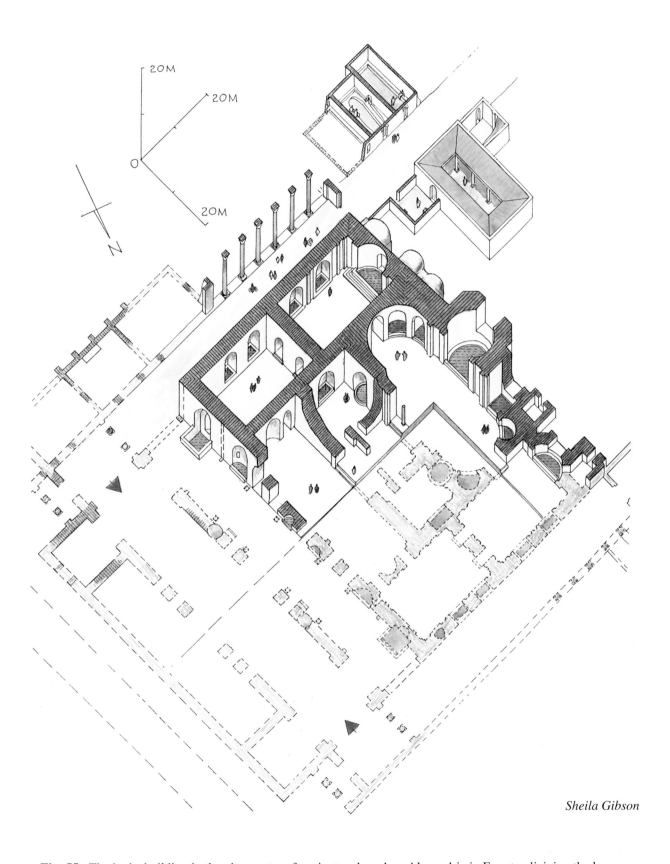

20M

20M

20M

O

Sheila Gibson

Fig. 55. The baths building in the city-centre of ancient and modern Alexandria in Egypt, adjoining the large educational complex, in the sixth century AD. There are small pools of water, shown in blue, rather than the larger pools of earlier baths buildings. To the top right is a public lavatory.

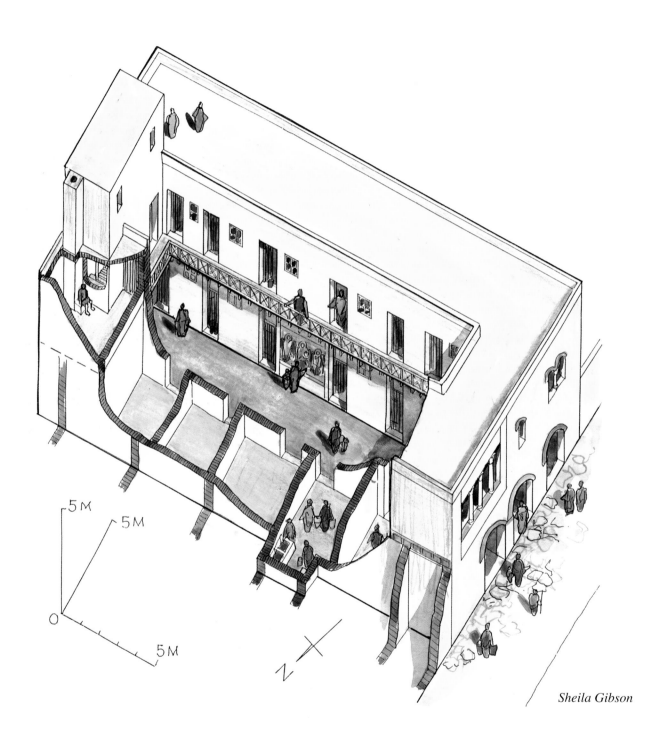

Sheila Gibson

Fig. 56. House D at Kom el-Dikka in the city-centre of Alexandria in Egypt, from about the sixth century AD.
There was a Christian shrine in the middle-courtyard with a painting of the Virgin Mary and Child.
The complex included workshops, a well and a latrine.

The end of the siege:

The adventures of Cloelia

My temples throb, my pulses boil,
I'm sick of Song and Ode and Ballad —
So Thyrsis, take the midnight oil,
And pour it on a lobster salad.

My brain is dull, my sight is foul,
I cannot write a verse, or read —
Then Pallas, take away thine Owl,
And let us have a Lark instead.

Thomas Hood (1799–1845), 'To Minerva'

After the encounter with Scaevola, Lars Porsenna sued for peace with the Romans, and both parties agreed the Etruscans would return home, taking with them Roman hostages to assure safe passage and peaceful co-existence. But one of the hostages, Cloelia (Cloelia, -ae, f.), led the others safely back to Rome, escaping, some say, on horseback. Livy says Porsenna accounted this an achievement more extraordinary than Horatius' defence of the bridge or Scaevola's immolation of his right hand. But this opinion may do more credit to Livy's and Porsenna's romantic hearts than their analytic heads. Presumably, the astonishment arises because Cloelia was a woman. Eventually, Porsenna agreed that, trumped though he may have been, it was still better to maintain the peace, and he left the Romans free to develop their empire.

Vocabulary

āgmen, āgminis, n.	column, band
cōnsēnsus, cōnsēnsūs, m.	agreement
dēdō, dēdere, dēdidī, dēditum	surrender
dēposcō, dēposcere, dēpoposcī, –	demand, require
fēmina, fēminae, f.	woman
honōrō, honōrāre, honōrāvī, honōrātum	honour, respect
obses, obsidis, m. and f.	hostage
restituō, restituere, restituī, restitūtum	restore
rumpō, rumpere, rūpī, ruptum	break
vertō, vertere, vertī, versum	turn, overturn

Ergō ita honōrātā virtūte, fēminae quoque ad pūblica decora excitātae, et Cloelia virgō, ūna ex obsidibus, cum castra Etruscōrum fōrte haud procul rīpā Tiberis locāta essent, frūstrāta custōdēs, dux āgminis virginum inter tēla hostium Tiberim trānāvit, sōspitēsque omnēs Rōmam ad propīnquōs restituit.[1]

Quod ubi rēgī nūntiātum est, prīmō incēnsus īrā, ōrātōrēs Rōmam mīsit ad Cloeliam obsidem dēposcendam:[2] aliās haud māgnī facere.[3] Deinde in admīrātiōnem versus, suprā Coclitēs Mūciōsque dīcere id facinus esse, et prae sē ferre quemadmodum,[4] sī nōn dēdātur obses, prō ruptō foedus sē habitūrum; sīc dēditam intāctam inviolātamque ad suōs remissūrum.[5]

---

[1] **ergō** – therefore; **quoque** – also; **pūblicus, -a, -um** – public; **excitō, excitāre, excitāvī, excitātum** – rouse; **excitātae – excitātae sunt; haud** – not; **procul** – at a distance (with an abl. of separation); **frūstror, frūstrārī, frūstrātus sum** – deceive; the participle **frūstrāta** modifies **Cloelia; dux** is in apposition with **Cloelia; tēlum, tēlī**, n. – weapon; **trānō, trānāre, trānāvī, —** – swim across; **sōspes, sōspitis** – safe; **propīnquī, propīnquōrum**, m. pl. – relatives.

[2] **quod = illud** in reference to Cloelia's courage; **prīmō** – at first (adv.); **ōrātor, ōrātōris**, m. – spokesman.

[3] **aliās** refers to the other prisoners aside from Cloelia; **māgnī** – gen. of value: 'of great account;' **facere** is a historical infinitive, here meaning 'consider.'

[4] **admīrātiō, admīrātiōnis**, f. – admiration, wonder; **suprā** – above, beyond (*with accus.*); **Coclitēs Mūciōsque** – the names of Horatius Cocles and Mucius Scaevola are used as if they were masculine plural adjectives: 'the deeds of Cocles and Scaevola'; **dīcere** is a historical infinitive; **prae ... ferre = praeferre** (prefer); the separation of the prefix from the main verb of a compound is called tmesis; **quemadmodum** – how (taking a rare accusative and infinitive construction); **prō** (*with abl.*) = as, the same as; **habitūrum = habitūrum esse.**

[5] **intāctus, -a, -um** – uninjured; **inviolātus, -a, -um** – unhurt; **ad suōs = ad suōs populōs; suōs** refers to Cloelia; **remittō, remittere, remīsī, remissum** – send back; **remissūrum = remissūrum esse.**

Utrimque cōnstitit fidēs;[6] et Rōmānī pīgnus pācis ex foedere restituērunt, et apud rēgem Etruscum nōn tūta sōlum sed honōrāta etiam virtūs fuit, laudātamque virginem parte obsidum sē dōnāre dīxit.[7] Ipsa quōs vellet legeret.[8]

Prōductīs omnibus, ēlēgisse impūbēs dīcitur[9] — quod et virginitātī decōrum et cōnsēnsū obsidum ipsōrum probābile erat.[10] eam aetātem potissimum līberārī ab hoste quae māximē opportūna iniūriae esset.[11]

Pāce redintegrātā, Rōmānī novam in fēminā virtūtem novō genere honōris, statuā equestrī, dōnāvēre.[12] In summā Sacrā Viā fuit posita virgō īnsīdēns equō.[13]

Livy 2. 13. 6–11

---

[6]   **utrimque** – on both sides; **cōnsistō** – here contains the idea of permanence: 'lasted' (*i.e.*, remained steadfast).

[7]   **pīgnus, pīgnoris or pīgneris**, n. – a person given as security, pledge; **pignus** is understood to be in apposition with **eam** (Cloelia), which is unexpressed; **Etruscus, -a, -um** – Etruscan; **nōn sōlum ... sed (etiam)** – not only ... but also; **tūtus, -a, -um** – safe; **virtūs** must refer to Cloelia; **dōnō, dōnāre, dōnāvī, dōnātum** – present x (*in the accus.*) with y (*in the abl.*).

[8]   **legeret** is a deliberative subjunctive: 'she should choose ....'

[9]   **prōdūcō, prōdūcere, prōdūxī, prōductum** – lead out; **ēligō, ēligere, ēlēgī, ēlēctum** – pick out; **impūbēs, impūbis** – under the age of puberty; youthful; **dīcitur** is used as an impersonal verb with indirect statement; Cloelia is to be understood as the subject of the indirect statement.

[10]   The antecedent of **quod** is the fact of Cloelia's decision to choose the very young; **decōrus, -a, -um** – becoming; **virginitās, virginitātis**, f. – maidenhood; virginity; **probābilis, probābile** – commendable.

[11]   **eam aetātem (= illam aetātem)** introduces another indirect statement, explanatory of the first indirect statement, using **dicitur** again as the main verb; **potissimum** – especially; **līberō, līberāre, līberāvī, līberātum** – free; the antecedent of **quae** is **aetātem**; **opportūnus, -a, -um** – apt, exposed; **iniūria, iniūriae**, f. – injustice, injury.

[12]   **redintegrō, redintegrāre, redintegrāvī, redintegrātum** – restore, renew; **novus, -a, -um** – new; **honor, honōris**, m. – honour; **statua, statuae**, f. – statue; **equester, equestris, equestre** – equestrian; **dōnō, -āre, -āvī, -ātum** – recognize; **dōnāvere = dōnāvērunt**.

[13]   **summus, -a, -um** – top of; **sacer, sacra, sacrum** – sacred; the Sacred Way was one of the main Roman thoroughfares; **īnsīdō, īnsīdere, īnsēdī, īnsessum** – sit on (*with dat.*).

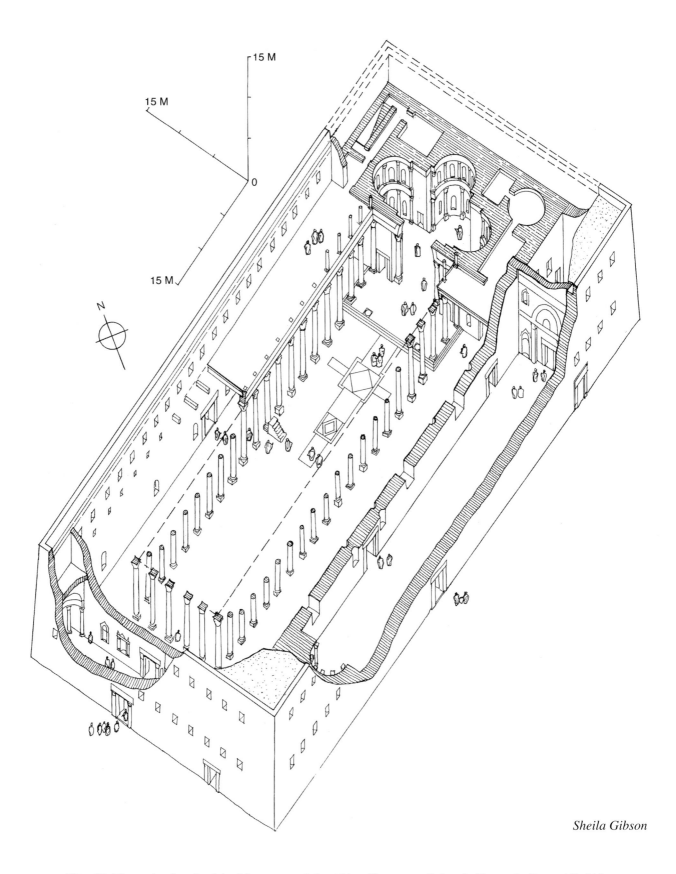

15 M

15 M

15 M

N

Sheila Gibson

Fig. 57. The main church of the Monastery of the Abbot Shenute at Sohag in Egypt, built ca. AD 440.

It is called the 'White Monastery' after the colour of its limestone walls.

Historical appendices

A chronology of Roman history
Significant points of geography
Some sentences and passages for memory

Can Queen Victoria Eat Cold Apple Pie?

Traditional school mnemonic for naming the seven hills of Rome:
the Capitoline, Quirinal, Viminal, Esquiline, Caelian, Aventine, and Palatine

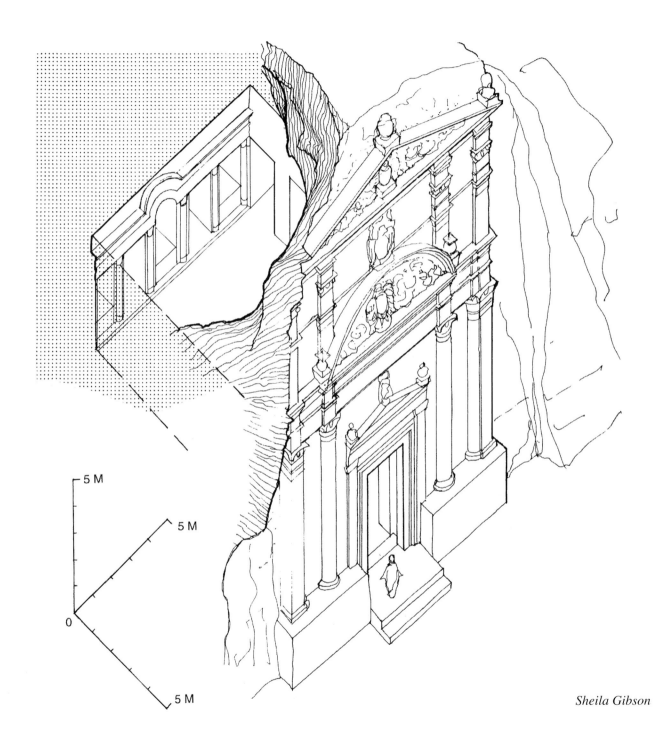

5 M

5 M

5 M

0

Sheila Gibson

Fig. 58. The Tomb of Sextius Florentinus at Petra in Jordan, built ca. AD 129. T. Aninius Sextius Florentinus was Roman governor of Arabia in AD 127. The tomb was commissioned by his son. His grave was probably the one in the centre of the back wall.

HISTORICAL APPENDIX 1
A CHRONOLOGY OF ROMAN HISTORY

Plaudite porcellī, porcōrum pigra propāgō.
Prōgreditur, plūrēs porcī pīnguēdine plēnī
Pūgnantēs pergunt, pecudem pars prōdigiōsa,
Perturbat pede petrōsās plērumque platēās,
Pars portentōsē populōrum prāta profānat.

Pūgna Porcōrum per P. Porcium Poētam (1831)

Historians in ancient Rome, at least from the first century BC, dated events with reference to years from 753 BC, the traditional date for the founding of Rome (ab urbe conditā or AUC). In the table below, years are reckoned in the conventional way, using BC (Before Christ) and AD (Annō Dominī, in the year of our Lord).

BC

753	Foundation of Rome, according to tradition
753–715	Reign of Romulus; creation of political and religious institutions; rape of the Sabine women
534–509	Reign of Tarquin the Proud, last of the kings
509	Beginning of the Roman Republic; establishment of the consulship
508/7	Lars Porsenna besieges Rome
499	Defeat of Latins at Lake Regillus
494	Secession of the plebeians; creation of the tribunate
450	Completion of the Twelve Tables, on which were inscribed the statutes of Rome
390	Gauls capture Rome; Camillus defeats the Gauls
366	First plebeian consuls
ca. 300	Roman silver coinage introduced
280	Pyrrhus of Epirus attacks Rome
275	Defeat of Pyrrhus
264–41	First Punic War; Rome gains control of Sicily
240	Livius Andronicus produces a comedy and tragedy at the Ludi Romani (Roman Games), the traditional beginning of Latin literature
218	Beginning of the Second Punic War; Hannibal marches on Italy

216	Battle of Cannae in which the Romans are defeated
211	Hannibal marches on Rome
202	Battle of Zama, at which Scipio Africanus defeats Hannibal; end of the Second Punic War with a treaty ratified at Rome in 201
149–146	Third Punic War
146	Destruction of Carthage and its annexation as a province of Africa; sack of Corinth; creation of Roman province of Macedonia
133	Tribunate and death of Tiberius Gracchus; Attalus III of Pergamum bequeathes his fortune to Rome; sack of Numantia
123	First tribunate of Gaius Gracchus
122	Second tribunate of Gaius Gracchus
111–105	Jugurthine War in Numidia (south of Carthage)
100	C. Marius becomes consul for the sixth time; birth of Julius Caesar
91	Start of the Social or Italic War, waged by Italian allies against Rome
88	Sulla seizes Rome; Marius flees to Africa
87–83	Sulla's military campaigns in Greece and Asia; end of Social War
86	Marius dies
83–80	Sulla's dictatorship
79	Death of Sulla
75	Annexation of Cyrene in Africa
73–71	Verres is governor of Sicily; revolt of Spartacus
70	Cicero's prosecution of Verres
67	Beginning of Pompey's eastern campaigns
65	Annexation of Syria
63	Consulship of Cicero; conspiracy of Catiline
62	Pompey's eastern setttlement and return to Rome
58–50	Caesar's Gallic campaigns
49	Caesar crosses the Rubicon
48	Battle of Pharsalus in Thessaly, in which Caesar defeats Pompey; murder of Pompey in Egypt; Caesar's liaison with Cleopatra (resulting in a son born in 47)
46	Caesar returns to Rome
44	Assassination of Caesar

43   Octavian marches on Rome and becomes consul; murder of Cicero

42   Deification of Julius Caesar

37   Marriage of Anthony and Cleopatra

31   Battle of Actium, in which Octavian defeats Anthony

30   Suicide of Cleopatra; Egypt becomes a Roman province

28   Octavian becomes princeps

27   Octavian is given the name Augustus

19   Death of Virgil

8   Death of Horace

AD

8   Banishment of Ovid

14   Death of Augustus; Tiberius becomes princeps

ca. 26   Pontius Pilate becomes prefect of Judaea

37   Death of Tiberius; Caligula becomes princeps

41   Death of Caligula, succeeded by Claudius

43   Claudius' invasion of Britain

54   Death of Claudius, succeeded by Nero

64   Outbreak of fire in Rome

68   Death of Nero, succeeded by Galba

69   Year of four emperors: Galba, Otho, Vitellius, Vespasian

70   The sack of Jeruusalem and destruction of the Temple

79   Titus succeeds Vespasian; eruption of Mt. Vesuvius

81   Domitian succeeds Titus

96–98   Rule of Nerva

98–117   Rule of Trajan

117–138   Rule of Hadrian

138–161   Rule of Antoninus Pius

161–180   Rule of Marcus Aurelius

180–192   Rule of Commodus, strangled on 31 December 192

193–211   Rule of Septimius Severus

211–217	Rule of Caracalla, initially with Geta, whom Caracalla murders
217–218	Rule of Macrinus
218–222	Rule of Elagabalus
222–235	Rule of Alexander Severus
235–285	Chaos and the rule of many (short-lived) emperors
284–305	Diocletian re-establishes control and starts a system of collegiate government known as the Tetrarchy (two senior rulers with two junior colleagues)
307–337	Rule of Constantine
312	Battle of the Milvian Bridge; Christianity becomes the official state religion
360–363	Rule of Julian the Apostate, who reinstates pagan religious practices
379–395	Rule of Theodosius I (the Great), who concludes a peace treaty with the Goths in 382
395	Empire splits into two states under Honorius (Western Empire) and Arcadius (Eastern or Byzantine Empire)
410	Alaric the Visigoth sacks Rome
476	Death of Romulus, last Emperor of the Western Empire
633–655	Arab conquests
1453	Fall of Constantinople and the end of the Byzantine Empire.

HISTORICAL APPENDIX 2
SIGNIFICANT POINTS OF GEOGRAPHY

The Art of Biography
Is different from Geography.
Geography is about Maps,
But Biography is about Chaps.

Edmund Clerihew Bentley (1875–1956)

Students should be aware of the locations of the following sites, areas, and geographical features:

Āfrica

Alexandrīa (urbs Aegyptī, also Alexandrēa)

Aquae Sextiae (urbs)

Aquitānia (pars Galliae)

Arar (flūmen)

Asia Minor

Assyria

Athēnae (urbs)

Babylōn

Belgica (pars Galliae)

Britannia

Byzantium (urbs)

Carthāgō (urbs)

Corsica (insula)

Crēta (insula)

Cyprus (insula)

Frētum Gaditānum

Gallia

Garumna (flūmen)

Hierosolyma (urbs)

Hispānia

Lacus Lemannus

Libya

Macedonia

Mare Aegaeum

Mare Hadriāticum (mare superum)

Mare Iōnicum

Mare Nostrum (mare internum)

Mare Tyrrhēnum (mare inferum)

Montēs Alpēs

Montēs Āpennīnī

Montēs Pyrēnaeī

Nīlus (flūmen)

Ōstia (portus Rōmae)

Padus (flūmen)

Phoenicē

Pontus (Euxīnus)

Prōvincia Rōmāna

Rhēnus (flūmen)

Rhodanus (flūmen)

Rōma (caput mundī)

Sardinia (insula)

Sicilia (insula)

Tiberis (flūmen)

HISTORICAL APPENDIX 3
SOME SENTENCES AND PASSAGES FOR MEMORY

Ere the parting hour go by,
Quick, thy tablets, Memory!

Matthew Arnold (1822–1888), 'A Memory Picture'

I. nescit vōx missa revertī.

Horace, *Ars Poetica* 390

A word once spoken cannot be recalled.

II. ex Āfricā semper aliquid novī.

Pliny, *Natural History* 8. 17. 42

There is always something new out of Africa.

III. rem tenē, verba sequentur.

Cato the Elder, as preserved in a fragment of the grammarian Festus

Keep at your subject; the words will come.

IV. homō sum: hūmānī nihil ā mē aliēnum putō.

Terence, *Self-Tormentor* 77

I am a human being; whatever pertains to humanity I consider my concern.

V. nōn amō tē, Sabidī, nec possum dīcere quārē;

hoc tantum possum dīcere: nōn amō tē.

Martial 1. 32

I do not love thee, Dr Fell.
The reason why, I cannot tell.
But this I know, and know full well:
I do not love thee, Dr Fell.

An apparently extemporaneous translation of the above epigram for John Fell (1625–1686) at Rugby

School by his pupil Tom Brown, threatened with expulsion unless he could construe Martial's Latin.

VI. quis? quid? ubi? quibus auxiliīs? cūr? quōmodo? quandō?

Cicero's principles for constructing an oration, as quoted by St Thomas Aquinas

Who? What? Where? With what help? Why? How? When?

VII. ēnse petit placidam sub lībērtāte quiētem.

Motto of the Commonwealth of Massachusetts

By the sword, she seeks a calm peace under freedom.

Edward Gibbon, in his memoirs, quotes this hexameter line as part of a couplet concerning the Swiss; Algernon Sidney, English ambassador to the court of Denmark in 1659–60, wrote the verse out in a book of mottoes in the Danish king's library. The ultimate origins of the line remain unclear.

VIII. sīc semper tyrannīs!

Motto of the state of Virginia

Thus ever to tyrants!

The sentence is ascribed on uncertain evidence to Brutus as he assassinated Caesar in 44 BC; it is also said to have been shouted by John Wilkes Booth when he shot Abraham Lincoln in 1865.

IX. sed fugit intereā, fugit irreparābile tempus.

Virgil, *Georgics* 3. 284

But time meanwhile is flying, flying beyond recall.

(Fairclough, trans., rev. by Goold)

X. Ōdī et amō. quārē id faciam, fōrtasse requīris.

Nesciō, sed fiērī sentiō et excrucior.

Catullus 85

I hate, and I love. Why do this, you ask? I don't know. But I feel it to be so, and it's torture.

XI.   ēripuit caelō fulmen scēptrumque tyrannīs.

> Hexameter line composed by Anne-Robert Jacques Turgot (1727–1781),
> French finance minister, on Benjamin Franklin.

He stole lightning from the heavens and the sceptre from tyrants.

XII.   Orātiō Dominica:

Pater noster, quī es in caelīs, sānctificētur nōmen tuum, adveniat rēgnum tuum, fiat voluntās tua sīcut in caelō et in terrā. Pānem nostrum supersubstantiālem dā nōbīs hodiē, et dīmitte nōbīs dēbita nostra, sīcut et nōs dīmittimus dēbitōribus nostrīs, et nē nōs indūcās in tentātiōnem, sed lībera nōs ā malō.

> Evangelium secundum Matthaeum 6. 9–13

The Lord's Prayer (*as traditionally given*):

Our Father, who art in heaven, hallowed be Thy name, Thy kingdom come, Thy will be done, on earth as it is in heaven. Give us this day our daily bread, and forgive us our trespasses, as we forgive those who trespass against us. And lead us not into temptation, but deliver us from evil.

XIII. ex nihilō nihil.

> Proverbial, perhaps derived from Lucretius, *On the Nature of Things* 2. 287:
> dē nīlō quoniam fierī nīl posse vidēmus.

Nothing comes from nothing.

XIV. verbum sapientī sat est.

> Proverbial, perhaps derived from Terence, *Phormio* 541: dictum sapientī sat est.

A word to the wise is sufficient.

XV.   nōn omnia possumus omnēs.

> Virgil, *Eclogues* 8. 63

We cannot all do everything.

XVI. per aspera ad astra.

Motto of NASA (National Aeronautics and Space Administration)

Through hardship to the stars.

The sentiment is probably proverbial; cf. Virgil, *Aeneid* 9. 641: sīc ītur ad astra; 12. 892-3: optā ardua pennīs/astra sequī; Seneca, *Hercules Furens* 437: nōn est ad astra ē terrīs via.

XVII. nāscentēs morimur fīnisque ab orīgine pendet.

Manilius, *Astronomica* 4. 16

At birth our death is sealed, and our end is consequent upon our beginning.

(Goold, trans.)

XVIII. Tū nē quaesieris, scīre nefās, quem mihi, quem tibi

fīnem dī dederint, Leuconoē, nec Babylōniōs

temptāris numerōs. ut melius, quidquid erit, patī,

seu plūrīs hiemēs seu tribuit Iuppiter ultimam,

quae nunc oppositīs dēbilitat pūmicibus mare

Tyrrhēnum: sapiās, vīna liquēs, et spatiō brevī

spem longam resecēs. dum loquimur, fūgerit invida

aetās: carpe diem, quam minimum crēdula posterō.

Horace, *Odes* 1. 11

Don't ask (we may not know), Leuconoe,
    What the gods plan for you or me.
        Leave the Chaldees to parse
        The sentence of the stars.

Better to bear the outcome, good or bad,
    Whether Jove purposes to add
        Fresh winters to the past
        Or to make this the last

Which now tires out the Tuscan sea and mocks
    Its strength with barricades of rocks.
        Be wise, strain clear the wine
        And prune the rambling vine

Of expectation. Life's short. Even while
    We talk Time, hateful, runs a mile.
        Don't trust tomorrow's bough
        For fruit. Pluck this, here, now.

(Michie, trans.)

Fig, 59. The 'Canopus' of Hadrian's Villa at Tivoli near Rome.

GLOSSARIES

LATIN TO ENGLISH
ENGLISH TO LATIN

Remuneration — O, that's the Latin word for three-farthings.

William Shakespeare (d. 1616), *Love's Labour Lost* 3. 1

'Hang-hog' is Latin for bacon, I warrant you.

William Shakespeare (d. 1616), *The Merry Wives of Windsor* 4. 1

Latin–English Glossary

Ā, ab, from, by (*prep. with abl.*)

Abdō, -ere, abdidī, abditum, hide

Abeō, -īre, abīvī, abitūrum, go away

Aborīginēs, aborīginum, m., native inhabitants

Absolvō, -ere, absolvī, absolūtum, acquit (*with abl.*); loosen

Absum, -esse, āfuī, āfutūrum, be absent, be distant

Ac, and; as *or* than (*after words of likeness or difference*)

Accēdō, -ere, accessī, accessūrum, go to

Accendō, -ere, accendī, accēnsum, set on fire, arouse

Accidit, -ere, accidit, it happens

Accingō, -ere, accinxī, accinctum, gird on, make ready for

Accipiō, -ere, accēpī, acceptum, receive

Accommodō, -āre, -āvī, -ātum, fit

Ācer, ācris, ācre, sharp, eager, fierce

Acerbitās, acerbitātis, f., bitterness

Aciēs, -ēī, f., sharp edge, eyesight, line of battle

Ad, to, for, near, in respect to (*prep. with accus.*)

Addō, -ere, addidī, additum, add, give

Addūcō, -ere, addūxī, adductum, lead to, influence

Adeō, so (*especially with adjs.*); what is more; *emphasizes preceding word, often not translated*

Adeō, -īre, adīvī, aditum, go to

Adferō, -ferre, attulī, adlātum, bring

Adficiō, -ere, adfēcī, adfectum, afflict; inspire

Adfīnitās, adfīnitātis, f., connection by marriage

Adfirmō, -āre, -āvī, -ātum, strengthen, confirm

Adhibeō, -ēre, adhibuī, adhibitum, bring to, apply

Adhūc, up to this point, still

Adiciō, -ere, adiēcī, adiectum, throw to, throw at

Adimō, -ere, adēmī, adēmptum, take away

Adipīscor, -ī, adeptus sum, get

Aditus, -ūs, m., approach

Adiungō, -ere, adiūnxī, adiūnctum, join

Adloquor, -ī, adlocūtus sum, address

Adluviēs, —, f., pool of water

Administrō, -āre, -āvī, -ātum, manage

Admīrātiō, admīrātiōnis, f., admiration, wonder

Admīror, -ārī, admīrātus sum, wonder, wonder at

Admittō, -ere, admīsī, admissum, let go, admit; commit (a crime)

Admoneō, -ēre, admonuī, admonitum, remind, advise, warn

Admoveō, -ēre, admōvī, admōtum, move to

Adpetō, -ere, adpetīvī, adpetītum, strive for, attack

Adprobō, -āre, -āvī, -ātum, approve

Adsector, -ārī, adsectātus sum, follow constantly, attend on

Adsideō, -ēre, adsēdī, —, sit near

Adsiduus, -a, -um, persistent

Adsum, -esse, adfuī, adfutūrum, be present, help

Adsūmō, -ere, adsūmpsī, adsūmptum, take up

Adulēscēns, adulēscentis, young

Adulēscentulus, -ī, m., a very young man

Adulter, adulterī, m., adulterer

Adulterium, -ī, n., adultery

Advena, -ae, m., stranger

Adveniō, -īre, advēnī, adventum, arrive

Adventus, -ūs, m., arrival

Adversārius, -a, -um, turned towards, opposed to

Adversus, -a, -um, facing, opposite, unfavourable; against (*prep. with accus.*)

Aedificō, -āre, -āvī, -ātum, build

Aedis, aedis, f., house

Aeger, aegra, aegrum, sick

Aequālis, -e, equal in age

Aequō, -āre, -āvī, -ātum, make equal

Aequus, -a, -um, level, just

Aestās, aestātis, f., summer

Aetās, aetātis, f., age

Aethēr, aetheris, m., upper air

Aetna, -ae, f., Mount Etna in Sicily

Āfricānus, -a, -um, African

Ager, agrī, m., field

Aggredior, -ī, aggressus sum, approach, attack, attempt

Āgmen, āgminis, n., column (of soldiers), band

Agō, -ere, ēgī, āctum, do, drive, discuss

Agricola, -ae, m., farmer

Āiō, ais, ait, —, —, āiunt, say

Alacritās, alacritātis, f., eagerness

Alba, -ae, f., Alba Longa, mother city of Rome, built by Ascanius

Albānī, -ōrum, m., inhabitants of Alba Longa

Albānus, -a, -um, of Alba Longa

Āles, ālitis, winged; bird (*as noun*)

Algidus, -ī, m., Mount Algidus

Aliēnō, -āre, -āvī, -ātum, alienate

Aliēnus, -a, -um, another's; unfavourable

Aliī ... aliī, some ... others

Aliquamdiū, for some considerable time

Aliquis, aliquid, someone, something

Aliquot, several (*undeclin.*)

Aliter, otherwise

Aliter atque (or ac), otherwise than

Aliter ... atque (or ac), otherwise than

Alius, -a, -ud, another, other

Alius ... alius, the one ... the other

Alō, -ere, aluī, altum, nourish

Altāria, altārium, n., altar

Alter, altera, alterum, the other, the second

Alter ... alter, the one ... the other

Altercātiō, altercātiōnis, f., dispute

Altitūdō, altitūdinis, f., height, depth

Altus, -a, -um, high, deep

Alūmen, alūminis, n., alum

Alveus, -ī, m., basket, container

Amābilis, -e, loveable, lovely

Amārus, -a, -um, bitter

Ambāgēs, ambāgis, f., roundabout way

Ambō, -ae, -ō, both

Amīcitia, -ae, f., friendship

Amictus, -ūs, m., mantle

Amīcus, -a, -um, friendly

Amīcus, -ī, m., friend

Āmittō, -ere, āmīsī, āmissum, send away, lose

Amnis, amnis, m., river

Amō, -āre, -āvī, -ātum, love

Amor, -ōris, m., love

Āmoveō, -ēre, āmōvī, āmōtum, put away

Amplus, -a, -um, large, magnificent

Anas, anatis, f., duck

Ancilla, -ae, f., slave-girl, servant

Angor, angōris, m., anguish

Angustus, -a, -um, narrow

Anima, -ae, f., air, life

Animadvertō, -ere, animadvertī, animadversum, notice

Animal, animālis, n., animal

Animus, -ī, m., mind, spirit, courage

Annus, -ī, m., year

Ante, before (*prep. with accus.*)

Anteā, previously

Antīquus, -a, -um, ancient

Aperiō, -īre, aperuī, apertum, open

Apis, apis, f., bee

Appāreō, -ēre, appāruī, appāritūrum, appear

Appellō, -āre, -āvī, -ātum, call

Appetō, *see* adpetō

Approbō, *see* adprobō

Apud, among, with (*prep. with accus.*)

Aqua, -ae, f., water

Arbitror, -ārī, arbitrātus sum, think

Arbor, arboris, f., tree

Arceō, -ēre, arcuī, —, keep ... from, hinder

Ardea, -ae, f., Ardea, a town near Rome

Ārdēns, ārdentis, burning

Ārdeō, -ēre, ārsī, ārsum, be on fire, burn

Arduus, -a, -um, steep, high

Argentum, -ī, n., silver

Arma, -ōrum, n., arms

Armō, -āre, -āvī, -ātum, arm

Arō, -āre, -āvī, -ātum, plough

Arvum, -ī, n., field

Arx, arcis, f., citadel

Ās, assis, m., as (*a coin of small value*)

Asia, -ae, f., Asia

Asper, aspera, asperum, rough, fierce

Assector, *see* adsector

Assideō, *see* adsideō

Assiduus, *see* adsiduus

Assūmō, *see* adsūmō

Āter, ātra, ātrum, black

Athēnae, -ārum, f., Athens

Atque, and; as *or* than (*after words of likeness or difference*)

Atrōx, atrōcis, cruel, violent

Attentus, -a, -um, attentive, industrious

Attica, -ae, f., Attica

Attonō, -āre, attonuī, attonitum, stun

Auctor, auctōris, m. and f., author, founder

Auctōritās, auctōritātis, f., authority, prestige

Audācia, -ae, f., boldness

Audāx, audācis, bold

Audeō, -ēre, ausus sum, dare

Audiō, -īre, -īvī, -ītum, hear

Auferō, -ferre, abstulī, ablātum, carry off

Augurium, -ī, n., bird-omen

Aula, -ae, f., hall

Aureus, -a, -um, golden

Aurum, -ī, n., gold

Auspicium, -ī, n., auspices, authority

Aut, or

Aut ... aut, either ... or

Autem, but, moreover

Auxilium, -ī, n., help

Aventīnum, -ī, m., Aventine, one of the seven hills of Rome

Aveō, -ēre, —, —, fare well; *imperative used as a form of salutation*

Āvertō, -ere, āvertī, āversum, turn away

Avidus, -a, -um, greedy, eager

Avis, -is, f., bird

Avītus, -a, -um, ancestral

Āvolō, -āre, -āvī, -ātum, fly away

Avunculus, -ī, m., maternal uncle

Avus, -ī, m., grandfather

Bacchus, -ī, m., Bacchus

Bandersnatcha, -ae, f., Bandersnatch

Barbarus, -a, -um, barbarian

Beātus, -a, -um, happy, rich

Bellō, -āre, -āvī, -ātum, wage war

Bellum, -ī, n., war

Bene, well

Beneficium, -ī, n., favour

Benīgnus, -a, -um, kind-hearted

Bēstia, -ae, m., beast

Bibliothēca, -ae, f., library

Bibō, -ere, bibī, —, drink

Bitūminātus, -a, -um, bitumenous

Bonus, -a, -um, good

Brevis, -e, short

Cadō, -ere, cecidī, casum, fall

Caecus, -a, -um, blind

Caedēs, caedis, f., slaughter

Caedō, -ere, cecīdī caesum, cut, kill

Caelum, -ī, n., sky

Caesar, Caesaris, m., Caesar

Calamitās, calamitātis, f., disaster

Calidus, -a, -um, hot

Callidus, -a, -um, clever

Campus, -ī, m., plain

Canis, canis, m. or f., dog

Canō, -ere, cecinī, —, sing

Cantō, -āre, -āvī, -ātum, sing

Capiō, -ere, cēpī, captum, take, form (a plan or conspiracy)

Capitōlium, i, n., Capitol hill, including the temple of Jupiter

Captīvus, -ī, m., prisoner

Caput, capitis, n., head

Carcer, carceris, m., prison

Careō, -ere, caruī, caritūrum, lack (*with abl.*)

Cāritās, cāritātis, f., dearness, high price

Carmen, carminis, n., song

Carthāgō, Carthāginis, f., Carthage

Cārus, -a, -um, dear

Castellum, -ī, n., fort

Castitās, castitātis, f., purity

Castra, -ōrum, n., camp

Cāsus, -ūs, m., event, misfortune, chance

Catēna, -ae, f., chain

Causa, -ae, f., cause

Causā, for the sake of (*with gen. beforehand*)

Caveō, -ēre, cāvī, cautum, beware

Caverna, -ae, f., cavity, cave

Cēdō, -ere, cessī, cessum, go, yield (*sometimes with dat.*)

Celeber, celebris, celebre, crowded, famous

Celer, celeris, celere, swift

Celeritās, celeritātis, f., speed

Celerō, -āre, —, —, hasten

Cēna, -ae, f., dinner

Cēnō, -āre, -āvī, -ātum, dine

Centum, a hundred (*undeclin.*)

Centuriō, centuriōnis, m., centurion

Cernō, -ere, crēvī, crētum, see

Certāmen, certāminis, n., struggle

Certō, -āre, -āvī, -ātum, strive

Certus, -a, -um, certain, fixed

Cervus, -ī, m., deer

Cēterī, -ae, -a, the other, the rest of

Cibārius, -a, -um, of food

Cingō, -ere, cinxī, cinctum, surround, gird on

Circā, around (*prep. with accus.*)

Circulus, -ī, m., circle

Circum, around (*prep. with accus.*)

Circumarō, -āre, -āvī, —, plough around

Circumdō, -are, circumdedī, circumdatum, surround

Circumferō, -ferre, circumtulī, circumlātum, direct about

Circumfundō, -ere, circumfūdī, circumfūsum, pour around

Circumplector, -ī, circumplexus sum, embrace

Circumspectō, -āre, -āvī, -ātum, look around

Circus, -ī, m., ring, space for chariot races, etc.

Citō, -āre, -āvī, -ātum, hurry

Cīvis, cīvis, m. or f., citizen

Cīvitās, cīvitātis, f., state

Clādēs, clādis, f., damage

Clāmor, clāmōris, m., shout

Clandestīnus, -a, -um, secret

Clārus, -a, -um, clear, bright, famous

Classis, classis, f., fleet

Claudō, -ere, clausī, clausum, close, shut in

Clēmentia, -ae, f., mercy

Cloāca, -ae, f., sewer

Coclēs, coclitis, m., person blind in one eye

Coepī, coepisse, coeptus sum, begin

Cōgitātiō, cōgitātiōnis, f., plan, design, thinking

Cōgitō, -āre, -āvī, -ātum, think, plan

Cōgnōmen, cōgnōminis, n., name

Cōgnōscō, -ere, cōgnōvī, cōgnitum, learn; know (*in perf.*)

Cōgō, -ere, coēgī, coāctum, force, collect

Cohors, cohortis, f., cohort (a tenth of a legion)

Cohortor, -ārī, cohortātus sum, urge

Colligō, -ere, collēgī, collēctum, collect

Colloquium, *see* conloquium

Collum, -ī, n., neck

Colō, -ere, coluī, cultum, cultivate, inhabit, worship

Coma, -ae, f., hair, leaves

Comes, comitis, m. and **f.,** companion

Cōmis, -e, courteous, affable

Cōmissātiō, cōmissātiōnis, f., revelling

Comitium, -ī, n., place of assembly

Commendō, -āre, -āvī, -ātum, entrust, recommend

Comminus, hand to hand

Commisātiō, *see* cōmissātiō

Commisceō, -ēre, commiscuī, commīxtum, mix together

Committō, -ere, commīsī, commissum, commit, entrust; begin (a contest)

Commoveō, -ēre, commōvī, commōtum, set in motion

Commūniō, -īre, -īvī, -ītum, fortify strongly

Commūnis, -e, common, general

Comparō, -āre, -āvī, -ātum, prepare, get

Comperiō, -īre, comperī, compertum, find

Compleō, -ēre, complēvī, complētum, fill, complete

Compōnō, -ere, composuī, compositum, put together, put to rest

Comprendō, *see* comprehendō

Comprehendō, -ere, comprehendī, comprehensum, seize firmly

Comprimō, -ere, compressī, compressum, repress, suppress

Concēdō, -ere, concessī, concessum, go, yield, grant

Concidō, -ere, concidī, —, fall

Conclāmō, -āre, -āvī, -ātum, cry aloud

Concordia, -ae, f., union

Concurrō, -ere, concurrī, concursum, run, run together

Concursus, -ūs, m., assembly

Conditor, conditōris, m., founder

Condō, -ere, condidī, conditum, establish, hide

Cōnferō, cōnferre, contulī, collātum, bring together, assign

Cōnfertus, -a, -um, crowded together

Cōnficiō, -ere, cōnfēcī, cōnfectum, do, make

Cōnfīdō, -ere, cōnfīsus sum, trust

Cōnfirmō, -āre, -āvī, -ātum, strengthen, say

Cōnflīgō, -ere, cōnflīxī, cōnflīctum, clash

Congredior, -ī, congressus sum, meet, clash

Cōniciō, -ere, cōniēcī, cōniectum, throw, throw together

Coniungō, -ere, coniūnxī, coniūnctum, join

Coniūrātiō, coniūrātiōnis, f., conspiracy

Coniūrō, -āre, -āvī, - ātum, conspire

Conligō, *see* colligō

Conloquium, -ī, n., conference

Conmisceō, *see* commisceō

Conmittō, *see* committō

Conmoveō, *see* commoveō

Conmūniō, *see* commūniō

Conparō, *see* comparō

Conpleō, *see* compleō

Conpōnō, *see* compōnō

Conprehendō, *see* comprehendō

Conprimō, *see* comprimō

Cōnor, -ārī, cōnātus sum, try

Cōnsalūtō, -āre, -āvī, -ātum, hail

Cōnscendō, -ere, cōnscendī, cōnscēnsum, climb up; go aboard (a ship)

Cōnsēnsus, -ūs, m., agreement

Cōnsentiō, -īre, cōnsēnsī, cōnsēnsum, agree

Cōnsīdō, -ere, cōnsēdī, cōnsessum, settle down, encamp

Cōnsilium, -ī, n., advice, plan, wisdom, council

Cōnsistō, -ere, cōnstitī, cōnstitum, stop, stand, make a
stand

Cōnsōlor, -ārī, cōnsōlātus sum, console

Cōnspectus, -ūs, m., sight

Cōnspiciō, -ere, cōnspēxī, conspectum, catch sight of

Cōnstat, -āre, cōnstitit, it is agreed, it is clear

Cōnstituō, -ere, cōnstituī, constitūtum, establish,
decide

Cōnsuētūdō, cōnsuētūdinis, f., custom

Cōnsul, cōnsulis, m., consul

Cōnsulō, -ere, cōnsuluī, cōnsultum, consult; take
thought for (*with dat.*)

Cōnsūmō, -ere, cōnsūmpsī, consūmptum, use up,
destroy

Cōnsurgō, -ere, cōnsurrēxī, cōnsurrēctum, rise up
together

Contemnō, -ere, contempsī, contemptum, scorn

Contendō, -ere, contendī, contentum, hasten, march,
struggle

Conterreō, -ēre, conterruī, conterritum, frighten
completely

Continenter, in unbroken succession

Contineō, -ēre, continuī, contentum, hold in

Contingō, -ere, contigī, contāctum, touch

Contor, -ārī, contātus sum, enquire

Contrā, against, opposite, in reply (*prep. with accus.*)

Contrōversia, -ae, f., lawsuit, dispute

Conveniō, -īre, convēnī, conventum, come together,
meet

Convertō, -ere, convertī, conversum, turn

Convīvium, -ī, n., dinner

Convolō, -āre, -āvī, -ātum, fly together

Coorior, -īrī, coortus sum, arise suddenly

Cōpia, -ae, f., abundance, supply; forces, resources
(*plural*)

Cōpiōsus, -a, -um, plentiful

Cor, cordis, n., heart

Corinthus, -ī, f., Corinth

Cornū, -ūs, n., horn; wing of an army

Corpus, corporis, n., body

Corrumpō, -ere, corrūpī, corruptum, spoil, debauch,
corrupt

Corvus, -ī, m., raven

Crēber, crēbra, crēbrum, frequent, numerous

Crēdō, -ere, crēdidī, crēditum, believe, entrust

Cremō, -āre, -āvī, -ātum, consume by fire

Creō, -āre, -āvī, -ātum, create, appoint

Crēscō, -ere, crēvī, crētum, grow

Crēta, -ae, f., Crete

Crīmen, crīminis, n., charge, crime

Cruciātus, -ūs, m., torture

Crūdēlis, -e, cruel

Crūdēlitās, crūdēlitātis, f., cruelty

Cruentus, -a, -um, bloody

Cubiculum, -ī, n., bed-chamber

Culpa, -ae, f., fault, blame

Culter, cultrī, m., knife

Cultus, -ūs, m., cultivation, dress (adornments),
worship

Cum, when, since, although

Cum, with (*prep. with abl.*)

Cum ... tum, not only ... but also

Cunctor, -ārī, cūnctātus sum, delay

Cūnctus, -a, -um, all, the whole

Cupiditās, cupiditātis, f., desire

Cupīdō, cupīdinis, f., desire

Cupiō, -ere, cupīvī, cupītum, desire

Cūra, -ae, f., care

Cūrō, -āre, -āvī, -ātum, provide for, take care

Currō, -ere, cucurrī, cursum, run

Currus, -ūs, m., chariot

Cursor, cursōris, m., runner

Cursus, -ūs, m., course

Curvus, -a, -um, curved

Custōdia, -ae, f., prison

Custōs, custōdis, m. and **f.,** guard

Damnō, -āre, -āvī, -ātum, condemn

Dē, down from, from, concerning (*prep. with abl.*)

Dēbeō, -ēre, dēbuī, dēbitum, owe, ought

Dēbitor, dēbitōris, m., debtor

Dēcēdō, -ere, dēcessī, dēcessum, depart, go away

Decem, ten (*undeclin.*)

Decemvir, -virī, m., decemvir, magistrate in a commission of ten

Dēcernō, -ere, dēcrēvī, dēcrētum, decide, decree

Decet, -ēre, decuit, it fits, it is fitting

Dēclārō, -āre, -āvī, -ātum, proclaim, announce

Decōrum, -ī, n., propriety

Dēcurrō, -ere, dēcucurrī, dēcursum, run down

Decus, decoris, n., beauty, glory

Dēdecus, dēdecōris, n., disgrace

Dēditiō, dēditiōnis, f., surrender

Dēdō, -ere, dēdidī, dēditum, surrender

Dēdūcō, -ere, dēdūxī, dēductum, lead away, launch (ships)

Dēfendō, -ere, dēfendī, dēfensum, defend

Dēfēnsor, dēfēnsōris, m., defender

Dēferō, -ferre, dētulī, dēlātum, bring down, report

Dēfīgō, -ere, dēfīxī, dēfīxum, fix firmly

Dēfluō, -ere, dēflūxī, dēfluxum, flow down

Dēfungor, -ī, dēfūnctus sum, discharge

Dēiciō, -ere, dēiēcī, dēiectum, throw down

Dein, then, next

Deinde, then, next

Dēleō, -ēre, dēlēvī, dēlētum, destroy

Dēliciae, -ārum, f., delight, darling

Dēlīctum, -ī, n., offence

Dēligō, -ere, dēlēgī, dēlēctum, choose

Dēmigrō, -āre, -āvī, -ātum, migrate, go away

Dēmōnstrō, -āre, -āvī, -ātum, show

Dēmum, at last

Dēnī, -ae. -a, ten each

Dēnique, at last

Dēns, dentis, m., tooth

Dēperdō, -ere, dēperdidī, dēperditum, lose utterly

Dēposcō, -ere, dēpoposcī, —, demand, require

Dēprehendō, -ere, dēprehendī, dēprehēnsum, arrest

Dēserō, -ere, dēseruī, dēsertum, abandon

Dēsīderium, -ī, n., desire

Dēsīderō, -āre, -āvī, -ātum, desire, miss

Dēsiliō, -īre, dēsiluī, —, jump down

Dēsinō, -ere, dēsiī, dēsitum, cease

Dēsistō, -ere, dēstitī, dēstitum, cease

Dēspērō, -āre, -āvī, -ātum, lose hope, despair of

Dēstituō, -ere, dēstituī, dēstitūtum, set apart

Dēsum, -esse, dēfuī, dēfutūrum, be lacking

Dēsuper, from above

Dētergeō, -ēre, dētersī, dētersum, wipe off

Dētrūdō, -ere, dētrūsī, dētrūsum, dislodge

Deus, -ī, m., god

Dexter, dextra, dextrum, right, favourable

Dīcō, -ere, dīxī, dictum, say, call

Dictātor, dictātōris, m., dictator

Diēs, -ēī, m. or **f.,** day

Difficilis, -e, difficult

Diffīdō, -ere, diffīsus sum, distrust, despair

Dīgnitās, dīgnitātis, f., authority, prestige

Dīgnus, -a, um, worthy

Dīiūdicō, -āre, -āvī, -ātum, judge between, decide

Dīligēns, dīligentis, diligent, careful

Dīligentia, -ae, f., carefulness, industry

Dīligō, -ere, dīlēxī, dīlēctum, love

Dīlūcēscō, -ere, dīlūxī, —, grow light

Dīmicō, -āre, -āvī, -ātum, fight

Dīmittō, -ere, dīmīsī, dīmissum, send away

Dīripiō, -ere, dīripuī, dīreptum, tear away, plunder

Discipulus, -ī, m., pupil

Discō, -ere, didicī, —, learn

Discrīmen, discrīminis, n., difference, crisis

Dissimilis, -e, unlike, dissimilar

Dissimulō, -āre, -āvī, -ātum, disguise

Dissolvō, -ere, dissolvī, dissolūtum, take apart, discharge

Diū, for a long time

Dīves, dīvitis, rich

Dīvidō, -ere, dīvīsī, dīvīsum, divide

Dīvīnitus, by divine providence

Dīvus, -a, -um, divine

Dō, dare, dedī, datum, give

Doceō, -ēre, docuī, doctum, teach, tell

Docilis, -e, taught easily

Doctor, doctōris, m., teacher

Doleō, -ēre, doluī, dolitūrum, grieve

Dolor, dolōris, m., pain, sorrow

Dolus, -ī, m., treachery

Domesticus, -a, -um, domestic

Dominātiō, dominātiōnis, f., mastery, lordship

Dominus, -ī, m., master

Domus, -ī or ūs, f., home

Dōnātīvum, -ī, n., largess (given by an emperor to his soldiers)

Dōnō, -āre, -āvī, -ātum, give, present X (*in the accus.*) with Y (*in the abl.*)

Dōnum, -ī, n., gift

Dormiō, -īre, -īvī, -ītum, sleep

Dubitō, -āre, -āvī, -ātum, hesitate (*with infinitive*); doubt (*with subjunctive*)

Dūcō, -ere, dūxī, ductum, lead, consider

Dulcis, -e, sweet

Dum, while (*with indicative.*); until, provided that (*with subjunctive*)

Duo, -ae, -o, two

Duodecimus, -a, -um, twelfth

Duplex, duplicis, double

Duplicō, -āre, -āvī, -ātum, make double, double

Dūrus, -a, -um, hard, hardy, cruel

Dux, ducis, m., leader

Ē, ex, out of (*prep. with. abl.*)

Ē rēpūblicā, for the good of the state (*see* rēs pūblica)

Ecce, see!

Edō, ēsse, ēdī, ēsum, eat

Ēdō, -ere, ēdidī, ēditum, give out, put on

Ēducō, -āre, -āvī, -ātum, educate

Ēdūcō, -ere, ēdūxī, ēductum, lead out

Efficiō, -ere, effēcī, effectum, accomplish, bring it about

Effugiō, -ere, effūgī, —, flee from, escape

Effundō, -ere, effūdī, effūsum, pour out

Ego (meī, mihi, mē, mē), I

Ēgredior, -ī, ēgressus sum, go out

Ēgregius, -a, -um, extraordinary

Ēiciō, -ere, ēiēcī, ēiectum, expel

Elephantus, -ī, m., elephant, ivory

Ēligō, -ere, ēlēgī, ēlēctum, pick out

Ēloquēns, ēloquentis, eloquent

Ēmicō, -āre, ēmicuī, ēmicātum, leap

Ēmittō, -ere, ēmīsī, ēmissum, send forth

Ēmō, -ere, ēmī, ēmptum, buy

Ēmorior, -ī, —, die

Ēn, see!

Enim, for, indeed

Eō, there (to that place)

Eō, īre, īvī or iī, itum, go

Eōdem, to the same place

Eques, equitis, m., horseman; cavalry (*plural*)

Equester, equestris, equestre, equestrian

Equitātus, -ūs, m., cavalry

Equus, -ī, m., horse

Ergā, toward (*prep. with accus.*)

Ergō, therefore

Errō, -āre, -āvī, -ātum, wander

Error, errōris, m., wandering, error

Et, and, also, even

Et ... et, both ... and

Etiam, also, even

Etruscī, -ōrum, m., Etruscans

Etruscus, -a, -um, Etruscan

Etsī, although, and yet

Euphrātēs, Euphrātis, m., Euphrates river

Eurus, -ī, m., south-east wind

Ēvādō, -ere, ēvāsī, ēvāsum, go out, escape

Ēveniō, -īre, ēvēnī, ēventum, come out, happen

Ēvertō, -ere, ēvertī, ēversum, overthrow

Ēvocō, -āre, -āvī, -ātum, call out

Ex, *see* ē

Exanimō, -āre, -āvī, -ātum, deprive of breath

Exasperō, -āre, -āvī, -ātum, roughen, exasperate

Excēdō, -ere, excessī, excessum, go out

Excelsus, -a, -um, lofty, high

Excīdō, -ere, excīdī, —, raze

Excipiō, -ere, excēpī, exceptum, catch, receive, follow, exempt

Excitō, -āre, -āvī, -ātum, rouse

Exemplum, -ī, n., precedent, example, warning

Exerceō, -ēre, exercuī, exercitum, exercise, train, employ, torment

Exercitus, -ūs, m., army

Exiguus, -a, -um, small

Eximō, -ere, exēmī, exēmptum, take away

Exīstimō, -āre, -āvī, -ātum, think

Expavēscō, -ere, expāvī, —, fear greatly

Expellō, -ere, expulī, expulsum, drive out; banish

Expetō, -ere, expetīvī, expetītum, strive after

Explōrātor, explōrātōris, m., scout

Expōnō, -ere, exposuī, expositum, expose, put forth

Exprimō, -ere, expressī, expressum, press, portray

Exprōmō, -ere, exprōmpsī, exprōmptum, disclose

Expūgnō, -āre, -āvī, -ātum, take by assault, storm

Expūrgō, -āre, -āvī, -ātum, purge, cleanse

Exsistō, -ere, exstitī, —, emerge, be

Exspectō, -āre, -āvī, -ātum, wait for

Exstinguō, -ere, exstinxī, exstinctum, exstinguish

Extrā, outside (*prep. with. accus.*)

Fabricō, -āre, -āvī, -ātum, construct

Fābula, -ae, f., tale

Facile, easily

Facilis, -e, easy

Facinus, facinoris, n., deed, crime

Faciō, -ere, fēcī, factum, do, make

Fallācia, -ae, f., lie

Fāma, -ae, f., fame, rumour

Famēs, famis, f., hunger

Fastīgium, -ī, n., (sloping) roof

Fateor, -ērī, fassus sum, confess

Fatīgō, -āre, -āvī, -ātūrum, weary

Fātum, -ī, n., fate

Faveō, -ēre, fāvī, fautum, favour (*with dat.*)

Fel, fellis, n., gall-bladder, gall, poison

Fēlīx, fēlīcis, happy, fruitful

Fēmina, -ae, f., woman

Femur, femoris, n., thigh

Ferē, about, generally

Ferīna, -ae, f., venison

Ferō, ferre, tulī, lātum, bear, carry, say

Ferōx, ferōcis, headstrong

Ferrum, -ī, n., iron, weapon

Ferus, -a, -um, wild, fierce

Festīnō, -āre, -āvī, -ātum, hasten

Fīcus, -ī or **ūs, m.,** fig-tree

Fidēlis, -e, trusty

Fīdēnae, -ārum, f., Fidenae, a town in Italy

Fīdēnātēs, Fīdēnātum, m., the Fidenates, an Italian tribe

Fidēs, -eī, f., faith, belief; *that which creates faith or belief:* loyalty, promise, protection, evidence, fulfilment

Fīdus, -a, -um, faithful, trustworthy

Fīlia, -ae, f., daughter

Fīlius, fīlī, m., son

Fīniō, -īre, -īvī, -ītum, put an end to

Fīnis, fīnis, m., end, boundary; territory (*plural*)

Fīnitimus, -a, -um, neighbouring

Fiō, fierī, factus sum, be made, be done

Flectō, -ere, flēxī, flexum, bend

Flētus, -ūs, m., weeping

Flō, flāre, flāvī, flātum, blow

Flōreus, -a, -um, flowery

Fluctus, -ūs, m., wave, sea

Fluitō, -āre, -āvī, —, float

Flūmen, flūminis, n., river

Fluō, -ere, flūxī, fluxum, flow

Foculus, -ī, m., brazier

Foedus, -a, -um, foul

Feodus, foederis, n., treaty, agreement

Fōrma, -ae, f., form, beauty

Fōrs, fōrtis, f., chance

Fōrte, by chance

Fortis, -e, brave

Fōrtūna, -ae, f., fortune

Fōrtūnātus, -a, -um, fortunate

Fossa, -ae, f., ditch

Fragilis -e, fragile

Fragor, fragōris, m., crashing

Frangō, -ere, frēgī, frāctum, break

Frāter, frātris, m., brother

Fremō, -ere, fremuī, —, roar, rage

Frequēns, frequentis, frequent, numerous

Frētus, -a, -um, relying on (*often with abl.*)

Frīgidus, -a, -um, cold, cool

Frūctus, -ūs, m., fruit, profit, enjoyment

Frūmentum, -ī, n., grain

Fruor, -ī, frūctus or **fruitūrus sum,** enjoy (*with abl.*)

Frūstrā, in vain

Frūstror, -ārī, frūstrātus sum, deceive

Fuga, -ae, f., flight

Fugiō, -ere, fūgī, —, flee, avoid

Fulgeō, -ēre, fulsī, —, shine

Fulgor, fulgōris, m., lightning

Fulgurō, -āre, -āvī, -ātum, lighten

Fulmen, fulminis, n., thunderbolt

Fulminō, -āre, —, —, hurl lightning

Fundāmentum, -ī, n., foundation

Fundō, -ere, fūdī, fūsum, pour, defeat

Fungor, -ī, fūnctus sum, perform

Fūnus, fūneris, n., death, destruction

Gaberbocchus, -ī, m., Jabberwocky

Gallia, -ae, f., Gaul

Gallus, -ī, m., a Gaul

Gaudeō, -ēre, gāvīsus sum, rejoice

Gaudium, -ī, n., joy

Geminī, -ōrum, m., twins

Geminus, -a, -um, twin

Genāva, -ae, f., Geneva

Gener, generī, m., son-in-law

Gēns, gentis, f., race, nation, family

Genū, -ūs, n., knee

Genus, generis, n., race, kind, offspring

Gerō, -ere, gessī, gestum, carry, carry on, wear

Gīgnō, -ere, genuī, genitum, bear, beget

Gīrus, -ī, m., ring, orbit

Gladiātor, gladiātōris, m., gladiator

Gladius, -ī, m., sword

Glōria, -ae, f., glory

Gracilis, -e, slender

Gradus, -ūs, m., step

Grāī, -ōrum, m., Greeks

Grassor, -ārī, grassātus sum, proceed against

Grātia, -ae, f., influence, gratitude

Grātiā, for the sake of (*with gen. beforehand*)

Grātulor, -ārī, grātulātus sum, congratulate, rejoice
(*often with dat.*)

Grātus, -a, -um, pleasing, grateful

Gravis, -e, heavy, grievous

Guttur, gutturis, n., throat

Gyrus, *see* gīrus

Habeō, -ēre, habuī, habitum, have, consider

Habitō, -āre, -āvī, -ātum, live, live in

Habitus, -ūs, m., appearance, dress, character

Hāc, by this way

Haereō, -ēre, haesī, haesūrum, cling, cling to

Haud, not

Haudquāquam, not at all

Hauriō, -īre, hausī, haustum, draw, drink, exhaust

Hibērus, -ī, m. the river Ebro

Hic, haec, hōc, this; he, she, it

Hīc, here

Hiems, hiemis, f., winter, storm

Hinc, from this place

Hispāniae, -ārum, f., Spain

Hodiē, today

Homō, hominis, m., man

Honestās, honestātis, f., honourableness

Honestus, -a, -um, good

Honor or **honōs, honōris, m.,** honour, sacrifice

Honōrō, -āre, -āvī, -ātum, honour, respect

Hōra, -ae, f., hour

Horrendus, -a, -um, dreadful

Hortor, -ārī, hortātus sum, urge

Hospes, hospitis, m. or **f.,** host, guest, stranger

Hospitālis, -e, relating to a guest

Hospitium, -ī, n., hospitality

Hostīlis, -e, hostile

Hostis, hostis, m., enemy

Hūc, to this place

Humilis, -e, humble

Iaceō, -ēre, iacuī, —, lie

Iaciō, -ere, iēcī, iactum, throw

Iactō, -āre, -āvī, -ātum, throw

Iam, already, now, soon

Iāniculum, -ī, n., Janiculum, a hill of Rome on the right
bank of the Tiber

Ibi, there

Īciō, -ere, īcī, ictum, strike

Ictus, -ūs, m., blow

Īdem, eadem, idem, the same; likewise

Idōneus, -a, -um, suitable

Igitur, therefore

Īgnārus, -a, -um, ignorant (of)

Īgnāvus, -a, -um, slothful

Īgnis, īgnis, m., fire

Īgnōrātiō, īgnōrātiōnis, f., ignorance

Īgnōrō, -āre, -āvī, -ātum, not know

Īgnōscō, -ere, īgnōvī, īgnōtum, pardon (*with dat.*)

Ille, illa, illud, that, he, she, it

Illīc, there, in that place

Illinc, from there

Illō, there (*motion to*)

Illūc, there (*motion to*)

Imāgō, imāginis, f., image

Immānis, -e, huge, savage

Immātūrus, -a, -um, unripe, immature

Immemor, immemoris, unmindful

Immēnsus, -a, -um, huge

Immineō, -ēre, —, —, overhang

Immittō, -ere, immīsī, immissum, let in, let go

Immortālitās, immortālitātis, f., immortality

Immūgiō, -īre, -īvī, —, bellow

Impedīmentum, -ī, n., hindrance; baggage (*plural*)

Impellō, -ere, impulī, impulsum, drive

Imperātōr, imperātōris, m., general

Imperium, -ī, n., command, power

Imperō, -āre, -āvī, -ātum, order

Impetrō, -āre, -āvī, -ātum, obtain, obtain one's request

Impetus, -ūs, m., attack

Impleō, -ēre, implēvī, implētum, fill

Impōnō, -ere, imposuī, impositum, put on

Importō, -āre, -āvī, -ātum, bring in

Impūbis, impūbis, under the age of puberty, youthful

Impudīcus, -a, -um, shameless

Impūne, with impunity

Īmus, -a, -um, lowest, bottom of

In, into, against (*prep. with accus.*); in, on (*prep. with abl.*)

In vicem, alternately

Inaugurō, -āre, -āvī, -ātum, take an augury in

Incalēscō, -ere, incaluī, —, grow hot

Incēdō, -ere, incessī, incessum, proceed

Incendō, -ere, incendī, incensum, set on fire, arouse

Incertus, -a, -um, uncertain

Inchoō, *see* incohō

Incidō, -ere, incidī, —, happen, occur

Incipiō, -ere, incēpī, inceptum, begin

Incitō, -āre, -āvī, -ātum, rouse

Inclīnō, -āre, -āvī, -ātum, bend, turn

Incōgnitus, -a, -um, unknown

Incohō, -āre, -āvī, -ātum, begin

Incolō, -ere, incoluī, —, inhabit

Incolumis, -e, safe

Increpitō, -āre, -āvī, -ātum, address angrily

Increpō, -āre, increpuī, increpitum, chide, harass

Incumbō, -ere, incubuī, incubitum, lie on, fall on

Incutiō, -ere, incussī, incussum, dash

Inde, from that place, then

Indicō, -āre, -āvī, -ātum, show, accuse

Indīcō, -ere, indīxī, indictum, proclaim

Indīgnitās, indīgnitātis, f., indignity

Indīgnus, -a, -um, unworthy (*often with abl.*)

Indō, -ere, indidī, inditum, place upon

Īnfāns, īnfantis, young

Īnfēlīx, īnfēlīcis, unlucky

Īnfēnsus, -a, -um, hostile

Īnferior, -ius, lower

Īnferō, -ferre, intulī, inlātum, bring in

Īnferus, -a, -um, below, underneath

Īnfestus, -a, -um, hostile

Īnfimus, -a, -um, lowest, bottom of

Īnfīrmō, -āre, -āvī, -ātum, weaken

Īnfōrmis, -e, unformed, shapeless

Ingenium, -ī, n., character, talent

Ingēns, ingentis, huge, dreadful

Ingredior, -ī, ingressus sum, go along, go into, begin

Iniciō, -ere, iniēcī, iniectum, cast in

Inimīcus, -a, -um, unfriendly

Initium, -ī, n., beginning

Iniūria, -ae, f., injustice

Iniūssū, without order

Inopia, -ae, f., lack

Inquam, inquis, inquit, say (*first, second, and third singular of a defective verb*)

Īnscius, -a, -um, not knowing

Īnsequor, -ī, īnsecūtus sum, follow

Īnsidiae, -ārum, f., ambush, treachery

Īnsīdō, -ere, īnsēdī, īnsessum, sit on

Īnsīgnis, -e, distinguished

Īnsolēns, īnsolentis, unaccustomed, insolent

Īnsōns, īnsontis, innocent

Īnspiciō, -ere, īnspēxī, īnspectum, look into

Īnstituō, -ere, īnstituī, īnstitūtum, establish, decide, prepare

Īnstō, -are, īnstitī, īnstatūrum, press on

Īnstruō, -ere, īnstrūxī, īnstrūctum, draw up, equip

Īnsula, -ae, f., island

Īnsum, -esse, īnfuī, īnfutūrum, be in

Īnsuper, above

Intāctus, -a, -um, uninjured

Integer, integra, integrum, fresh, intact, blameless

Intellegō, -ere, intellēxī, intellēctum, understand

Intendō, -ere, intendī, intentum, stretch

Inter, between, among (*prep. with accus.*)

Interdum, now and then

Intereā, meanwhile

Interficiō, -ere, interfēcī, interfectum, kill

Intericiō, -ere, interiēcī, interiectum, intervene

Interim, meantime, in the meanwhile

Interimō, -ere, interēmī, interēmptum, kill

Interpōnō, -ere, interposuī, interpositum, put between

Interrogō, -āre, -āvī, -ātum, ask

Interrumpō, -ere, interrūpī, interruptum, break, sever

Interveniō, -īre, intervēnī, interventum, intrude upon (*with dat.*)

Intrā, inside (*prep. with accus.*)

Intrō, -āre, -āvī, -ātum, go into

Inūtilis, -e, useless

Invādō, -ere, invāsī, invāsum, go into

Inveniō, -īre, invēnī, inventum, find

Investīgō, -āre, -āvī, -ātum, track, search after

Invidia, -ae, f., envy, hatred

Inviolātus, -a,, -um, unhurt

Invīsō, -ere, invīsī, —, see, visit

Invītō, -āre, -āvī, -ātum, invite

Ipse, -a, -um, -self; very (*as in "the very man"*)

Īra, -ae, f., anger, angry impulse

Īrāscor, -ī, īrātus sum, be angry (*with dat.*)

Īrātus, -a, -um, angry

Irrumpō, -ere, -irrūpī, irruptum, burst

Is, ea, id, he, she, it; such (*anticipating a result clause*)

Iste, ista, istud, that, that of yours

Istīc, there (*no motion*)

Istinc, from there

Istūc, there (*motion to*)

Ita, thus, so

Italia, -ae, f., Italy

Itaque, accordingly, and so

Item, likewise

Iter, itineris, n., way, journey

Iterum, again

Iubeō, -ēre, iussī, iūssum, order

Iububbus, -ī, m., Jubjub

Iūcundus, -a, -um, pleasant

Iūdex, iūdicis, m., judge, juryman

Iūdicō, -āre, -āvī, -ātum, judge, decide

Iugulō, -āre, -āvī, -ātum, cut the throat

Iugum, -ī, n., yoke, ridge

Iungō, -ere, iūnxī, iūnctum, join

Iuppiter, Iovis, m., Jupiter

Iūrō, -āre, -āvī, -ātum, swear

Iūs, iūris, n., justice, right, duty

Iūstus, -a, -um, regular

Iuvenālis, -e, youthful

Iuvenis, -e, young

Iuvenis, iuvenis, m., young man

Iuventa, -ae, f., youth

Iuventūs, iuventūtis, f., young people

Iuvō, -āre, iūvī, iūtum, help

Iūxtā, near (*prep. with accus.*)

Labor, labōris, m., work, suffering

Labōrō, -āre, -āvī, -ātum, strive, be hard pressed

Lacrima, -ae, f., tear

Lambō, -ere, —, —, lick

Lampas, lampadis, f., torch (*Poets often use the Greek declension.*)

Lāna, -ae, f., wool, spinning

Languidus, -a, -um, sluggish

Lapis, lapidis, m., stone

Lateō, -ēre, latuī, —, lie hidden

Latīnī, -ōrum, m., Latins

Latīnus, -a, -um, Latin

Latus, latēris, n., side

Lātus, -a, -um, wide

Laurentīnus, -a, -um, of the Laurentians (inhabitants of Latium)

Laus, laudis, f., praise, glory

Lāvīnium, -ī, n., Lavinium, city in Latium founded by Aeneas

Lāvīnius, -a, -um, of Lavinium in Latium

Lectus, -ī, m., bed

Lēgātiō, lēgātiōnis, f., embassy

Lēgātus, -ī, m., lieutenant, ambassador

Legiō, legiōnis, f., legion

Lēgō, -āre, -āvī, -ātum, appoint

Legō, -ere, lēgī, lēctum, collect, choose, read, skim along

Lēnis, -e, soft, gentle, mild

Lēnitās, lēnitātis, f., softness, gentleness, mildness

Levis, -e, light

Lēx, lēgis, f., law

Libenter, willingly

Liber, librī, m., book

Līber, lībera, līberum, free

Līberālitās, līberālitātis, f., kindness, generosity

Līberī, līberōrum, m., children

Līberō, -āre, -āvī, -ātum, free

Lībērtās, lībērtātis, f., freedom

Libīdō, libīdinis, f., desire, passion

Lībō, -āre, -āvī, -ātum, taste, pour a libation

Licet, -ēre, licuit or **licitum est,** it is permitted

Līctor, līctōris, m., lictor

Līgneus, -a, -um, wooden

Līgnum, -ī, m., wood

Līmen, līminis, n., threshold, gate, palace

Lingua, -ae, f, tongue

Littera, -ae, f., letter (of the alphabet); letter (document) (*plural*)

Lītus, lītōris, n., shore

Locō, -āre, -āvī, -ātum, place, establish

Locus, -ī, m.; loca, -ōrum, n. (*in plural*)**,** place

Longē, far

Longus, -a, -um, long

Loquor, -ī, locūtus sum, speak

Lūceō, -ēre, lūxī, —, shine

Lūctor, -ārī, lūctātus sum, wrestle, struggle

Lūcubrō, -āre, -āvī, -ātum, work by lamp-light

Lūdibrium, -ī, n., mockery

Lūdus, -ī, m., game

Lūmen, lūminis, n., light, eye

Lupa, -ae, f., wolf

Lūsus, -ūs, m., gaming

Lūx, lūcis, f., light

Lūxus, -ūs, m., excess, extravagance

Lympha, -ae, f., water

Māchina, -ae, f., machine

Mācte, blessed (*undeclin.*)

Maestus, -a, -um, sad

Magis, more

Magister, magistrī, m., master

Magistrātus, -ūs, m., public office, official

Māgnitūdō, māgnitūdinis, f., size

Māgnoperē, greatly

Māgnus, -a, -um, large, great

Māior, māius, larger, greater

Mālō, mālle, māluī, —, prefer

Malus, -a, -um, bad

Mamma, -ae, f., teat

Mandō, -āre, -āvī, -ātum, order, entrust (*often with dat.*)

Maneō, -ēre, mānsī, mānsum, remain, await

Manus, -ūs, f., hand, a band of men

Mare, maris, n., sea

Marītus, -ī, m., husband

Mārs, Mārtis, m., Mars

Māter, mātris, f., mother

Māteria, -ae, f., material

Mātrimōnium, -ī, n., marriage

Mātūrō, -āre, -āvī, -ātum, hasten

Māximus, -a, -um, largest, greatest

Medicāmentum, -ī, n., medicine

Medicus, -ī, m., physician

Medius, -a, -um, middle

Melior, melius, better

Meminī, meminisse, —, remember (*often with gen.*)

Memorābilis, -e, memorable

Memoria, -ae, f., memory

Mēns, mentis, f., mind, intention

Mēnsis, mēnsis, m., month

Mentiō, mentiōnis, f., mention

Mentior, -īrī, mentītus sum, lie

Mereō, -ēre, meruī, meritum, deserve, earn, serve (as a soldier)

Mereor, -ērī, meritus sum, deserve, earn, serve (as a soldier)

Mergō, -ere, mersī, mersum, plunge, overwhelm

Metuō, -ere, metuī, —, fear

Metus, -ūs, m ., fear

Meus, -a, -um, my

Mīles, mīlitis, m., soldier

Mīlia, mīlum, n., thousands

Mīlitō, -āre, -āvī, -ātum, be a soldier, serve in the army

Mīlle, a thousand (*undeclin.*)

Mīlliārium, -ī, n., a milestone

Mina, -ae, f., mina (Greek weight of a hundred Attic drachmas, used as money)

Minae, -ārum, f., threats

Mināx, minācis, threatening

Minimus, -a, -um, smallest

Minitābundus, -a, -um, threatening

Minor, minus, smaller

Minus, less

Mīrābilis, -e, wonderful

Mīrāculum, -ī, n., wonder, marvel

Mīror, -ārī, mīrātum sum, wonder, wonder at

Mīrus, -a, -um, wonderful

Misceō, -ēre, miscuī, mīxtum, mix, confuse

Missa, -ae, f., The Mass

Mītēscō, -ere, —, —, soften

Mītis, -e, soft, gentle, mild

Mittō, -ere, mīsī, missum, send, let go

Modus, -ī, m., manner, measure, limit

Moenia, moenium, n., walls

Mōlēs, mōlis, f., mass

Mōlior, -īrī, mōlītus sum, build, undertake

Mollis, -e, soft, gentle, mild

Moneō, -ere, monuī, monitum, warn, advise

Mōns, mōntis, m., mountain

Mōnstrum, -ī, n., monster, omen

Monumentum, -ī, n., memorial

Morbus, -ī, m., sickness, disease

Moribundus, -a, -um, dying

Morior, -ī, mortuus sum, die

Moror, -ārī, morātus sum, delay

Mors, mortis, f., death

Mortālis, -e, mortal

Mōs, mōris, m., custom

Mōtus, -ūs, m., movement, disturbance, uprising

Moveō, -ēre, mōvī, mōtum, move

Mox, soon, subsequently

Mucrō, mucrōnis, m., sword

Muliebris, -e, womanly

Mulier, mulieris, f., woman

Multitūdō, multitūdinis, f., multitude

Multum, much

Multus, -a, -um, much

Mūnīmentum, -ī, n., defence, protection

Mūniō, -īre, mūnīvī, mūnītum, fortify

Mūnus, mūneris, n., duty, gift

Mūrus, -ī, m., wall

Mūtō, -āre, -āvī, -ātum, change

Nam, for

Namque, for

Nāscor, -ī, nātus sum, be born

Nāsus, -ī, m., nose

Nātiō, nātiōnis, f., tribe

Nātūra, -ae, f., nature

Nātus, -ī, m., son

Nauta, -ae, m., sailor

Nāvis, nāvis, f., ship

-ne, *sign of a question;* whether

Nē, lest; that ... not

Nē ... quidem, not even

Nebula, -ae, f., mist

Nec, and ... not, nor

Nec ... nec, neither ... nor

Necessārius, -a, -um, necessary

Necesse, necessary

Necō, -āre, -āvī, -ātum, kill

Necopīnātus, -a, -um, unexpected

Negō, -āre, -āvī, -ātum, deny, refuse

Nēmō, nēminis or **nūllīus, nēminī, nēminem, nūllō** or **nēmine, m.,** no one

Nepōs, nepōtis, m., grandson, descendant

Neque, and not, nor

Neque ... neque, neither ... nor

Nequeō, -īre, nequīvī, —, be unable

Nēquīquam, in vain

Neuter, neutra, neutrum, neither (of two)

Nī, unless, if not

Nihil, n., nothing; not (*undeclin.*)

Nihilō minus, no less, none the less

Nimium, excessively, very

Ningit, -ere, ninguit, it snows

Nisi, unless, if not

Niteō, -ēre, nituī, —, shine

Nitrōsus, -a, -um, nitrous

Nō, nāre, nāvī, —, swim

Nōbilis, -e, noble

Nōbilitās, nōbilitātis, f., nobility

Noceō, -ēre, nocuī, nocitūrum, harm

Noctū, at night

Nocturnus, -a, -um, nocturnal

Nōlō, nōlle, nōluī, —, be unwilling

Nōmen, nōminis, n., name

Nōminō, -āre, -āvī, -ātum, name, call

Nōminātīvus, -a, -um, nominative

Nōn, not

Nōn sōlum ... sed (etiam), not only ... but also

Nōnne, *Sign of a question requiring an affirmative answer*

Nōs, nostrum or **nostrī, nōbīs, nōs, nōbīs,** we, us

Noster, nostra, nostrum, our

Notus, -ī, m., south wind

Nōtus, -a, -um, known, famous

Novem, nine (*undeclin.*)

Novitās, novitātis, f., newness

Novus, -a, -um, new, strange

Nox, noctis, f., night

Noxa, -ae, f., fault, hurt

Nūdus, -a, -um, bare

Nūllus, -a, -um, no

Num, *sign of a question requiring a negative answer;* whether

Nūmen, nūminis, n., divine will, god

Numerus, -ī, m., number

Numquam, never

Nunc, now

Nūncupō, -āre, -āvī, -ātum, announce publicly

Nūntiō, -āre, -āvī, -ātum, report

Nūntius, -ī, m., messenger, message

Nurus, -ūs, f., daughter-in-law

Ob, on account of (*prep. with accus.*)

Obeō, -īre, obīvī, obitum, go to, meet, die

Obferō, *see* offerō

Obiciō, -ere, obiēcī, obiectum, throw against, expose

Oblinō, -ere, oblēvī, oblitum, defile

Oblīquus, -a, -um, slanting, awry

Oblīvīscor, -ī, oblītus sum, forget (*often with gen.*)

Oborior, -īrī, obortus sum, arise

Obruō, -ere, obruī, obrutum, whelm, bury

Obscūrus, -a, -um, dark, obscure, uncertain

Obses, obsidis, m., hostage

Obsideō, -ēre, obsēdī, obsessum, besiege, occupy

Obsidiō, obsidiōnis, f., siege, blockade

Obsistō, -ere, obstitī, obstitum, oppose

Obstinō, -āre, -āvī, -ātum, be persistent, resolve

Obstupefaciō, -ere, obstupefēcī, obstupefactum, become senseless

Obtestor, -ārī, obtestātus sum, call as a witness

Obtineō, -ēre, obtinuī, obtentum, hold

Obtruncō, -āre, -āvī, -ātum, cut down

Obvertō, -ere, obvertī, obversum, turn towards

Obvius, -a, -um, against, meeting (*with dat.*)

Occāsiō, occāsiōnis, f., opportunity

Occīdō, -ere, occīdī, occīsum, kill

Occupō, -āre, -āvī, -ātum, seize

Occurrō, -ere, occurrī, occursum, run against, meet

Octāvus (-a, -um) - decimus (-a, -um), eighteenth

Octō, eight (*undeclin.*)

Oculus, -ī, m., eye

Ōdī, ōdisse, ōsūrum, hate

Odium, -ī, n., hatred

Offerō, -ferre, obtulī, oblātum, present

Officiōsus, -a, -um, obliging

Ōlim, formerly, some time

Ōmen, ōminis, n., omen

Omnīnō, entirely

Omnis, -e, all, every

Opera, -ae, f., work

Opīniō, opīniōnis, f., opinion

Opīnor, -ārī, opīnātus sum, suppose

Oportet, -ēre, oportuit, it is necessary

Oppidum, -ī, n., town

Oppōnō, -ere, opposuī, oppositum, put against

Opportūnus, -a, -um, apt, exposed

Opprimō, -ere, oppressī, oppressum, overwhelm

Oppūgnātiō, oppūgnātiōnis, f., attack

Oppūgnō, -āre, -āvī, -ātum, attack

Ops, opis, f., help, aid; wealth, resources (*plural*)

Optimus, -a, -um, best

Optō, -āre, -āvī, -ātum, long for, choose

Opulentus, -a, -um, rich, wealthy, powerful

Opus, operis, n., work; siege-work

Opus est, there is need of (*with abl.*)

Ōra, -ae, f., shore

Ōrātiō, ōrātiōnis, f., speech

Ōrātor, ōrātōris, m., spokesman

Orbis, orbis, m., circle, world

Ōrdine, regularly, properly

Ōrdō, ōrdinis, m., line, order

Orīgō, orīginis, f., origin

Orior, -īrī, ortus sum, arise, spring from

Ōrnātus, -ūs, m., dress, equipment

Ōrō, -āre, -āvī, -ātum, beg

Ōs, ōris, n., mouth

Os, Ossis, n., bone

Ostendō, -ere, ostendī, ostentum, show

Ōstium, -ī, n., entrance

Ōtium, -ī, n., leisure, peace

Paelex, paelicis, f., mistress, concubine

Paene, almost

Palātium -ī, n., Palatine hill, one of the seven hills of Rome

Palūs, palūdis, f., swamp

Pār, paris, equal, like

Parcō, parcere, pepercī, parsum, spare, refrain from

Parēns, parentis, m. and f., parent

Pāreō, -ere, pāruī, —, obey

Pariter, equally, side by side

Parō, -āre, -āvī, -ātum, prepare, get

Pars, partis, f., part, direction, side

Particeps, participis, m. sharer

Partus, -ūs, m., birth, offspring

Parum, little, too little

Parumper, for a little while

Parvus, -a, -um, small

Pāscō, -ere, pāvī, pāstum, feed

Passim, generally, everywhere

Pāstor, pastōris, m., herdsman

Patefaciō, -ere, patefēcī, patefactum, open, expose

Pateō, -ēre, patuī, —, lie open

Pater, patris, m., father

Patior, -ī, passus sum, allow, suffer

Patria, -ae, f., fatherland

Patrius, -a, -um, father's, native

Paucī, -ae, -a, few

Paulisper, for a little while

Paulum, a little

Pauper, pauperis, poor

Pavidus, -a, -um, trembling, fearful

Pavor, pavōris, m., panic

Pāx, pācis, f., peace

Peccātum, -ī, n., fault

Peccō, -āre, -āvī, -ātum, sin

Pectus, pectoris, n., breast

Pecūnia, -ae, f., money

Pecus, pecoris, n., herd

Pecus, pecudis, f., beast; herd (*in plural*)

Pedes, peditis, m., footsoldier; infantry (*plural*)

Pēior, pēius, worse

Pellō, -ere, pepulī, pulsum, drive, rout

Penātēs, penātium, m., guardian deities of the household

Penes, in the house with (*prep. with accus.*)

Penetrō, -āre, -āvī, -ātum, penetrate

Penitus, deep within, utterly

Per, through (*prep. with accus.*)

Percontor, -ārī, percontātus sum, enquire

Perdō, -ere, perdidī, perditum, destroy, lose

Perdūcō, -ere, perdūxī, perductum, lead through

Pereō, -īre, perīvī, peritum, perish

Perferō, -ferre, pertulī, perlātum, endure, bring

Perficiō, -ere, perfēcī, perfectum, do, make

Perfuga, -ae, m., deserter

Pergama, -ōrum, n., Pergamum in Asia Minor; Troy (*by metonymy*)

Pergō, -ere, perrēxī, perrēctum, continue, proceed

Perīculum, -ī, n., danger

Perinde, just as, in like manner

Perindiē, on the day after tomorrow

Perītus, -a, -um, experienced (*often with gen.*)

Permaneō, -ēre, permānsī, permānsūrum, remain

Permittō, -ere, permīsī, permissum, permit, entrust (*often with dat.*)

Perniciēs, -ēī, f., destruction

Perpetuus, -a, -um, continuous, everlasting

Persequor, -ī, persecūtus sum, follow

Persōna, -ae, f., person

Persōnālis, persōnale, personal

Persuādeō, -ēre, persuāsī, persuāsum, persuade

Perturbō, -āre, -āvī, -ātum, throw into confusion

Perveniō, -īre, pervēnī, perventum, arrive

Pēs, pedis, m., foot

Pessimus, -a, -um, worst

Pestifer, pestifera, pestiferum, pestilential

Petō, -ere, petīvī, petītum, seek, attack, ask

Petrōsus, -a, -um, rocky

Piger, pigra, pigrum, slow, lazy

Pīgnus, pīgnoris or **pīgneris, n.,** a person given as

security, pledge

Pīnguēdō, pīnguēdinis, f., fatness, oiliness

Pīnguis, -e, fat, rich

Pīrāta, -ae, m., pirate

Placeō, -ēre, placuī, placitum, please (*with dat.*)

Placidus, -a, -um, calm

Plācō, -āre, -āvī, -ātum, quiet

Plangor, plangōris, m., beating, mourning

Platea, -ae, f., broad way, street

Plaudō, -ere, plausī, plausum, applaud

Plēnus, -ā, -um, full

Plērus, -a, -um, composing the greater part; most of (*in plural*)

Pluit, -ere, plūvit, it is raining

Plūrimum, principally, in the highest degree

Plūrimus, -a, -um, most

Plūs, plūris, more

Pōculum, -ī, n., cup

Poena, -ae, f., penalty, punishment

Poēta, -ae, m., poet

Polliceor, -ērī, pollicitus sum, promise

Pondus, ponderis, n., weight

Pōnō, -ere, posuī, positum, put, put down

Pōns, pōntis, m., bridge

Pontus, -ī, m., sea

Populātiō, populātiōnis, f., devastation

Populus, -ī, m., people

Porcellus, -ī, m., little pig

Porcus, -ī, m., pig

Portentōsus, -a, -um, monstrous, portentous

Portō, -āre, -āvī, -ātum, carry

Portus, -ūs, m., harbour

Poscō, -ere, poposcī, —, demand

Possum, posse, potuī, —, be able, can

Post, after, behind (*prep. with accus.*); afterwards (*adv.*)

Posteā, afterward

Posterī, -ōrum, m., future generations

Posterior, posterius, later

Posterus, -a, -um, following

Postquam, after

Postrēmō, at last

Postrēmus, -a, -um, last

Postulō, -āre, -āvī, -ātum, demand

Potēns, potentis, powerful

Potestās, potestātis, f., power

Potior, -īrī, potītus sum, get possession of (*with abl.*)

Potissimum, especially

Pōtō, -āre, -āvī, -ātum, drink

Prae, in front of, in comparison with, because of (*prep. with abl.*)

Praebeō, -ēre, praebuī, praebitum, offer, show, furnish

Praecipiō, -ere, praecēpī, praeceptum, order, instruct, anticipate, receive in advance

Praecipitō, -āre, -āvī, -ātum, hurl, hasten

Praecipuē, especially

Praeda, -ae, f., booty

Praedīcō, -ere, praedīxī, praedictum, warn, predict

Praedō, praedōnis, m., plunderer

Praefectus, -ī, m., prefect

Praeferō, -ferre, praetulī, praelātum, prefer

Praeficiō, -ere, praefēcī, praefectum, put in charge of

Praemium, -ī, n., reward

Praesēns, praesentis, present, helpful

Praesidium, -ī, n., guard, protection

Praestat, -āre, praestitit, it is better

Praestō, -āre, -stitī, -stitum, excel, show (courage), perform (duty)

Praesum, -esse, -fuī, —, be in charge of

Praeter, past, except, contrary to (*prep. with accus.*)

Praetereā, besides

Praetextus, -a, -um, bordered, fringed

Prātum, -ī, n., meadow

Prāvus, -a, -um, crooked, bad

Precātiō, precātiōnis, f., prayer

Precor, -ārī, precātus sum, pray

Prehendō, -ere, prehendī, prehensum, grasp

Premō, -ere, pressī, pressum, press, overwhem

Pretium, -ī, n., price, reward

Prex, precis, f., prayer

Prīdiē, on the day before

Prīmō, at first

Prīmōris, -e, foremost

Prīmum, firstly

Prīmus, -a, -um, first

Prīnceps, prīncipis, m., leader

Prīncipātus, -ūs, m., leadership

Principium, -ī, n., beginning

Prīscus, -a, -um, old

Prior, prius, first, earlier

Priusquam, before

Prius ... quam, before

Prō, for, in front of (*prep. with abl.*)

Probābilis, -e, commendable

Prōcēdō, -ere, prōcessī, —, proceed

Procella, -ae, f., violent wind

Procer, proceris, m., noble

Prōcreō, -āre, -āvī, -ātum, breed, beget

Procul, at a distance

Prōcumbō, -ere, prōcubuī, prōcubitum, fall down

Prōdigiōsus, -a, -um, unnatural, wonderful

Prōdūcō, -ere, prōdūxī, prōductum, lead out

Proelium, -ī, n., battle

Profānō, -āre, -āvī, -ātum, render unholy

Profectō, certainly

Proficīscor, -ī, profectus sum, set out

Prōfluō, -ere, prōfluxī, —, flow forth

Profugus, -ā, -um, in flight, fugitive

Profundus, -a, -um, deep

Prōgredior, -ī, prōgressus sum, advance

Prohibeō, -ēre, prohibuī, prohibitum, keep away, prevent

Proinde, just as, in like manner

Prōlābor, -ī, prōlapsus sum, slip forwards

Prōmittō, -ere, prōmīsī, prōmissum, send forth, promise

Prōnūntiō, -āre, -āvī, -ātum, announce

Prōpāgō, -āre, -āvī, -ātum, spread, extend

Prope, near (*adverb or prep. with accus.*)

Properē, hastily

Properō, -āre, -āvī, -ātum, hasten

Propīnquī, -ōrum, m., relatives

Propīnquus, -a, -um, near

Propitius, -a, -um, favourable

Proprius, -a, -um, one's own, appropriate, lasting

Propter, on account of (*prep. with accus.*)

Prōpūgnō, -āre, -āvī, -ātum, fight

Prōsequor, -ī, prōsecūtus sum, follow, honour

Prōsiliō, -īre, prōsiluī, —, leap forth

Prōspiciō, -ere, prōspēxī, prōspectum, look out, look out and see

Prōsum, prōdesse, prōfuī, prōfutūrus, benefit

Prōtendō, -ere, prōtendī, prōtentum, stretch forth

Prōvideō, -ēre, prōvīdī, prōvīsum, foresee, provide

Prōvincia, -ae, f., province

Prōvocō, -āre, -āvī, -ātum, call forth

Proximus, -a, -um, next, nearest

Pūbēs, pūbis, f., young men

Pūblicus, -a, -um, public

Pudīcitia, -ae, f., chastity, modesty

Pudīcus, -a, -um, chaste, modest

Pudor, pudōris, m., shame, modesty

Puella, -ae, f., girl

Puer, puerī, m., boy

Puerīlis, -e, childish, boyish

Pūgna, -ae, f., fight

Pūgnō, -āre, -āvī, -ātum, fight

Pulcher, pulchra, pulchrum, beautiful

Pulsō, -āre, -āvī, -ātum, strike

Puppis, puppis, f., stern, ship

Pūrgātiō, purgātiōnis, f., cleansing

Putō, -āre, -āvī, -ātum, think

Quā, where

Quācumque, by whatever way, wherever

Quaerō, -ere, quaesīvī, quaesītum, look for, enquire

Quālis, -e, what kind of; as

Quam, than, as, how; form of **quī**; as ... as possible (*with superlative*)

Quam ob rem, therefore, why

Quamquam, although, and yet

Quamvis, although; very (*with adjectives and adverbs*)

Quandō, when, since

Quantus, -a, -um, how great, how much; as (*correlative with tantus*)

Quārē, therefore, why

Quasi, just as, just as if, as it were

Quattuor, four (*undeclin.*)

-Que, and

-que ... -que, both ... and

Quem ad modum, how, as; *used as an exclamation*

Queō, -īre, quīvī, quitum, be able

Querēla, -ae, f., complaint

Queror, -ī, questus sum, complain

Quī, quae, quod, who, which (*relative pronoun*); what ...? (*interrogative adj.*)

Quia, because

Quīcumque, quaecumque, quodcumque, whoever, whatever

Quid, what, why

Quīdam, quaedam, quoddam, a certain

Quidem, indeed; (*often not translated*)

Quīn, indeed (*with indicative*); but that (*with subjunctive*)

Quīnque, five (*undeclin.*)

Quīntus, -a, -um, fifth

Quippe, in fact, for

Quis, who

Quisquam, quicquam, anyone, anything (*usually after a negative*)

Quisque, quidque or **quicque,** each, everyone

Quisquis, quicquid, whoever, whatever

Quō, where (to what place); whereby

Quō modo, how, as

Quō tempōre, when

Quoad, while, until, as far as

Quod, which, what, this, it, the fact that, because

Quondam, formerly, sometimes

Quoniam, since

Quoque, also

Quot, how many

Rapiō, -ere, rapuī, raptum, seize, take away

Ratiō, ratiōnis, f., way, reason, consideration

Rebellō, -āre, -āvī, —, revolt

Recēdō, -ere, recessī, recessum, go back

Recipiō, -ere, recēpī, receptum, take back, receive

Recordor, -ārī, recordātus sum, remember

Rēctus, -a, -um, straight, upright

Reddō, -ere, reddidī, redditum, give back, render

Redeō, -īre, redīvī, reditum, go back, return

Redigō, -ere, redēgī, redāctum, reduce, render

Redintegrō, -āre, -āvī, -ātum, restore, renew

Redivīvus, -a, um, renewed

Redūcō, -ere, redūxī, reductum, lead back

Referō, -ferre, rettulī, relātum, bring back, report

Rēgia, -ae, f., palace

Rēgīna, -ae, f., queen

Regiō, regiōnis, f., region

Rēgius, -a, -um, royal

Rēgnō, -āre, -āvī, -ātum, rule

Rēgnum, -ī, n., rule, kingdom

Regō, -ere, rēxī, rēctum, rule

Rēiciō, -ere, rēiēcī, rēiectum, throw back

Relinquō, -ere, relīquī, relictum, leave

Reliquiae, -ārum, f., remains

Reliquus, -a, -um, the remaining, the rest of

Remaneō, -ēre, remānsī, —, remain

Remittō, -ere, remīsī, remissum, send back, relax

Removeō, -ēre, remōvī, remōtum, remove

Remūneror, -ārī, remūnerātus sum, repay

Remus, -ī, m., Remus

Renūntiō, -āre, -āvī, -ātum, report

Reor, rērī, ratus sum, think

Repente, suddenly

Repentīnus, -a, -um, sudden

Reperiō, -īre, repperī, repertum, find

Repetō, -ere, repetīvī, repetītum, return to, recall

Repōnō, -ere, reposuī, repositum, put back

Reprehēnsō, -āre, —, —, hold back repeatedly

Repudiō, -āre, -āvī, -ātum, reject

Requīrō, -ere, requīsīvī, requīsītum, look for

Rēs, reī, f., thing, affair

Rēs pūblica, reī pūblicae, f., state

Rescindō, -ere, rescidī, rescissum, tear, cut down

Resistō, -ere, restitī, —, resist

Resonō, -āre, -āvī, —, sound, resound

Respondeō, -ēre, respondī, respōnsum, answer

Respōnsum, -ī, n., answer

Restituō, -ere, restituī, restitūtum, restore

Retineō, -ēre, retinuī, retentum, hold back

Retrahō, -ere, retrāxī, retractum, drag back

Retrō, back

Reveniō, -īre, revēnī, —, return

Revertor, -ī, reversus sum, return

Revinciō, -īre, revinxī, revinctum, bind

Revīvīscō, -ere, revīxī, —, revive

Revocō, -āre, -āvī, -ātum, call back

Rēx, rēgis, m., king

Rīpa, -ae, f., bank (of a stream)

Rōbustus, -a, -um, of oak; hard

Rogō, -āre, -āvī, -ātum, ask

Rōma, -ae, f., Rome

Rōmānus, -a, -um, Roman

Rōmulāris, -e, of Romulus

Rōmulus, -ī, m., Romulus

Rōs, rōris, m., dew

Rūmīnālis, -e, of Rumina (a Roman goddess)

Rūmor, rūmōris, m., rumour

Rumpō, -ere, rūpī, ruptum, break

Ruō, -ere, ruī, ruātum, throw up, throw down, fall, rush

Rūrsus, back, again

Rūs, rūris, n., country

Rūsticus, -a, -um, rustic

Sabīnī, -ōrum, m., Sabines

Sacer, sacra, sacrum, sacred

Sacerdōs, sacerdōtis, m. and f., priest

Sacrificium, -ī, n., sacrifice

Saeclum, -ī, n., age

Saeculum, -ī, n., age

Saepe, often

Saepiō, -īre, saepsī, saeptum, fence in

Saeviō, -īre, -īvī, -ītum, rage

Sagitta, -ae, f., arrow

Sāl, salis, m., salt, sea

Salūs, salūtis, f., safety

Salūtātiō, salūtātiōnis, f., greeting, saluting

Salvus, -a, -um, safe, unviolated

Sanciō, -īre, sānxī, sānctum, confirm

Sānctus, -a, -um, sacred, holy

Sānē, certainly

Sanguis, sanguinis, m., blood

Sapientia, -ae, f., wisdom

Satelles, satellitis, m., bodyguard

Satiō, -āre, -āvī, -ātum, fill, satisfy

Sat, enough

Satis, enough

Saxum, -ī, n., rock

Scelerātus, -a, -um, wicked

Scelus, sceleris, n., crime

Scientia, -ae, f., knowledge

Scīlicet, of course (*sometimes sarcastic*)

Sciō, -īre, scīvī, scītum, know, know how

Scīscitor, -ārī, scīscitātus sum, enquire repeatedly

Scrība, -ae, m., secretary

Scrībō, -ere, scrīpsī, scrīptum, write

Scūtum, -ī, n., shield

Secundum, following after (*prep. with accus.*)

Secundus, -a, -um, second, favourable

Sed, but

Sēdecim, sixteen (*undeclin.*)

Sedeō, -ēre, sēdī, sessum, sit

Sēdēs, sēdis, f., seat, abode

Semel, once

Sēmet, *strengthened form of* sē

Semper, always

Sempiternus, -a -um, eternal

Senātor, senātōris, m., senator

Senātus, -ūs, m., senate

Senex, senis, old

Sensus, -ūs, m., feeling, sense

Sententia, -ae, f., opinion, plan

Sentiō, -īre, sēnsī, sēnsum, feel, perceive

Sepeliō, -īre, sepelīvī, sepultum, bury

Septem, seven (*undeclin.*)

Sequor, -ī, secūtus sum, follow

Serō, -ere, sēvī, satum, sow

Sērus, -ā, -um, late

Serviō, -īre, servīvī, servītum, serve (*with dat.*)

Servitium, -ī, n., body of slaves

Servō, -āre, -āvī, -ātum, save, guard

Servus, -ī, m., slave

Seu, or if

Seu ... seu, whether ... or; either ... or; if ... or if

Sevēritās, sevēritātis, f., severity, austerity

Sex, six (*undeclin.*)

Sī, if

Sīc, thus, so

Siccus, -a, -um, dry

Sīcut, just as

Sīdus, sīderis, n. star

Sīgnum, -ī, n., sign, standard, statue

Sileō, -ēre, siluī, –, be silent

Silvius, -a, -um, Of the Silvian kings of Alba Longa

Similis, -e, like

Simul, at the same time

Simul ... simul, both ... and

Simulācrum, -ī, n., image, ghost

Sine, without (*prep. with abl.*)

Singulī, -ae, -a, single, one at a time

Sinister, sinistra, sinistrum, left, unfavourable

Sinō, -ere, sīvī, situm, allow

Sistō, -ere, stitī, statum, stop, set

Sitiō, -īre, sitīvī, —, thirst

Situs, -ūs, m., position

Socius, -ī, m., comrade, ally

Socrus, -ūs, f., mother-in-law

Sōl, sōlis, m., sun

Sōleō, -ēre, sōlitus sum, be accustomed

Sōlitūdō, sōlitūdinis, f., desert

Sollicitō, -āre, -āvī, -ātum, stir up

Solum, -ī, n., ground

Sōlus, -a, -um, alone

Solvō, -ere, solvī, solūtum, loosen, set sail, perform

Somnus, -ī, m., sleep

Sonitus, -ūs, m., sound

Sonōrus, -a, -um, noisy

Sonus, -ī, m., sound

Sōpiō, -īre, -īvī, -ītum, put to sleep

Sordidus, -a, -um, dirty

Soror, sorōris, f., sister

Sors, sortis, f., lot, fate

Sōspes, sōspitis, safe

Speciēs, speciēī, f., appearance

Spectātus, -a, -um, examined, esteemed

Spectō, -āre, -āvī, -ātum, look, look at

Speculor, -ārī, speculātus sum, spy

Speculum, -ī, n., mirror

Spērō, -āre, -āvī, -ātum, hope, expect

Spēs, speī, f., hope

Spoliō, -āre, -āvī, -ātum, strip, rob

Spolium, -ī, n., spoils

Sponte, voluntarily

Spūmō, -āre, -āvī, -ātum, foam

Stabilis, -e, stable

Stabulum, -ī, n., quarters

Stāgnum, -ī, n., pool of standing water

Statiō, statiōnis, f., post, station

Statim, immediately

Statua, -ae, f., statue

Statuō, -ere, statuī, statūtum, establish, decide

Sternō, -ere, strāvī, strātum, spread out, slay

Stīpendium, -ī, n., wage

Stirpis or stirps, stirpis, m. and f., offspring

Stō, -āre, stetī, statum, stand

Stringō, -ere, strinxī, strictum, draw tight, draw (a
  sword), touch, trim

Struō, -ere, strūxī, strūctum, build, arrange

Studeō, -ēre, studuī, —, be eager for, be devoted to

Studium, -ī, n., eagerness

Stuprō, -āre, -āvī -ātum, debauch, ravish

Stuprum, -ī, n., defilement

Sub, under (*prep. with accus. and abl.*)

Subdō, -ere, subdidī, subditum, subdue, substitute

Subeō, -īre, subīvī, subitum, go under, come to,
  undergo, follow

Subiciō, -ere, subiēcī, subiectum, put under

Subitō, suddenly

Subitus, -a, -um, sudden

Sublicius, -a, -um, resting upon piles

Submergō, -ere, submērsī, submersum, sink

Submittō, -ere, submīsī, submissum, lower

Submoveō, -ēre, submōvī, submōtum, remove

Subsidium, -ī, n., help, reinforcement

Subveniō, -īre, subvēnī, subventum, come to; help,
  aid, assist

Succēdō, -ere, successī, successum, go under, go up to,
  succeed

Succendō, -ere, succendī, succēnsum, set on fire

Sūdor, sūdōris, n., sweat

Suffundō, -ere, suffūdī, suffūsum, pour, stain

—, suī, sibi, sē, sē, *reflexive pronoun, third person:* (of,
  etc.) himself, herself, itself, themselves

Sum, esse, fuī, futūrum, be

Summus, -a, -um, last, highest, top of

Sūmō, -ere, sūmpsī, sūmptum, take, inflict
  (punishment)

Sūmptus, -ūs, m., expense

Super, above (*prep. with accus.*)

Superbus, -a, -um, proud

Superior, -ius, previous, higher

Superī, -ōrum, m., gods

Superincidō, -ere, —, —, fall on top of

Superō, -āre, -āvī, -ātum, overcome, surpass, be
  plentiful, survive

Supersum, -esse, superfuī, superfutūrum, remain, survive

Superus, -a, -um, upper

Supplicium, -ī, n., punishment

Suprā, above (*prep. with accus.*)

Suprēmus, -a, -um, last, highest, top of

Surripiō, -ere, surripuī, surreptum, snatch, withdraw

Suscipiō, -ere, suscēpī, susceptum, take up, undertake

Sustineō, -ēre, sustinuī, sustentum, withstand, hold up

Suus, -a, -um, his own, her own, its own, their own

Sweatō, -āre, -āvī, -ātum, sweat

Syrācūsae, -ārum, f., Syracuse in Sicily

Taberna, -ae, f., shop, hut

Taceō, -ēre, tacuī, tacitum, be silent

Tālis, -e, such

Tam, so

Tamen, nevertheless

Tamquam, just as, just as if, on the grounds that

Tandem, at last

Tantum, so much; only

Tantus, -a, -um, so great, so much

Tantus ... quantus, so much ... as

Tēctum, -ī, n., roof, house

Tēlum, -ī, n., weapon

Temerē, rashly

Tempestās, tempestātis, f., storm, weather

Templum, -ī, n., temple

Temptō, -āre, -āvī, -ātum, try

Tempus, tempōris, n., time; temple (of the head)

Tendō, -ere, tetendī, tentum, stretch, shoot, hasten

Tenebrae, -ārum, f., darkness

Teneō, -ēre, tenuī, —, hold

Tenuis, -e, thin, light

Ter, three times

Tergum, -ī, n., back

Terminus, -ī, m., boundary

Terra, -ae, f., land

Terreō, -ēre, terruī, territum, terrify

Terror, terrōris, m., fear

Tertius, -a, -um, third

Testis, testis, m. and f., witness

Testor, -ārī, testātus sum, bear witness, call to witness

Theātrum, -ī, n., theatre

Tiberīnus, -a, -um, of the Tiber

Tiberis, Tiberis. m., the river Tiber

Timeō, -ēre, timuī, —, fear

Timor, timōris, m., fear

Toga, -ae, f., toga

Togātus, -a, -um, civilian

Tollō, -ere, sustulī, sublātum, raise, remove, put out of the way

Tonō, -āre, -āvī, -ātum, thunder

Tondeō, -ēre, totondī, tōnsum, cut

Tōnsor, tōnsōris, m., barber

Torreō, -ere, torruī, tostum, roast

Tot, so many (*undeclin.*)

Tōtus, -a, -um, all, the whole

Tractō, -āre, -āvī, -ātum, handle

Trādō, -ere, trādidī, trāditum, surrender, pass on

Trāgula, -ae, f., javelin, dart

Trahō, -ere, trāxī, tractum, draw, draw down, drag

Trāiciō, -ere, trāiēcī, trāiectum, throw, shoot

Trānō, -āre, -āvī, —, swim across

Trāns, across (*prep. with accus.*)

Trānseō, -īre, trānsīvī, trānsitum, go across

Trānsfuga, -ae, m. or f., deserter

Trānsigō, -ere, trānsēgī, trānsāctum, drive through

Trānsiliō, -īre, trānsiluī, —, leap

Trānsitus, -ūs, m., passage

Trecentēsimus (-a, -um) et alter (altera, alterum), three hundred and second

Trecentēsimus (-a, -um) et quīntus (-a, -um) - decimus (-a, -um), three hundred and fifteenth

Trecentī, -ae, -a, three hundred

Trepidus, -a, -um, trembling, anxious

Trēs, tria, three

Tribūnal, tribūnālis, n., platform

Tribūnus, -ī, m., tribune

Tribuō, -ere, tribuī, tribūtum, attribute, grant

Trīcēsimus (-a, -um) - octāvus (-a, -um), thirty-eighth

Trīstis, -e, sad, grim

Trōia, -ae, f., Troy

Trūdō, -ere, trūsī, trūsum, push

Trux, trucis, savage

Tū, tuī, tibi, tē, tē, you (*singular*)

Tum, then

Tumultuōsus, -a, -um, disquieting

Tumultus, -ūs, m., tumult

Tunc, then

Turba, -ae, f., crowd

Turbō, -āre, -āvī, -ātum, disturb, scatter

Turpiculus, -a, -um, rather vile

Turpis, -e, shameful

Turpitūdō, turpitūdinis, f., shamefulness

Turris, turris, f., tower

Tūtēla, -ae, f., protection

Tūtum, -ī, n., safety

Tūtus, -a, -um, protected, safe

Tuus, -a, -um, your (*singular*)

Tyrannus, -ī, m., tyrant

Ubi, when, where

Ūllus, -a, -um, any

Ūltimus, -a, -um, farthest

Ultor, ultōris, m., avenger

Umquam, ever

Ūnā, also

Unde, from where

Undique, from all sides, on all sides

Unguis, unguis, m., a man's nail; a bird's claw

Ūnicus, -a, um, only, single

Ūniversus, -a, -um, all, the whole

Unquam, ever

Ūnus, -a, -um, one

Urbs, urbis, f., city

Usquam, at any place

Usque, all the way, all the time

Ūsus, -ūs, m., use, experience

Ut, as, when, how (*with indicative*); that, so that, how (*with subjunctive*)

Uter, utra, utrum, which (of two)?

Uterque, utraque, utrumque, each (of two), both

Utī, as, when how (*with indicative*); that, so that, how (*with subjunctive*)

Ūtilis, -e, useful

Utinam, *sign of a wish*

Utique, at any rate

Ūtor, -ī, ūsus sum, use (*with abl.*)

Utrimque, on both sides

Uxor, uxōris, f., wife

Vacō, -āre, -āvī, -ātum, be empty, be free

Vacuus, -a, -um, empty

Vadimōnium, -ī, n., promise, security

Vādō, -ere, —, —, go

Vador, -ārī, vadātus sum, bind over by bail

Vāgītus, -ūs, m., crying

Validus, -a, -um, strong

Vāllum, -ī, n., wall

Vānitās, vānitātis, f., emptiness, falsity

Varius, -a, -um, varied

Vāstō, -āre, -āvī, -ātum, lay waste

Vāstus, -a, -um, huge, desolate

Vehō, -ere, vēxī, vēctum, carry (*active*); be carried, ride, sail (*passive*)

Vēientēs, Vēientium, m., Veientes, inhabitants of Veii

Vel, or, even

Vel ... vel, either ... or

Vēlōx, vēlōcis, swift

Vēlum, -ī, n., sail

Velut, just as

Vēndō, -ere, vēndidī, vēnditum, sell

Venēnum, -ī, n., poison

Venia, -ae, f., favour, pardon

Veniō, -īre, vēnī, ventum, come

Ventus, -ī, m., wind

Venus, veneris, f., grace, charm; Venus

Verberō, -āre, -āvī, -ātum, beat

Verbum, -ī, n., word

Verēcundia, -ae, f., respect

Vereor, -ērī, veritus sum, fear

Vērō, indeed (*often not translated*)

Versō, -āre, -āvī, -ātum, turn, ponder

Vertō, -ere, vertī, versum, turn, overturn

Vērum, but

Vērus, -a, -um, true

Vescor, -ī, —, eat (*with abl.*)

Vestālis, Vestālis, f., Vestal priestess

Vester, vestra, vestrum, your (*plural*)

Vestibulum, -ī, n., fore-court

Vestīgium, -ī, n., footstep

Vestis, vestis, f., garment, covering

Vetō, -āre, vetuī, vetitum, forbid

Vetus, veteris, old

Vetustus, -a, -um, ancient

Via, -ae, f., way

Viātor, viātōris, m., wayfarer, traveller

Vīctor, vīctōris, m., conqueror

Vīctōria, -ae, f., victory

Vīctrix, vīctricis, f., conqueror

Vīctus, -ūs, m., food, way of life

Vīcus, -ī, m., village

Videō, -ēre, vīdī, vīsum, see

Videor, -ērī, vīsus sum, seem, seem best, be seen

Vīgintī, twenty (*undeclin.*)

Vigor, vigōris, m., vigour

Vīlis, -e, cheap

Vinciō, -īre, vinxī, vinctum, bind

Vincō, -ere, vīcī, vīctum, conquer

Vindicō, -āre, -āvī, -ātum, claim, rescue, punish, avenge

Vīnum, -ī, n., wine

Violēns, violentis, impetuous, violent

Violō, -āre, -āvī, -ātum, harm

Vir, virī, m., man

Virga, -ae, f., twig, wand

Virginitās, virginitātis, f., virginity

Virgō, virginis, f., maiden

Virīlis, -e, male

Virtūs, virtūtis, f., courage, virtue

Vīs, —, —, vim, vī; vīrēs, vīrium, vīribus, vīrēs, vīribus, f., force, violence; strength (*plural*)

Vīsō, -ere, vīsī, vīsum, see, visit

Vīta, -ae, f., life

Vitium, -ī, n., flaw, vice

Vītō, -āre, -āvī, -ātum, avoid

Vīvō, -ere, vīxī, —, live

Vīvus, -a, -um, living

Vix, scarcely, with difficulty

Vocō, -āre, -āvī, -ātum, call

Volō, velle, voluī, —, wish

Volscī, -ōrum, m., Volsci, people in the south of Latium

Voluntās, voluntātis, f., will, good will, consent

Vōs, vestrum (vestrī), vōbīs, vōs, vōbīs, you (*plural*)

Vōx, vōcis, f., voice, word

Vulgātus, -a, -um, common

Vulgō, -āre, -āvī, -ātum, make general, make common

Vulgus, -ī, m. and **n.,** multitude

Vulnerō, -are, -avi, -atum, wound

Vulnus, vulneris, n., wound

Vultur, vulturis, m., vulture

Vultus, -ūs, m., face, expression

ENGLISH–LATIN GLOSSARY

A certain, quīdam, quaedam, quoddam

A little, paulum

Abandon, dēserō

Abode, sēdēs

About, ferē

Above, īnsuper

Above, super (prep. with accus.)

Above, suprā (prep. with accus.)

Abundance, cōpia

Accomplish, efficiō

Accordingly, itaque

Accuse, indīcō

Acquit, absolvō (with abl.)

Across, trāns (prep. with accus.)

Add, addō

Address angrily, increpitō

Address, adloquor

Admiration, admīrātiō

Admit, admittō

Adulterer, adulter

Adultery, adulterium

Advance, prōgredior

Advice, cōnsilium

Advise, admoneō

Advise, moneō

Affair, rēs

Afflict, adficiō

After, post (prep. with accus.)

After, postquam

Afterward, posteā

Afterwards, post

Again, iterum

Again, rūrsus

Against, adversus (prep. with accus.)

Against, contrā (prep. with accus.)

Against, in (prep. with accus.)

Against, obvius (with dat.)

Age, aetās

Age, saeclum

Age, saeculum

Agree, cōnsentiō

Agreement, cōnsēnsus

Agreement, foedus

Aid, ops

Aid, subveniō

Air, anima

Alba Longa, Alba

Alienate, aliēnō

All, cunctus

All, omnis

All, tōtus

All, ūniversus

All the time, usque

All the way, usque

Allow, patior

Allow, sinō

Ally, socius

Almost, paene

Alone, sōlus

Already, iam

Also, et

Also, etiam

Also, quoque

Also, ūnā

Altar, altāria

Alternately, in vicem

Although, cum

Although, etsī

Although, quamquam

Although, quamvīs

Alum, alūmen

Always, semper

Ambassador, lēgātus

Ambush, īnsidiae

Among, apud (prep. with accus.)

Among, inter (prep. with accus.)

Ancestral, avītus

Ancient, antīquus

Ancient, vetustus

And ... not, nec

And not, neque

And so, itaque

And yet, etsī

And yet, quamquam

And, ac

And, atque

And, et

And, -que

Anger, īra

Angry, īrātus

Angry impulse, īra

Anguish, angor

Animal, animal

Announce, dēclārō

Announce, prōnūntiō

Announce publicly, nūncupō

Another, alius

Another's, aliēnus

Answer, respondeō

Answer, respōnsum

Anticipate, praecipiō

Anxious, trepidus

Any, ūllus

Anyone, quisquam (usually after a negative)

Anything, quicquam (usually after a negative)

Appear, appāreō

Appearance, habitus

Appearance, speciēs

Applaud, plaudō

Apply, adhibeō

Appoint, creō

Appoint, lēgō

Approach, aditus

Approach, aggredior

Appropriate, proprius

Approve, adprobō

Apt, opportūnus

Ardea, Ardea

Arise suddenly, coorior

Arise, oborior

Arise, orior

Arm, armō

Arms, arma

Army, exercitus

Around, circā (prep. with accus.)

Arouse, accendō

Arouse, incendō

Arrange, struō

Arrest, dēprehendō

Arrival, adventus

Arrive, adveniō

Arrive, perveniō

Arrow, sagitta

As, ac (after words of likeness or difference)

As, as (a coin of small value)

As, atque (after words of likeness or difference)

As, quam

As, quem ad modum

As, quō modo

As, ut (with indicative)

As ... as possible, quam (with superlative)

As far as, quoad

As it were, quasi

Asia, Asia

Ask, interrogō

Ask, petō

Ask, rogō

Assembly, concursus

Assign, cōnferō

Assist, subveniō

At a distance, procul

At any place, usquam

At any rate, utique

At first, prīmō

At last, dēmum

At last, dēnique

At last, postrēmō

At last, tandem

At night, noctū

At the same time, simul

Athens, Athēnae

Attack, adpetō

Attack, aggredior

Attack, impetus

Attack, oppūgnātiō

Attack, oppūgnō

Attack, petō

Attempt, aggredior

Attend on, adsector

Attentive, attentus

Attica, Attica

Attribute, tribuō

Aurum, gold

Auspices, auspicium

Austerity, sevēritās

Author, auctor

Authority, auctōritās

Authority, auspicium

Authority, dīgnitās

Avenge, vindicō

Avenger, ultor

Aventine, Aventīnum

Avoid, fugiō

Avoid, vītō

Await, maneō

Awry, oblīquus

Bacchus, Bacchus

Back, retrō

Back, rūrsus

Back, tergum

Bad, malus

Bad, prāvus

Baggage, impedīmenta (plural)

Band, āgmen

Band of men, manus

Bandersnatch, Bandersnatcha

Banish, expellō

Bank (of a stream), rīpa

Barbarian, barbarus

Barber, tōnsor

Bare, nūdus

Basket, alveus

Battle, proelium

Be, exsistō

Be, sum

Be a soldier, mīlitō

Be able, possum

Be able, queō

Be absent, absum

Be accustomed, sōleō

Be angry, īrāscor

Be born, nāscor

Be carried, vehō (passive)

Be devoted to, studeō

Be distant, absum

Be done, fiō

Be eager for, studeō

Be empty, vacō

Be free, vacō

Be hard pressed, labōrō

Be in, īnsum

Be in charge of, praesum

Be lacking, dēsum

Be made, fiō

Be on fire, ārdeō

Be persistent, obstinō

Be plentiful, superō

Be present, adsum

Be seen, videor

Be silent, sileō

Be silent, taceō

Be unable, nequeō

Be unwilling, nōlō

Bear, ferō

Bear, gīgnō

Bear witness, testor

Beast, bēstia

Beast, pecus

Beat, verberō

Beating, plangor

Beautiful, pulcher

Beauty, decus

Beauty, fōrma

Because, quia

Because, quod

Because of, prae (prep. with abl.)

Become senseless, obstupefaciō

Bed, lectus

Bed-chamber, cubiculum

Bee, apis

Before, ante (prep. with accus.)

Before, prius ... quam

Before, priusquam

Beg, ōrō

Beget, gīgnō

Beget, prōcreō

Begin, coepī

Begin (a contest), committō

Begin, inchoō

Begin, incipiō

Begin, incohō

Begin, ingredior

Beginning, initium

Beginning, principium

Behind, post (prep. with accus.)

Belief, fidēs

Believe, crēdō

Bellow, immūgiō

Below, īnferus

Bend, flectō

Bend, inclīnō

Benefit, prōsum

Besides, praetereā

Besiege, obsideō

Best, optimus

Better, melior

Between, inter (prep. with accus.)

Beware, caveō

Bind, revinciō

Bind, vinciō

Bind over by bail, vador

Bird, avis

Bird-omen, augurium

Birth, partus

Bitter, amārus

Bitterness, acerbitās

Bitumenous, bitūminātus

Black, āter

Blame, culpa

Blameless, integer

Blessed, mācte (undeclin.)

Blind, caecus

Blockade, obsidiō

Blood, sanguis

Bloody, cruentus

Blow, flō

Blow, ictus

Body, corpus

Body of slaves, servitium

Bodyguard, satelles

Bold, audāx

Boldness, audācia

Bone, os

Book, liber

Booty, praeda

Bordered, praetextus

Both, ambō

Both ... and, et ... et

Both ... and, -que ... -que

Both ... and, simul ... simul

Bottom of, īmus

Bottom of, īnfimus

Boundary, fīnis

Boundary, terminus

Boy, puer

Boyish, puerīlis

Brave, fortis

Brazier, foculus

Break, frangō

Break, interrumpō

Break, rumpō

Breast, pectus

Breed, prōcreō

Bridge, pōns

Bright, clārus

Bring, adferō

Bring, perferō

Bring back, referō

Bring down, dēferō

Bring in, importō

Bring in, īnferō

Bring it about, efficiō

Bring to, adhibeō

Bring together, cōnferō

Broad way, platea

Brother, frāter

Build, aedificō

Build, mōlior

Build, struō

Burn, ārdeō

Burning, ārdēns

Burst, irrumpō

Bury, obruō

Bury, sepeliō

But, autem

But, sed

But, vērum

But that, quīn (with subjunctive)

Buy, ēmō

By, ā, ab (prep. with abl.)

By chance, fōrte

By divine providence, dīvīnitus

By this way, hāc

By whatever way, quācumque

Caesar, Caesar

Call, appellō

Call, dīcō

Call, nōminō

Call, vocō

Call as a witness, obtestor

Call back, revocō

Call forth, prōvocō

Call out, ēvocō

Call to witness, testor

Calm, placidus

Camp, castra

Capitol hill, Capitōlium

Care, cūra

Careful, dīligēns

Carefulness, dīligentia

Carry, ferō

Carry, gerō

Carry, portō

Carry, vehō (active)

Carry off, auferō

Carry on, gerō

Carthage, Carthāgō

Cast in, iniciō

Catch sight of, cōnspiciō

Catch, excipiō

Cause, causa

Cavary, equitātus

Cave, caverna

Cavity, caverna

Cease, dēsinō

Cease, dēsistō

Centurion, centuriō

Certain, certus

Certainly, profectō

Certainly, sānē

Chain, catēna

Chance, cāsus

Chance, fōrs

Change, mūtō

Character, habitus

Character, ingenium

Charge, crīmen

Chariot, currus

Charm, venus

Chaste, pudīcus

Chastity, pudīcitia

Cheap, vīlis

Chide, increpō

Childish, puerīlis

Children, līberī

Choose, dēligō

Choose, legō

Choose, optō

Circle, orbis

Citadel, arx

Citizen, cīvis

City, urbs

Civilian, togātus

Claim, vindicō

Clash, cōnflīgō

Clash, congredior

Claw, unguis (of a bird)

Cleanse, expūrgō

Cleansing, pūrgātiō

Clear, clārus

Clever, callidus

Climb up, cōnscendō

Cling, haereō

Cling to, haereō

Close, claudō

Cohort, cohors (a tenth of a legion)

Cold, frīgidus

Collect, cōgō

Collect, colligō

Collect, legō

Column, āgmen

Come, veniō

Come out, ēveniō

Come to, subeō

Come to, subveniō

Come together, conveniō

Command, imperium

Commendable, probābilis

Commit (a crime), admittō

Commit, committō

Common, commūnis

Common, vulgātus

Complain, queror

Complaint, querēla

Complete, compleō

Comprising the greater part, plērus

Comrade, socius

Concerning, dē (prep. with abl.)

Concubine, paelex

Condemn, damnō

Conference, conloquium

Confess, fateor

Confirm, adfirmō

Confirm, sanciō

Congratulate, grātulor (often with dat.)

Connection by marriage, adfīnitās (affīnitās)

Conquer, vincō

Conqueror, vīctor

Conqueror, vīctrix

Consent, voluntās

Consider, dūcō

Consider, habeō

Consideration, ratiō

Console, cōnsōlor

Conspiracy, coniūrātiō

Conspire, coniūrō

Construct, fabricō

Consul, cōnsul

Consult, cōnsulō

Consume by fire, cremō

Container, alveus

Continue, pergō

Continuous, perpetuus

Contrary to, praeter (prep. with accus.)

Cool, frīgidus

Corinth, Corinthus

Corrupt, corrumpō

Council, cōnsilium

Country, rūs

Courage, animus

Courage, virtūs

Course, cursus

Courteous, cōmis

Covering, vestis

Crashing, fragor

Create, creō

Crete, Crēta

Crime, crīmen

Crime, facinus

Crime, scelus

Crisis, discrīmen

Crooked, prāvus

Crowd, turba

Crowded, celeber

Crowded together, cōnfertus

Cruel, atrōx

Cruel, crūdēlis

Cruel, dūrus

Cruelty, crūdēlitās

Cry aloud, conclāmō

Crying, vāgītus

Cultivate, colō

Cultivation, cultus

Cup, pōculum

Curved, curvus

Custom, cōnsuētūdō

Custom, mōs

Cut, caedō

Cut, tondeō

Cut down, obtruncō

Cut down, rescindō

Cut by the throat, iugulō

Damage, clādēs

Danger, perīculum

Dare, audeō

Dark, obscūrus

Darkness, tenebrae

Darling, dēliciae

Dart, trāgula

Dash, incutiō

Daughter, fīlia

Day, diēs

Dear, cārus

Dearness, cāritās

Death, fūnus

Death, mors

Debauch, corrumpō

Debauch, stuprō

Debtor, dēbitor

Deceive, frūstror

Decemvir, decemvir

Decide, cōnstituō

Decide, dēcernō

Decide, dīiūdicō

Decide, īnstituō

Decide, iūdicō

Decide, statuō

Decree, dēcernō

Deed, facinus

Deep, altus

Deep, profundus

Deep within, penitus

Deer, cervus

Defeat, fundō

Defence, mūnīmentum

Defend, dēfendō

Defender, dēfēnsor

Defile, oblinō

Defilement, stuprum

Delay, cunctor

Delay, moror

Delight, dēliciae

Demand, dēposcō

Demand, poscō

Demand, postulō

Deny, negō

Deprive of breath, exanimō

Depth, altitūdō

Descendant, nepōs

Desert, sōlitūdō

Deserter, perfuga

Deserter, trānsfuga

Deserve, mereō

Deserve, mereor

Design, cōgitātiō

Desire, cupiditās

Desire, cupīdō

Desire, cupiō

Desire, dēsīderium

Desire, dēsīderō

Desire, libīdō

Desolate, vāstus

Despair, diffīdō

Despair of, dēspērō

Destroy, cōnsūmō

Destroy, dēleō

Destroy, perdō

Destruction, fūnus

Destruction, perniciēs

Devastation, populātiō

Dew, rōs

Dictator, dictātor

Die, ēmorior

Die, morior

Die, obeō

Difference, discrīmen

Difficult, difficilis

Diligent, dīligēns

Dine, cēnō

Dinner, cēna

Dinner, convīvium

Direct about, circumferō

Direction, pars

Dirty, sordidus

Disaster, calamitās

Discharge, dēfungor

Discharge, dissolvō

Disclose, exprōmō

Discuss, agō

Disease, morbus

Disgrace, dēdecus

Disguise, dissimulō

Dislodge, dētrūdō

Dispute, altercātiō

Dispute, contrōversia

Disquieting, tumultuōsus

Dissimilar, dissimilis

Distinguished, īnsīgnis

Distrust, diffīdō

Disturb, turbō

Disturbance, mōtus

Ditch, fossa

Divide, dīvidō

Divine, dīvus

Divine will, nūmen

Do, agō

Do, cōnficiō

Do, faciō

Do, perficiō

Dog, canis

Domestic, domesticus

Double, duplex

Double, duplicō

Doubt, dubitō (with subjunctive)

Down from, dē (prep. with abl.)

Drag, trahō

Drag back, retrahō

Draw, hauriō

Draw, trahō

Draw (a sword), stringō

Draw down, trahō

Draw tight, stringō

Draw up, īnstruō

Dreadful, horrendus

Dreadful, ingēns

Dress, cultus

Dress, habitus

Dress, ōrnātus

Drink, bibō

Drink, hauriō

Drink, pōtō

Drive, agō

Drive, impellō

Drive, pellō

Drive, trānsigō

Drive out, expellō

Dry, siccus

Duck, anas

Duty, iūs

Duty, mūnus

Dying, moribundus

Eager, ācer

Eager, avidus

Eagerness, alacritās

Eagerness, studium

Earn, mereō

Earn, mereor

Easily, facile

Easy, facilis

Eat, edō

Eat, vescor (with abl.)

Ebro river, Hibērus

Educate, ēducō

Eight, octō

Eighteenth, octāvus-decimus

Either ... or, aut ... aut

Either ... or, seu ... seu

Either ... or, vel ... vel

Elephant, elephantus

Eloquent, ēloquēns

Embassy, lēgātiō

Embrace, circumplector

Emerge, exsistō

Employ, exerceō

Emptiness, vānitās

Empty, vacuus

Encamp, cōnsīdō

End, fīnis

Endure, perferō

Enemy, hostis

Enjoy, fruor (with abl.)

Enjoyment, fructus

Enough, sat

Enough, satis

Enquire, contor

Enquire, percontor

Enquire, quaerō

Enquire repeatedly, scīscitor

Entirely, omnīnō

Entrance, ōstium

Entrust, commendō

Entrust, committō

Entrust, crēdō

Entrust, mandō (often with dat.)

Entrust, permittō (often with dat.)

Envy, invidia

Equal in age, aequālis

Equal, pār

Equally, pariter

Equestrian, equester

Equip, īnstruō

Equipment, ōrnātus

Error, error

Escape, effugiō

Escape, ēvādō

Especially, potissimum

Especially, praecipuē

Establish, condō

Establish, cōnstituō

Establish, īnstituō

Establish, statuō

Esteemed, spectātus

Eternal, sempiternus

Etruscans, Etruscī

Etruscan, Etruscus

Euphrates river, Euphrātēs

Even, et

Even, etiam

Even, vel

Event, cāsus

Ever, umquam

Ever, unquam

Everlasting, perpetuus

Every, omnis

Everywhere, passion

Evidence, fidēs

Examined, spectātus

Example, exemplum

Exasperate, exasperō

Excel, praestō

Except, praeter (prep. with accus.)

Excess, lūxus

Excessively, nimium

Exempt, excipiō

Exercise, exerceō

Exhaust, hauriō

Expect, spērō

Expel, ēiciō

Expense, sūmptus

Experience, ūsus

Experienced, perītus (often with gen.)

Expose, expōnō

Expose, obiciō

Expose, patefaciō

Exposed, opportūnus

Expression, vultus

Exstinguish, exstinguō

Extend, propāgō

Extraordinary, ēgregius

Extravagance, lūxus

Eye, lūmen

Eye, oculus

Eyesight, aciēs

Face, vultus

Facing, adversus

Faith, fidēs

Faithful, fīdus

Fall down, prōcumbō

Fall, cadō

Fall, concidō

Fall, ruō

Fall on, incumbō

Fall on top of, superincidō

Falsity, vānitās

Fame, fāma

Family, gēns

Famous, celeber

Famous, clārus

Famous, nōtus

Far, longē

Fare well, aveō

Farmer, agricola

Farthest, ultimus

Fat, pīnguis

Fate, fātum

Fate, sors

Father, pater

Fatherland, patria

Father's, patrius

Fatness, pīnguēdō

Fault, culpa

Fault, noxa

Fault, peccātum

Favour, beneficium

Favour, faveō (with dat.)

Favour, venia

Favourable, dexter

Favourable, propitius

Favourable, secundus

Fear, metuō

Fear, metus

Fear, terror

Fear, timeō

Fear, timor

Fear, vereor

Fear greatly, expavēscō

Fearful, pavidus

Feed, pāscō

Feel, sentiō

Feeling, sēnsus

Fence in, saepiō

Few, paucī

Fidenae, Fīdēnae

Fidenates, Fīdenātēs

Field, ager

Field, arvum

Fierce, ācer

Fierce, asper

Fifth, quīntus

Fight, dīmicō

Fight, prōpūgnō

Fight, pūgna

Fight, pūgnō

Fig-tree, fīcus

Fill, compleō

Fill, impleō

Fill, satiō

Find, comperiō

Find, inveniō

Find, reperiō

Fire, īgnis

First, prīmus

First, prior

Firstly, prīmum

Fit, accommodō

Five, quīnque (undeclin.)

Fix firmly, dēfīgō

Fixed, certus

Flaw, vitium

Flee, fugiō

Flee from, effugiō

Fleet, classis

Flight, fuga

Float, fluitō

Flow, fluō

Flow down, dēfluō

Flow forth, prōfluō

Flowery, flōreus

Fly away, āvolō

Fly together, convolō

Foam, spūmō

Follow, excipiō

Follow, īnsequor

Follow, persequor

Follow, prōsequor

Follow, sequor

Follow, subeō

Follow constantly, adsector

Following, posterus

Following after, secundum (prep. with accus.)

Food, vīctus

Foot, pēs

Footsoldier, pedes

Footstep, vestīgium

For, ad (prep. with accus.)

For, enim

For, nam

For, namque

For, quippe

For a little while, parumper

For a little while, paulisper

For a long time, diū

For some considerable time, aliquamdiū

For the good of the state, ē rēpūblicā

For the sake of, causā (with gen. beforehand)

For the sake of, grātiā (with gen. beforehand)

Forbid, vetō

Force, cōgō

Force, vīs

Forces, cōpiae (plural)

Fore-court, vestibulum

Foremost, prīmōris

Foresee, prōvideō

Forget, oblīvīscor

Form, capiō (a plan or conspiracy)

Form, fōrma

Formerly, ōlim

Formerly, quondam

Fort, castellum

Fortify, mūniō

Fortify strongly, commūniō

Fortunate, fōrtūnātus

Fortune, fōrtūna

Foul, foedus

Foundation, fundāmentum

Founder, auctor

Founder, conditōr

Four, quattuor

Fragile, fragilis

Free, līber

Free, līberō

Freedom, lībērtās

Frequent, crēber

Frequent, frequēns

Fresh, integer

Friendly, amīcus

Friendship, amīcitia

Frighten completely, conterreō

Fringed, praetextus

From, ā or ab (prep. with abl.)

From, dē (prep. with abl.)

From above, dēsuper

From all sides, undique

From that place, inde

From there, illinc

From there, istinc

From this place, hinc

From where, unde

Fruit, fructus

Fruitful, fēlīx

Fugitive, profugus

Fulfilment, fidēs

Full, plēnus

Furnish, praebeō

Future generations, posterī

Gall, fel

Gall-bladder, fel

Game, lūdus

Gaming, lūsus

Garment, vestis

Gate, līmen

Gaul, Gallia

Gaul, Gallus

General, commūnis

General, imperātōr

Generally, ferē

Generally, passim

Generosity, līberālitās

Geneva, Genāva

Gentle, lēnis

Gentle, mītis

Gentle, mollis

Gentleness, lēnitās

Get, adipīscor

Get, comparō

Get, parō

Get possession of, potior (with abl.)

Ghost, simulācrum

Gift, dōnum

Gift, mūnus

Gird on, accingō

Gird on, cingō

Girl, puella

Give, addō

Give, dō

Give, dōnō

Give back, reddō

Give out, ēdō

Gladiator, gladiātor

Glory, decus

Glory, glōria

Glory, laus

Go, cēdō

Go, concēdō

Go, eō

Go, vādō

Go aboard (a ship), cōnscendō

Go across, trānseō

Go along, ingredior

Go away, abeō

Go away, dēcēdō

Go away, dēmigrō

Go back, recēdō

Go back, redeō

Go into, ingredior

Go into, intrō

Go into, invādō

Go out, ēgredior

Go out, ēvādō

Go out, excēdō

Go to, accēdō

Go to, adeō

Go to, obeō

Go under, subeō

Go under, succēdō

Go up to, succēdō

God, deus

God, nūmen

Gods, superī

Golden, aureus

Good, bonus

Good, honestus

Good will, voluntās

Grace, venus

Grain, frūmentum

Grandfather, avus

Grandson, nepōs

Grant, concēdō

Grant, tribuō

Grasp, prehendō

Grateful, grātus

Great, māgnus

Greater, māior

Greatest, māximus

Greatly, māgnoperē

Greedy, avidus

Greeks, Grāī

Greeting, salūtātiō

Grieve, doleō

Grievous, gravis

Grim, trīstis

Ground, solum

Grow, crēscō

Grow hot, incalēscō

Grow light, dīlūcēscō

Guard, custōs

Guard, praesidium

Guard, servō

Guardian deities of the household, penātēs

Guest, hospes

Hail, cōnsalūtō

Hair, coma

Hall, aula

Hand, manus

Hand to hand, comminus

Handle, tractō

Happen, ēveniō

Happen, incidō

Happy, beātus

Happy, fēlīx

Harass, increpō

Harbour, portus

Hard, dūrus

Hard, rōbustus

Hardy, dūrus

Harm, noceō

Harm, violō

Hasten, celerō

Hasten, contendō

Hasten, festīnō

Hasten, mātūrō

Hasten, praecipitō

Hasten, properō

Hasten, tendō

Hastily, properē

Hate, ōdī

Hatred, invidia

Hatred, odium

Have, habeō

He, hic

He, ille

He, is

Head, caput

Headstrong, ferōx

Hear, audiō

Heart, cor

Heavy, gravis

Height, altitūdō

Help, adsum

Help, auxilium

Help, iuvō

Help, ops

Help, subsidium

Help, subveniō

Helpful, praesēns

Herd, pecus

Herdsman, pāstor

Here, hīc

Hesitate, dubitō (with infinitive)

Hide, abdō

Hide, condō

High, altus

High, arduus

High price, cāritās

Higher, superior

Highest, summus

Highest, suprēmus

Hinder, arceō

Hindrance, impedīmentum

His own, her own, its own, their own, suus

Hold, obtineō

Hold, teneō

Hold back, retineō

Hold back repeatedly, reprehēnsō

Hold in, contineō

Hold up, sustineō

Holy, sānctus

Home, domus

Honour, honor (honōs)

Honour, honōrō

Honour, prōsequor

Honourableness, honestās

Hope, spērō

Hope, spēs

Horn, cornū

Horse, equus

Horseman, eques

Hospitality, hospitium

Host, hospes

Hostage, obses

Hostile, hostīlis

Hostile, īnfēnsus

Hostile, īnfestus

Hot, calidus

Hour, hōra

House, aedis

House, tēctum

How, quam

How, quem ad modum

How, quō modo

How, ut (with indicative)

How, ut (with subjunctive)

How great, quantus

How many, quot

How much, quantus

Huge, immānis

Huge, immēnsus

Huge, ingēns

Huge, vāstus

Humble, humilis

Hundred, centum (undeclin.)

Hunger, famēs

Hurl, praecipitō

Hurl lightning, fulminō

Hurry, citō

Hurt, noxa

Husband, marītus

Hut, taberna

I, ego

If, sī

If ... or if, seu ... seu

If not, nī

If not, nisi

Ignorance, īgnōrātiō

Ignorant (of), īgnārus

Image, imāgō

Image, simulācrum

Immature, immātūrus

Immediately, statim

Immortality, immortālitās

Impetuous, violēns

In, in (prep. with abl.)

In comparison with, prae (prep. with abl.)

In fact, quippe

In flight, profugus

In front of, prae (prep. with abl.)

In front of, prō (prep. with abl.)

In like manner, perinde

In like manner, proinde

In reply, contrā (prep. with accus.)

In respect to, ad (prep. with accus.)

In that place, illīc

In the highest degree, plūrimum

In the house with, penes (prep. with accus.)

In unbroken succession, continenter

In vain, frūstrā

In vain, nēquīquam

Indeed, enim

Indeed, quidem

Indeed, quīn (with indicative)

Indeed, vērō (often not translated)

Indignity, indīgnitās

Industrious, attentus

Industry, dīligentia

Infantry, peditēs

Inflict (punishment), sūmō

Influence, addūcō

Influence, grātia

Inhabit, colō

Inhabit, incolō

Inhabitants of Alba Longa, Albānī

Injustice, iniūria

Inside, intrā (prep. with accus.)

Insolent, īnsolēns

Inspire, adficiō

Instruct, praecipiō

Intact, integer

Intention, mēns

Intervene, intericiō

Into, in (prep. with accus.)

Intrude upon, interveniō (with dat.)

Invite, invītō

Iron, ferrum

Island, īnsula

It, hōc

It, id

It, illud

It, quod

It fits, decet

It happens, accidit

It is agreed, cōnstat

It is better, praestat

It is clear, cōnstat

It is fitting, decet

It is necessary, oportet

It is permitted, licet

It is raining, pluit

It snows, ningit

Italy, Italia

Ivory, elephantus

Jabberwocky, Gaberbocchus

Janiculum, Iāniculum

Javelin, trāgula

Join, adiungō

Join, coniungō

Join, iungō

Journey, iter

Joy, gaudium

Jubjub, Iububbus

Judge, iūdex

Judge, iūdicō

Judge between, dīiūdicō

Jump down, dēsiliō

Jupiter, Iuppiter

Juryman, iūdex

Just, aequus

Just as, perinde

Just as, proinde

Just as, quasi

Just as, sīcut

Just as, tamquam

Just as, velut

Just as if, quasi

Just as if, tamquam

Justice, iūs

Keep ... from, arceō

Keep away, prohibeō

Kill, caedō

Kill, interficiō

Kill, interimō

Kill, necō

Kill, occīdō

Kind, genus

Kind-hearted, benīgnus

Kindness, līberālitās

King, rēx

Kingdom, rēgnum

Knee, genū

Knife, culter

Know, cōgnōscō (in perf.)

Know, sciō

Know how, sciō

Knowledge, scientia

Known, nōtus

Lack, careō (with abl.)

Lack, inopia

Land, terra

Large, amplus

Large, māgnus

Larger, māior

Largess (given by an emperor to his soldiers),
    dōnātīvum

Largest, māximus

Last, postrēmus

Last, summus

Last, suprēmus

Lasting, proprius

Late, sērus

Later, posterior

Latin, Latīnus

Latins, Latīnī

Launch (ships), dēdūcō

Lavinium, Lāvīnium

Law, lēx

Lawsuit, contrōversia

Lay waste, vāstō

Lazy, piger

Lead away, dēdūcō

Lead back, redūcō

Lead out, ēdūcō

Lead out, prōdūcō

Lead through, perdūcō

Lead to, addūcō

Lead, dūcō

Leader, dux

Leader, prīnceps

Leadership, prīncipātus

Leap, ēmicō

Leap, trānsiliō

Leap forth, prōsiliō

Learn, cōgnōscō

Learn, discō

Leave, relinquō

Leaves, coma

Left, sinister

Legion, legiō

Leisure, ōtium

Less, minus

Lest, nē

Let in, immittō

Let go, admittō

Let go, immittō

Let go, mittō

Letter, litterae (document)

Letter, littera (of the alphabet)

Level, aequus

Library, bibliothēca

Lick, lambō

Lictor, līctor

Lie, fallācia

Lie, iaceō

Lie, mentior

Lie hidden, lateō

Lie on, incumbō

Lie open, pateō

Lieutenant, lēgātus

Life, anima

Life, vīta

Light, levis

Light, lūmen

Light, lūx

Light, tenuis

Lighten, fulgurō

Lightning, fulgor

Like, similis

Likewise, īdem

Likewise, item

Limit, modus

Line, ōrdō

Line of battle, aciēs

Little, parum

Little pig, porcellus

Live, habitō

Live, vīvō

Live in, habitō

Living, vīvus

Lofty, excelsus

Long, longus

Long for, optō

Look, spectō

Look around, circumspectō

Look at, spectō

Look for, quaerō

Look for, requīrō

Look into, īnspiciō

Look out and see, prōspiciō

Look out, prōspiciō

Loosen, absolvō

Loosen, solvō

Lordship, dominātiō

Lose, āmittō

Lose, perdō

Lose hope, dēspērō

Lose utterly, dēperdō

Lot, sors

Love, amō

Love, amor

Love, dīligō

Loveable, amābilis

Lovely, amābilis

Lower, īnferior

Lower, submittō

Lowest, īmus

Lowest, īnfimus

Loyalty, fidēs

Machine, māchina

Magistrate, decemvir (in a commission of ten)

Magnificent, amplus

Maiden, virgō

Make, cōnficiō

Make, faciō

Make, perficiō

Make a stand, cōnsistō

Make common, vulgō

Make double, duplicō

Make equal, aequō

Make general, vulgō

Make ready for, accingō

Male, virīlis

Man, homō

Man, vir

Manage, administrō

Manner, modus

Mantle, amictus

March, contendō

Marriage, mātrimōnium

Mars, Mārs

Marvel, mīrāculum

Mass, Missa

Mass, mōlēs

Master, dominus

Master, magister

Mastery, dominātiō

Material, māteria

Meadow, prātum

Meantime, interim

Meanwhile, intereā

Measure, modus

Medicine, medicāmentus

Meet, congredior

Meet, conveniō

Meet, obeō

Meet, occurrō

Meeting, obvius (with dat.)

Memorable, memorābilis

Memorial, monumentum

Memory, memoria

Mention, mentiō

Mercy, clēmentia

Messenger, nūntius

Middle, medius

Migrate, dēmigrō

Mild, lēnis

Mild, mītis

Mild, mollis

Mildness, lēnitās

Milestone, mīlliārium

Mina, mina (Greek weight of a hundred Attic drachmas, used as money)

Mind, animus

Mind, mēns

Mirror, speculum

Misfortune, cāsus

Miss, dēsīderō

Mist, nebula

Mistress, paelex

Mix, misceō

Mix together, commisceō

Mockery, lūdibrium

Modest, pudīcus

Modesty, pudīcitia

Modesty, pudor

Money, pecūnia

Monster, mōnstrum

Monstrous, portentōsus

Month, mēnsis

More, magis

More, plūs

Moreover, autem

Mortal, mortālis

Most, plūrimus

Most of, plērī

Mother, māter

Mother-in-law, socrus

Mount Algidus, Algidus

Mount Etna, Aetna

Mountain, mōns

Mourning, plangor

Mouth, ōs

Move, moveō

Move to, admoveō

Movement, mōtus

Much, multum

Much, multus

Multitude, multitūdō

Multitude, vulgus

My, meus

Nail of a man, unguis

Name, cōgnōmen

Name, nōmen

Name, nōminō

Narrow, angustus

Nation, gēns

Native, patrius

Native inhabitants, Aborīginēs

Nature, nātūra

Near, ad (prep. with accus.)

Near, iūxtā (prep. with accus.)

Near, prope

Near, prope (prep. with accus.)

Near, propīnquus

Nearest, proximus

Necessary, necessārius

Neck, collum

Neighbouring, fīnitimus

Neither (of two), neuter

Neither ... nor, nec

Neither ... nor, neque ... neque

Never, numquam

Nevertheless, tamen

New, novus

Newness, novitās

Next, dein

Next, deinde

Next, proximus

Night, nox

Nine, novem (undeclin.)

Nitrous, nitrōsus

No, nūllus

No less, nihilō minus

No one, nēmō

Nobility, nōbilitās

Noble, nōbilis

Noble, procer

Nocturnal, nocturnus

Noisy, sonōrus

Nominative, nōminātīvus

None the less, nihilō minus

Nor, nec

Nor, neque

Nose, nāsus

Not, haud

Not, nihil

Not, nōn

Not at all, haudquāquam

Not even, nē ... quidem

Not know, īgnōrō

Not knowing, īnscius

Not only ... but also, cum ... tum

Not only ... but also, nōn sōlum ... sed (etiam)

Nothing, nihil

Notice, animadvertō

Nourish, alō

Now, iam

Now, nunc

Now and then, interdum

Number, numerus

Numberous, crēber

Numerous, frequēns

Obey, pāreō

Obliging, officiōsus

Obscure, obscūrus

Obtain, impetrō

Obtain one's request, impetrō

Occur, incidō

Of (*etc.*) himself, herself, itself, themselves, — , suī, sibi, sē, sē

Of Alba Longa, Albānus

Of course, scīlicet (sometimes sarcastic)

Of food, cibārius

Of Lavinium, Lāvīnius

Of oak, rōbustus

Of Romulus, Rōmulāris

Of Rumina (a Roman goddess), Rūmīnālis

Of the Laurentians, Laurentīnus

Of the Silvian kings of Alba Longa, Silvius

Of the Tiber, Tiberīnus

Offence, dēlictum

Offer, praebeō

Official, magistrātus

Offspring, genus

Offspring, partus

Offspring, stirpis (stirps)

Often, saepe

Oiliness, pīnguēdō

Old, prīscus

Old, senex

Old, vetus

Omen, mōnstrum

Omen, ōmen

On, in (prep. with abl.)

On account of, ob (prep. with accus.)

On account of, propter (prep. with accus.)

On all sides, undique

On both sides, utrimque

On the day after tomorrow, perindiē

On the day before, prīdiē

On the grounds that, tamquam

Once, semel

One, ūnus

One at a time, singulī

One's own, proprius

Only, tantum

Only, ūnicus

Open, aperiō

Open, patefaciō

Opinion, opīniō

Opinion, sententia

Opportunity, occāsiō

Oppose, obsistō

Opposed to, adversārius

Opposite, adversus

Opposite, contrā (prep. with accus.)

Or, aut

Or, vel

Or if, seu

Orbit, gīrus (gyrus)

Order, imperō

Order, iubeō

Order, mandō (often with dat.)

Order, ōrdō

Order, praecipiō

Origin, orīgō

Other, alius

Otherwise, aliter

Otherwise than, aliter atque (or ac); aliter ... atque (or ac)

Ought, dēbeō

Our, noster

Out of, ē (prep. with abl.)

Out of, ex (prep. with abl.)

Outside, extrā (prep. with accus.)

Overcome, superō

Overhang, immineō

Overthrow, ēvertō

Overturn, vertō

Overwhelm, mergō

Overwhelm, opprimō

Overwhelm, premō

Owe, dēbeō

Pain, dolor

Palace, līmen

Palace, rēgia

Palatine, Palātium

Panic, pavor

Pardon, īgnōscō (with dat.)

Pardon, venia

Parent, parēns

Part, pars

Pass on, trādō

Passage, trānsitus

Passion, libīdō

Past, praeter (prep. with accus.)

Peace, ōtium

Peace, pāx

Penalty, poena

Penetrate, penetrō

People, populus

Perceive, sentiō

Perform (duty), praestō

Perform, fungor

Perform, solvō

Pergamum, Pergama

Perish, pereō

Permit, permittō (often with dat.)

Persistent, adsiduus

Person, persōna

Person blind in one eye, coclēs

Person given as security, pīgnus

Personal, persōnālis

Persuade, persuādeō

Pestilential, pestifer

Physician, medicus

Pick out, ēligō

Pig, porcus

Pirate, pīrāta

Place, locō

Place, locus

Place of assembly, comitium

Place upon, indō

Plain, campus

Plan, cōgitātiō

Plan, cōgitō

Plan, cōnsilium

Plan, sententia

Platform, tribūnal

Pleasant, iūcundus

Please, placeō (with dat.)

Pleasing, grātus

Pledge, pīgnus

Plentiful, cōpiōsus

Plough, arō

Plough around, circumarō

Plunder, dīripiō

Plunderer, praedō

Plunge, mergō

Poet, poēta

Poison, fel

Poison, venēnum

Ponder, versō

Pool of standing water, stāgnum

Pool of water, adluviēs

Poor, pauper

Portentous, portentōsus

Portray, exprimō

Position, situs

Post, statiō

Pour, fundō

Pour, suffundō

Pour a libation, lībō

Pour around, circumfundō

Pour out, effundō

Power, imperium

Power, potestās

Powerful, opulentus

Powerful, potēns

Praise, laus

Pray, precor

Prayer, precātiō

Prayer, prex

Precedent, exemplum

Predict, praedīcō

Prefect, praefectus

Prefer, mālō

Prefer, praeferō

Prepare, comparō

Prepare, īnstituō

Prepare, parō

Present, dōnō

Present, offerō

Present, praesēns

Press, exprimō

Press, premō

Press on, īnstō

Prestige, auctōritās

Prestige, dīgnitās

Prevent, prohibeō

Previous, superior

Previously, anteā

Price, pretium

Priest, sacerdōs

Principally, plūrimum

Prison, carcer

Prison, custōdia

Prisoner, captīvus

Proceed, pergō

Proceed, prōcēdō

Proceed against, grassor

Proclaim, dēclārō

Proclaim, indīcō

Profit, fructus

Promise, fidēs

Promise, polliceor

Promise, prōmittō

Promise, vadimōnium

Properly, ōrdine

Propriety, decōrum

Protected, tūtus

Protection, fidēs

Protection, mūnīmentum

Protection, praesidium

Protection, tūtēla

Proud, superbus

Provide, prōvideō

Provide for, cūrō

Provided that, dum (with subjunctive)

Province, prōvincia

Public, pūblicus

Public office, magistrātus

Punish, vindicō

Punishment, poena

Pupil, discipulus

Purge, expūrgō

Purity, castitās

Push, trūdō

Put, pōnō

Put against, oppōnō

Put an end to, fīniō

Put away, āmoveō

Put back, repōnō

Put between, interpōnō

Put down, pōnō

Put forth, expōnō

Put in charge of, praeficiō

Put on, ēdō

Put on, impōnō

Put out of the way, tollō

Put to rest, compōnō

Put to sleep, sōpiō

Put together, compōnō

Put under, subiciō

Quarters, stabulum

Queen, rēgīna

Quiet, plācō

Race, gēns

Race, genus

Rage, fremō

Rage, saeviō

Raise, tollō

Rashly, temerē

Rather vile, turpiculus

Raven, corvus

Ravish, stuprō

Raze, excīdō

Read, legō

Reason, ratiō

Recall, repetō

Receive, accipiō

Receive, excipiō

Receive, recēdō

Receive in advance, praecipiō

Reduce, redigō

Refrain from, parcō

Refuse, negō

Region, regiō

Regular, iūstus

Regularly, ōrdine

Reinforcement, subsidium

Reject, repudiō

Rejoice, gaudeō

Rejoice, grātulor (often with dat.)

Relating to a guest, hospitālis

Relatives, propīnquī

Relax, remittō

Relying on, frētus (often with abl.)

Remain, maneō

Remain, permaneō

Remain, remaneō

Remain, supersum

Remains, reliquiae

Remember, meminī (often with gen.)

Remember, recordor

Remind, admoneō

Remove, removeō

Remove, submoveō

Remove, tollō

Remus, Remus

Render, reddō

Render, redigō

Render unholy, profānō

Renew, redintegrō

Renewed, redivīvus

Repay, remūneror

Report, dēferō

Report, nūntiō

Report, referō

Report, renūntiō

Repress, comprīmō

Require, dēposcō

Rescue, vindicō

Resist, resistō

Resolve, obstinō

Resound, resonō

Resources, cōpiae (plural)

Resources, opēs (plural)

Respect, honōrō

Respect, verēcundia

Resting upon piles, sublicius

Restore, redintegrō

Restore, restituō

Return, redeō

Return, reveniō

Return, revertor

Return to, repetō

Revelling, cōmissātiō (commissātiō)

Revive, revīvīscō

Revolt, rebellō

Reward, praemium

Reward, pretium

Rich, beātus

Rich, dīves

Rich, opulentus

Rich, pīnguis

Ride, vehō (passive)

Ridge, iugum

Right, dexter

Right, iūs

Ring, circus

Ring, gīrus (gyrus)

Rise up together, cōnsurgō

River, amnis

River, flūmen

Roar, fremō

Roast, torreō

Rob, spoliō

Rock, saxum

Rocky, petrōsus

Roman, Rōmānus

Rome, Rōma

Romulus, Rōmulus

Roof, fastīgium

Roof, tēctum

Rough, asper

Roughen, exasperō

Roundabout way, ambāgēs

Rouse, excitō

Rouse, incitō

Royal, rēgius

Rule, rēgnō

Rule, regō

Rumour, fāma

Rumour, rūmor

Run, concurrō

Run, currō

Run against, occurrō

Run down, dēcurrō

Run together, concurrō

Runner, cursor

Rush, ruō

Rustic, rūsticus

Sabines, Sabīnī

Sacred, sacer

Sacred, sānctus

Sacrifice, sacrificium

Sad, maestus

Sad, trīstis

Safe, incolumis

Safe, salvus

Safe, sōspēs

Safe, tūtus

Safety, salūs

Safety, tūtum

Sail, vehō (passive)

Sail, vēlum

Sailor, nauta

Salt, sāl

Saluting, salūtātiō

Satisfy, satiō

Savage, immānis

Savage, trux

Save, servō

Say, āiō

Say, cōnfīrmō

Say, dīcō

Say, ferō

Say, inquam

Scarcely, vix

Scatter, turbō

Scorn, contemnō

Scout, explōrātor

Sea, fluctus

Sea, mare

Sea, pontus

Sea, sāl

Search after, investīgō

Seat, sēdēs

Second, secundus

Secret, clandestīnus

Secretary, scrība

Security, vadimōnium

See!, ecce

See!, ēn

See, cernō

See, invīsō

See, videō

See, vīsō

Seek, petō

Seem, videor

Seem best, videor

Seize, occupō

Seize, rapiō

Seize firmly, comprehendō

Self, ipse

Sell, vēndō

Senator, senātor

Send, mittō

Send away, āmittō

Send away, dīmittō

Send back, remittō

Send forth, ēmittō

Send forth, prōmittō

Sense, sēnsus

Servant, ancilla

Serve, serviō (with dat.)

Serve (as a soldier), mereō

Serve (as a soldier), mereor

Serve in the army, mīlitō

Set, sistō

Set apart, dēstituō

Set in motion, commoveō

Set on fire, incendō

Set on fire, accendō

Set on fire, succendō

Set out, proficīscor

Set sail, solvō

Settle down, cōnsīdō

Seven, septem (undeclin.)

Sever, interrumpō

Several, aliquot (undeclin.)

Severity, sevēritās

Sewer, cloāca

Shame, pudor

Shameful, turpis

Shameless, impudīcus

Shapeless, īnfōrmis

Sharer, particeps

Sharp edge, aciēs

Sharp, ācer

She, ea

She, haec

She, illa

Shield, scūtum

Shine, fulgeō

Shine, lūceō

Shine, niteō

Ship, nāvis

Ship, puppis

Shoot, tendō

Shoot, trāiciō

Shop, taberna

Shore, lītus

Shore, ōra

Short, brevis

Shout, clāmor

Show (courage), praestō

Show, dēmōnstrō

Show, indīcō

Show, ostendō

Show, praebeō

Shut in, claudō

Sick, aeger

Sickness, morbus

Side, latus

Side, pars

Side by side, pariter

Siege, obsidiō

Siege-work, opus

Sight, cōnspectus

Sign of a question requiring a negative answer, num

Sign of a question requiring an affirmative answer, nōnne

Sign of a question, -ne

Sign of a wish, utinam

Sign, sīgnum

Silver, argentum

Sin, peccō

Since, cum

Since, quandō

Since, quoniam

Sing, canō

Sing, cantō

Single, singulī

Single, ūnicus

Sink, submergō

Sister, soror

Sit, sedeō

Sit near, adsideō

Sit on, īnsīdō

Six, sex (undeclin.)

Sixteen, sēdecim (undeclin.)

Size, māgnitūdō

Skim along, legō

Sky, caelum

Slanting, oblīquus

Slaughter, caedēs

Slave, servus

Slave-girl, ancilla

Slay, sternō

Sleep, dormiō

Sleep, somnus

Slender, gracilis

Slip forwards, prōlābor

Slothful, īgnāvus

Slow, piger

Sluggish, languidus

Small, exiguus

Small, parvus

Smaller, minor

Smallest, minimus

Snatch, surripiō

So, ita

So, sīc

So, tam

So great, tantus

So many, tot (undeclin.)

So much ... as, tantus ... quantus

So much, tantum

So much, tantus

So that, ut (with subjunctive)

So, adeō (especially with adjs.)

Soft, lēnis

Soft, mītis

Soft, mollis

Soften, mītēscō

Softness, lēnitas

Soldier, mīles

Some ... others, aliī ... aliī

Some time, ōlim

Someone, aliquis

Something, aliquid

Sometimes, quondam

Son, fīlius

Son, nātus

Son-in-law, gener

Song, carmen

Soon, iam

Soon, mox

Sorrow, dolor

Sound, resonō

Sound, sonitus

Sound, sonus

South wind, notus

South-east wind, Eurus

Sow, serō

Space for chariot races, circus

Spain, Hispāniae

Spare, parcō

Speak, loquor

Speech, ōrātiō

Speed, celeritās

Spinning, lāna

Spirit, animus

Spoil, corrumpō

Spoils, spolium

Spokesman, ōrātor

Spread, prōpāgō

Spread out, sternō

Spring from, orior

Spy, speculor

Stable, stabilis

Stain, suffundō

Stand, cōnsistō

Stand, stō

Standard, sīgnum

Star, sīdus

State, cīvitās

State, rēs pūblica

Station, statiō

Statue, sīgnum

Statue, statua

Steep, arduus

Step, gradus

Stern, puppis

Still, adhūc

Stir up, sollicitō

Stone, lapis

Stop, cōnsistō

Stop, sistō

Storm, expūgnō

Storm, hiems

Storm, tempestās

Straight, rēctus

Strange, novus

Stranger, advena

Stranger, hospes

Street, platea

Strength, vīrēs

Strengthen, adfirmō

Strengthen, cōnfirmō

Strengthened form of sē, sēmet

Stretch, intendō

Stretch, tendō

Stretch forth, prōtendō

Strike, īciō

Strike, pulsō

Strip, spoliō

Strive, certō

Strive, labōrō

Strive after, expetō

Strive for, adpetō

Strong, validus

Struggle, certāmen

Struggle, contendō

Struggle, lūctor

Stun, attonō

Subdue, subdō

Subsequently, mox

Substitute, subdō

Succeed, succēdō

Such, is, ea, id (anticipating a result clause)

Such, tālis

Sudden, repentīnus

Sudden, subitus

Suddenly, repente

Suddenly, subitō

Suffer, patior

Suffering, labor

Suitable, idōneus

Summer, aestās

Sun, sōl

Supply, cōpia

Suppose, opīnor

Suppress, comprimō

Surpass, superō

Surrender, dēditiō

Surrender, dēdō

Surrender, trādō

Surround, cingō

Surround, circumdō

Survive, superō

Survive, supersum

Swamp, palūs

Swear, iūrō

Sweat, sūdor

Sweet, dulcis

Swift, celer

Swift, vēlōx

Swim, nō

Swim across, trānō

Sword, gladius

Sword, mucrō

Syracuse, Syrācūsae

Take, capiō

Take, sūmō

Take an augury in, inaugurō

Take apart, dissolvō

Take away, adimō

Take away, eximō

Take away, rapiō

Take back, recēdō

Take by assault, expūgnō

Take care, cūrō

Take thought for, cōnsulō (with dat.)

Take up, adsūmō

Take up, suscipiō

Tale, fābula

Talent, ingenium

Taste, lībō

Taught easily, docilis

Teach, doceō

Teacher, doctor

Tear, lacrima

Tear, rescindō

Tear away, dīripiō

Teat, mamma

Tell, doceō

Temple (of the head), tempus

Temple, templum

Ten, decem (undeclin.)

Ten each, dēnī

Terrify, terreō

Territory, fīnēs (plural)

Than, ac (after words of likeness or difference)

Than, atque (after words of likeness or difference)

Than, quam

That, ille, illa, illud

That, iste, ista, istud

That, ut (with subjunctive)

That ... not, nē

That of yours, iste, ista, istud

The fact that, quod

The one ... the other, alius ... alius

The one ... the other, alter ... alter

The other, alter

The other, cēterī

The remaining, reliquus

The rest of, cēterī

The rest of, reliquus

The same, īdem

The second, alter

The whole, cūnctus

The whole, tōtus

The whole, ūniversus

Theatre, theātrum

Then, dein

Then, deinde

Then, inde

Then, then

Then, tum

There, eō

There, ibi

There, illīc

There, illō (motion to)

There, illūc (motion to)

There, istīc (no motion)

There, istūc (motion to)

There is need of, opus est (with abl.)

Therefore, ergō

Therefore, igitur

Therefore, quam ob rem

Therefore, quārē

Thigh, femur

Thin, tenuis

Thing, rēs

Think, arbitror

Think, cōgitō

Think, exīstimō

Think, putō

Think, reor

Thinking, cōgitātiō

Third, tertius

Thirst, sitiō

Thirty-eighth, trīcēsimus-octāvus

This, hic, haec, hōc

This, quod

Thousand, mīlle (undeclin.)

Thousands, mīlia

Threatening, mināx

Threatening, minitābundus

Threats, minae (plural)

Three hundred and fifteenth, trecentēsimus et quīntus

Three hundred and second, trecentēsimus et alter

Three hundred, trecentī

Three times, ter

Three, trēs

Threshold, līmen

Throat, guttur

Through, per (prep. with accus.)

Throw against, obiciō

Throw at, adiciō

Throw back, rēiciō

Throw down, dēiciō

Throw down, ruō

Throw into confusion, perturbō

Throw to, adiciō

Throw together, cōniciō

Throw up, ruō

Throw, cōniciō

Throw, iaciō

Throw, iactō

Throw, trāiciō

Thunder, tonō

Thunderbolt, fulmen

Thus, ita

Thus, sīc

Tiber river, Tiberis

Time, tempus

To, ad (prep. with accus.)

To that place, eō

To the same place, eōdem

To this place, hūc

To what place, quō

Today, hodiē

Toga, toga

Tongue, lingua

Too little, parum

Tooth, dēns

Top of, summus

Top of, suprēmus

Torch, lampas

Torment, exerceō

Torture, cruciātus

Touch, contingō

Touch, stringō

Toward, ergā (prep. with accus.)

Tower, turris

Town, oppidum

Track, investīgō

Train, exerceō

Traveller, viātor

Treachery, dolus

Treachery, īnsidiae

Treaty, foedus

Tree, arbor

Trembling, pavidus

Trembling, trepidus

Tribe, nātiō

Tribune, tribūnus

Trim, stringō

Troy, Pergama (by metonymy)

Troy, Trōia

True, vērum

Trust, cōnfīdō

Trustworthy, fīdus

Trusty, fidēlis

Try, cōnor

Try, temptō

Tumult, tumultus

Turn, convertō

Turn, inclīnō

Turn, versō

Turn, vertō

Turn away, āvertō

Turn towards, obtruncō

Turned towards, adversārius

Twelfth, duodecimus

Twenty, vīgintī (undecl.)

Twig, virga

Twin, geminus

Twins, geminī

Two, duo

Tyrant, tyrannus

Unaccustomed, īnsolēns

Uncertain, incertus

Uncertain, obscūrus

Uncle, avunculus (maternal)

Under, sub (prep. with accus. and abl.)

Under the age of puberty, impūbis

Undergo, subeō

Underneath, īnferus

Understand, intellegō

Undertake, mōlior

Undertake, suscipiō

Unexpected, necopīnātus

Unfavourable, adversus

Unfavourable, aliēnus

Unfavourable, sinister

Unformed, īnfōrmis

Unfriendly, inimīcus

Unhurt, inviolātus

Uninjured, intāctus

Union, concordia

Unknown, incōgnitus

Unless, nī

Unless, nisi

Unlike, dissimilis

Unlucky, īnfēlīx

Unmindful, immemor

Unripe, immātūrus

Until, dum (with subjunctive)

Until, quoad

Unviolated, salvus

Unworthy, indīgnus (often with abl.)

Up to this point, adhūc

Upper, superus

Upper air, aethēr

Upright, rēctus

Uprising, mōtus

Urge, cohortor

Urge, hortor

Us, nōs

Use, ūsus

Use, ūtor (with abl.)

Use up, cōnsūmō

Useful, ūtilis

Useless, inūtilis

Utterly, penitus

Varied, varius

Veientes, Vēientēs

Venison, ferīna

Venus, Venus

Very, ipse

Very, nimium

Very, quamvis (with adjectives and adverbs)

Very young man, adulēscentulus

Vestal priestess, Vestālis

Vice, vitium

Victory, vīctōria

Victor, vīctor

Vigour, vigor

Village, vīcus

Violence, vīs

Violent, atrōx

Violent, violēns

Violent wind, procella

Virginity, virginitās

Virtue, virtūs

Visit, invīsō

Visit, vīsō

Voice, vōx

Voluntarily, sponte

Vosci, Volscī

Vulture, vultur

Wage war, bellō

Wage, stīpendium

Wait for, exspectō

Wall, mūrus

Wall, vāllum

Walls, moenia (plural)

Wand, virga

Wander, errō

Wandering, error

War, bellum

Warn, admoneō

Warn, moneō

Warn, praedīcō

Warning, exemplum

Water, aqua

Water, lympha

Wave, fluctus

Way, iter

Way, ratiō

Way, via

Way of life, vīctus

Wayfarer, viātor

We, nōs

Weaken, īnfīrmō

Wealth, opēs (plural)

Wealthy, opulentus

Weapon, ferrum

Weapon, tēlum

Wear, gerō

Weary, fatīgō

Weather, tempestās

Weeping, flētus

Weight, pondus

Well, bene

What, quid

What, quod

What ...?, quī, quae, quod (interrogative adj.)

What is more, adeō

What kind of, quālis

Whatever, quodcumque

Whelm, obruō

When, cum

When, quandō

When, quō tempŏre

When, ubi

When, ut (with indicative)

Where, quā

Where, quō (to what place)

Where, ubi

Whereby, quō

Wherever, quācumque

Whether, -nē

Whether, num

Whether ... or, seu ... seu

Which, quod

While, dum (with indicative)

While, quoad

Who, quī, quae, quod (relative pronoun)

Who, quis

Whoever, quīcumque, quaecumque

Why, quam ob rem

Why, quārē

Why, quid

Wicked, scelerātus

Wide, lātus

Wife, uxor

Will, voluntās

Willingly, libenter

Wind, ventus

Wine, vīnum

Wing of an army, cornū

Winged, āles

Winter, hiems

Wipe away, dētergeō

Wisdom, cōnsilium

Wisdom, sapientia

Wish, volō

With, apud (prep. with accus.)

With, cum (prep. with abl.)

With difficulty, vix

With impunity, impūne

Withdraw, surripiō

Without, sine (prep. with abl.)

Without order, iniūssū

Withstand, sustineō

Witness, testis

Wolf, lupa

Woman, fēmina

Woman, mulier

Womanly, muliebris

Wonder, admīror

Wonder, mīrāculum

Wonder, mīror

Wonder at, admīror

Wonder at, mīror

Wonder, admīrātiō

Wonderful, mīrābilis

Wonderful, mīrus

Wood, līgnum

Wooden, līgneus

Wool, lāna

Word, verbum

Word, vōx

Work, labor

Work, opera

Work, opus

Work by lamp-light, lūcubrō

World, orbis

Worse, pēior

Worship, colō

Worship, cultus

Worst, pessimus

Worthy, dīgnus

Wound, vulnerō

Wound, vulnus

Wrestle, lūctor

Write, scrībō

Year, annus

Yield, cēdō (sometimes with dat.)

Yield, concēdō

Yoke, iugum

You, tū (singular)

You, vōs (plural)

Young, adulēscēns

Young, īnfāns

Young man, iuvenis

Young men, pūbēs

Young people, iuventūs

Your, tuus (singular)

Your, vester (plural)

Youth, iuventa

Youthful, impūbis

Youthful, iuvenālis

GENERAL INDEX

Probably, passim

Entry in the general index of R. Meiggs, *The Athenian Empire* (1972)

Numbers refer to pages

Epilogue

Ancient Sages, pardon these
Somewhat doubtful quantities.

Hubert J. de Burgh, 'Half Hours with the Classics' in *Echoes from Kottabos* (1906)

Notes

Notes